Beyond Simple Belief

GOD'S TRANSFORMING PROCESS TO GENUINE FAITH

JF JEFF ETCHBERGER

WITH

JL JULIE LOPES

ISBN 978-1-0980-5964-4 (paperback)
ISBN 978-1-0980-5965-1 (digital)

Christian Faith Publishing, Inc.
832 Park Avenue
Meadville, PA 16335
www.christianfaithpublishing.com

Scripture quotations are from the ESV® Bible, Text Edition® (2016) (the Holy Bible, English Standard Version®), copyright © 2001 by Crossway, a publishing ministry of Good News Publishers. Used by permission. All rights reserved.

Printed in the United States of America

CONTENTS

PREFACE

We believe that the Bible is the Word of God, fully inspired and without error in the original manuscripts, written under the inspiration of the Holy Spirit, and that it has supreme authority in all matters of faith and conduct for all people, for all time (2 Tim. 3:16, Mark 13:31). Based upon this view of Scripture, we have incorporated the principles below in the writing of this work:

- We consistently refer to each of the persons of the Godhead as they are referred to in Scripture.
- We have provided long blocks of Scripture text (for those who are reading without a Bible available) to facilitate the reading of the actual word of God, rather than our summary or restatement of it.
- We see throughout Scripture that God uses *repetition* of various declarations, promises, and teaching points that he deems are important for accomplishing the work of transformation of our faith. Thus, we too use repetition to emphasize the important points of the transformation process in the life of each biblical character.

The main purpose of this book is to help you, the reader, glean a biblical understanding of *God's process* for the transformation of belief into genuine faith as revealed in Scripture. Thus, our definition of the term *transformation* emerges out of the Scripture passages referenced and will be consistently clarified throughout this work.

CHAPTER I
What Happened to Us

This book is the result of twenty to thirty years of theological study and ministry by each of the authors. It specifically focuses on the topic of spiritual transformation: how God transforms *simple belief,* that which enables us to *believe in* Jesus Christ as the Son of God who died for our sins, into *genuine faith* like that of Abraham, Jacob, and others recorded in Hebrews 11. This kind of faith enables us to *surrender fully to God in trusting obedience to his will* for our lives. It is worth a bit of explanation about how we arrived at this place of writing a book together.

Jeff's Story

My focus on this topic began in the summer of 1991 when I left a twenty-year career in government and the private sector to attend Fuller Theological Seminary (FTS) in Pasadena, California. I immediately began absorbing volumes of lecture materials as well as assigned reading as a hunger for the Word of God rapidly grew in me. I could not believe how dramatically my life changed in a short time as a result of reading and studying. Although my wife (Kristi) and I were convinced that we were doing what God was calling us to do, I struggled to figure out the *why* of everything that happened during the previous two years that led us to make such a significant midlife career change.

During my second summer at FTS, Dr. James Loder, a theologian from Princeton Seminary, came to campus as a guest lecturer.

He had just written a book entitled *The Transforming Moment*.[1] In the book, he tells the story of a serious life experience that brought about significant spiritual transformation in him.[2] At the time it occurred, he was a tenured professor of theology at Princeton Seminary, the most liberal Presbyterian seminary in the country.

The story focuses on a short trip he was taking with his wife and two young daughters in their camper. Late in the afternoon he noticed a middle-aged woman standing by a car with a flat tire on the side of the road. He pulled his car onto the shoulder and went back to see if he could help her. Struggling to get the jack to work on the front-left side of the car, he walked to the front-right tire to see if he could figure out how to get the jack to work appropriately. Just has he knelt by the tire, a car driven by an older man approached on the road, with the sound of screeching brakes; the driver had fallen asleep at the wheel. His car crashed into the rear of the older Oldsmobile on which Dr. Loder was working. The force of the impact pushed the Olds on top of him, landing on his chest, and then pushed him and the Olds fifteen feet into the back of their camper. In the midst of this action, Dr. Loder was aware of what was about to happen and worked to position himself in such a way as to keep the car from falling on his head and shoulders. And then, despite the shock over what had just happened, his wife, empowered by the Holy Spirit, sufficiently lifted the front end of the old, very heavy Olds so that Dr. Loder could free himself from under it.

He walked to the embankment near where his two daughters sat crying, fully believing "this disaster has a purpose."[3] He was able to comfort his three-year-old daughter by telling her a story.[4] He was still sitting there when the emergency medical people arrived. He was able to walk himself to the stretcher and was taken by ambulance to the hospital. He had multiple extremely serious injuries. However, two days later, with indications of healing taking place,

---

[1] James Loder, *The Transforming Moment*, 2nd ed. (Colorado Springs: Helmers & Howard, 1989).
[2] Loder, 9–13.
[3] Loder, *Transforming Moment*, 10.
[4] Ibid., 11.

the head surgeon cancelled plans for skin grafts on his back, saying, "A good surgeon knows when to get out of the way and let God do the healing."[5] Dr. Loder describes the event of the accident and the quick healing that began almost immediately as "fact and meaning" coming together to "compose a convicting experience."[6] He says of this life event, "I had been and am convicted."[7]

The impact of what had occurred transformed Dr. Loder's life and thinking. This fully tenured liberal theologian, one who had been highly trained in theology, who knew about God, was transformed into one who came to *know God personally* through this experience; the God he knew about became real to him. As a result of this experience, he became a conservative evangelical ordained pastor whose thoughts and teaching became focused on addressing this question: how does God transform individuals into what he created them to be—genuine believers in his son Jesus Christ? The result of spending time with Dr. Loder that summer, both in and out of the classroom, hearing his testimony and studying his book, was that I began to examine events in my own life from a new perspective.

I have always believed that I was a Christian; I cannot remember a time when I did not believe this to be true. I even remember attending church and Sunday school while in elementary school. As an adult, I sang in the church choir, served as an elder, and was Clerk of Session. Throughout my life, I had always tried to live my life according to Christian beliefs. But in 1989, a friend invited me to attend her church one Sunday. Upon later reflection, I had to acknowledge that I heard the whole gospel that day for the first time in my life. This realization led me to immediately begin to struggle with the question of whether or not I was a genuine born-again believer, or if I had been a Christian "in name only" for my entire life up to that point.

As a result of my interaction with Dr. Loder, I too began to focus my reading and study along the same lines as his, seeking to

---

5   Ibid., 12.
6   Ibid.
7   Ibid., 13.

understand how God transforms us into genuine believers in Jesus Christ. What quickly became apparent was that spiritual transformation can occur at a single moment in time, such as for the thief on the cross (Luke 23:42–43), or it can take much longer, as evidenced by Dr. Loder's personal testimony. I had always been uncomfortable listening to people describe their conversion as occurring on a specific date and time because this was not my own experience. It was enlightening for me to hear someone talk about a *transformation process* rather than a *conversion event*. Hearing and reading Dr. Loder's work about transformation began to shed light on what was now happening in my own life.

Following seminary, while serving as a pastor at my first church in Southern California, I attended a weekend retreat for pastors where another theologian, Dr. Ben Campbell Johnson from Columbia Theological Seminary in Atlanta, spoke about how to discern the will of God. His emphasis was on how God guides and directs believers in daily life. A significant tool that Dr. Johnson presented was a paradigm that helps an individual look back at the milestones in their life, regardless of how many (or few) there have been. He explained that we can begin to see how God works in our lives if we examine what has happened *between* the respective milestones, seeking to understand what occurred during that time to prepare us to achieve the next milestone. He explained that God works differently in each person's life; there is no "one way" that works for everyone. By utilizing this paradigm, a person can start to learn how God guides and directs them individually in daily life.

Following the weekend retreat, some things began to fall into place in my thinking as I began to integrate what I had learned from Dr. Loder regarding a faith transformation process and the paradigm learned from Dr. Johnson. I realized that I had been asking the wrong question. I had been asking the question of why: why had God allowed the events of the past several years to happen—both bad and good? This is typically what people ask when something terrible happens in their life. However, it now became evident that the correct question to ask is, what is God trying to teach me to prepare me for the next season of my life, to transform me?

Considering what I had learned from both men, I began to look back at the milestones in my own life. I began to see how God had been at work through all that had occurred. And I began to understand the answer to another question that I was then struggling with: was God actively directing the series of events that have transpired in my life, or was I just taking a series of circumstances and attributing them to the work of God? For the first time, I truly began to see how God had been, and was currently, actively involved in my own personal daily life.

Several years later, as new milestones occurred in my life, I continued to struggle with questions regarding spiritual transformation. My colleague and friend from seminary, Julie Lopes, sent me a book by Dr. Robert Clinton from Fuller Seminary, *The Making of a Leader*.[8] The thesis of Dr. Clinton's book is that God uses wilderness experiences, times of pain and suffering, to transform and prepare people for what he has planned in the next season of their life. By combining the concepts learned from Dr. Clinton with those from Dr. Loder regarding transformation, and examining the prior events of my own life through the lens of the milestone paradigm learned from Dr. Johnson, I finally began to understand how to make sense of the foundational question I was asking: how does God transform us? This process that I was beginning to understand is seen in Scripture, where we are told that beyond simple belief, which opens the way to salvation, comes *transformation* (the word used in some Bible translations is *sanctification*).

At this point, I teamed up with Julie to explore these issues together, in the context of events happening in our own lives, since events in her life had also motivated her to study the process of spiritual transformation. What had started for me as a solitary process soon became a joint quest to understand how God transforms simple belief into genuine faith as revealed throughout Scripture. We began rereading Scripture searching for evidence of God's transforming work in the lives of individuals and looking for evidence of transformation of our faith in the midst of our own life circumstances.

---

[8]   J. Robert Clinton, *The Making of a Leader: Recognizing the Lessons and Stages of Leadership Development* (Colorado Springs: NavPress, 1988).

Julie's Story

Like Jeff, I cannot remember any time in my life when I did not believe in God. I grew up going to church. I took the spiritual side of my life very seriously, often feeling quite close to God. However, I did not consider myself to be a "Christian," but rather a "Catholic," as I was raised in the Catholic Church. I had a well-developed sense of "right" and "wrong," yet my life was one of continual failures, unable to live up to the standard of "doing right" all the time. As I grew into adulthood, I knew about God, and about Jesus, but I was living a very secular life. My belief in God simply did not influence my daily life in any significant way. I was doing what I thought I was supposed to do: get a college degree and find a career, in the midst of being a wife and mother—generally seeking to be "a good person." Although I continued to go to church on a regular basis, attending church did not result in any observable influence on how I lived daily life. There was a very real disconnect between attending church on Sunday and how I lived life the rest of the week. It seemed that when I left church on Sunday, I left God in the church.

If asked, I would describe the door by which God took Jeff into the topic of spiritual transformation as one of *pastoral theology*. The door God took me through was a bit different, which I would describe as *psychological theology*. That path began to open up in front of me, starting in the 1990s, through a series of significant events.

The first significant event, however, occurred earlier when I returned to college to finish my undergraduate degree after twelve years of life as a wife and mother. After some research and prayer, I shifted my degree program from childhood development to psychology. I had two years of coursework to complete in order to finish my degree, but being a working mother and wife, it took ten years to do so. In 1994 I completed my BA in psychology from California State University, Los Angeles. I knew I was not made to devote my life to counseling, so I often wondered what I would do with this degree.

As I was coming to the end of my psychology degree program in 1994, I began to develop a deep longing to attend Fuller Theological Seminary (FTS) in Pasadena, California. I applied for admission late in the year and was accepted into the master of divinity (MDiv) degree program.

In one of my Fuller classes, I was required to read Dr. Robert Clinton's book, *The Making of a Leader*, a model of leadership development that can be seen by studying the lives of several biblical characters. One of the important concepts of his model that made a long-lasting impression on me is what Clinton called "boundary" times[9] in our lives, the shorter times of transition between the longer "main" seasons of our lives. I was most struck by the idea that God takes us through a *transformation* process, which strengthens and matures our faith, when we are in transition from one season of life to another. This transformation is necessary in order to be ready for the next season of life that is coming to us.

About this time, I also took a class taught by Dr. James Loder, which required me to read James Fowler's book, *Stages of Faith*,[10] which describes a maturing process of faith similar to the maturing process we see in psychological development. There are seasons of "childhood," "adolescence," and "adulthood" in our journey of faith, as in our psychological development. The most significant point for me from that class was this: there is a *maturing process* to our life of faith. In light of what I had learned from Dr. Loder and Dr. Clinton, I began to wonder what "spiritual maturity" looked like in my own life. Through the difficult times of life, was I moving toward greater spiritual maturity over time or not?

Other significant events occurred in my life over time. God led me to a book on prayer and temperament. It was my first foray into intentionally integrating the spiritual/theological realm and the psychological realm, even though my undergraduate and graduate degree paths were already bringing about some measure of integration of these two disciplines. At about this same time, I changed my degree at Fuller from MDiv to MA in theology (MAT). I also applied for and was accepted into a certificate program (in the form

---

[9] Clinton, *Leader*, 49.
[10] James W. Fowler, *Stages of Faith: The Psychology of Human Development and the Quest for Meaning* (New York: HarperOne, 1981).

of a cohort) for a concentrated focus of study in spirituality and spiritual direction. The coursework for this cohort fit perfectly with my long-standing interest in psychology, and my growing interest in, and focus on, how to help others "grow up" spiritually.

In one of the spiritual direction classes, as required reading I was introduced to the book *The Critical Journey* by Janet Hagberg and Robert Guelich,[11] which describes a six-stage model of spiritual formation. I was taking this class at a time when I was personally in a very difficult place in my own life: total exhaustion and burnout, questioning my place in the world and the purpose of my life. *The Critical Journey* became a very important anchor in my life for many years to come, simply because it provided an explanation for the turmoil and unanswered questions I was living with. I could see from my own life that spiritual formation was all about the *growth* or *transformation of my faith*, and that this transformation occurred in the midst of daily life challenges. My journey was teaching me that simple belief, the simple acknowledgement of the *reality* of God, was not the same as mature faith (what Jeff has called *genuine faith*), which according to my reading of Scripture seemed to demand surrender to, and obedience to, God's will for my life.

The power of *The Critical Journey* as a way of understanding the process of spiritual formation and transformation is a big topic for another time. However, what is important here is that in this model there is a season of the spiritual journey that has two parts, described as "stage 4" and "the wall."[12] Together they explain what God is doing in our lives during times of major life struggles. These are often times of transition when many things seem to be falling apart, when one season of life is coming to an end and the next season has not yet fully dawned, when life is "a mess." According to this model, God is working during these times to gradually move us from a life of "doing" the right things to a life of "being" a person of mature faith.[13] I saw

---

[11] Janet O. Hagberg and Robert A. Guelich, *The Critical Journey: Stages in the Life of Faith*, 2nd ed. (Salem: Sheffield Publishing Company, 2005).

[12] Hagberg and Guelich, *Journey*, 92–130.

[13] This is a very simplistic summary of the seasons of the spiritual transformation process and represents only one aspect of a much more profound season of

this stage of the spiritual journey coinciding with the "boundary" times from Clinton's model of leadership development. I began to understand that the difficult circumstances in my life had an intentional purpose, that those difficult circumstances came to me from the hand of God for the specific purpose of maturing my faith.

At about the time I entered the spirituality/spiritual direction program at Fuller, I also went through a certification program separate from Fuller to work with a particular temperament model based in part on the work of Isabel Myers and Katharine Briggs. This certification process took me deep into temperament and leadership styles based on the work of Linda Berens.[14] Interestingly, I had long been a passionate student of both leadership development and temperament; I studied these topics separately for several years. And now, while I was pursuing a theological degree, I was also immersing myself in a new model of temperament and leadership styles. Being a person with a strong spiritual side, I began to wonder how our God-given temperament influenced our individual journey with God. And that led to questioning how that journey with God moved us along unique paths from basic faith to mature (genuine) faith.

Through these years, Jeff (and Kristi) and I had ongoing conversations about our own faith struggles in the midst of difficult life circumstances. We were sharing with each other our insights about our own journeys, and we spoke into each other's lives to encourage one another to stay the course, to stay in step with God in the midst of the pain and struggle, to trust that he was doing an intentional work in us through daily life circumstances. Through these conversations, and in the midst of life's challenges, I learned to ask the ques-

---

spiritual transformation. For the purposes of this chapter, I have chosen to focus only on this one aspect.

[14] Linda V. Berens, *Understanding Yourself and Others: An Introduction to the 4 Temperaments*, 4.0 ed. (West Hollywood: Radiance House, 2010); *Understanding Yourself and Others: An Introduction to Interaction Styles*, 2.0 ed. (West Hollywood: Radiance House, 2008). In many years of working with Berens's information on interaction styles, I have come to see them as clear description of *leadership* styles, how we work together in groups or teams. My use of the term *leadership styles* instead of *interaction styles* is the result of teaching for several years about leadership styles using Berens's information.

tion again and again, "What is God doing?" I had learned that God is *always* intentionally doing something in our lives. The question was not *if* he was doing something, but *what* was he doing?

Jeff and I realized rather quickly that we had both been on individual but parallel paths for several years, both of us learning from different perspectives about spiritual transformation. Through our ongoing discussions about what was happening in our lives, and in light of what we had gleaned from the authors mentioned above, we both began to see and understand that there is a process of transformation of faith that occurs in the midst of daily life circumstances. The challenging circumstances of our own lives led us to dig deeper into Scripture to see what God's word had to say about the process of faith transformation. Over time, God brought specific biblical texts about transformation repeatedly to mind during our conversations. Our subsequent search of scriptural passages revealed that a general *transformation process* does indeed occur. And that transformation process is necessary for a person to move toward spiritual maturity.

What Scripture Revealed

The first biblical text to look at in seeking to understand what Scripture has to say about the faith transformation process is John 8. Jesus is in the temple and has been talking about the Father and his relationship with the Father. John tells us that many Jews believed in Jesus as a result of his words (John 8:30). Then John continues, "So Jesus said to the Jews who had believed in him, 'If you abide in my word you are truly my disciples'" (John 8:31). What Jesus is saying here is significant and startling. He is essentially saying that there are "true" disciples and "untrue" disciples (but note they are still called *disciples*). He is not talking about *nonbelievers*; nonbelievers are not considered disciples. Jesus is saying that within those who "believe," there are both genuine and nongenuine disciples.

Jonathan Edwards, considered by many to be the foremost theologian in American history, wrote "A Treatise Regarding Religious

Affections," written in 1746.[15] In Part II of that work, he argues that there is no issue that should be of more significant concern to every person than to know the distinguishing characteristics of those who are *genuinely born again*. He says that people who have those characteristics (those that possess true virtue and holiness, which is acceptable in the sight of God) are in favor with God, and thus can be assured of inheriting eternal life. He observes that although this issue is of great importance, and that there is clear and abundant teaching in the Word of God about being born again, many professing Christians remain in considerable disagreement regarding this vital issue.

Part II of Edwards's treatise examines in detail twelve affections (emotions or feelings) that many professing Christians have been deceived into believing are indicators of genuine faith. One such example is that many Christians believe that the intensity of their emotional response in a faith setting *proves genuine faith*. In other words, intense emotional responses in faith situations means one's faith is genuine. Yet Edwards asserts that Scripture clearly shows such affections *do not* prove genuine faith. He argues that such belief—what we are calling simple belief—results in being a hypocrite: *appearing* to have genuine faith, but not truly *possessing* it when viewed from a biblical perspective.[16]

Dr. John Piper, considered by many to be the foremost theologian and pastor alive in America today, has proved to be a great source of inspiration and biblical understanding to both of us through his prolific preaching and books. In one sermon, he addresses the question "What does it mean to be a disciple?"[17] He states that in the theological arena in America today, there is teaching about two tiers of Christian belief: the first tier is called *conversion*; the second tier

---

[15] Jonathan Edwards, *A Treatise Concerning Religious Affections in Three Parts* (np, 1746); Part II, pp. 21–53, Christian Classics Ethereal Library, online publisher, http://www.ccel.org/ccel/edwards/affections.i.html.

[16] Edwards, *Affections*, 21–53.

[17] John Piper, "This Man Receives Sinners and Eats with Them," audio sermon (August 13, 1995), minutes 22–25, http://www. desiringgod. org/messages/ this-man-receives-sinners-and-eats-with-them.

is called *discipleship*. He observes that people can live between tiers 1 and 2, and never get to tier 2. In this way of thinking, people can go through a conversion process but never become true disciples. Thus, there are many people who think that becoming a Christian is a low-level act of intellectual espousal of, or mental assent to, doctrinal truth. This is then followed by a simple declaration that they *believe* specific facts—such as Jesus died on the cross for their sin and that he is God. They believe that they will go to heaven if they *merely believe such facts*. And they think that the purpose of preaching and biblical teaching is to move people from this first level of belief to tier 2, to become disciples. To state it again, Piper is saying that in this line of thinking/teaching, one can believe without being a disciple. Piper states that such thinking is the reason there are so many weak and carnal churches in America. Further, he argues that such belief is dead wrong from a biblical perspective. That is the reason we refer to this line of thinking, believing basic facts (or giving "mental assent") about who God is, or who Jesus is and what he did, as "simple belief" throughout this book.

Piper argues that by examining Luke's gospel and Acts for what *disciple* means, it is evident that such "two-tier" thinking is not consistent with Scripture. The best text to support this is from Acts 11 in which Luke observes, "And in Antioch, the disciples were first called Christians" (Acts 11:26). That's Luke's understanding of what *disciple* means: disciples are Christians; Christians are disciples. The two cannot be separated. Thus, Piper concludes that the word *disciple* in the mouth of Jesus did not refer *only* to someone with a "second-tier" allegiance to him. Rather, a disciple is a genuine believer whose faith is in the process of being transformed.

By combining the thinking of Edwards and Piper, we conclude that people who possess only simple belief, who think that becoming a Christian is a low-level act of intellectual espousal of (or mental assent to) doctrinal truth, followed by some act that indicates they believe specific gospel facts (e.g., signed a faith commitment card in a worship service), are the nongenuine disciples that Jesus refers to in John 8:31. According to Edwards, these are the hypocrites that only *appear* to have genuine faith without *actually* possessing it.

The next text that we need to consider in the faith transformation process is Matthew 7. Jesus says:

> "Every tree that does not bear good fruit is cut down and thrown into the fire. Thus you will recognize them by their fruits.
>
> Not everyone who says to me, 'Lord, Lord,' will enter the kingdom of heaven, but the one who *does the will of my Father* who is in heaven. On that day many will say to me, 'Lord, Lord, did we not prophesy in your name, and cast out demons in your name, and do many mighty works in your name?' And then will I declare to them, 'I never knew you; depart from me, you workers of lawlessness.'" (Matt. 7:19–23, italics added)

We believe that this is one of the hardest texts in all of Scripture. Basically it says that nongenuine disciples have been deceived into thinking that because of the work they do in Jesus's name that they are going to enter the kingdom of God; they are going to go to heaven. However, Jesus's words say otherwise: simply doing works in his name is not sufficient.

This text should challenge every professing Christian who reads it to ask, "Is that me? Am I one of those? Am I a genuine disciple?" Jesus says here that being a disciple is not only about *what you do*; it's about *who you are*, and whether he knows you (this "knowing" infers an intimate knowing, which is very different from an intellectual "knowing about" another). The driving force behind our writing of this book is this Mathew text, what it says about genuine believers, and how it challenges the prevailing belief today in the American church about what it means to be a Christian.

The next text we need to consider in the study of faith transformation is in the Gospel of John, chapter 1, where we find John describing true belief in Jesus:

> He was in the world, and the world was made through him, yet the world did not know him. He came to his own, and his people did not receive him. But to all who did receive him, who believed in his name, he gave the right to *become* children of God, who were born, not of blood nor of the will of the flesh nor of the will of man, but of God. (John 1:10–13, italics added)

What does John mean when he says, "He gave the right to become children of God" to "all who did receive him, who believed in his name" (v. 12)? Here we need to take a short detour into the Greek text. The Greek word translated "to become" is *gínomai*, which means "to emerge from or *to transition* from one condition to another." It signifies a process over time, a *"change of condition, state, or place."* It implies *"motion, movement, or growth."*[18] It does not infer that there is a particular state of being that we have achieved. Rather, it infers a *process of becoming.* Thus, this passage describes simple belief as the *starting point* for transition or movement toward greater spiritual growth or maturity in the life of an individual. It infers that belief is not all there is to genuine Christian faith. The apostle Peter also uses *gínomai* when he writes about Jesus in 2 Peter:

> His divine power has granted to us all things that pertain to life and godliness, through the knowledge of him who called us to his own glory and excellence, by which he has granted to us his precious and very great promises, so that through them you may *become* partakers of the divine

---

[18] *Strong's Concordance*, 1096, *ginomai*: to come into being, to happen, to become, https://biblehub. com/greek/1096. htm.

nature, having escaped from the corruption that
is in the world because of sinful desire. (2 Pet.
1:3–4, italics added)

In another passage, Peter uses a different Greek word, *auxanó*,
which means "to grow."[19] Here he expresses the same transitional
thought as John by saying, "Like newborn infants, long for the pure
spiritual milk, that by it you may *grow up* into salvation—if indeed
you have tasted that the Lord is good" (1 Pet. 2:2–3, italics added).
By combining together what Peter and John both say in these texts, it
becomes clear that believing is *the beginning* of movement, of *transitioning*, from one condition of faith to another in the life of one who
now believes. This transitioning takes time. But note that these texts
do not state that simple belief is *all* that is required for a person to be
a child of God, a genuine believer.

The apostle Paul sounds a very similar note when he writes,
"And we all, with unveiled face, beholding the glory of the Lord, *are
being transformed* into the same image from one degree of glory to
another. For this comes from the Lord, who is the Spirit" (2 Cor. 3:18,
italics added). However, rather than using *gínomai*, he uses the Greek
word *metamorphóō*, which means "being transformed." *Metamorphóō*
is formed from the combination of two Greek words, *metá*, which
means "*change after being with*," and *morphóō*, which means "*changing form* in keeping with inner reality."[20] These two words, combined
into *metamorphóō*, give us the sense of an *ongoing process* of change
or transformation. Interestingly, this is the word from which we get
our English word *metamorphosis*, which means "*a profound change in
form from one stage to the next*" or "*any complete change in appearance
[or] character*."[21] Also, it is essential to note that Paul uses the passive
present tense of the verb to express that the transformation to which
he refers is *ongoing and thus not yet complete*. Additionally, the passive

19 *Strong's Concordance*, 837, *auxanó*: to make to grow, https://biblehub.com/greek/837.htm.
20 Ibid., 3339, *metamorphoó*: to transform, https://biblehub. com/greek/3339. htm.
21 *Webster's Encyclopedic Unabridged Dictionary of the English Language* (New York: Gramercy Books, 1996), 1207.

tense infers that the work of transformation is being done to us by God.[22] We do not make transformation happen ourselves.

When we combine the information above, we find that Paul is saying that those who believe in Jesus, like himself, *are being transformed* after "beholding the glory of the Lord" (2 Cor. 3:18). Paul is saying that when we see the truth, the *glory*, of who Jesus really is, a transformational process begins in us, a process that John introduces, and Peter expands upon in the texts discussed above. Further, it reveals that God's work of transformation is *ongoing* in the life of the genuine believer.

Returning to chapter 3 in John's gospel, he records Jesus as saying, "Whoever believes in the Son has eternal life; whoever does not obey the Son shall not see life, but the wrath of God remains on him" (John 3:36). According to this text, the one who has genuine belief (which we are calling "genuine saving faith" or "genuine faith") will see eternal life, *and* such belief *results in obedience to God*. These two aspects of genuine faith are connected and cannot be separated; genuine believers *will* obey God. Thus, Jesus is saying that simple belief (mental assent alone) that does not result in obedience to God is not genuine saving faith.

From this lengthy discussion, we assert along with Scripture that simple belief, which does not result in obedience to the will of God, is not equivalent to genuine saving faith. Mental assent to the truth of who Jesus is and what he has done through his death and resurrection *that does not lead to* a changed life, a life *surrendered to the will of God*—demonstrated in *obedience to God*—is not genuine saving faith. Additionally, we assert that a process of "becoming" (transformation) *must occur* for such obedience to occur.

Once again, John Piper's writing is helpful in further understanding this concept. He argues that *belief* "in the saving sense always includes the *heartfelt embrace* of what is believed; knowing doesn't always include that."[23] He goes on to say that knowing

---

[22] See John 6:63–65.

[23] John Piper, *A Peculiar Glory: How the Christian Scriptures Reveal Their Complete Truthfulness* (Wheaton: Crossway, 2016), 136, italics added.

historical facts and doctrinal truth alone does not equate to "saving belief"—belief that leads to salvation.[24] Yet he *is* saying that believing and knowing *cannot be separated*. Saving belief is based on a foundation of (intellectual) knowledge *that leads to* more in-depth (heartfelt) knowing.[25] John's first epistle reveals this connection between historical facts and spiritual belief in his own life. He starts his epistle with, "That which was from the beginning, which we have heard, which we have seen with our eyes, which we looked upon and have touched with our hands, concerning the word of life—" (1 John 1:1). From this we learn that John's faith is grounded in experiential evidence (or "knowing" from experience), which enables him to say that he has "come to know and to believe the love that God has for us" (1 John 4:16).

Piper points out that simply believing in historical facts about Jesus is not sufficient for genuine saving faith. He refers to what James says, "You believe that God is one; you do well. Even the demons believe—and shudder!" (James 2:19). From this text, Piper argues that believing in the existence of divine reality—even the sacred truth of the gospel or the Bible—*does not mean* that a person's belief will lead to salvation.[26] In other words, such simple belief as we have described cannot be considered to be the same as genuine *saving faith*.

Now let's consider Romans 4. Paul states, "The promise to Abraham and his offspring that he would be heir of the world did not come through the law but through the righteousness of faith" (Rom. 4:13). He goes on to explain that this promise "depends on faith, in order that the promise may rest on grace and be guaranteed to all his offspring—not only to the adherent of the law but also to the one who shares the faith of Abraham, who is the father of us all" (Rom. 4:16). Paul is saying that genuine faith is more than righteous

---

[24] Piper, *Peculiar Glory*, 138.
[25] An example of this connectedness between believing and knowing can be seen in John 17:6–9.
[26] Piper, *Peculiar Glory*, 136.

acts according to the law; it requires *trust* that God will be faithful to his promises. Paul then says this about Abraham:

> He did not weaken in faith when he considered his own body, which was as good as dead (since he was about a hundred years old), or when he considered the barrenness of Sarah's womb. No unbelief made him waver concerning the promise of God, but he grew strong in his faith as he gave glory to God, fully convinced that God was able to do what he had promised. (Rom. 4:19–21)

Here Paul explains that Abraham was faced with a human impossibility. What did he do? Paul focuses on Abraham's *trust* in God's word, his promises (vv. 20–21). Thus, because of his "faith" and "full conviction," Abraham showed that his belief in God encompassed a level of *trust* that God can give a son to a one hundred-year-old man and a barren (and aged) woman. This level of trust marks the emergence of genuine faith in Abraham.

At this point, consideration of the various texts discussed above should reveal that there are both genuine and nongenuine believers, and that simple belief that does not result in obedience to God's will is not equivalent to genuine belief, which is the same as saving faith. Mere mental assent to specific facts is *not* all that is required for a person to be a child of God. Instead, "believing" in the "saving" sense always includes the heartfelt embrace of what is believed.[27] Additionally, *believing in God also encompasses trusting God.* Genuine belief is the beginning of movement, of transitioning from one condition to another, in the life of the one who now believes. It is a process of becoming, of growing, of maturing, of transformation over time that must occur for obedience to occur. Thus, simple belief in the existence of divine reality—even the divine truth of the gospel or the Bible—does not necessarily mean that a person believes in a way that leads to salvation. The "process of becoming" (transforma-

---

[27] Piper, *Peculiar Glory*, 137.

tion) moves a person's faith beyond simple belief comprised of mental assent to facts, to belief that encompasses *trust* in God, *surrender* to his will, and a heartfelt *embrace* of what is believed, that results in *obedience* to the one believed.

How Transformation Occurs

Having said this, the next obvious question is how does this transformation take place? To find an answer to that question, we turn to John 3, where Nicodemus asks Jesus:

> "How can a man be born when he is old? Can he enter a second time into his mother's womb and be born?" Jesus answered, "Truly, truly, I say to you, unless one is born of water and the Spirit, he cannot enter the kingdom of God. That which is born of the flesh is flesh, and that which is born of the Spirit is spirit. Do not marvel that I said to you, 'You must be born again.' The wind blows where it wishes, and you hear its sound, but you do not know where it comes from or where it goes. So it is with everyone who is born of the Spirit." (John 3:4–8)

Jesus attributes the transformation that occurs in a person who is "born again" to the work of the Holy Spirit. Thus, transformation that leads to true saving faith is not the work of human effort and will; it is only the work of God through his Holy Spirit. In John 6, Jesus says:

> "It is the Spirit who gives life; the flesh is no help at all. The words that I have spoken to you are spirit and life. But there are some of you who do not believe." (For Jesus knew from the beginning who those were who did not believe, and who it was who would betray him.) And he said,

"This is why I told you that no one can come to me unless it is granted him by the Father." (John 6:63–65)

What Jesus says here about who will believe and who will not believe, "unless it is granted him by the Father" (v. 65), is difficult for us to accept, unless it is tied together with the first part of the text where he says, "It is the Spirit who gives life" (v. 63). Jesus is saying that God does not just *provide the means* of salvation and transformation, but that God is also the *provider*, the agent of this transforming work. God alone does the work within an individual that results in saving faith. Also consider what Paul writes in Philippians:

Therefore, my beloved, as you have always obeyed, so now, not only as in my presence but much more in my absence, work out your own salvation with fear and trembling, for it is God who works in you, both to will and to work for his good pleasure. (Phil. 2:12–13)

When this text is quoted, verse 12 is as far as people usually go: "work out your own salvation with fear and trembling," which by itself seems to infer human effort and will is needed. But verse 13 begins with the keyword *for*, which is often overlooked; it means "because." What follows provides the reason for what was said in the preceding verse. In this case, it means that the reason an individual should work out their faith with fear and trembling is because "it is *God who works in you, both to will and to work* for his good pleasure" (v. 13, italics added). And we see in 2 Thessalonians that Paul states, "God chose you as the first fruits to be saved, through sanctification by the Spirit" (2 Thess. 2:13). Here then, Paul provides the answer to the question about how transformation occurs. God has chosen those who become children of God for salvation through the transforming work of the Holy Spirit.

As Christians, we talk about the sovereignty of God and the will of God. But do we recognize when *God is at work in our lives?* Do we realize, accept, and trust what Scripture says, that *God is engaged and active* in our lives? Does God become *real* for us? Do we continually ask the question "Where is God in this?" in the midst of all of life's situations and circumstances? Until we can answer *that* question, we cannot come to a genuine understanding of what God is doing in our lives. But before we are willing to ask that question, we must get to the point where God is more than an abstract, objective idea. We must move to the place where we can say with deep, heartfelt conviction, "God is real for me."

Getting to that point changes everything about our lives, as it did for the apostle Paul. He writes in 1 Corinthians 15, "But by the grace of God I am what I am, and his grace toward me was not in vain. On the contrary, I worked harder than any of them, though it was not I, but the grace of God that is with me" (1 Cor. 15:10). This is Paul's great confession: despite all that he achieved, all that he did, here he is saying, "It's not me. It's not about what I did." Instead, it began for Paul on the Damascus road when Jesus Christ became real to him. And Paul was one of the most religious men of his day, following the laws that governed Jewish daily life better than most. That's what Pharisees and scribes were, the most religious people of their day. But most Pharisees and scribes were quite good at separating their intellect from their hearts. They knew Scripture! Satan too knows Scripture better than any of us. So, we must understand that yes, "faith comes by hearing and hearing through the word of God" (Rom. 10:17). But it doesn't stop there. As we have seen, believing (or mental assent) is just the beginning. Scripture teaches us that *transformation* must come; growth must occur to transform that simple belief into genuine saving faith. If it doesn't, we ought to be asking ourselves, why not? And, we would be wise to consider what the absence of transformation of our faith means for our salvation.

The next text we need to look at is in 1 Corinthians 3. There Paul writes:

> What then is Apollos? What is Paul? Servants
> through whom you believed, as the Lord assigned
> to each. I planted, Apollos watered, but *God gave*

the growth. So neither he who plants nor he who waters is anything, but only God who gives the growth. (1 Cor. 3:5–7, italics added)

This fact is repeated continuously in Scripture: to become a genuine believer, a person must undergo the process of transformation. And many texts make it explicit that it is God who does the work of transformation.

Recognizing God's Transforming Work

At this point, the question naturally arises: how can we recognize God at work in our lives? As we have just discussed, Scripture is clear in saying that it is God through the Holy Spirit who performs the work of transformation in a person's life. But Scripture provides no straightforward explanation about *how* that work is accomplished. However, it is possible to examine the lives of biblical characters to answer that question. We must go beyond reading Scripture for the purpose of understanding the historical context of Israel and look at the life stories of biblical characters to learn from their life experiences how God brought about their spiritual transformation (i.e., transformation of their faith).

That is the work of this book: to reexamine some of the familiar biblical stories of well-known and important individuals, with a focus on how God brought about his transforming work through daily life events to move them from simple, objective belief to genuine faith anchored in deep trust, which enabled them to obey God. Through it all, we will keep asking again and again "Where is God in this?" to see how he was actively involved in daily life events working to transform each one into the individual he created them to be. We hope that as you read, you will look at each story with us and ask along the way how God might be working in your own life in similar ways to transform your belief into faith.

A Final Word

As we work through these biblical stories, it is important to remember that the transformation process is unique to each person; there is no one *way* for everyone, which is why this book is so important. Although we will see similarities in the transformation process among the character studies, there are also noticeable and important differences. As you read, please keep in mind that although God may have worked one way in a biblical character's life, it does not mean that he will only work in the same way in your life, or in ours. We all must be open to how God might choose to accomplish his transforming work in each of us.

Finally, we wish to conclude this introduction with one final text from John 15, Jesus's most extended discourse on abiding, discipline, and being a disciple, using the metaphor of pruning. He says:

> "I am the true vine, and my Father is the vinedresser. Every branch in me that does not bear fruit he takes away, and every branch that does bear fruit he prunes, that it may bear more fruit. Already you are clean because of the word that I have spoken to you. Abide in me, and I in you. As the branch cannot bear fruit by itself, unless it abides in the vine, neither can you, unless you abide in me. I am the vine; you are the branches. Whoever abides in me and I in him, he it is that bears much fruit, for apart from me you can do nothing. If anyone does not abide in me he is thrown away like a branch and withers; and the branches are gathered, thrown into the fire, and burned. If you abide in me, and my words abide in you, ask whatever you wish, and it will be done for you. By this my Father is glorified, that you bear much fruit and so prove to be my disciples." (John 15:1–8)

Both of us have recognized the truth of these words many times in our own lives and in the lives of others. Through our study of what Scripture says about the individual stories of transformation, Jeff through his ministry of pastoral counseling and Julie through her ministry of spiritual mentoring, we believe that every moment of pruning has resulted in bearing more fruit. For the purposes of this book, that fruit is the transformation of our faith, which moves us toward a deeper and broader way of living in this world. It leads us further into a life of obedience to the will of God.

Thus, the purpose of putting our thoughts and words to paper in this book is to share what we have personally experienced and observed so that others may benefit from those insights. We have found this information especially helpful for anyone who has or is currently struggling to understand "Where is God in this?" with regard to the pain, suffering, and wilderness experiences of daily life. It is our genuine desire and prayer that as you read the following chapters, the insights shared about the transformation process will bless your life as it has our own.

CHAPTER 2
Abraham

Abraham is a towering figure in the history of the Christian faith. His story is an excellent place to start a study of how God works in and through everyday life events to reveal himself to us, to transform us from simple belief to genuine faith. God desires to transform Abraham's faith to the point where he is willing to obey God's instructions to him, without question. How does this transformation of Abraham's faith to the point of unquestioned obedience occur? That is what this chapter is all about.

The core essence of transformed faith means increasing intimacy with God over time. It also means deepening dependence on God and not on oneself. This deepening intimacy and dependency happen as God reveals himself in order to become real to us amid life's challenges. As we experience God's presence with us and learn more about his character, he works within us to enable us to trust him more. We discover that he *will* fulfill his promises to us. As our trust grows, we find we are willing and able to surrender our plans for our life, and instead accept and embrace God's plans for us. We can do this only to the degree that we trust his goodness toward us, his love, grace, mercy, and forgiveness. It is *his* path for our lives that enables us to live fully as the person he has created us to be and to live out his call on our lives, as he works to accomplish his purposes in his world through us.

Abraham's story is immersed in God's faithfulness to fulfill his promises. So, before we get started on our study of Abraham, a word about God's promises is needed. God's Word (Scripture) is full of promises to his people. God uses his promises to reveal himself to us. In the process of fulfilling those promises over time, he proves his faithfulness, thus revealing more of his character to us. All of this works to transform our faith. As a result, we are willing and able to trust God more in the following days; we are better able to surrender our plans and our will for our lives to him in exchange for his plans and his will for us. We can learn much about this process of spiritual transformation from Abraham's journey of faith—indeed from all of the biblical characters we will study in this book.

Abraham's Family Background

Abraham's story is a story of promises given and reaffirmed again and again by God, with the partial fulfillment of those promises in Abraham's lifetime. We are introduced to Abraham when he was not known by that name, but rather as Abram. Genesis 11:27–32 gives us a summary of Abram's family situation at the beginning of this biblical story. Under the leadership and direction of his father, Terah, the family left Ur of the Chaldeans. Archaeological investigations reveal that this was "a well-developed urban culture" in Abram's time.[1] How long Terah's family lived in this ancient city in southern Babylonia is not known. Given the size of the family, it would seem that they had lived there for some time, perhaps for generations. This passage also does not tell us why Terah decided to uproot his family and move from his home city to an unknown rural land. In any case, to pack up and move an entire clan from a place with family roots to a strange land approximately one thousand miles away is a rather massive undertaking. Finally, we read that their intended destination was Canaan, but they stopped and settled in Haran (v. 31), about halfway to Canaan. That was quite a trip!

In Joshua 24:1–3, we learn one more important fact about Abram's family situation not mentioned in the Genesis passage. While Terah and his family lived in Ur of the Chaldeans, they "served other gods" (v. 2). Since we are focusing on Abram's faith, it is helpful to

---

[1]   Ur was a significant port city on the Persian Gulf; "Ur," Ancient History Encyclopedia, Joshua J. Mark, April 28, 2011, https://www.ancient.eu/ur/.

know what his past faith practices were before the beginning of God's transformational work in him. Joshua gives us a clear indication that Terah's family had integrated fully into the religious practices of the region in which they lived, and had their spiritual practices anchored in worshipping other gods.[2] It is in the context of daily life, including worshiping other gods, that the One True God will manifest himself to Abram for particular and intentional purposes.

This brief introduction to the general background of Abram's family lays the broad groundwork for the spiritual (faith) transformation that Abram will experience throughout the rest of his life, as his story unfolds for us through the next eleven chapters of Genesis.

God's Initial Promise, Abram's Response

God's specific dealings with Abram begin in Genesis 12 with a detailed invitation to *do* something, along with God's promise of blessing and Abram's response to God's call:

> Now the LORD said to Abram, "Go from your country and your kindred and your father's house to the land that I will show you. And I will make of you a great nation, and I will bless you and make your name great, so that you will be a blessing. I will bless those who bless you, and him who dishonors you I will curse, and in you all the families of the earth shall be blessed."
> So Abram went as the LORD had told him. (Gen. 12:1–4)

According to this passage, God invites Abram to step out in faith, to go to a land that is unknown to him. Additionally, God includes in that call a promise that reveals God's intended purposes for Abram's life: God will use Abram for the benefit of all nations.

---

2   To "serve" any god in any way is an act of worship. Thus, Terah and his family "worshipped" other gods.

The very next thing we read is that Abram obeys God's instruction. There is no objection. There is no questioning. He somehow recognizes that God is speaking to him, and he obeys.

Centuries later, we learn from the author of Hebrews that this one act of obedience by Abram (later known as Abraham) was considered a *response of faith* (Heb. 11:8). Our vantage point in time means that we know where the story about Abram's faith will end up: he becomes a great example of righteousness through faith. Therefore, questions necessarily arise: is there a difference between what appears to be an initial response of faith and trust in Jehovah God early in his life, and the faith required thirty-three years later to offer his son of promise as a sacrifice, in obedience to the command of that same God? Is there a difference between the type (and degree) of faith demonstrated in each situation? There is indeed a difference. Thus, other questions arise: how did Abram move from this initial act of obedience to the *word* of God, to the point where he was willing to be obedient *to God*, to ultimately be willing to sacrifice his son who was God's provision for the fulfillment of God's promise to him? What transformational work did God do in Abram, and how did he do it, to bring Abram to this future point of radical obedience? These are the questions that this chapter seeks to answer.

Let us take a closer look at God's promise to Abram. There are two elements of the promise that are important to our discussion. First, God says, "From you I will make a great nation" (v. 2), which means Abram is going to be prosperous and have offspring. The theological term used to refer to this part of the promise is *progeny*. Included in God's promise is that a great nation will grow from Abram's offspring. Second, God says that he is going to give Abram "the land that I will show you" (v. 1), which we eventually learn is Canaan. *Land* and *progeny* (offspring) are the two core elements of God's promise to Abram. The most critical element in Abram's mind is offspring, which becomes evident as his story unfolds. So indeed, that is the crucial element of his life that God uses to drive the entire process of transforming Abram's faith. In fact, in Genesis 12:4–5 we learn that his age (seventy-five) and the name of his wife (Sarai), as well as being childless, are the three facts of Abram's "everyday life" that God uses to reveal himself to Abram, and thus grow Abram's faith through the next thirty-three years of his life.

The first important point of Abram's story is his age. God is not concerned with our chronological age. He is interested in our "spiritual age," where we are in our journey toward genuine faith and our relationship with him. Abram's initial call at the age of seventy-five should be an encouragement to each of us. God can and does continue to transform our faith throughout our lives, regardless of our chronological age. The question is not how old (or young) we are, but whether we have the spiritual eyes and ears to see and hear God's call to us during life's daily events.

What does Abram's obedience of faith look like? "Abram took Sarai his wife, and Lot his brother's son, and all their possessions that they had gathered, and the people that they had acquired in Haran; and they set out to go to the land of Canaan" (Gen. 12:5). Abram hears God's instruction; he packs up his family and possessions and leaves Haran. Notice what their possessions include: the people that they have acquired while living in Haran. That refers to indentured servants. It is a sign that Abram's (and Lot's) wealth is beginning to grow.

Acts of Worship

The next thing we learn about Abram's story is that he and his family arrive in Canaan, specifically at Shechem. We also learn that the Canaanites were living in the land (v. 6). It is important to notice that the land is occupied by another people group who (presumably) consider it to be their land and their home. It is in this context that God appears to Abram a second time and says to him, "To your offspring, I will give this land" (v. 7).

What is Abram's response to God appearing and speaking to him a second time? An act of worship: he "built there an altar to the LORD, who had appeared to him" (v. 7). In religious life, building an altar to any god is for making sacrifices, which is an act of worship to that god. Here we see Abram, who came from a land where he "worshiped other gods," now building an altar to the LORD (in the

Old Testament this term refers to Yahweh). Such observable behavior as a simple act of worship is essential to notice; it reveals that the process of transformation is beginning to take place in Abram. This step of spiritual growth is the result of God "appearing" and "speaking" to him. So it is with us. From this one small piece of Abram's story, we can see that God reveals himself to his people through everyday life events. He desires to move us to recognize him as the One True God, which leads us to worship Him.

Abram's Faith Falters

Abram's story continues in Genesis 12 with Abram moving on to Bethel, pitching his tent, building another altar to the LORD, and then he calls "upon the name of the LORD" (v. 8). His act of worship has now expanded to include *calling on the name* of the LORD. God is becoming more personal and thus more real to Abram. That infers a growing relationship between Abram and God, another step in the process of transformation, in which God is becoming more of a *person* and less of an *idea*.

However, Abram's faith falters. Amid a potentially life-threatening situation, he asks his wife to lie to save his own life:

> Now there was a famine in the land. So Abram went down to Egypt to sojourn there, for the famine was severe in the land. When he was about to enter Egypt, he said to Sarai his wife, "I know that you are a woman beautiful in appearance, and when the Egyptians see you, they will say, 'This is his wife.' Then they will kill me, but they will let you live. Say you are my sister, that it may go well with me because of you, and that my life may be spared for your sake."[3] (Gen. 12:10–13)

---

3   Asking Sarai to say she is Abram's sister is not a complete lie. In fact, she was his half sister, having the same father, but different mothers. In Judaism, the

It seems appropriate at this point to ask "Where is God in this?" Does this famine occur by chance or by the will of God? Scripture does not say. We do not know if God has told Abram to go to Egypt. It is apparent, however, that God does not stop him from going. We will soon see that God does, indeed, have a purpose in Abram going to Egypt. Thus, the sovereignty of God supports the conclusion that God is somehow actively involved in this chain of events.

There is another question to ponder: Why does Abram ask Sarai to lie? Verse 12 reveals that he fears for his life: "They will kill me." As this episode continues, we find that Abram's fears are valid. Sarai is indeed seen as quite desirable and is "taken into Pharaoh's house" (Gen. 12:14–15). Thus, for *Sarai's sake*, Pharaoh is kind toward Abram. Usually, we would look at Abram's actions and consider them justified in light of the cultural norms of that time. That would be the human perspective, but God sees things differently. Verse 17 states, "But the LORD afflicted Pharaoh and his house with great plagues because of Sarai, Abram's wife."

We need to examine Abram's actions from God's perspective, from the context of the promise, rather than from a human perspective or cultural norms. His actions reveal that he doubts God's promise to him. How can the promise of offspring be fulfilled if he dies? Abram's request that Sarai lie to protect his life is an indication that his faith is quite weak. He has heard the promise from God and seems to accept it as truth to some degree. The evidence of this is that his faith in God has begun to grow: he worshipped God in response to the promise.

If Abram *trusts* the promise of offspring and *trusts* that the one who gave the promise will be faithful to that promise, he will not fear for his life now. Genuine faith includes *both belief and trust*. The role of these components of faith is to facilitate the process of transforming our faith to the point of surrender to God's will, which leads to acts of obedience. And so it is with Abram. We see indication here

---

bloodline comes down through the mother. So it is possible that Abram did not view this request as asking Sarai to lie. Yet, it is clear that he is afraid for his own safety and thus asks Sarai to tell a partial truth, which we, today, view as a lie.

that he has some level of belief, *mental assent*, to the truth of God's promise to him—at least at the time when he received the promise. His behavior now reveals that he is still acting from a place of doubt (lack of faith), and thus asks Sarai to lie for his safety. His mental belief has not yet moved to heart-level trust. As a result, he fears for his life rather than trusting God to keep him safe in order to fulfill God's promise to him.

The result of Abram's weak faith is that others suffer "great plagues" (Gen. 12:17). The text does not tell how Pharaoh knows that Abram lied, yet he does know. He also knows that Abram's lie is behind God's actions against him and his household. As a result, Pharaoh calls Abram to appear before him and confronts him with his lie (vv. 18–19). From the text, we can see that God intentionally set up this series of daily life events and allows Abram to walk right into them, to teach Abram a lesson as part of the transformation process. What is that lesson? That God *will* fulfill his promise to Abram by preventing any event from occurring that would cause God's promise to fail, such as Pharaoh taking Sarai to be his wife.

Pharaoh ultimately kicks Abram out of Egypt, yet he lets Abram keep all of the flocks, herds, and other things he gave Abram when he took Sarai as his wife. It is interesting to note that because of the famine and the move to Egypt, Abram ends up with more possessions. Does he suffer loss because of the drought? No. Is he punished for the lie that he told? Not if we view "punishment" as a loss, a loss that is a consequence of sin. Does he learn a lesson of trust from what happened? As the story continues, it will become readily apparent that he has not learned this lesson, not yet. Abram is a slow learner, and so are we.

Indicators of Further Transformation

In Genesis 13, Abram goes back to the Negeb (the desert in the land of Canaan), specifically to Bethel, where he built the altar when he first arrived in Canaan (v. 3). We learn the extent of Abram's wealth (v. 2), which grew as a result of his time in Egypt. We also see another act of worship that indicates his faith in God still exists.

Here at Bethel, he calls "upon the name of the LORD" (v. 4). It is significant that after all he experienced in Egypt—asking Sarai to lie for him and then having his wife taken from him—Abram comes back to the place where he was when he first received God's promise, and again worships God, again calls upon the name of the LORD. As was previously mentioned, such an act for one who formally worshipped other gods is an indication of the progress of transformation in Abram. So, we may not know for sure if the experiences in Egypt taught him a vital faith lesson. However, what is clear from the text is that although his experiences in Egypt tested his faith in God, they did not destroy his faith. It might seem that they somehow solidified his belief in God, as evidenced by this act of worship.

The middle section of Genesis 13, verses 5–12, is the story of Abram separating from his nephew Lot, who has been with him since he left Haran. As Abram prospers, accumulating flocks and herds, so does Lot. Thus, their combined flocks and herds are now too big for them to dwell together; they each need to find land that will appropriately support their flocks and herds. What does Abram do? He gives Lot the choice of taking the fertile land to the left of where they stand, which is described as having water, grass, and fields, versus taking the land to the right, which is the Negeb, the desert. It is here that a new set of subtle changes in Abram's faith become apparent. According to cultural norms, as the head of the family, he has the right to choose the area where he wants to settle. Instead, he lets Lot choose first. That is another indication of the ongoing transformation of Abram's faith. We have already seen Abram begin to worship the LORD. Here we see what appears to be the emergence of *trust in God*, the kind of trust that leads one to think, "God can fulfill his promise regardless of whether or not Lot chooses the choicest land."

Notice how God responds to Abram's emerging trust:

> The LORD said to Abram, after Lot had separated from him, "Lift up your eyes and look from the place where you are, northward and southward and eastward and westward, for all the land that you see I will give to you and to your off-

spring forever. I will make your offspring as the dust of the earth, so that if one can count the dust of the earth, your offspring also can be counted. Arise, walk through the length and the breadth of the land, for I will give it to you." So Abram moved his tent and came and settled by the oaks of Mamre, which are at Hebron, and there he built an altar to the LORD. (Gen. 13:14–18)

After Abram separates from Lot, God comes immediately to Abram and renews the promises he has previously made, of both land and offspring. Note that God changes the terminology he uses in renewing the promise. He starts by reaffirming the promise regarding land, but this time expands the promise. It is not just "this land" as God previously stated the promise (Gen. 12:7), but "all the land that you see" in all directions (Gen. 13:15), "northward and southward and eastward and westward" (v. 14). God also reaffirms his promise of offspring, but again states it differently: "I will make your offspring as the dust of the earth" (v. 16). By restating his promises to Abram with expanded details, it seems God is affirming his faithfulness to do as he has promised. God is not only going to "give this land," but all the land Abram can see in every direction. He is not just going to give Abram offspring; they will be too numerous to count.

In response to God's affirmation of his promises, Abram again engages in the act of worship. After moving on to "the oaks of Mamre," he again builds "an altar to the LORD" (v. 18). This repetitive act of worship in Abram's life is a way of acknowledging God concretely. It appears that a life habit of worship is developing, providing further evidence that ongoing transformation is occurring.

In Genesis 14, the area where Lot lives with his family, including Sodom and Gomorrah, are attacked and overcome by enemy kings of the surrounding area. Lot and his family and all his possessions are taken away as captives, along with the other residents of that area. When Abram hears the news, he goes to rescue Lot and his family and the rest of the people taken with him (v. 13–16). He does this with only 318 trained men "born in his house" (v. 14). Interestingly, Abram asks no one else outside of his family for assistance with rescuing a family member. He takes only his trained men. He seems to know that he does not have to rely on men outside of his family to accomplish the rescue of Lot and the others. Indeed, Abram and his men are victorious in their rescue efforts, routing the enemy forces and rescuing all the captives and their possessions. Abram's apparent reliance only upon people under his authority may be an indication that his trust in God to protect him is growing. It may be a sign that continuing transformation is taking place, as God is gradually becoming more real to Abram personally. With each "visit" from God, it seems he can trust God a little more, as though his *rational belief in God's promises* is being transformed into *heart-level trust in God himself* to protect him and enable him to be successful in the ensuing fight.

Abram returns from his victory over the marauding kings. They must be feeling good, having defeated the enemy forces with just his men. A revealing exchange ensues between Abram and Melchizedek, king of Salem, who is also "priest of God Most High" (Gen. 12:18). Melchizedek blesses Abram and says:

> Blessed be Abram by God Most High,
> Possessor of heaven and earth;
> and blessed be God Most High,
> who has delivered your enemies into your hand!
> (Gen. 14:18–20)

Upon hearing this blessing and declaration of *who God is* and *what God has done* in his life, Abram gives the priest a tenth of everything (v. 20). That represents the spiritual practice of tithing. Additionally, he refuses the legitimate spoils of war, saying, "Lest you should say, 'I have made Abram rich'" (v. 23). It seems Abram is trying to avoid having any person other than God be in a position to take credit for his growing wealth and status in the area. He is willing to engage in spiritual practices as a response to the blessing. Both of these reveal that transformation continues to take place in Abram.

There is another indicator of ongoing transformation evident in this part of Abram's story. He is offered the spoils of war by the king of Sodom, which was a tradition in the ancient Near East. Only the men who go out to battle normally receive a share of the spoil, as compensation for engaging in the fight. However, Abram reveals that prior to going to war, he made a vow to the LORD, saying, "I have lifted my hand to the LORD, God Most High, Possessor of heaven and earth, that I would not take a thread or a sandal strap or anything that is yours" (vv. 22–23). Here is a critical point in the process of transforming Abram's faith. Here we see that Abram has moved from worshiping God by building altars and calling on the name of the LORD, to making a vow to the LORD before a battle—a vow that dictates his behavior after the victorious battle. When offered the spoils of war, he did not take what was by custom his right to take, to not negate that vow.

Through this series of events, we can see the results of God transforming Abram's faith. Before going to battle, he makes a vow to take nothing for himself as compensation for the victory he hoped to achieve. Then God sends a priest to him to teach him that God gave him the victory so that Abram would not think that he had achieved this great victory in his own strength and wisdom. Through life events and the words of others, God is making more of himself known to Abram personally. God is continuing to become more real for Abram through these life experiences, and in the process, his heart and his faith are being transformed. He has moved from being a person who asked another to lie to potentially spare his own life, to refusing to accept what is rightfully his in order to remain faithful to his vow to God.

Affirmation of Promise and Covenant

In Genesis 15, we see God's response to what Abram did in chapter 14:

> After these things the word of the LORD came to Abram in a vision: "Fear not, Abram, I am your shield; your reward shall be very great." But Abram said, "O Lord GOD, what will you give me, for I continue childless, and the heir of my house is Eliezer of Damascus?" And Abram said, "Behold, you have given me no offspring, and a member of my household will be my heir." And behold, the word of the LORD came to him: "This man shall not be your heir; your very own son shall be your heir." (Gen. 15:1–4)

Returning victorious from battle, Abram honors his vow to God. In return, God again speaks to Abram with words of reassurance, saying, "Your reward shall be very great" (v. 1). However, in Abram's mind, there is only one kind of reward. So, he asks God, "What will you give me, for I continue childless" (v. 2). Even though we have seen evidence of Abram's faith being transformed, his lack of trust in God's faithfulness to fulfill his promise remains evident. God's word alone is not yet sufficient for Abram to fully trust God's promise.

God then restates his promise of an heir for a third time, again in different terms, as a way of reassuring Abram that God is, indeed, faithful: "And he brought him outside and said, 'Look toward heaven, and number the stars, if you are able to number them.' Then he said to him, 'So shall your offspring be'" (v. 5). What was Abram's response to this third affirmation of God's promise to him? He "believed the LORD, and [God] counted it to him as righteousness" (v. 6). We continue to see God's patience with Abram, frequently reaffirming his promise as a way of building Abram's faith beyond mere mental assent. Gradually Abram's heart is being affected, and thus, his faith is being transformed as he learns more about God's character, beyond what God has promised to *who God is*. Here is the point: each time Abram encounters God, he is learning more about *who God is*. Thus, God is becoming more and more real to him; his trust in God is deepened and strengthened as he slowly learns with each encounter that God will be faithful to his word.

Although Abram believes what the LORD has said, he is still questioning how he is to *know* that he and his offspring will possess the land (v. 8). God responds to this questioning with a "real-life event" designed to build deeper trust in Abram. God invites him to bring animals to him and cut them in two. He then causes Abram to sleep. The story continues:

> Then the LORD said to Abram, "Know for certain that your offspring will be sojourners in a land that is not theirs and will be servants there, and they will be afflicted for four hundred years. But I will bring judgment on the nation that they serve, and afterward they shall come out with great possessions. As for you, you shall go to your fathers in peace; you shall be buried in a good old age. And they shall come back here in the fourth generation, for the iniquity of the Amorites is not yet complete." (Gen. 15:13–16)

While Abram is in a deep sleep, God moves from reaffirming his promises to making a covenant commitment to Abram:

> When the sun had gone down and it was dark, behold, a smoking fire pot and a flaming torch passed between these pieces. On that day the LORD made a covenant with Abram, saying, "To your offspring I give this land, from the river of Egypt to the great river, the river Euphrates, the land of the Kenites, the Kenizzites, the Kadmonites, the Hittites, the Perizzites, the

Rephaim, the Amorites, the Canaanites, the Girgashites and the Jebusites." (Gen. 15:17–19)

From a human perspective, this is a significant move on God's part. No longer does God only promise land and offspring to Abram. Instead, he executes a covenant with Abram. Abram would have viewed the covenant as a more significant level of commitment than just a promise. Please note, however, that from God's perspective, making a promise has the same binding effect upon *himself* as a covenant. To God, his word is binding, whether given as a promise or as a covenant; neither requires anything from Abram in return. God executes the covenant for Abram's benefit. It is designed to build his trust in God's faithfulness to his word, as reflected in the phrase, "Know for certain" (v. 13). God not only reassures Abram that he is going to have offspring, but he also reveals what will happen to those future offspring. Through this process, Abram is experiencing more of God's real character. God seeks to build Abram's trust by moving from making a promise to Abram to executing a covenant commitment to him. In doing so, God commits himself to fulfill the terms of the covenant. All of the promises and revelation through covenant are designed to further build Abram's trust in God's faithfulness to his word.

Here is a significant and fantastic point about this part of Abram's story. Abram still does not have a sufficient level of trust that God will fulfill his word. However, God is not mad at him for his lack of trust; he does not rebuke Abram. God continues the process of intentionally and incrementally transforming Abram's faith over time. And he does so with each of us.

Human Solution to a Divine Promise

By Genesis 16, it has been sixteen years since God's initial promise to Abram; he is now eighty-six years old. In this chapter, we come to the events involving Sarai and her maidservant Hagar. Sarai's actions demonstrate her lack of trust in the promise of God. Sarai is ten years younger than Abram, so at this time, she is seventy-six years old and well past childbearing age. She loves her husband, and from the text, it seems apparent that she wants Abram to have a son. So, she takes matters into her own hands:

> Now Sarai, Abram's wife, had borne him no children. She had a female Egyptian servant whose name was Hagar. And Sarai said to Abram, "Behold now, the LORD has prevented me from bearing children. Go in to my servant; it may be that I shall obtain children by her." And Abram listened to the voice of Sarai. So, after Abram had lived ten years in the land of Canaan, Sarai, Abram's wife, took Hagar the Egyptian, her servant, and gave her to Abram her husband as a wife. And he went in to Hagar, and she conceived. (Gen. 16:1–4a)

Note that Sarai believes God is preventing her from bearing children, but still believes God's promise to Abram to have offspring. Her faith is not strong enough to trust in God's timing and God's way of fulfilling his promise to Abram. She does not believe God will cause *her* to bear Abram a son at such an advanced age, so she devises a rational solution to a divine situation. We can all learn from Sarai that attempting to manipulate circumstances to fulfill God's promise by human means is never the best thing to do.

This passage again reveals Abram's wavering faith when influenced by Sarai's suggestion. He does not have the faith and, therefore, the courage to say *no* to Sarai. Rather than accepting her solution to this faith situation, he might have said to Sarai (if he were as trusting now as he will be later in his life), "My trust is in the LORD. The LORD has established a covenant with me. His reputation, his character, his glory, his honor is fully on the line. I trust him to fulfill that covenant commitment that he has made with me in his way and in his time." However, Abram does not think this way. He does not believe that this is accurate because he agrees with Sarai's suggestion. Thus, the whole episode with Abram and Hagar ensues, and she finds herself pregnant. Indeed, a son is born to Abram, but not through God's planned process, not by God's promised action.

One would think that Sarai would be pleased that her maidservant bears a son for Abram. After all, isn't that why she suggested this course of action, for Abram to have an heir? However, rather than being pleased, Sarai gets jealous; she wants to banish Hagar from their household. Once again, Abram acquiesces to Sarai's demands. However, God intervenes and redeems Hagar and her son (Gen. 16:7–11, 15; 17:20). Hagar's son, Ishmael, is not included in God's promise to Abram. Still, God is merciful to Ishmael. God will give him a parallel but separate promise.

One of the lessons of this part of Abram's story is that God intends to fulfill his promises to us, but *in his time and in his way.* When he seems to delay fulfilling those promises, we often become impatient and seek out ways to make God's promises become a reality through our effort. Moreover, in the process, we say we are merely acting on God's behalf. In reality, however, our impatience reveals a lack of trust and faith in God's faithfulness. When we seek to speed up God's timing, we often end up creating more of a mess, not just in our own lives, but often in the lives of others. In his sovereignty and love, God blesses those caught in our schemes, yet he will not accept our attempts to fulfill his promises on his behalf through our self-effort. His delay is usually designed to strengthen and deepen our faith as we wait for him to do as he has promised. The better blessing is to wait upon the LORD and his timing.

Fourth Affirmation of God's Promise

Another thirteen years pass before the story picks up again in Genesis 17. Abram is now ninety-nine years old when God appears to him again:

> When Abram was ninety-nine years old the
> LORD appeared to Abram and said to him, "I am
> God Almighty; walk before me, and be blameless,
> that I may make my covenant between me and

you, and may multiply you greatly." Then Abram fell on his face. And God said to him, "Behold, my covenant is with you, and you shall be the father of a multitude of nations. No longer shall your name be called Abram, but your name shall be Abraham, for I have made you the father of a multitude of nations. I will make you exceedingly fruitful, and I will make you into nations, and kings shall come from you. And I will establish my covenant between me and you and your offspring after you throughout their generations for an everlasting covenant, to be God to you and to your offspring after you. And I will give to you and to your offspring after you the land of your sojournings, all the land of Canaan, for an everlasting possession, and I will be their God."
(Gen. 17:1–8)

What is the very first thing that God does when he appears again to Abram? He renews the covenant for the *fourth* time. However, notice that the language that God uses is getting increasingly large. This time he says that he will make Abram be the "father of a multitude of nations" (v. 4) and he will be "exceedingly fruitful" (v. 6). The descriptive words are getting more grandiose as God renews the covenant again and again with Abram.

The second thing God does at this time is to change Abram's name to Abraham. The act of naming is significant in Scripture, going back to Adam, who named Eve in the garden and as well as all the animals. Naming is a recognition of authority; the one who names another has authority over the one named.[4] Additionally, names in Scripture are often known to represent a description of that

---

4   Genesis 1:28: God gave dominion (authority) over "every living thing that moves upon the earth." Genesis 2:19: God brought all living creatures to Adam "to see what he would call them; and whatever the man called every living creature, that was its name."

person.[5] By changing Abram's name to *Abraham*, God is saying to him, "I am sovereign over you, so much so that I am going to change your name." God is demonstrating another aspect of his character to Abram: God is in authority over him.

Remember, God is working to get Abram to trust him completely and unconditionally and with good reason. Thirteen years have passed since God last reaffirmed his promise to Abram (after Ishmael was born). If Abram did not trust God to fulfill his promise then, seemingly nothing has transpired in the interim to change that. We see a few verses later evidence of Abraham's continuing lack of genuine faith: he falls on his face and laughs and questions within himself if a child can be born to a man as old as he is (v. 17). He also questions Sarai's ability to have a child at her age. Abraham still does not trust God to fulfill his promise. Thus, God steps in and changes his name to demonstrate his authority over this situation, indeed over all of Abraham's life.

In Genesis 17:9–14, God takes a third step to provide further evidence of his commitment to his covenant with Abraham: he requires Abraham to circumcise the foreskin of all males "born in your house or bought with your money" (v. 12). That will be a constant physical reminder to all men in Abraham's family, and eventually for the entire nation of Israel, of the covenant God made with Abraham. By doing so, God is, in essence, saying to Abraham, "If you have trouble remembering my word, my promise to you, then here is a physical reminder of my covenant with you."

We can see that over time, God does not speak harshly or rebuke Abraham for his recurring lack of trust in God's word to him, but instead very lovingly, throughout twenty-nine years, he first makes a promise, then refines the promise with a more expansive description of it. He then turns the promise into a covenant in which God commits *himself alone* to fulfill, and then again renews the covenant commitment, emphasizing God's sovereignty and character by a name change, along with the physical reminder of the covenant through

---

5   One Hebrew meaning of *Abraham* is "father of many."

circumcision. God uses all of these different ways to build Abraham's trust that God will, indeed, be faithful to his promises.

How does Abraham respond? By again being obedient to do what God told him to do:

> Then Abraham took Ishmael his son and all those born in his house or bought with his money, every male among the men of Abraham's house, and he circumcised the flesh of their foreskins that very day, as God had said to him. Abraham was ninety-nine years old when he was circumcised in the flesh of his foreskin. And Ishmael his son was thirteen years old when he was circumcised in the flesh of his foreskin. That very day Abraham and his son Ishmael were circumcised. And all the men of his house, those born in the house and those bought with money from a foreigner, were circumcised with him. (Gen. 17:23–27)

No questions, no argument. Abraham does it—that very day.

God does the same thing for Sarai: he changes her name to *Sarah* (Gen. 17:15). He then says to Abraham, "I will give you a son by her. I will bless her, and she shall become nations; kings of peoples shall come from her" (v. 16). Sarai has not trusted God's promise either. She demonstrated that by convincing Abram to have a child with her maidservant Hagar.

Nevertheless, God has not wavered in his commitment to his initial promise to Abram. Almost three decades later, God is still committed to fulfilling his promise. Despite all of this, there still seems to be a lack of trust in Abraham:

> Then Abraham fell on his face and laughed and said to himself, "Shall a child be born to a man who is a hundred years old? Shall Sarah, who is ninety years old, bear a child?" And Abraham said to God, "Oh that Ishmael might live before you!"

God said, "No, but Sarah your wife shall bear
you a son, and you shall call his name Isaac. I will
establish my covenant with him as an everlasting covenant for his offspring after him." (Gen.
17:17–19)

By his statement, Abraham reveals that he thinks Ishmael might
be the one through whom God will fulfill his covenant promise as an
everlasting covenant. Ishmael is indeed Abraham's offspring; he just
was not an offspring of Sarah, nor is he the offspring through whom
God will fulfill his promise to Abraham. Again, rather than chastis-
ing Abraham for his lack of trust, God says *no* and, instead, lovingly
tries to move Abraham to a higher level of trust. He reaffirms that
Sarah will be the one to bear God's promised son by revealing that
son's name, thus again demonstrating his authority over the fulfillment of his promise and the promised offspring. God again states
that it is through *this* son that God will fulfill his promise and covenant to Abraham. Through all of this, God seems to be saying, "Do
you honestly think, after all I have just said, that I will not fulfill my
promise to you?"

Please remember, we are examining these texts from the perspective of "Where is God in this?" and "How does God transform
Abraham's simple belief to genuine faith?" Notice again the gentle,
loving way in which God is training Abraham to trust God's word
to him and, therefore, to *trust God himself.* This step-by-step transformational process is moving Abraham ever closer to the mountain
on which he will be asked to sacrifice his promised son, although he
does not know it.

What can we learn from Abraham's story to this point? We, like
Abraham, usually do not know what God is preparing us for through
daily life events. The transformation process that leads from simple
belief to genuine faith is the process of God revealing himself to us
in incremental ways throughout our daily life experiences, in order
to grow our trust and deepen our faith in *who he is for us as our God.*

Final Affirmation of the Promise

In the opening of Genesis 18, the LORD, accompanied by two angelic beings, comes to Abraham's camp. Recognizing that they are important men, Abraham engages in cultural hospitality by inviting them to rest and has food prepared to serve them. The story continues:

> They said to him, "Where is Sarah your wife?" And he said, "She is in the tent." The LORD said, "I will surely return to you about this time next year, and Sarah your wife shall have a son." And Sarah was listening at the tent door behind him. Now Abraham and Sarah were old, advanced in years. The way of women had ceased to be with Sarah. So Sarah laughed to herself, saying, "After I am worn out, and my lord is old, shall I have pleasure?" The LORD said to Abraham, "Why did Sarah laugh and say, 'Shall I indeed bear a child, now that I am old?' Is anything too hard for the LORD? At the appointed time I will return to you, about this time next year, and Sarah shall have a son." But Sarah denied it, saying, "I did not laugh," for she was afraid. He said, "No, but you did laugh." (Gen. 18:9–15)

Once again God comes to Abraham, this time to announce that the time has finally arrived for the fulfillment of God's promise to him; namely, within a year he will have a son with Sarah. Sarah laughs to herself in unbelief, but the LORD hears it. So, he asks Abraham, "Why did Sarah laugh… Is anything too hard for the LORD" (vv. 13–14)? In reality, God is asking Abraham, "Does she still not trust me?" Still, when Sarah denies having laughed, the LORD delivers a gentle rebuke to her, saying only, "No, but you did laugh." In other words, "Your response reveals that you do not yet trust my word."

Can one blame Sarah? She is ninety years old, and the text says that she could no longer bear children; it is a physical impossibility from a human perspective. Thus, God gently rebukes her and Abraham by asking, "Is anything too hard for the LORD" (v. 14)? This is a crucial question to keep in mind as God transforms each of us.

More Trust-Building Events

The focus of the story now moves to Sodom and Gomorrah. God has been receiving complaints about the moral corruption in these cities through the prayers of his people, and it is to these cities that the three men go. It is evident that Abraham understands the moral situation and suspects what is going to happen. Unmistakably he is concerned for the welfare of Lot and his family; he intercedes with God, asking God if he will indeed destroy the righteous with the unrighteous:

> Then Abraham drew near and said, "Will you indeed sweep away the righteous with the wicked? Suppose there are fifty righteous within the city. Will you then sweep away the place and not spare it for the fifty righteous who are in it? Far be it from you to do such a thing, to put the righteous to death with the wicked, so that the righteous fare as the wicked! Far be that from you! Shall not the Judge of all the earth do what is just?" And the LORD said, "If I find at Sodom fifty righteous in the city, I will spare the whole place for their sake." (Gen. 18:23–26)

Abraham's ongoing questioning continues to lower the number of righteous people that might be minimal enough for God to change his mind about passing judgment on the unrighteous for the sake of the righteous. Abraham's final question is, "'Suppose ten are found there.' [God] answered, 'For the sake of ten I will not destroy it.' And the LORD went his way, when he had finished speaking to Abraham, and Abraham returned to his place" (vv. 32–33).

Abraham likely does not have any interest in those cities other than the safety of his nephew and his nephew's family. Abraham's motivation in speaking to the LORD in this way is solely to save Lot. God acquiesces to Abraham's concerns, finally agreeing not to destroy the cities if there is a minimum of ten righteous people found there. However, the LORD's motivation in engaging in this conversation with Abraham is for the continuing transformation of his faith:

> The LORD said, "Shall I hide from Abraham what I am about to do, seeing that Abraham shall surely become a great and mighty nation, and all the nations of the earth shall be blessed in him? For I have chosen him, that he may command his children and his household after him to keep the way of the LORD by doing righteousness and justice, so that the LORD may bring to Abraham what he has promised him." (Gen. 18:17–19)

God is effectively saying, "Righteous and just as my actions will be, I do not want to destroy the trust that I am building in Abraham." Thus, he allows Abraham to drill down to a minimal number of righteous people, and God agrees to this request. Here is another step of building trust, of God making himself real to Abraham through specific life experiences.

In Genesis 19, the two angels visit the city (the LORD remained behind talking with Abraham), and Lot greets them (v. 1). A mob comprised of the men of the city come to Lot's house seeking to "know" the two newcomers to the city. Lot instead offers his two daughters to the mob to "do with them as you please" (v. 8), even though his daughters are betrothed to be married (v. 14). This offer does not mollify the mob, and ultimately, the angels throw the men into confusion by blinding them in order to save Lot and his family from the mob. Consequently, the angels seal the fate of the cities. They urge Lot to take his family out of the city before the destruction begins (v. 12). Once Lot and his family are safely moved to their new city, Zoar, the LORD rains down fire and sulfur on Sodom, Gomorrah, and the surrounding fields and pastures, destroying everything (vv. 15–25). Verse 29 says that "when God destroyed the cities of the valley, God remembered Abraham and sent Lot out of the midst of the overthrow when he overthrew the cities in which Lot had lived."

The next morning, Abraham stood overlooking the valley and saw the destruction that had taken place. What he saw was a physical demonstration of God's power, which reveals to Abraham who God genuinely is—a mighty God. The manifestation of God's power in the physical world is one way in which God reveals himself to us. He uses that demonstration to move us from unbelief to belief, and from simple belief to trust. In this case, God's demonstration of his power to Abraham was likely used to remind Abraham again that God is all-powerful; there is nothing that God cannot do. Thus, this demonstration of power provides further confirmation to Abraham that God will be faithful to his promises; he is powerful enough to fulfill his promises. This demonstration of God's power as a part of the process of transforming our faith is a theme that is seen again and again in different biblical stories.

This part of Abraham's story reminds us of God's purpose that we have seen from the beginning: to cultivate deep abiding faith in Abraham. Abraham was undoubtedly aware of God's intention to destroy Sodom and Gomorrah, based on his attempt to talk God out of destroying the righteous with the wicked (Gen. 18:23–32). Looking down on the valley below the next day, Abraham sees the power of God come face-to-face with the mercy and compassion of God, which he displayed to Abraham the day before by acknowledging that he would, indeed, set aside his wrath for the sake of the righteous. Moreover, by saving Lot and his family from certain destruction, God takes an additional step in building unconditional trust in Abraham.

Abraham's Faith Falters Again

In Genesis 20, Abraham sojourns in Gerar and encounters Abimelech, king of Gerar. Here we discover that Abraham's faith is still quite inconsistent; he fears for his life once again in a foreign land and again lies about Sarah being his sister. So once again, God intervenes to protect the future fulfillment of his promise to Abraham. God visits Abimelech in a dream, tells him Sarah is another man's wife, and reveals that it was God who kept the king from sinning by not having touched Sarah. God then instructs Abimelech to return Sarah to Abraham and promises Abimelech that Abraham will pray for him because he is a prophet (see Gen. 20:3–11).

Abimelech immediately goes and confronts Abraham with his deception, and ultimately gives Abraham freedom to live in the land wherever he chooses. Additionally, Abimelech gives Abraham a large amount of silver as a sign of Sarah's innocence. Finally, Abraham prays for Abimelech, as God foretold in the dream. That prayer brings healing to Abimelech's household, in which the women had become barren because of Sarah's presence (see Gen. 20:8–18). That must have had an impact both upon Abraham and Abimelech; removing the barrenness of women is a significant answer to prayer.

However, for our purposes, the critical element here is not what was accomplished by prayer, but *the act of prayer itself.* We have seen on several previous occasions how Abraham worshiped God, how he "called upon the name of the LORD," which is an act of worship. Here in this text, we see for the first time that Abraham's relationship with God and his belief and trust in God have slowly grown to the point that he now enters into prayer for another person. Indeed, choosing to pray for God to intervene in the life of another reveals a certain level of trust in the relationship between God and the one who prays; it requires a certain amount of trust and faith in *who God is*—his heart of compassion and mercy, and *his faithfulness* to answer those prayers.

Unmistakably Abraham has been conversing with God ("conversation" is a form of prayer). For example, in the past few chapters, he has talked to God about Sarah's barrenness, and he tried to stop the planned destruction of Sodom and Gomorrah by negotiating with God. Here Abraham is praying on behalf of Abimelech and his household. He has moved from discussing personal problems with God to praying for others—in essence, asking God to intervene in the life circumstances of others outside of his own family. From this we see indication of continuing transformation in Abraham.

It might be worthwhile to briefly summarize some key points of Abraham's life up to this point. He is one hundred years old; thirty years have passed since he left Ur of the Chaldeans. Twenty-five years have passed since he received God's promise for the first time. Abraham has at times been obedient to God, and just as often, he has displayed little to no faith or trust in God. As we move through the rest of the story of Abraham's life, we will see how God continues to transform him slowly, yet patiently. By continuing to experience God's mercy and patience, Abraham's faith continues to be transformed.

Promise Fulfilled and Faith Tested

In Genesis 21, God begins to fulfill both main parts of the long-awaited promise (progeny and land). Abraham is now one hundred years old, and Sarah is ninety. They are in the land of Canaan, and now Abraham has a son by Sarah. They name the child Isaac as previously instructed (Gen. 17:19) and, on the eighth day, is circumcised according to the command of God as a physical sign of the covenant made to Abraham. They then throw a grand celebration, for this birth has been anticipated for twenty-five years.

During the party, Sarah is sitting there (most likely holding Isaac in her arms) and looks across the crowd to see Hagar laughing. There is no indication in the text to tell us why Hagar is laughing. Her son Ishmael is now thirteen years old. Hagar has received from God her promise concerning her son. There is no indication that she is laughing at Sarah, but Sarah responds as if Hagar *is* laughing at her.

Therefore, she tells Abraham to get rid of her. What was Abraham's response to his wife's request, and how did God respond to Abraham?

> And the thing was very displeasing to Abraham on account of his son. But God said to Abraham, "Be not displeased because of the boy and because of your slave woman. Whatever Sarah says to you, do as she tells you, for through Isaac shall your offspring be named. And I will make a nation of the son of the slave woman also, because he is your offspring." So Abraham rose early in the morning and took bread and a skin of water and gave it to Hagar, putting it on her shoulder, along with the child, and sent her away. And she departed and wandered in the wilderness of Beersheba. (Gen. 21:11–14)

From a cultural perspective of the ancient Near East, Ishmael is Abraham's son, just as Isaac is. When Sarah told Abraham to get rid of Hagar, Abraham likely looked at Ishmael and thought, "But this is my son!" God understands the heart of Abraham and immediately responds, in essence saying, "Do not be worried. I am great enough and will take care of Hagar and Ishmael too." Notice that the promise God gives regarding Ishmael is parallel to that given to Abraham: land and progeny (offspring); yet it is separate from the promise that the birth of Isaac will begin to fulfill. Thus, God's promise to Ishmael does not come forward to today through the biblical line of the patriarchs. God treats Ishmael similarly to Isaac; he will become a nation and occupy land that will be given to him, although that land will not be as good as the land promised to Isaac. He will continuously wander and regularly experience conflict with his neighbors, but he *will* become a nation. Moreover, that nation *will* occupy a land of its own. One can see the fulfillment of this promise throughout history to this very day, as the descendants of Ishmael eventually settled in what we now call the Middle East: Saudi Arabia, Iraq, and Iran.

Now let us focus upon the impact this incident must have had on transforming Abraham's faith. Remember, we are examining his story by asking the questions "Where is God in this?" and "How is God transforming Abraham's faith?" through ordinary, daily situations and circumstances. By speaking to Abraham quickly after Sarah insists that he send Hagar and Ishmael away, God continues to reveal himself to Abraham, continues to build his trust. God's words to Abraham seem to be intended to calm his father's heartfelt concern for his son Ishmael. God understands that, to Abraham, both boys are his sons. God promises Abraham that *this* son will also receive blessings from God; he will not be forgotten or set aside.

Moving further into Genesis 21, Abraham again encounters Abimelech, who has observed that Abraham is prospering and attributes that to God, saying, "God is with you in all that you do" (v. 22). At every turn, through many daily life events, God is working to transform Abraham's faith and trust, and the blessings of Abraham's relationship with God are evident to others. Here God uses Abimelech, king of the Philistines, to gently remind Abraham that "all that you have is because of *me*."

Immediately following this reminder of what God has done for Abraham, an incident occurs between the two men that represents a test of Abraham's faith and indicates further transformation in Abraham:

> When Abraham reproved Abimelech about a well of water that Abimelech's servants had seized, Abimelech said, "I do not know who has done this thing; you did not tell me, and I have not heard of it until today." So Abraham took sheep and oxen and gave them to Abimelech, and the two men made a covenant. Abraham set seven ewe lambs of the flock apart. And Abimelech said to Abraham, "What is the meaning of these seven ewe lambs that you have set apart?" He said, "These seven ewe lambs you will take from my hand, that this may be a wit-

ness for me that I dug this well." Therefore that place was called Beersheba, because there both of them swore an oath. So they made a covenant at Beersheba. Then Abimelech and Phicol the commander of his army rose up and returned to the land of the Philistines. Abraham planted a tamarisk tree in Beersheba and called there on the name of the LORD, the Everlasting God. And Abraham sojourned many days in the land of the Philistines. (Gen. 21:25–34)

In this passage, Abraham and Abimelech resolve a dispute among their servants over a well. Access to water is essential in arid lands. It also represents an element of power: the owner of the land has power over those who travel through the land, for they can control access to vital water supplies. Thus, this critical issue needs resolution because it is related to God's covenant promise to Abraham that his offspring will live in *this* land. If there is no access to water, a shepherd cannot graze his flocks and herds. This vital issue could have sorely tested Abraham, yet Abraham responds to the conflict directly with confidence and gentleness, an additional indication of his growing trust in God. He then plants a tamarisk tree on the spot and again calls "on the name of the LORD, the Everlasting God" (v. 33), which is an act of worship. Note that this time the term *everlasting* is used when referring to God. It seems Abraham's faith has taken another small step forward, as this new description of *"who God is"* reveals another growth step in Abraham's experiential understanding of God.

We often quickly pass over such texts, those that seem to be "simply" stating facts about a person's life experience. However, by continually asking the question "Where is God in this?" one can see evidence of God's transforming work through such seemingly innocuous daily life events. The story of Abraham began when he was rooted in a culture with religious practices that served "other gods," but he has been transformed through the succeeding years to the point where an act of worship is a natural response for him after an encounter with God. No one tells him to plant the tamarisk tree or to call upon the name of the LORD, much less to refer to God as the "Everlasting God" (v. 33). Still, those acts testify to Abraham's growing understanding that *God is real in his life.* Because of this, his trust in God is also growing.

Faith Tested Again

The climax of Abraham's story occurs in Genesis 22. He is now 108 years old. Thirty-eight years have passed since he followed his father, Terah, out of Ur of the Chaldeans; thirty-three years since God gave him the promise of a son who would be the beginning of a great nation. His promised son was born and has grown. He is now a young man[6] when God says to Abraham, "Take your son, your only son Isaac, whom you love, and go to the land of Moriah, and offer him there as a burnt offering on one of the mountains of which I shall tell you" (Gen. 22:2). The essence of God's instruction to Abraham is yet another test of faith—and trust—in which God is asking, "Do you really believe my promise to you and my repeated assurances that I will fulfill my promise? Do you really trust me, trust my faithfulness? Will you accept what I tell you to do and do it?" Keep in mind that Abraham has already argued with God regarding his plan for the destruction of Sodom and Gomorrah. Here he is now being told to go sacrifice his son, his "only" son (according to God's words), the son through whom God was supposed to fulfill his promise to Abraham. Would he do as God has now instructed, without argument or negotiation?

Apparently, without questioning or hesitation, Abraham obeys what God tells him to do: "So Abraham rose early in the morning,

---

[6] Scripture does not tell us exactly how old Isaac is at this time. The Hebrew term for "lad" can mean a baby, a boy, or a young man (see Gen. 21:5,12). Early church historian Josephus states, "Now Isaac was twenty-five years old" when Abraham obeys God's command to sacrifice Isaac. Thus we have chosen to identify him as "a young man." *The Genuine Works of Flavius Josephus, the Jewish Historian* (William Whiston, M.A., London, 1737), 1.13.2, page 22, http://penelope.uchicago.edu/josephus/ant-1.html.

saddled his donkey, and took two of his young men with him, and his son Isaac. And he cut the wood for the burnt offering and arose and went to the place of which God had told him" (Gen. 22:3). After three days of travel and nearing their destination, Isaac asks, "'My father!'…'Behold, the fire and the wood, but where is the lamb for a burnt offering?' Abraham said, 'God will provide for himself the lamb for a burnt offering, my son'" (vv. 7–8). Abraham does not hesitate to respond to Isaac's question. That is confidence. That is trust. He is saying to his son, "It is going to be all right. It will all work out." His response is one of assurance. It seems to come out of much deeper trust in God's faithfulness than he has had up to this point. This trust has grown as a result of God's continued affirmation that he *will* fulfill his promise and covenant. It is the result of the transforming work that God has accomplished in Abraham during the past thirty-three years.

It is God's response to Abraham's unwavering obedience that provides the key to understanding the scope of the transformation God has accomplished in Abraham:

> Then Abraham reached out his hand and took the knife to slaughter his son. But the angel of the LORD called to him from heaven and said, "Abraham, Abraham!" And he said, "Here I am." He said, "Do not lay your hand on the boy or do anything to him, for now I know that you fear God, seeing you have not withheld your son, your only son, from me." (Gen. 22:10–12)

Notice that Isaac says nothing during this time. He certainly must be aware of what is about to happen, especially when Abraham binds his hands and feet, lays him on the altar, and then raises the knife to kill him. However, the angel of God stops him from doing so.

It is crucial to understand the angel's comments to Abraham if we are going to truly appreciate the transforming work God has already accomplished in Abraham. Was he "afraid" of what was about to happen as we understand fear today? Proverbs 1:7 states, "The fear of the LORD is the beginning of knowledge." This fear is not one of being afraid that "if I do not do this, I will be punished or condemned by God." Instead, it is a fear that says, "Without God, there will be no one to guide and direct me." At this point it seems that *God has become completely real for Abraham*. He does not need to know how God is going to save Isaac, his son of promise, even though he is right to say to Isaac, "God will provide for himself the lamb for the burnt offering" (Gen. 22:8); God does provide. Here we see that when one genuinely fears the LORD, it reveals that God has become so real that regardless of what God asks, one will obey without objection or hesitation because trust in God's faithfulness and goodness have grown deep in one's heart.

The angel of the LORD speaks again to Abraham:

> And the angel of the LORD called to Abraham a second time from heaven and said, "By myself I have sworn, declares the LORD, because you have done this and have not withheld your son, your only son, I will surely bless you, and I will surely multiply your offspring as the stars of heaven and as the sand that is on the seashore. And your offspring shall possess the gate of his enemies, and in your offspring shall all the nations of the earth be blessed, because you have obeyed my voice." So Abraham returned to his young men, and they arose and went together to Beersheba. (Gen. 22:15–19)

The angel of the LORD, swears an oath to Abraham, which from God's perspective is the same as a promise or a covenant. When *we* swear an oath, we do so by that thing in our lives that is more important than ourselves. As Christians, we swear by God because he is the single most important and influential being in our lives. However, God does not have anyone higher than he is by whom to swear an oath. Thus, God swears "by myself," in essence saying, "By my name and for my glory, I swear this to you because I have read your heart, and I see that you truly trust me."

Notice also in his oath that the LORD says, "I will surely bless you, and I will surely multiply your offspring" (v. 17). The word *surely* is used two times in succession. Here is the final reaffirmation of the promise made to Abram thirty-three years earlier, and again God changes and expands the verbiage he uses. Note that it is difficult in English to see the significance of the use of the word *surely* because that word does not exist in Hebrew. In Hebrew, emphasis is made by what would be in English stating the same word twice; the words *bless* and *multiply* would be repeated. Thus, the phrase literally would read, "I will bless bless you, and I will multiply multiply your offspring." In this way, God says to Abraham, "Let there be no doubt in your mind what I am going to do for you and your offspring."

So, the story of Abraham is complete, but notice what it took to get Abraham to this point. The process of transformation began thirty-eight years before when he left Ur of the Chaldeans with his father, and God repeatedly renewed the promises and covenants during the next thirty-three years. Looking back over those years, is it conceivable that Abraham would have been ready thirty-three years earlier to respond to God's command to sacrifice Isaac without the slow process of transformation that God took him through? As we read the story of Abraham, asking the question "Where is God in this?" we can see the subtle changes that occur during those thirty-three years as God transforms Abraham into the man who to this day is considered the great patriarch of our Christian faith.

Lessons Learned from the Story of Abraham

At the beginning of this chapter, our story started when Abram was seventy-five years old, yet God took thirty-three years to gradually develop his faith. Eventually that faith enabled him to be willing to sacrifice his son of promise. That should be encouraging news for all of us, both old and young, as our age is not essential to God. He will work in anyone's life, at any age, to reveal himself to us, in order that we come to *know God* so that we might trust him and thus follow him wherever he may lead us. Abram's story should serve to encourage people who have walked this earth for a while: God's purposes for our lives go on as long as we are alive.

Here are some things to consider as you reflect on your journey with God in light of what we learn from Abraham's story:

1. God works to transform us beyond simple belief to genuine faith in the LORD. As Hebrews 11 points out, Abraham demonstrated that he "believed" in God by his obedience in leaving Haran when told by God to do so. However, God wanted more than that for Abraham. He wanted Abraham's faith and trust in him to grow to a level where nothing—not even the life of Isaac—was more important to him than his love for God. The desire to obey God's will without question or hesitation was God's intention for Abraham, even though he personally never experienced the full reality of all the promises God made to him. And so it is for each of us: our age does not matter. God desires that we experience his faithfulness and goodness through daily life events *so that* we will do as God asks us to do in this world, regardless of how old or young we are.

   Consider: Where are you in your faith? Do you "see" and "hear" God revealing himself to you through daily life events? Do you struggle to surrender, to do as God invites you to do? Is your faith intermittently strong and weak, as was Abraham's? All of our life events are used by God to reveal himself to us for the sake of deepening our trust and faith in him alone. Regardless of where you are in your life, trust that God will continue to be intentional about the path he lays before you in order to transform and strengthen your trust and faith in him.

2. God accomplishes his work to transform us with great patience and gentleness. God took thirty-three years to transform Abraham from simple belief to genuine faith.

God did not rush Abraham. He allowed him to make mistakes—a series of mistakes—and experience the consequences of those mistakes. Following each mistake, God came to reassure Abraham as a way of becoming real to him and to build his trust. As a result, Abraham had to learn to be patient and not allow the lengthy delay in seeing God's promises fulfilled prevent him from experiencing deepening trust in God.

Consider: How are you doing with being patient, waiting upon God? If God is sovereign over all things (and he is), then he is sovereign over your life events and the process of transforming your simple belief into genuine faith. If God is patient with us and our slowness to learn, should we not be patient as God accomplishes the work of transformation in us?

3.   As God works to transform us, indicators of that transformation become apparent in our lives. The effects of transformation became apparent in Abraham as he began to engage in various acts of worship. Abraham was willing to allow Lot to choose the choice land in which to settle. He swore an oath to God not to take any of the spoils from his victory over the enemies who had taken Lot and his family as captives. He began to recognize and acknowledge how his prosperity was due to God's blessing upon him. Signs of transformation such as these continued until, in faith, he declared that "God will provide for himself the sheep for the burnt offering" (Gen. 22:8). The progress of Abraham's transformation may have been slow and inconsistent, but as God transformed him over time, Abraham's faith grew steadily and ultimately became steadfast.

Consider: What indicators of ongoing transformation do you see as you reflect on your own life to date? In what ways have you developed various forms of worship as a regular part of your life, in response to an increasing revelation of *who God is*? In what ways have you been willing to increasingly trust God, demonstrated by your willingness to do whatever he asks of you or to go wherever he may lead you?

Our prayer is that the lessons learned from Abraham will inform and guide you as God accomplishes his work of transforming your faith. As you reflect upon how God is transforming you, remember that God deals with us both in similar ways as others, and in ways unique to each of us. As we continue to examine the stories of other biblical characters, it will be apparent that God does, indeed, meet each of us where we are, and intentionally work to transform us in order to deepen and strengthen our faith, our trust in *who God is for us*.

CHAPTER 3
Jacob

God takes more than one hundred years to transform Jacob from a manipulative, self-centered young man into a man to whom God is real and trustworthy. It takes a lifetime for Jacob to experience God as *his* God, to trust God to fulfill his promises to Jacob. This transformation of Jacob's faith eventually enables him to accept without reservation God's sovereign will for his life, even if it is in retrospect, near the end of his life. As with Abraham, the spiritual lesson God works to teach Jacob throughout his life is that God intends to fulfill his promises to Jacob and his offspring. However, the *process* God uses to bring Jacob to genuine faith is quite different.

In this chapter, we will examine the life of Jacob, who, like Abraham, also appears in the honor roll of faith in Hebrews 11:21, "By faith Jacob, when dying, blessed each of the sons of Joseph, bowing in worship over the head of his staff." The writer of Hebrews makes no further comment about Jacob's faith in this text. We must look at many events in his long life story to see the unique process God takes him through, to see how his faith is transformed from his youth to the end of his life at the age of 147. It is an exciting story. As it unfolds, we ask the question again and again, as we did throughout Abraham's story, "Where is God in this?"

Contextual Background

Before we begin to study how God transforms Jacob's faith, we need to understand a few contextual points about Jacob's family and some cultural customs of the time. Specifically, it is helpful to understand God's prophecy to Rebekah, the differences between Jacob and his brother Esau, and the difference between Rebekah and Isaac's love for their sons. It is also essential to understand the cultural meaning of the birthright of a firstborn son and the significance of the father's blessing.

Prophecy: For insight into these contextual points, we begin in Genesis 25:19–23. In this passage, the family lines of Isaac, Jacob's father, are listed. We then learn that (1) Isaac married Rebekah at the age of forty, (2) Isaac prayed to the LORD because Rebekah was barren, and (3) the LORD answered Isaac's prayer; she conceived twins. They struggled within her to such a degree that she sought the LORD in prayer to understand why this was so.

The LORD answered her with a prophecy about her two as yet unborn children (Gen. 25:23). That prophecy contained three critical points that help explain Rebekah's dominant role in her sons' lives, especially in Jacob's life: (1) each of her sons will be the father of two people groups that will become "nations," (2) one is stronger than the other, and (3) the older shall serve the younger. Remember too that what happens in Jacob's life is part of the process of God fulfilling his original promise to Abraham, through Isaac and Rebekah, and then through Jacob—the promise of offspring too numerous to count.

Differences: Genesis 25:27 describes the differences between Rebekah's sons: "When the boys grew up, Esau was a skillful hunter, a man of the field, while Jacob was a quiet man, dwelling in tents." Esau is a rugged outdoorsman, while Jacob is a gentler, softer kind of individual. We will soon see that he was also cunning. Jacob, the younger son, uses coercion and deception to attempt to bring about the fulfillment of God's prophecy to Rebekah by human effort and manipulation. He schemes to steal Esau's birthright from him. This part of Jacob's character plays a significant role in how God transforms him.

The additional contextual point is that the division between Rebekah's two sons foretold in the prophecy began to emerge in the affections of Isaac and Rebekah toward their sons. Isaac loved his rugged outdoor son, Esau, while Rebekah loved the softer, gentler personality in Jacob (v. 28). We will see that Rebekah believed God's prophetic word to her about the future of her sons, and that belief empowered and guided her determination to see the prophecy fulfilled. It is likely the reason she became a very active participant in the events of Jacob's early life (before Isaac's death).

Birthright: The fact that the "older shall serve the younger" (v. 23) is the most crucial part of the prophecy; it is a reversal of customary familial relationships in the ancient Near East. According to ancient tradition, all sons remained under the rule and authority of their father until his death. The *eldest* son then assumed the patriarchal role in the family, including control of all assets (including livestock and people). This *birthright* of the *first*born son was critical for nomadic families such as Isaac's family. When the assets of a family were composed of sheep, goats, donkeys, and camels, all family members and household servants were needed to manage and control the flocks and herds. The oldest son was responsible for carrying on the patriarchal role to ensure the stability of the family after the death of the father. Thus, this prophecy stating that the *younger* will rule the *older* is quite unusual, and therefore noteworthy; it is critical to understanding certain events in Jacob's life.

Birthright versus Father's Blessing: Before we move into the heart of Jacob's faith story, it is helpful to understand the difference between a *birthright* and a *father's blessing*, as both play a dominant role in Jacob's life. In Old Testament biblical culture, as was previously mentioned, the *birthright* was an honor and right given to the firstborn son. It bestowed "head of household" status and the right to inherit a double portion of the father's estate upon the father's death, and thus eventually become the person of authority over the entire family. The father's *blessing*, however, carried necessary implications regarding the children's inheritance, family standing, and potential for their future. Blessings came in the form of a type of prayer spoken over the child and were considered a high honor. It would include words of encouragement, details of the child's inheritance, and prophetic words concerning their future life. Keep in mind that the spoken word carries power, power to destroy, and power to build up (Prov. 12:6), to bring life and death (Prov. 18:21). Also, remember,

God *spoke* the world into existence (Gen. 1:3–26, Heb. 11:3). Thus, losing a blessing (i.e., *not receiving* a blessing) was viewed as a curse on one's life and was considered to be a severe event. A birthright belonged to the firstborn son, but any child could receive a blessing. Having this general understanding of the difference between a birthright and a blessing will enhance our understanding of actions and attitudes that we will see in Jacob's story, right from the very beginning.

As we move through the story of Jacob, it will be essential to keep in mind the question "Where is God in this?" and to ask it often. The prophecy God gave Rebekah is the root of everything significant that occurs in Jacob's life. Keeping the prophecy in mind brings pieces of Jacob's story together that otherwise might not make sense; events that seem insignificant will take on noticeable importance. In the story of Jacob, God's way of facilitating the fulfillment of the prophecy by what he does and does not do in specific circumstances may be surprisingly different than what we might expect.

Losing the Birthright

One of the familiar parts of Jacob's story, and where we begin our study, is found in Genesis 25, where Jacob's youth and his tendency toward cunning and manipulative behavior is revealed:

> Once when Jacob was cooking stew, Esau came in from the field, and he was exhausted. And Esau said to Jacob, "Let me eat some of that red stew, for I am exhausted!" (Therefore his name was called Edom[1].) Jacob said, "Sell me your birthright now." Esau said, "I am about to die; of what use is a birthright to me?" Jacob said, "Swear to me now." So he swore to him and sold his birthright to Jacob. Then Jacob gave Esau

---

[1] This is a Hebrew wordplay. The Hebrew word for *Edom* is similar to the Hebrew word for *red*.

bread and lentil stew, and he ate and drank and
rose and went his way. Thus Esau despised his
birthright. (Gen. 25:29–34)

Certainly, Esau's behavior is foolish and impulsive; Jacob's use
of coercion reveals he is willing to be dishonest to get what he wants.
Neither son is innocent in what happens in this situation.

Notice that in God's dealings with Abraham,[2] God frequently took action to keep Abraham from making mistakes that
had the potential to derail the fulfillment of God's promises to him.
However, here with Jacob, God does not intervene to prevent Jacob
from stealing the birthright. Why? Because through Jacob's actions,
God's prophecy—his will for Jacob—is somehow being fulfilled.
In Abraham's case, God made promises about what *he* would do to
fulfill his promises to Abraham. In Jacob's case, the prophecy was
given to Rebekah, not to Jacob; God did not state what *he would do*
to fulfill that prophecy. The critical theological point is that God is
sovereign over all that occurs in our lives, when he takes action and
intervenes to fulfill his plans, *and* when he seems to remain silent and
lets life's circumstances seemingly unfold under human influences
alone. Thus, we might conclude that there was more than one way,
all acceptable to God, in which Jacob might end up ruling his older
brother. It seems that God chose to permit Jacob's action because
he knew that action would ultimately lead to the fulfillment of his
prophecy to Rebekah. If we lose sight of this, then everything that
happens from this point on in Jacob's life is due to the human manipulation of Rebekah and/or Jacob, rather than from the hand of God.
If that is the case, then one would have to conclude that they are not
people with genuine faith in God, and thus wonder why the honor
roll of faith in Hebrews 11 includes Jacob.

---

[2] See chapter 2, "Abraham," for the details of God's actions with him.

Stealing the Blessing

At the beginning of Genesis 27, the interpersonal dynamics between Jacob and Esau become even more difficult. Isaac longs to give a blessing to his oldest son, Esau, before he dies (v. 4), as was the custom. Remember, Isaac loves Esau more than Jacob. As previously mentioned, a father's blessing is different from the firstborn son's birthright. Isaac knows that his life is coming to an end, and he desires to give Esau his blessing. Rebekah overhears Isaac telling Esau what he wants to do, along with his instructions to Esau to hunt game and prepare his favorite meal (v. 5). She fears that God will not fulfill his prophecy if Isaac's plan succeeds. She, therefore, decides to circumvent Isaac's plan by asking Jacob to go to the herd and select two goats so she can prepare a meal, a much faster process than hunting. That would enable Jacob to take Esau's place and receive the planned blessing before Esau returns. Jacob doubts that he will be able to fool his father because of his different physical makeup from that of his brother. Rebekah has already thought of the potential problems with her plan and explains to Jacob how they will overcome the differences. After hearing her full plan, Jacob hesitantly goes along with her scheme (vv. 6–17).

The story continues in Genesis 27:18–29. Jacob takes the meal to his father, and because of Isaac's poor eyesight, he is confused about several things. Isaac questions how it is that "Esau" (who is Jacob) returns so quickly from hunting (v. 20). He comments that the voice is not right; he checks out the skin, and finally, he checks out the smell of the clothing. Due to Rebekah's foresight, Isaac eventually becomes convinced enough that it is Esau who stands before him (vv. 21–23). Is it reasonable to think that the deception is successful? Perhaps, for he loves Esau over Jacob; he is old with poor eyesight and hearing, and he deeply desires to give Esau his blessing. It is significant to notice what does not happen here: God does not expose the deception, nor does he intervene to stop it. His lack of intervention seems to suggest that God is okay with this situation unfolding under human manipulation.

It is vital to note Jacob's response in Genesis 27:20 when Isaac asks how it is that "Esau" has returned so quickly from hunting. Jacob answers, "Because the LORD *your* God granted me success" (italics added). His response reveals something of the state of Jacob's faith at this point in his life. God is the God of his father, Isaac. One key element in spiritual transformation is that God must become real to the individual through personal experience.[3] At this point in Jacob's life, God is not yet real to him *personally*. He *knows about God* objectively and believes to some degree that this God is real; God does exist. However, he does not yet *know God* through subjective, personal experience.

As the story continues, Isaac gives the blessing to Jacob, thinking he is giving it to Esau:

> Then his father Isaac said to him, "Come near
> and kiss me, my son." So he came near and kissed
> him. And Isaac smelled the smell of his garments
> and blessed him and said,
>
> "See, the smell of my son
> is as the smell of a field that the LORD has blessed!
> May God give you of the dew of heaven
> and of the fatness of the earth
> and plenty of grain and wine.
> Let peoples serve you,
> and nations bow down to you.
> Be lord over your brothers,
> and may your mother's sons bow down to you.
> Cursed be everyone who curses you,
> and blessed be everyone who blesses you!" (Gen. 27:26–29)

Based on the content of this blessing, we have to wonder: is Isaac aware of God's prophecy to Rebekah? Is that why he goes along with the suspected deception? The answer to these questions must be

---

[3] As discussed in chapter 2, paragraph 2.

no. Remember that Isaac believes (or at least wants to believe) that he is blessing Esau, the older son. Then notice that line 8 of the blessing states, "Be lord over your brothers, and may your mother's sons bow down to you." This part of the blessing is in direct conflict with God's prophecy, which stated that "the older will serve the younger" (Gen. 25:23). So, we must conclude that Isaac is not aware of God's prophecy to Rebekah about Jacob.

Isaac ultimately believes the deception. Right after Jacob leaves his father, Esau returns from hunting, prepares Isaac's favorite meal, takes it to him, and invites him to eat. Then:

> His father Isaac said to him, "Who are you?" He answered, "I am your son, your firstborn, Esau." Then Isaac trembled very violently and said, "Who was it then that hunted game and brought it to me, and I ate it all before you came, and I have blessed him? Yes, and he shall be blessed." As soon as Esau heard the words of his father, he cried out with an exceedingly great and bitter cry and said to his father, "Bless me, even me also, O my father!" But he said, "Your brother came deceitfully, and he has taken away your blessing." Esau said, "Is he not rightly named Jacob?[4] For he has cheated me these two times. He took away my birthright, and behold, now he has taken away my blessing." Then he said, "Have you not reserved a blessing for me?" Isaac answered and said to Esau, "Behold, I have made him lord over you, and all his brothers I have given to him for servants, and with grain and wine I have sustained him. What then can I do for you, my son?" Esau said to his father, "Have you but one blessing, my father? Bless me, even me also, O my father." And Esau lifted up his voice and wept. (Gen. 27:32–38)

---

4   The name *Jacob* means "to cheat or deceive."

Once the deception becomes known, Esau responds with bitterness, anger, and grief. Notice that Isaac does not waver in the face of Esau's emotional response. Even though he acknowledges that Jacob obtained the blessing deceitfully, Isaac reaffirms the blessing (v. 33); he does not try to wriggle out of it or to undo what he has done. He is very straightforward when he says to Esau, "Your brother came deceitfully, and he has taken away your blessing" (v. 35). It is critical to notice once again that God does not intervene at this point. He allows Isaac to remain steadfast in giving the blessing to Jacob. To have done otherwise would mean that the prophecy would not come to fulfillment.

Isaac gives a blessing to Esau, but it is one that is much weaker than the one given to Jacob (vv. 39–40). It does not contain the promise of land and prosperity that he gave to Jacob. Thus, Esau reacts angrily over the lesser blessing. However, does that mean he will not prosper at all? As we again ask the question "Where is God in this?" we have to look forward to Genesis 33:9 (twenty years in the future) and see the bigger picture, to see that Esau eventually does indeed prosper.

Often God lets a great deal of time pass before he again reveals something of what he is doing in a person's life. When we ask the question about God's activity or inactivity, questioning his presence or absence in a situation, it is essential to keep an eye on the bigger picture, the longer timeframe of one's life. Doing so enables us to see more of what God has done in the past and helps us see what God might be doing in the present situation. Moreover, with the help of various life stories in Scripture, we can learn that God will *eventually* fulfill his promises to his people. Thus we, today, are better able to trust God's faithfulness to fulfill his promises to *us*, even though we cannot see how our life story will play out. We can learn from biblical stories that God is, indeed, faithful to his people, in his time, and in his way.

The Beginning of Transformation

Although Esau does receive a blessing from his father, his anger leads him to vow to kill Jacob after Isaac dies. Once again, Rebekah intervenes on Jacob's behalf after being told what Esau planned to do:

> So she sent and called Jacob her younger son and said to him, "Behold, your brother Esau comforts himself about you by planning to kill you. Now therefore, my son, obey my voice. Arise, flee to Laban my brother in Haran and stay with him a while, until your brother's fury turns away— until your brother's anger turns away from you, and he forgets what you have done to him. Then I will send and bring you from there. Why should I be bereft of you both in one day?" (Gen. 27:42b–45)

Incredibly, Rebekah brings Isaac into her plans for Jacob's safety. She whines to him about her hatred of the Hittite women Esau has married and fears that if Jacob does not leave the area, he may also marry a Hittite woman (v. 46). Isaac, for his part in this drama, calls Jacob to him once again and gives him instructions and an additional blessing:

> "Arise, go to Paddan-aram to the house of Bethuel your mother's father, and take as your wife from there one of the daughters of Laban your mother's brother. God Almighty bless you and make you fruitful and multiply you, that you may become a company of peoples. May he give the blessing of Abraham to you and to your offspring with you, that you may take possession of the land of your sojournings that God gave to Abraham!" Thus Isaac sent Jacob away. And he went to Paddan-aram. (Gen. 28:2–5)

Not only does Isaac agree to do what Rebekah asks of him, he again blesses Jacob, utilizing the language of God's covenant with both Abraham and Isaac: promising land and offspring. This blessing is successfully delivered, as compared to the first one, clearly indicating that Isaac accepts the fact that the inheritance and the blessing now belong to Jacob. Without delay, Jacob leaves for Paddan-aram (v. 5).

Now occurs one of the most famous texts in Jacob's story. While on his way to Paddan-aram, he finds a place to sleep for the night and has a vivid dream:

> Taking one of the stones of the place, he put it under his head and lay down in that place to sleep. And he dreamed, and behold, there was a ladder set up on the earth, and the top of it reached to heaven. And behold, the angels of God were ascending and descending on it! And behold, the LORD stood above it and said, "I am the LORD, the God of Abraham your father and the God of Isaac. The land on which you lie I will give to you and to your offspring. Your offspring shall be like the dust of the earth, and you shall spread abroad to the west and to the east and to the north and to the south, and in you and your offspring shall all the families of the earth be blessed. Behold, I am with you and will keep you wherever you go, and will bring you back to this land. For I will not leave you until I have done what I have promised you." (Gen. 28:11b–15)

This is the first time we see God speaking to Jacob personally, even if in a dream. Several essential things occur in this dream, all of which have very personal relevance for Jacob. First, God reveals himself to Jacob as the God of his fathers, Abraham and Isaac. Jacob was familiar with *this* God, thus ensuring Jacob knows who is speaking to him. Additionally, God makes several promises to him, promises of land to him and his offspring, that *his* offspring will be quite numerous, and that through them all people will be blessed. Perhaps the most significant point concerning the transformation of Jacob's faith is God's promise to *be with him, to protect him, and to bring him back to this land* that he has just given Jacob. The final powerful promise is that God will stay with Jacob until *he* has done all that he has promised to do (v. 15). We learned in the story of Abraham that *God reveals himself to individuals to establish a personal relationship as part of the transformation process that leads to genuine faith.* Thus, the fulfillment of God's last promise will prove to be a significant transforming moment for Jacob.

Indeed, we get some evidence of the beginning of transformation occurring in Jacob. For the first time, in Genesis 28, we see signs of spiritual transformation taking place in him upon waking from his dream. First, he acknowledges God's presence in that place, saying, "Surely the LORD is in this place, and I did not know it … How awesome is this place! This is none other than the house of God, and this is the gate of heaven" (vv. 16–17). Notice that for the first time, God appears on Jacob's radar screen in a way that ensures Jacob "gets it." No longer is God confined to stories from his father or his mother. No, this is a very personal, subjective experience of God.

Jacob then engages in what seems to be the first actions that reveal a measure of transforming faith emerging in him:

> So early in the morning Jacob took the stone that he had put under his head and set it up for a pillar and poured oil on the top of it. He called the name of that place Bethel, but the name of the city was Luz at the first. Then Jacob made a vow, saying, "If God will be with me and will keep me in this way that I go, and will give me bread to eat and clothing to wear, so that I come again to my father's house in peace, then the LORD shall be my God, and this stone, which I have set up for a pillar, shall be God's house. And of all that you give me I will give a full tenth to you." (Gen. 28:18–22)

Jacob engages in acts of worship: he builds a pillar and pours oil on the top of it, in response to the promises God made to him—to "keep him" wherever he goes and to bring him "back to this land" (v. 15). Jacob's actions in response to God, revealing himself, are evidence that his faith is beginning to be transformed. Jacob's demands of God are not excessive; he merely wants clothing, food, and a safe journey until he again returns to this same place. God's promises are far more than what Jacob asks for: he renews with Jacob the same covenant promises of land and progeny that he made to Abraham and Isaac.

Jacob then makes a vow to tithe: "a full tenth" (v. 22). It is significant that the first word of his vow is *if.* Stating his vow in this way reveals where Jacob's faith is at this point in his life. He is saying that *if* God proves to be faithful to his word, *then* Jacob will indeed accept and embrace him as *his* God. Here is God's reason for appearing and speaking to Jacob: to make himself real to Jacob *so that* he will see and know God for who he is—faithful to his word. Only then will Jacob be willing and able to accept God *as his God.*

God has begun the process of becoming real to Jacob, thereby marking the beginning of God's transforming work in him. This work will take a long time, longer than it did with Abraham.

Jacob Deceived

The story continues in Genesis 29 when Jacob arrives in Haran, his mother's hometown. He immediately goes to the meeting place in town, the well, looking for members of the household of Laban, who are shepherds. He inquires of those waiting to water their sheep if Laban is still alive. At that moment, Rachel, Laban's daughter, is bringing their sheep to be watered. Jacob is immediately attracted to her. After identifying himself as the son of Laban's sister, Rebekah, Rachel takes Jacob to meet her father, his uncle, who is exceedingly glad to meet his sister's son. Jacob stays with them a month (Gen. 29:1–14). At the end of a month, Laban speaks to Jacob:

> "Because you are my kinsman, should you there-
> fore serve me for nothing? Tell me, what shall

your wages be?" Now Laban had two daughters. The name of the older was Leah, and the name of the younger was Rachel. Leah's eyes were weak, but Rachel was beautiful in form and appearance. Jacob loved Rachel. And he said, "I will serve you seven years for your younger daughter Rachel." Laban said, "It is better that I give her to you than that I should give her to any other man; stay with me." So Jacob served seven years for Rachel, and they seemed to him but a few days because of the love he had for her. (Gen. 29:15–20)

Jacob serves the seven years as agreed, and then asks Laban to give him Rachel to be his wife. Laban throws a wedding feast to celebrate the occasion. At the end of the celebration, Jacob lies down and waits for his bride to come to him, to "know" her in the way Scripture refers to the intimate marriage relationship. He falls asleep after doing so. However, the next morning, Jacob realizes that it was Leah, not Rachel, who lay with him the night before. Jacob confronts Laban, but Laban excuses his actions by saying, "It is not so done in our country, to give the younger before the firstborn. Complete the week of this one, and we will give you the other also in return for serving me another seven years" (vv. 26–27). Jacob completes the week with Leah. He then works another seven years, and Rachel becomes his wife. Laban's deception cost Jacob a total of fourteen years of service for his two wives (and two servants that came with his wives). He gets nothing else out of these marriages.

Notice at this point that if we ask where God is in all of this, we must observe that God again does not intervene as these events transpire. Is God allowing Jacob to experience what it is like to be deceived, as he had deceived Isaac? That is certainly a possibility. However, the text includes no comment in that regard. What may be more likely is that Laban's deception and what results from it (the number of Jacob's offspring that come from two wives and their handmaidens) is once again related to the prophecy given to Rebekah: from Jacob would come "nations" (Gen. 25:23). God does not intervene because he intends to work through these events to bring about the fulfillment of his promise.

The text now introduces an interlude that is worth noting. It sets forth the dysfunctional relationships in Jacob's household between his two wives. They play expected critical roles in the fulfillment of God's promise of offspring to Jacob. However, the relationship between them is loaded with drama.

Jealousy, Barrenness, and Children

To summarize Genesis 29:31–30:24, there are feelings of being unloved (Leah), jealousy (both women), the despondency of barrenness (Rachel), and God intervening in each woman's life, as well as using their handmaidens, to eventually give Jacob twelve sons. Specifically, Leah, the older sister and Jacob's first wife (a position of preference in the ancient Near East), feels unloved because of Jacob's noticeably more profound and abiding love for Rachel. Rachel feels superior to Leah because of this, even though she is the younger of the two and the second wife. Both women experience barrenness. In their jealousy of one another, both believe that bearing Jacob's offspring is the one thing that will make them more valuable in his eyes than the other. When God enables Leah to conceive, Rachel becomes despondent at her barrenness. Ultimately God also enables Rachel to conceive, which heightens Leah's attempts to capture Jacob's attention and affections.

There are several key observations to be made about how the specifics of this intrigue unfold. First, God is not disengaged from these events as they transpire, nor was he absent from the events of the previous twenty years. The text attributes the birth of Leah's first child to God's action in response to her feelings over how her husband treated her: "When the LORD saw that Leah was hated, he opened her womb" (Gen. 29:31).

Second, and more importantly, is her reaction to the birth of Ruben, her firstborn son, as noted in her choice of his name, which means "see": "Because the LORD has *looked* upon my affliction; for now my husband will love me" (v. 32, italics added). Leah feels unloved. She believes that the way to get her husband to love her is by giving birth to sons, which were very important in the ancient Near East. Leah continues to bear him a total of four sons, but there is no indication that Jacob's feelings for Leah change as she has hoped.

As for Rachel, she is frustrated with being unable to bear children. She envies her sister Leah for her ability to bear children and decides to take matters into her own hands. In Genesis 30:1–3, she pleads with Jacob, demanding that he give her children, clearly demonstrating that she believes *Jacob* is responsible for her barrenness. Jacob's response in verse 2 is revelatory: "Am I in the place of God, who has withheld from you the fruit of the womb?" He indicates for the first time since his encounter with God at Bethel years before that God is now more dominant in his thinking. He understands that *God* is somehow involved in how life events transpire over time, at least in these most recent events. Rachel demonstrates her continuing lack of faith by giving Jacob her maidservant Bilhah so that she "may give birth on my behalf" (v. 3). We see here echoes of Sarai's lack of faith, when she offered Hagar to Abram for the same reason (Gen. 16:2).

Over time, Rachel's maidservant Bilhah gives birth twice, and Leah gives birth two more times. By this time, Jacob has a total of eight sons: six by Leah and two by Bilhah. As a result, Rachel's desperation increases. She is likely questioning whether or not Jacob's love for her can be sustained through her continued barrenness.

This barrenness continues to create rising tensions between Rachel and Leah, which prompts Rachel to once again try to manipulate life events to effect change in her situation.

> In the days of wheat harvest Reuben went and found mandrakes[5] in the field and brought them to his mother Leah. Then Rachel said to Leah, "Please give me some of your son's mandrakes." But she said to her, "Is it a small matter that you have taken away my husband? Would

---

5   Mandrakes were commonly known for their use as an aphrodisiac.

you take away my son's mandrakes also?" Rachel
said, "Then [Jacob] may lie with you tonight in
exchange for your son's mandrakes." When Jacob
came from the field in the evening, Leah went out
to meet him and said, "You must come in to me,
for I have hired you with my son's mandrakes."
So he lay with her that night. And God listened
to Leah, and she conceived and bore Jacob a fifth
son. (Gen. 30:14–17)

The desperation in both women has risen to such a level that
they are willing to bargain for the opportunity to lay with Jacob.
Rachel is desperate to have a child, believing that bearing a child is
needed in order to preserve his love for her. Leah is desperate to have
Jacob simply love her. Thus, they bargain over mandrakes. Of course,
what they're really bargaining for is Jacob's affection, trying to determine who will lie with Jacob that night.

In Genesis 30, we see that, after Leah bears a sixth son and a
daughter, God is still involved in this ongoing situation. He is not yet
finished with Rachel.

Then God remembered Rachel, and God listened
to her and opened her womb. She conceived and
bore a son and said, "God has taken away my
reproach." And she called his name Joseph, saying, "May the LORD add to me another son!"
(Gen. 30:22–24)

In her response to finally bearing a son for Jacob, she says, "God
has taken away my reproach" (v. 23). However, her focus is not on
the redemption that must now certainly come to her because she is
no longer barren. Rather, her focus is on having *another* son. Her
response reveals what is most important to her, and it reveals something of the level of her faith. God is just a means to achieving her
goal, which is to catch up with Leah. She deeply desires to ensure
Jacob's continuing love for her by having more sons.

Notice that God allows the desperation in both Leah and Rachel, and the hostility and competition between them, to exist. If we ask at this point "Where is God in this?" it becomes clear that, through these difficult circumstances, God has begun to fulfill his covenant promise of numerous offspring for Jacob. Notice also that these texts show both Leah and Rachel explicitly attributing the births to God (Gen. 29:31–35, 30:23–24). Jacob has not yet taken possession of the land, but he now has eleven sons. The promise was not specific about who would bear these offspring for Jacob, unlike the prophecy to Abram in which God insisted that he would fulfill his promise of offspring through Sarai. Here, both Leah and Rachel are used by God to fulfill his promise to Jacob. Thus, one of the critical elements of God's promise to Jacob, numerous offspring, is being fulfilled.

Where is Jacob's faith at this point? He still seems to have an objective perspective of God, seeing God as one who, at times, influences how life unfolds. However, there is little evidence that God is becoming truly *personal to Jacob* in any significant way as his offspring continue to multiply. How easy it is to lose sight of God's hand at work in our lives over time. We see in Jacob's mental assent to the reality of God, but there is no indication yet of personal, heart-level trust in Jacob. We do not yet see him actively trusting that God knows what he is doing; he is not yet trusting God to fulfill his promises. There is still more transformation of faith that needs to occur.

God's Prosperity Plan

The focus of the text now returns to Jacob's relationship with Laban, the father of Leah and Rachel. In Genesis 30:25–34, we will see more signs of ongoing transformation in Jacob during his years working for Laban.

Right after Joseph is born, we find Jacob asking Laban to release him, to let him take his wives and children and return home; it is time to care for his own family by returning to his family's home and country (v. 25). He affirms that Laban is aware of his years of faithful service and that Laban has prospered by Jacob's care for his livestock. Indeed, through divination, Laban says that the LORD told him that he has prospered because of Jacob. So, Laban invites Jacob to define what his wages will be (v. 28).

They enter into a discussion about Jacob's wages as payment for his service. However, history has proven to Jacob that he cannot trust Laban to stick to his word, so Jacob devises a plan. He asks that he be allowed to select all the speckled and spotted sheep and goats, along with every black lamb, from Laban's current herds. The distinctive markings will make it easy in the future for Laban to determine if Jacob has stolen from Laban's flocks, which would be nonspeckled sheep and goats, and white lambs. If Laban accepts this agreement, Jacob offers to stay longer to care for Laban's herds. Laban agrees to this plan (vv. 31–34).

The critical point here is that Jacob uses this plan to attest to his character, "So my honesty will answer for me later" (v. 33). Here is a clear indication that some transformation has taken place in Jacob since his dealings with his brother, Esau. Additionally, he does not trust Laban's character to uphold the promises he has just made to Jacob (remember how he ended up married to Leah instead of Rachel). So, he wants to ensure that when the day comes to leave and return to his home, there will be no ground for Laban to accuse him of dishonesty.

As the story continues, we immediately see that Jacob was right to suspect Laban's willingness to live by the agreement. Laban is already planning how he can cheat Jacob. Instead of letting Jacob select the goats for his herd, he carries out his plan:

> But that day Laban removed the male goats that were striped and spotted, and all the female goats that were speckled and spotted, every one that had white on it, and every lamb that was black, and put them in the charge of his sons. And he set a distance of three days' journey between himself and Jacob, and Jacob pastured the rest of Laban's flock. (Gen. 30:35–36)

After this action, Laban rightfully believes that Jacob would not get many speckled, spotted, or entirely black sheep, as he has removed them all from the herds that Jacob would tend. However, Jacob has a rather remarkable plan of his own:

> Then Jacob took fresh sticks of poplar and almond and plane trees, and peeled white streaks in them, exposing the white of the sticks. He set the sticks that he had peeled in front of the flocks in the troughs, that is, the watering places, where the flocks came to drink. And since they bred when they came to drink, the flocks bred in front of the sticks and so the flocks brought forth striped, speckled, and spotted. And Jacob separated the lambs and set the faces of the flocks toward the striped and all the black in the flock of Laban. He put his own droves apart and did not put them with Laban's flock. Whenever the stronger of the flock were breeding, Jacob would lay the sticks in the troughs before the eyes of the flock, that they might breed among the sticks, but for the feebler of the flock he would not lay them there. So the feebler would be Laban's, and the stronger Jacob's. Thus the man increased greatly and had large flocks, female servants and male servants, and camels and donkeys. (Gen. 30:37–43)

That is an unbelievable plan. How could an experienced shepherd such as Jacob possibly think that such a plan would produce the desired results? Incredibly, six years pass, and Jacob accumulates large flocks and herds, despite the improbability of his plan succeeding. We have to ask at this point, "Where is God in this?" The answer is in Jacob's explanation to his wives about the events of the past six years:

> "You know that I have served your father with all my strength, yet your father has cheated me and

changed my wages ten times. But God did not permit him to harm me. If he said, 'The spotted shall be your wages,' then all the flock bore spotted; and if he said, 'The striped shall be your wages,' then all the flock bore striped. Thus, God has taken away the livestock of your father and given them to me." (Gen. 31:6–9)

Here we might also ask: how is it that God has become so prominent in Jacob's thinking and understanding about what has transpired during the previous six years? When we first heard of the plan, it was Jacob's plan. Now, Jacob is ascribing his success to God. We find the answer in what he tells Rachel and Leah about his personal experience of God, which occurred sometime after he negotiated the "wages plan" with Laban:

"In the breeding season of the flock I lifted up my eyes and saw in a dream that the goats that mated with the flock were striped, spotted, and mottled. Then the angel of God said to me in the dream, 'Jacob,' and I said, 'Here I am!' And he said, 'Lift up your eyes and see, all the goats that mate with the flock are striped, spotted and mottled, for I have seen all that Laban is doing to you. I am the God of Bethel, where you anointed a pillar and made a vow to me. Now arise, go out from this land and return to the land of your kindred.'" (Gen. 31:10–13)

God comes to Jacob a second time in a dream. He identifies himself as the same God that Jacob encountered at Bethel (where he made a vow to God) and explains why his plan is working, why the offspring of the sheep and goats are striped, spotted, and mottled.

In light of the accusations of Rachel's and Leah's brothers that Jacob has been stealing from their father (Gen. 31:1), and as a result of this second personal experience of God, Jacob acknowledges to his wives that it is *God* who is responsible for the growth of his flocks. Thus, we see in retrospect that the plan he offered six years earlier for determining his wages was God's plan and not his own.

Faith Strengthened

This scene is a vital moment in the spiritual transformation taking place in Jacob. We don't know the exact timing of this second encounter with God. We do know that Jacob's first personal encounter with God occurred twenty years before this point in time (fourteen years working to earn the right to marry Leah and Rachel, and another six years to build up his wealth before returning home).

The dream he describes here occurred sometime during the past six years after he negotiated the agreement for his wages with Laban. It is possible that Jacob did not know for some time why his plan was working, and that it was not until "the angel of God" explained it to him in a dream that he understood. Only then could he attribute his prosperity rightly to the work of God. Thus, his willingness to explain to his wives in such a detailed manner what *God had done* is a vital indicator of the spiritual transformation occurring in his life. His faith in God to act in his own life is growing, slowly. It is a prime example of how God intervenes in our daily lives, orchestrating events, revealing himself to us in various ways, making himself known to us, thus strengthening and transforming our faith.

It is noteworthy that it has, indeed, been *twenty years* since God first appeared to Jacob as he was fleeing from his brother Esau. The transformation process takes quite some time. Indeed, it occurs in God's time, not ours; it takes a lifetime. As with Jacob, so it is with us. Sometimes God's transformational work proceeds so slowly we lose sight of God's hand at work in the circumstances of our lives. Sometimes it takes a dream, or some other breakthrough by God, to help us see how he has been working on our behalf over time. It is a holy moment when we see with clarity the truth of God's presence in our lives, his hand at work in our circumstances, in order to *strengthen and deepen our faith and trust in him as our God.*

Another indication of the transformation taking place in Jacob's faith is the way in which he refers to God in the first part of Genesis 31: "the God of my father" (v. 5), "God" (vv. 7, 9), and "the angel of God" (v. 11). It is this last description that is eventually revealed to be "the God of Bethel, where you anointed a pillar and made a vow to me" (v. 13). The first phrase, "the God of my father," reveals that God is still not quite real to Jacob personally, but he does recognize the God who is speaking to him and acting in his life situations. He then moves to say, "God." That is a small move, but one that may reveal that an essential step of transformation is taking place in Jacob. He has moved from using *a description of God* to *naming God*. For each of us, it is often the unnoticed little things that indicate the extent to which the process of transformation is occurring over time. For Jacob, we see that God has not yet become real enough to him to actually trust God. Therefore, God is not yet *his* God. But he does acknowledge that God has been at work through his life's circumstances for the past six years. This is a significant milestone in Jacob's life.

As another important part of the transformation of Jacob's faith, it seems God wants to make certain Jacob knows without a doubt that this God who is speaking to him about the flock is the same God who revealed himself to Jacob twenty years before. Apparently, God will do whatever it takes to reveal the truth of who he is to his people.

Jacob's Faith versus Rachel's Faith

In Genesis 31:17–19, we read that Jacob leaves Haran in obedience to God's command and starts the return trip to the land of his family (Gen. 31:3). His obedience is another indication that transformation is taking place in Jacob's faith. He hears the instruction of God, and then obeys. Obedience to God's commands, or surrender to God's way of life, is a clear indication that genuine faith is taking root, going beyond *simple belief* to deeper *trust* in the person of God. Only when we *trust God* are we willing and able to surrender in faith to his plans for our lives. As we step out in trusting obedience, we eventually discover God's faithfulness. The more we trust by acting in obedience, the more we experience God's faithfulness, which then strengthens our faith and willingness to obey.

We also learn in these verses that Rachel's faith in the God of Abraham and Isaac is not the same as Jacob's. She takes her father's household gods with her when they leave Haran (v. 20). The text is unclear about why she does this. It seems *her* faith is still rooted in her family's religious practices, even though she and Leah encourage Jacob to follow God's command to return home (v. 16). In that encouragement, Rachel validates God's word to Jacob to return home, which might lead us to think that she too has some measure of true faith in God. Yet her action of taking the household gods reveals that she has *no personal belief or trust in God*. This is an example of how one can give mental assent to the concept of God, even accept the reality of God in another's life, without having any genuine *personal* belief or trust in that same God.

This part of Rachel's story demonstrates that we can believe that God is worthy of recognition and obedience *in the life of another*, yet completely miss his presence and direction in our own life. Acknowledging God intellectually, abstractly, thus potentially giving the appearance of also believing in God, is not the same as having genuine faith rooted in trust that governs our actions in daily life. The process of transforming faith moves us from that objective, impersonal acceptance of God to the place of accepting and trusting that he is also *God to us personally*. Rachel's actions of taking the family's gods belie her superficial belief in the God of Abraham and Isaac, in the God who is becoming gradually more real to her husband Jacob.

Wavering Faith

Three days after Jacob and his family leave Haran, word comes to Laban concerning their departure. He pursues them for seven days and ultimately catches up with them:

> And Laban said to Jacob, "What have you done,
> that you have tricked me and driven away my
> daughters like captives of the sword? Why did

you flee secretly and trick me, and did not tell me, so that I might have sent you away with mirth and songs, with tambourine and lyre? And why did you not permit me to kiss my sons and my daughters farewell? Now you have done foolishly. It is in my power to do you harm. But the God of your father spoke to me last night, saying, 'Be careful not to say anything to Jacob, either good or bad.' And now you have gone away because you longed greatly for your father's house, but why did you steal my gods?" Jacob answered and said to Laban, "Because I was afraid, for I thought that you would take your daughters from me by force. Anyone with whom you find your gods shall not live. In the presence of our kinsmen point out what I have that is yours, and take it." Now Jacob did not know that Rachel had stolen them. (Gen. 31:26–32)

This is an interesting scene. Laban catches up with Jacob and is quite agitated. What he says to Jacob is correct: Jacob once again engaged in deceitful behavior. He did leave Haran with his wives, children, and livestock without notice and without allowing them to have a proper farewell celebration. Laban also charges Jacob with taking his household gods. No wonder he is agitated! However, he restrains his comments and actions as he admits, "The God of your father spoke to me last night" (v. 29), warning him to be careful with what he said to Jacob. Once again, God intervenes against Laban, for the good of Jacob and his family. Laban would have conducted himself much differently if God had not spoken to him, for he states, "It is in my power to do you harm" (v. 29). That was his intent when departing his home in pursuit of Jacob, but he acts differently than he intended because of God's intervention and warning.

Laban's experience of God is crucial because of the response that emerges from Jacob; it reveals the condition of Jacob's faith. Hearing Laban's admission would have been the perfect opportunity for Jacob to say to him that the angel of God appeared to him as well, telling him to "return to the land of your kindred" (Gen. 31:3), but Jacob does not say this. Instead, he excuses his actions by saying, "I was afraid" (v. 31). That indicates a level of weakness in Jacob's faith. Although it is growing, his faith is not yet strong enough for him to take action that exhibits genuine *trust in God* to fulfill his promise to keep Jacob safe (Gen. 28:15). God has intervened two times on his behalf, and after each intervention, Jacob has acknowledged that God has blessed him while he worked for Laban. His faith is not yet strong enough to hold him as an anchor in the face of potential harm. His fear is stronger than his faith.

This scene represents a bit of a step backward for Jacob's faith. However, we must not be too quick to judge Jacob in his wavering faith, for we do the same thing. We often testify to others of our experiences of God as we periodically see his hand at work in our lives. However, when we face perceived threats to our safety and security, we revert to human ways of dealing with our fear. We, like Jacob, are undergoing a process that God intends to use to transform and strengthen our faith, to move us from the mental assent that God does exist to trust that is rooted in heart-level, experiential understanding that God is trustworthy. This level of trust emerges when God becomes real to us personally.

In the following verses (Gen. 31:38–42), after Laban searches and does not find his family's gods in Jacob's possessions, Jacob becomes emboldened to confront Laban with his manipulation of the terms of Jacob's wages. He reviews his faithfulness to Laban, defending his righteous actions in light of Laban's manipulative actions during the past twenty years. Jacob finally gets around to acknowledging that God has been on his side, protecting him from Laban's schemes, and that this is the real reason for his prosperity. In an almost imperceptible way, Jacob's faith may be undergoing a meaningful change that is moving him toward knowing God personally.

Laban is taken aback by Jacob's words. Realizing he has no evidence to support his charges of theft against Jacob, he changes the direction of the conversation and establishes a commitment between himself and Jacob not to harm each other.

> Then Laban said to Jacob, "See this heap and the pillar, which I have set between you and me. This heap is a witness, and the pillar is a witness, that I will not pass over this heap to you, and you will not pass over this heap and this pillar to me, to do harm. The God of Abraham and the God of Nahor, the God of their father, judge between us." So Jacob swore by the Fear of his father Isaac, and Jacob offered a sacrifice in the hill country and called his kinsmen to eat bread. They ate bread and spent the night in the hill country. (Gen. 31:51–54)

Notice that in the execution of this agreement, Laban refers to God as "the God of Abraham and the God of Nahor, the God of their father" (v. 53). Although Laban agrees with Jacob about the description of God, for him God is objective; he is someone else's God, but one for whom he has gained some respect. In contrast, and in light of his unqualified use of "God" in the preceding verses, one might expect Jacob's reference to God to be different, to reveal in some way that God is more personal and real to him, but this is not so. Again, Jacob moves to an objective reference about God, as he swears by "the Fear of his father Isaac"[6] (v. 53). This objective, less-than-personal description of God reveals something of a spiritual struggle that may be going on within Jacob. At times he seems to move toward a more personal, experiential view of God. Then he reverts to a more objective description of God.

This type of inconsistency is typical in the slow, arduous process of spiritual transformation. The critical point here is that the same can be true for each of us today. The process of transformation

---

[6] The phrase "the Fear of Isaac" is generally believed to refer to Isaac's fear of the LORD. Thus it is taken to be a reference to Isaac's faith in God.

requires us to work through painful life experiences designed to turn the eyes of our hearts toward *God alone* so that we experience more of *who God is*. In various life challenges, we, like Jacob, struggle (and often fail) to be consistent in our lived-out faith by trusting God. However, in inconsistent progress, ongoing transformation *is* taking place. We can trust that God is, indeed, working in our lives to continually reveal his presence and his character to us, to make himself known to us, for the sake of developing our faith in him alone throughout our lives.

Fear Threatens Faith

In Genesis 32:1–2, after Jacob and Laban go their separate ways, the angels of God appear to Jacob. So just as he did at Bethel, Jacob worships, by giving the place a name that reflects his meaningful experience of God, Mahanaim.[7] The naming of that place to mark his recognition of it as "God's camp" is an act of worship. In the context of what happens next, it is reasonable to think that the appearance of the angels of God to Jacob was intended to reassure him of God's presence with him as he approaches his father's home, and specifically his brother Esau, in the land of Canaan. However, their appearance does not initially have the intended effect. Although Jacob worships God after his encounter with the angels, we see just how frightened Jacob is for his safety, and the safety of his family as events continue to unfold in Genesis 32:3–20.

In Genesis 32:3–5, Jacob sends messengers to go ahead of his entourage to notify Esau of his pending arrival. He intends to deflect any hostile response that Esau may have to Jacob returning home. Verse 7 tells us that Jacob was "afraid and distressed" when he heard that Esau and four hundred men were coming to meet him. That fear is quite understandable. Remember the events that took place twenty years before: Jacob stole Esau's birthright and their father's blessing from him through deceit and manipulation. Esau intended to kill

---

[7] *Mahanaim* means "two camps." For Jacob, this word may have held the meaning of "God's camp" and "Jacob's camp."

Jacob after their father died (Gen. 27:36, 41). Jacob's faith in God at this time is not strong enough to overcome his anxiety over how Esau might react to his return.

Jacob's fear is so great that he divides his family and possessions into two groups (Gen. 27:7, 13–18), thinking that if Esau destroys one group in anger and retaliation, at least the other group may escape and be safe (v. 8). The next day he sends servants ahead of him with a variety of livestock to meet Esau and the four hundred men as a peace offering and gift. Here we need to ask a few questions: Is Jacob merely trying to appease Esau's potential anger, or does he seek to mend a broken relationship with Esau? Has his faith grown enough to enable him to seek reconciliation with Esau, or is Jacob still in self-preservation mode? Who is Jacob relying on for his safety: God, his efforts, or Esau's potential forgiveness?

We get a clear picture of Jacob's distress and the intentions of his heart in the prayer that Jacob prays to God:

> And Jacob said, "O God of my father Abraham and God of my father Isaac, O LORD who said to me, 'Return to your country and to your kindred, that I may do you good,' I am not worthy of the least of all the deeds of steadfast love and all the faithfulness that you have shown to your servant, for with only my staff I crossed this Jordan…Please deliver me from the hand of my brother, from the hand of Esau, for I fear him, that he may come and attack me…But you said, 'I will surely do you good, and make your offspring as the sand of the sea, which cannot be numbered for multitude.'" (Gen. 32:9–12)

Jacob fears for his life, as well as for the future fulfillment of God's promise to him. In the face of that fear, he finally turns to God in prayer for protection, reminding God of his promise to Jacob.

Here is a tremendously important moment in Jacob's life. It reveals that significant transformation has taken place. He recognizes his unworthiness before God, which drives him to pray, to ask God for help. Additionally, he prays to *God*—not just to the God of Abraham or his Father Isaac, but to the God who *spoke to him personally*, and to whom he now addresses as "LORD." Yes, he is crying out because of his continuing fear of Esau; he has no idea of the emotional state of his brother. Also, we will soon see he still seems to be relying on his wisdom and efforts to find a way to appease Esau's anticipated anger and potential retaliation. However, Jacob is returning to his family's home in obedience to God's command. He seems ready to face whatever awaits him.

The critical point is that he finally demonstrates sufficient trust in God to *cry out to God* for help, recalling God's promises to him. Even in his fear, he chooses to act in obedience to God. This prayer represents a notable change in him from the first time he prayed to God, in which he told God that if God would bring him safely back to the land, that he, Jacob, would believe in him (Gen. 28:20–21). Jacob has now returned to his homeland and has just taken a step of faith to trust God. This level of trust emerges only out of experientially *knowing* that God is real and worthy of our trust. God's intended transformation of Jacob's faith is definitely progressing. He has moved beyond belief to a small measure of trust, enough to turn to God, asking God to protect him and his family from the brother whom he still fears. Although we see inconsistent manifestations of faith taking place in Jacob over time, transformation *is* taking place.

Jacob Becomes Israel

In the next part of Jacob's story, God again intervenes in a significant way:

> The same night he arose and took his two wives,
> his two female servants, and his eleven children,
> and crossed the ford of the Jabbok. He took them
> and sent them across the stream, and everything
> else that he had. And Jacob was left alone. And
> a man wrestled with him until the breaking of

the day. When the man saw that he did not prevail against Jacob, he touched his hip socket, and
Jacob's hip was put out of joint as he wrestled
with him. Then he said, "Let me go, for the day
has broken." But Jacob said, "I will not let you go
unless you bless me." And he said to him, "What
is your name?" And he said, "Jacob." Then he
said, "Your name shall no longer be called Jacob,
but Israel, for you have striven with God and with
men, and have prevailed." Then Jacob asked him,
"Please tell me your name." But he said, "Why is
it that you ask my name?" And there he blessed
him. So Jacob called the name of the place Peniel,
saying, "For I have seen God face to face, and yet
my life has been delivered." (Gen. 32:22–30)

This episode is well-known by many and, as we will see, is a
watershed event in Jacob's life. There are many vital points in this
passage about the process of transformation. First, it is notable that
Jacob sends everyone across the river, but he remains behind, alone
for the night. It is in this "aloneness" that God meets him. And so
it is at times with us: when we are alone, we are often positioned
well for an unanticipated personal experience with God to unfold.
Intellectual understanding *concerning* God often comes from more
corporate or public experience. However, profound transformation
often comes when we are alone with God. It is from these personal
experiences alone with God that he becomes more real to us; it is
when our intimacy with God deepens, which enables us to be willing
to trust God with more of our lives. As we will eventually see, this
experience with God is pivotal in God becoming more real to Jacob.

Next, we learn that "a man" wrestles with Jacob. We do not
know if Jacob was asleep or awake during this event; however, Jacob's
experience is not a unique occurrence in Scripture. This text describes
the visitor as "a man," similar to the description of the visitors to
Abraham in Genesis 18: "The LORD appeared to him ... Three
men were standing in front of him" (vv. 1–2). At times God appears

to people in Scripture in the form of people, thus inserting himself physically into real-world events, into our personal lives.

Jacob wrestles with the man seemingly throughout the night. Near morning, the man causes Jacob's hip to be "put out of joint" (Gen. 32:25), thus demonstrating the power of the man with whom Jacob wrestled. That is significant in that we are never left untouched when we experience the One True God. Jacob is affected by a physical impairment that will likely serve as a reminder of his genuine encounter with God (v. 31). We do not always retain a physical reminder, but *a change of some kind does occur* when we experience the presence and power of the living God.

Before releasing the man and letting him leave, Jacob pleads for a blessing (v. 26). This request reveals that he now understands to some degree that he has had a personal encounter with God and that he values the importance of a blessing from God.

We then read that the man changes Jacob's name to *Israel*, reflecting Jacob's experience with God[8] (v. 28). That reminds us of Jacob's earlier name change of *Luz* to *Bethel* (Gen. 28:19), and God changing the names of Abram and Sarai to *Abraham* and *Sarah* (Gen. 17:5). Again, the act of naming is important from a biblical perspective. The name of a person reveals the essence or character of that person. Jacob was once known as a cheat and a thief (the meaning of *Jacob*). Now, following his encounter with the living God, he will be known as one who has wrestled with God and has survived (Gen. 32:28). Just as with Abraham, changing Jacob's name is a sign of God's authority over him.

In verse 29, Jacob then asks for the name of the man. Why did Jacob ask for his name? Why is knowing his name important? We may presume that Jacob sought to confirm his growing suspicion that he did, indeed, wrestle directly with God. Moreover, why did the heavenly visitor refuse to reveal his name? God has no name other than "I am." Consider this possibility: because there is no other being in authority over God, he did not have to answer Jacob's question. That would indicate that Jacob is under God's authority, but God is

---

[8] One accepted meaning for the name *Israel* is "the one who strives with God."

independent of any other authority. God alone is sovereign over all creation, for all time; he will do what he will do.

The man grants Jacob's request and blesses him. We do not know the content of the blessing. Also, we can only imagine the effect of this blessing on Jacob. What we do know is that Jacob was not willing to let the man go until the man blessed him. How do any of us feel when God grants our request? Known by God, heard by God? Answered prayer is another way in which God makes himself real to us personally. We can suppose that this was also true for Jacob, for in the next verse, as a result of this blessing, he names that place Peniel,[9] a name that reflects the significance of Jacob's experience with God: "I have seen God face to face" (v. 30). This naming of the place is a spontaneous act of worship, just as he did at Luz/Bethel (Gen. 28:19); it is seemingly in response to his encounter with God.

The various points of this passage, when seen together, represent significant progress in the transformation of Jacob's faith. This interchange with God in the form of a man, the insistence that the man bless Jacob, the change in Jacob's name, and the naming of the place as an act of worship—all reveal that Jacob has had a significant personal and intimate encounter with God. As a result, God is becoming real and personal to Jacob; his faith is being transformed and strengthened in the process. That is the spiritual transforming work God is doing in him, transforming his faith through personal, intimate experiences with God.

There is still room for more growth. Although Jacob now recognizes God's presence and action in his life, we do not yet have any indication that he *trusts* God to keep him safe or to fulfill his promises to Jacob any more than he has demonstrated so far. The degree of his trust in God will become evident in his next notable life event.

---

[9] *Peniel* means "the face of God." *Peneul* (32:31) is an alternative spelling for *Peniel*.

Jacob Meets Esau

In the beginning of Genesis 33, we see evidence of how much, or how little, Jacob trusts God to protect him and his family:

> And Jacob lifted up his eyes and looked, and behold, Esau was coming, and four hundred men with him. So he divided the children among Leah and Rachel and the two female servants. And he put the servants with their children in front, then Leah with her children, and Rachel and Joseph last of all. He himself went on before them, bowing himself to the ground seven times, until he came near to his brother. (Gen. 33:1–3)

After Jacob's recent experiences with God, we would reasonably expect Jacob to demonstrate less fear of Esau and more trust in God's promise to protect him and bring him safely home. We have seen Jacob praying for God to protect him as he returned to his homeland because of his acknowledged fear of Esau's reaction to seeing him again (Gen. 32:11–12). We have also seen evidence of a more profound conviction of God's active presence in his life, demonstrated by his acts of worship after wrestling with God-as-man (Gen. 32:24–30). However, we do not yet see Jacob demonstrating *more trust in God.*

Even after his prayer for God's help and protection, Jacob still relies on Esau to meet him with acceptance, rather than relying on God to orchestrate the circumstances to ensure fulfillment of his promise. He *prays* for God's intervention, and then he *acts* as though the outcome of this situation is dependent upon his actions and Esau's response to his presence. Jacob thought to himself, "I may appease him with the present that goes ahead of me … perhaps he will accept me" (Gen. 32:20). These actions do not indicate at this point a high level of trust in God's faithfulness to act on his behalf.

Notice also that Jacob places the family in order of importance to him, from the least important to the most important. He is still afraid of Esau's response to his presence, and thus still fears for the safety of those he loves most. This event in Jacob's life reveals that evidence of transforming faith emerges slowly in life events even after a tangible, meaningful experience of God's presence with us. Jacob is still not walking with confidence in God's promise of protection, even though he has demonstrated that he has accepted and received those promises.

Esau's reaction to seeing Jacob certainly is not what Jacob expected, given Jacob's careful arrangement of different family groups:

> But Esau ran to meet him and embraced him and fell on his neck and kissed him, and they wept. And when Esau lifted up his eyes and saw the women and children, he said, "Who are these with you?" Jacob said, "The children whom God has graciously given your servant." Then the servants drew near, they and their children, and bowed down. Leah likewise and her children drew near and bowed down. And last Joseph and Rachel drew near, and they bowed down. Esau said, "What do you mean by all this company that I met?" Jacob answered, "To find favor in the sight of my lord." But Esau said, "I have enough, my brother; keep what you have for yourself." Jacob said, "No, please, if I have found favor in your sight, then accept my present from my hand. For I have seen your face, which is like seeing the face of God, and you have accepted me. Please accept my blessing that is brought to you, because God has dealt graciously with me, and because I have enough." Thus he urged him, and he took it. (Gen. 33:4–11)

As Esau and his men draw near, Esau runs to Jacob, exuberantly greets him and embraces him (v. 4). He does the exact opposite of what Jacob feared that he would do. As the family draws near to them, Esau asks who they are. Jacob introduces them by saying, "The children whom God has graciously given your servant," thereby acknowledging God's role in providing wives, servants, children, and possessions. When Esau asks about the meaning of all that he sees, Jacob indicates by his response, "To find favor with my lord" (v. 8), that he still believes that *he* needs to do something to help guarantee his safety and Esau's favor. One might presume this is because Jacob had stolen his brother's heritage and father's blessing from him twenty years before.

Esau's response, that he has enough and urges Jacob to keep his possessions (v. 9), reveals the actual state of Esau's feelings for his brother. It seems the slights and hurts of the past have been forgiven and/or forgotten. He seems genuinely delighted to see his brother once again.

By asking the question "Where is God in this?" we can see that God has intervened in Esau's life over time to prosper him and change his feelings toward Jacob. In this way, God provides the means to fulfill his promise of protection to Jacob as he returns home.

Once again, we learn an essential point in the ongoing transforming work that is happening in Jacob, which we can apply to our own transformation process. God intervenes in life events to give us moments of assurance of his presence through active participation in our lives. When we experience an unexpected outcome, we need to ask, how did that happen? Why did I not get the response I was expecting? Where is God in this situation; what is he doing? In the situation above, God changed Esau's heart. As a result, he protected Jacob; the anticipated threat from Esau disappeared. Jacob must have been asking, "What caused the change in my brother?" The spiritual/theological perspective is that God intervened to keep his promise to Jacob of protection and safety.

It is interesting to note that God intervenes in these unfolding life events, changing Esau's heart toward Jacob (in order to transform Jacob's faith), but there is no evidence of faith in Esau. However, God still works through Esau, giving him a joyful heart toward Jacob and his family, to fulfill part of his promise to Jacob.

Another critical point is that, because God is all-knowing, he knew Jacob would respond out of fear, despite all of his assurances to be with Jacob and to keep him safe on his journey home. Still, God does not intervene to keep Jacob from fearing for his life, or the lives of his family members. God allows Jacob to continue to struggle with the issue of trusting God so that his work to change Esau's heart toward Jacob, and thus fulfill his promise to keep Jacob safe, would stand out in stark contrast to Jacob's continuing lack of trust in God. The stark differences between Jacob's heart of fear and Esau's forgiving and welcoming heart seem to be intended to demonstrate to Jacob that God is, indeed, faithful to his word.

Did Jacob see this truth at the moment? Did his faith become more profound as a result of this unexpected response from Esau? No, at least not yet. His response to Esau's question, "To find favor with my lord" (v. 8), reveals that, at the moment, Jacob is not tuned in to God's active involvement in what has just transpired. That can be seen as a parallel event to Abraham's transformation process when he lied to Abimelech about Sara being his sister (Gen. 20:1–13). God seems to have a process of transforming the faith of his people: he gives promises and establishes a covenant; he reaffirms the covenant and reassures promises, and then he tests one's faith through challenging life circumstances. Abraham failed to trust God for his safety, so he lied to Abimelech. So Jacob seems to have failed to trust God with the outcome of his long-awaited encounter with Esau, also fearing for his safety and the safety of his family. Despite a measure of apparent ongoing transformation in Jacob, there is room for more to take place. God is not yet finished transforming Jacob's faith.

Safety Threatened

In Genesis 34, Jacob continues his journey into the land of promise (Canaan) and settles there. As the text continues, Shechem, the son of one of the kings of a nearby Gentile nation, abuses Jacob's daughter Dinah. Two of her brothers exact revenge by wiping out all the men residing there. Notice Jacob's reaction to these events:

> Then Jacob said to Simeon and Levi, "You have brought trouble on me by making me stink to the inhabitants of the land, the Canaanites and the Perizzites. My numbers are few, and if they gather themselves against me and attack me, I shall be destroyed, both I and my household." (Gen. 34:30)

The brothers' response to Jacob, "Should he treat our sister like a prostitute?" (v. 31), indicates they feel that they have responded appropriately to the abuse of their sister Dinah. They do not fear retaliation by the surrounding people. Instead, they seem focused on avenging the wrong done to their sister. However, Jacob's response emerges from fear (again) and reveals that his concerns are entirely different. He is upset with his two sons because "my numbers are few" (v. 30). He worries that the inhabitants of the land will seek to destroy him and his family, which would threaten the fulfillment of God's promise to him. He again demonstrates his continuing lack of trust in God's word to keep him safe and to fulfill his promises. Even though God has promised to protect him, even though God demonstrated through Esau's acceptance of Jacob that he would keep his promises to him, Jacob is still fearful for his safety and thus still doubts God's willingness and/or ability to keep him safe. The promise and power of God to protect Jacob and his family still do not seem to enter into Jacob's thinking as he responds to the events happening around him. Jacob needs more transformation of his faith to occur.

Faith Strengthened Again

Jacob and Esau separate in Genesis 35. Esau returns to his home while Jacob diverts to Bethel, as directed by God:

> God said to Jacob, "Arise, go up to Bethel and dwell there. Make an altar there to the God who

appeared to you when you fled from your brother Esau." So Jacob said to his household and to all who were with him, "Put away the foreign gods that are among you and purify yourselves and change your garments. Then let us arise and go up to Bethel, so that I may make there an altar to the God who answers me in the day of my distress and has been with me wherever I have gone." So they gave to Jacob all the foreign gods that they had, and the rings that were in their ears. Jacob hid them under the terebinth tree that was near Shechem.

And as they journeyed, a terror from God fell upon the cities that were around them, so that they did not pursue the sons of Jacob. And Jacob came to Luz (that is, Bethel), which is in the land of Canaan, he and all the people who were with him, and there he built an altar and called the place El-bethel, because there God had revealed himself to him when he fled from his brother. (Gen. 35:1–7)

These events reveal four aspects of God's transforming work taking place in Jacob. First, Jacob instructs all the members of his household to surrender their foreign gods and the rings that were in their ears (v. 2). That is a way of purifying the family clan from the influences of pagan religious practices. As the head of the family, Jacob is becoming the spiritual leader of his family, calling them all to participate in the cleansing process. This act of purification also reveals that Jacob somehow believes holiness is required as he and his family take action to do as God has instructed: go and build an altar (v. 1).

Second, for the first time, Jacob's reference to God is personal, referring to him as "the God who answers *me* in the day of my distress and has been with *me* wherever I have gone" (v. 3, italics added). God is becoming more real to Jacob personally; he no longer refers to

God as the God of Abraham or his father, Isaac. He is now making statements that reveal his growing personal relationship with God.

Third, God responds to Jacob's genuine declaration of faith, reaffirming his power and protection, by causing terror to fall upon the people of the cities around him (v. 5). God thus ensures safety for Jacob and his family and reveals his active participation in Jacob's life events.

Finally, when they arrive at Bethel, Jacob builds another altar to God (in response to God's instruction [v. 1]) and calls the place El-bethel,[10] signifying Jacob's understanding of *who this God is* who has instructed him to do so. We have seen these "acts of worship" from Jacob before (building an altar and renaming the place because of his personal experience of God, giving a name that represents something of the importance of that experience to him). These actions emerge out of increasing awareness of who God is becoming to him *personally* and are his testimony about what God has done for him.

God responds to Jacob's acts of worship, which represent his increasingly transformed faith:

> God appeared to Jacob again, when he came from Paddan-aram, and blessed him. And God said to him, "Your name is Jacob; no longer shall your name be called Jacob, but Israel shall be your name."[11] So he called his name Israel. And God said to him, "I am God Almighty: be fruitful and multiply. A nation and a company of nations shall come from you, and kings shall come from your own body. The land that I gave to Abraham and Isaac I will give to you, and I will give the land to your offspring after you." Then God went up from him in the place where he had spoken with him. And Jacob set up a pillar in the place

---

10 *El bethel* means "God of Bethel."

11 The name *Israel* means "may God prevail," "he struggles with God," or "God perseveres." All seem to reflect the ongoing "wrestling" with God that Jacob has experienced in his life.

where he had spoken with him, a pillar of stone. He poured out a drink offering on it and poured oil on it. So Jacob called the name of the place where God had spoken with him Bethel. (Gen. 35:9–15)

God's response to Jacob's acts of worship is to appear to him again, in the same place where God first met Jacob in a personal way (Gen. 28:13–22). During this encounter, God confirms that he has changed Jacob's name to Israel (Gen. 35:10), he reaffirms who he is ("I am God Almighty," v. 11), and he restates his covenant promise of numerous offspring in the form of a command ("be fruitful and multiply," v. 11). God's objective is to continue to build trust in Jacob, step by step, to bring him to the point where Jacob does not doubt that God is real and that he *will* fulfill his promises to Jacob. At this point, Jacob's faith is not that strong. Still, we do see small steps of spiritual growth and transformation taking place in this passage. Jacob responds to this new experience of God with more acts of worship: he "set up a pillar of stone; poured out a drink offering on it and poured oil on it" (v. 14). These actions reveal that he is beginning to develop habits of specific acts of worship in response to recognized personal encounters with God.

Acts of worship in response to a personal, revelatory experience of God are some of the indicators that the work of transformation is ongoing in an individual's life. They were evident in the life of Abraham and are now evident in the life of Jacob. We will continue to see them repeated in the lives of other biblical characters. Thus, the question arises: can we see the same indicators occurring in our own lives? When we see how Abraham, Jacob, and other biblical characters respond to personal experiences of God, we can ask ourselves if we are responding in the same manner to our own experiences of God.

We have seen a series of events that seem to represent a frequent pattern in the life of faith. God acts, which causes our faith to grow and deepen. In response to our deepening faith, we worship God. God then intervenes at later times to reaffirm what we have learned about who he is—his power and his faithfulness to fulfill his promises to us. In response to that intervention and revelation, we worship God. This continuing cycle over our lifetime—God acts, and we respond in worship—is the ebb and flow of God's transformational process throughout our lifetime. God orchestrates this process on our behalf for the specific purpose of transforming our simple belief into genuine faith that is rooted in trust.

Faith Tested Again

Jacob's story continues when Rachel dies giving birth to Benjamin. Her death becomes a stumbling block for Jacob; he loses Rachel, the love of his life. As we ask "Where is God in this?" we must wait to see its impact on the events that will occur and upon the continuing transforming work taking place in Jacob's life. We will see that the death of Rachel is a devastating event in Jacob's life because, from his perspective, his love for Rachel is the foundation for everything in his life. Following her death, he projects that importance onto Joseph, and subsequently Benjamin.

Although from this point Jacob's story becomes intertwined with that of Joseph, Rachel's son, we can continue to follow the process of transformation occurring in Jacob's life at various points within the story of Joseph.

In Genesis 37, Joseph is introduced as Jacob's favorite son: "Now Israel[12] loved Joseph more than any other of his sons because he was the son of his old age. He also made him a robe with many colors." Joseph's brothers hate him because of Israel's obvious special love for him (v. 4).

The story of his brothers' hatred unfolds in verses 5–20. As a precocious teenager, Joseph has two dreams revealing future events that he brags about to his ten older brothers. In his youthful arrogance, he tells them that the dreams mean that he will one day rule

---

[12] From this point to the end of this chapter, the name *Israel* is used interchangeably with *Jacob*, to reflect how these two names are used in the Scripture passages discussed.

over them. The dreams anger his brothers so much that they conspire to get rid of him.

One day when his father sends Joseph to his brothers as they are shepherding the flocks, they throw him into a pit. Initially, they plan to kill him, but then change their minds. Instead they sell Joseph to Ishmaelite traders going to Egypt (vv. 21–28). The brothers then lie to Jacob about what happened to Joseph. They bring Joseph's robe back to Jacob, torn and covered in animal blood. Jacob accepts this as proof that his favorite son has died (vv. 29–33). The story continues, "Then Jacob tore his garments and put sackcloth on his loins and mourned for his son many days. All his sons and all his daughters rose up to comfort him, but he refused to be comforted and said, 'No, I shall go down to Sheol to my son, mourning'" (vv. 34–35).

Jacob's response to this incident again reveals the status of his faith. His grief and despair lead to hopelessness. In essence, he is saying his life is over, worthless, even though Rachel's son Benjamin is still alive, as are all of his other sons. That indicates Joseph's importance to Jacob. There is no evidence that Jacob has the promise of many offspring in mind as he reacts to the apparent loss of his beloved son, or that God might fulfill his promises through his remaining sons. With this news, his response reveals that his love for Joseph is more important to him than trusting God's promises and faithfulness. What is most important, it seems, is that he believes his life is over if Joseph is no longer alive.

Famine Tests Faith

Jacob appears again in Genesis 42 when the famine hits the land of Canaan, and he decides that they need grain for their family. In verses 1–4, he sends ten of his sons down to Egypt to buy grain, all but Benjamin. Jacob believes Joseph is dead, so Jacob views Benjamin as his last connection to Rachel, the love of his life. He refuses to endanger Benjamin's life by sending him to Egypt with his brothers. There is no indication that Benjamin did not get along with his brothers or that, like Joseph, was spoiled and precocious. He was simply Jacob's last connection to Rachel.

Notice that God is silent throughout this situation. There are no visitations by God to again reassure and encourage Jacob or to heal his pain and relieve his suffering. Instead, God allows Jacob to move forward—to react and respond to developing circumstances—in his humanness. That means Jacob continues to feel the pain and loss of Rachel and Joseph and fears the possible loss of Benjamin as well. God's lack of intervention on Jacob's behalf does not mean God is not with him, nor does it mean God is not actively directing the unfolding of life's events. Sometimes God deepens and strengthens our faith by *not* removing the pain too soon. He uses it for our ultimate good while continuing to reign sovereign over all that unfolds in our lives.

The story continues in chapter 42, verses 6–25. Jacob's ten sons go down to Egypt to buy food. They come to Joseph because he is the one who sells grain to the people (41:56–57, 42:6). His brothers do not recognize him, but he recognizes them (vv. 7, 8). He is harsh with them, accuses them of being spies, and holds them in custody for three days (vv. 9–17). He extracts information from them during questioning that his little brother, Benjamin, is alive and demands that they bring him to Egypt in order to prove that they are not spies in the land. He lets nine of them return home with grain for their family, retaining one brother (Simeon) as an incentive for them to return with Benjamin (vv. 18–20). He tells them that if they return without their "other brother" that they will not see Simeon again. He then arranges to fill their bags with grain, but he also puts their money back into their bags (vv. 24–25).

The nine brothers have no choice but to return home and explain to Jacob everything that has transpired and request that he permit Benjamin to return to Egypt with them (vv. 26–34).

> And Jacob their father said to them, "You have bereaved me of my children: Joseph is no more, and Simeon is no more, and now you would take Benjamin. All this has come against me." Then Reuben said to his father, "Kill my two sons if I do not bring him back to you. Put him in my

hands, and I will bring him back to you." But he said, "My son shall not go down with you, for his brother is dead, and he is the only one left. If harm should happen to him on the journey that you are to make, you would bring down my gray hairs with sorrow to Sheol." (Gen. 42:36–38)

Notice that Jacob does not mention God in his response; he does not remember the covenant promises in his response to this turn of events. There is no recounting of how God has protected him from his brother Esau or how God has prospered him. Jacob's perspective on this situation is myopic. He is even willing to write off Simeon as dead. Jacob refuses to allow Benjamin to accompany his brothers back to Egypt, stating, "He is the only one left" (v. 38). There is no consideration shown for the other surviving sons. His focus is solely on keeping Benjamin safe, his final connection to Rachel. It becomes exceedingly clear through these texts that Jacob's love for Rachel continues after her death and is much more important to him than trusting God.

Once again, it is appropriate to ask "Where is God in this?" As we have seen, Jacob's *belief* in God has grown over time, but his *trust* in God's faithfulness to fulfill his promises has not grown much. His belief in God is apparent at various moments in his life: he has accepted his experiences of God as real; he has worshiped God at various times in response to those authentic experiences of God. However, his belief that God is real has not strengthened his *trust in God's faithfulness* to him. This is evident from his insistence to continue to value Rachel, Joseph, and finally Benjamin, more than God and God's promises to him.

To summarize, increasing *trust in God* is a crucial indicator that spiritual transformation is taking place in an individual's life. Trust in *who God is* requires more than a simple belief that God exists. As we have seen from various stories from Jacob's life, God can be real to a person, and yet that individual can still not trust God to be faithful to his promises. We spend most of our spiritual lives moving slowly from unbelief to belief, to trust. This path of spiritual transformation is one that God orchestrates for each of us; it is a lifelong process.

The challenge of Jacob's faith at this time is this: God is sovereign; he has control over the famine and the lives of his family members. God knows the famine will leave Jacob with only two choices: either allow Benjamin to go to Egypt with his brothers or allow all of his family to die from starvation. Either way, Jacob is faced with his deep fears. God is inviting Jacob to consider God's sovereignty and his faithfulness to his promises amid these fears. His choices seem to be to hold on to his own beliefs and fears, and everyone faces dying from starvation; or, trust God, his wisdom and his ways, and all will live—including Benjamin. In his desperation to keep Benjamin with him, Jacob seems to be ignoring the real possibility that starvation also threatens Benjamin's life.

God is inviting Jacob to surrender to God that which he now holds most dear: the life of Benjamin. By God's silence, God continues to push Jacob into a spiritual "wilderness," inviting Jacob to trust his faithfulness and trustworthiness. Through these heart-wrenching life events, God continues to challenge and thus build Jacob's faith, to take him beyond simple *belief in God* to genuine *trust and acceptance of God's will for his life.* Here is an opportunity for Jacob to remember God's faithfulness in the past, and to trust that he will be faithful in the immediate future. That is the next step in the transformation of Jacob's faith.

Notice that this is the second wilderness experience into which God has taken Jacob. The first was the twenty years he spent working for Laban after fleeing from his brother Esau. However, this time is different; this wilderness revolves around providing grain for his family to survive. The first wilderness experience resulted in God becoming real to him, and his genuine *belief* in God developed. However, genuine *trust* in God did not occur during that time. So God has taken Jacob into the wilderness again to continue the work of transformation, to develop and strengthen his trust in God's faithfulness *so that* he can become the man of faith that God created him to be.

Trust Emerges

In Genesis 43, we find that time has passed, and the family's grain supply is gone. Jacob's sons must go down to Egypt to buy more grain, or they will not only lose their flocks and herds but will begin to lose the lives of family members. Because of what God revealed to Joseph as he interpreted Pharaoh's dreams before the famine began,[13] he knew that the famine was not just in Egypt but also in the land of Canaan where his family lived. He knew his brothers would have to return to Egypt to buy more grain. So Joseph has been waiting for his brothers' return visit.

In Genesis 43:1–10, Israel instructs his sons to return to Egypt to buy more grain. Judah reminds him that the man from whom they must buy grain (Joseph) had said that they would not see his face again if they did not bring their little brother with them (v. 3). The brothers refuse to go back to Egypt without Benjamin.

After Judah pledges himself as a guarantee of his brother's safety, Israel finally relents and agrees to send Benjamin with his brothers on the second trip to Egypt:

> Then their father Israel said to them, "If it must be so, then do this: take some of the choice fruits of the land in your bags, and carry a present down to the man, a little balm and a little honey, gum, myrrh, pistachio nuts, and almonds. Take double the money with you. Carry back with you the money that was returned in the mouth of your sacks. Perhaps it was an oversight. Take also your brother, and arise, go again to the man. May God Almighty grant you mercy before the man, and may he send back your other brother and Benjamin. And as for me, if I am bereaved of my children, I am bereaved." (Gen. 43:11–14)

---

[13] See Genesis 41 for the details of Pharaoh's dreams and Joseph's interpretations and the rise of Joseph to the second highest position in Egypt. Also see chapter 4 in this book for more details of Joseph's life.

Here is a vibrant text concerning what we have been examining in the life of Israel and his growing faith. Israel is finally persuaded to let Benjamin go to Egypt by the combination of his family's dire need for grain in order to survive and Judah's guarantee for Benjamin's safety by putting his own life on the line for Benjamin's life. There is no evidence of Israel looking for God's *presence and action* in this series of life events. We see no reflection on his part about what God has previously done for him. It seems Israel makes his decision to send Benjamin with the others for purely pragmatic reasons. From his human perspective, it seems there is no other alternative except death. From a faith perspective, Israel still does not seem to recognize God's involvement in what is happening in his life circumstances. He concludes, "If I am bereaved of my children, I am bereaved" (v. 14). In this statement, there is no evidence of *trust in God* to protect him and his offspring so that God can fulfill his promises to him in the future. Instead, he seems resigned to fate, to the real possibility that all of his sons might die.

Notice what Israel does just before his "bereaved" statement. He appeals for God's mercy, stating, "May God Almighty grant you mercy before the man, and may he send back your other brother and Benjamin (v. 14)." That is a form of prayer, beseeching God indirectly to protect his sons. Previously, a significant milestone in Israel's life of faith occurred when he prayed for the first time. He prays again in this text, yet he exhibits no confidence that God actually will fulfill his request. It seems to demonstrate his continuing lack of trust in God's faithfulness. In essence, Israel acknowledges by this prayer that he has experienced God's mercy in the past and now draws upon that experience as a foundation for his beseeching prayer. He is, in essence, pleading with God to keep his sons safe. Jacob has learned in some measure that God has the power to do so, but his "bereaved" statement reveals how little actual trust he has in God's faithfulness to fulfill his promises to him and his offspring.

Although Israel relents and agrees to the terms of the journey, and thus agrees to send Benjamin back to Egypt with his brothers, it seems he does not make this choice because he recognizes God's sovereignty in the events as they transpire. Instead, it seems he has no other choice except to face certain death by starvation. When God's will does not coincide with our plans or expectations, we must still be willing to accept God's sovereignty over our life in order to exhibit genuine faith. This situation in Israel's life reflects the genuine struggle we must go through to come to the point of trusting God's sovereignty over all aspects of our life, and thus accept his will for us. Here we see elements of real heart-level understanding and trust slowly developing in Israel as he moves beyond simple belief.

This process of transforming faith often includes seemingly impossible situations that teach us to trust who God is and his intentions for us. God leads us into such circumstances in order to prove to us that his way for us is better than our own and to prove his faithfulness to us. Through such circumstances, we become willing to consider acceding to God's authority over our lives. It is the *process of the struggle*, moving through the struggle of faith itself, that brings forth the transformation of our faith. It leads us to a more in-depth and stronger trust in God's faithfulness. The only way for our faith to grow into mature faith is to walk through tough life circumstances, seek to see God's presence and involvement in those circumstances (even when he seems silent), and then choose to surrender to his path for us. It is in this process, as we trust, accept, and surrender to God's will, that he proves his faithfulness to us personally. Until we experience this process, we are not likely to accede to God's sovereignty, and therefore we are not likely to accept his path for us. It is in retrospect, after stepping out in faith, after we have moved through tough circumstances, that we see the goodness of God's plan for us.

In the circumstances discussed above, during God's silence, we see Israel taking that step of faith. In some measure, he is accepting God's sovereignty, regardless of the outcome. Israel does not know if his desperately desired outcome will come to pass; his deepest fear is that it will not. Still, he makes the only choice that has the possibility of turning out well. It happens to be the path that requires him to trust God, even if indirectly. Deep in his heart, he reluctantly surrenders to God's plan.

That is what the work of transformation is all about: moving beyond simple belief to genuine trust and acceptance of God's will for our lives. No one completes the transformational move from belief to trust quickly, but rather it is the essence of our lifelong journey with God.

Joseph and Brothers Reunited

As the story continues, the brothers go down to Egypt with Benjamin, with a present for "the man" (e.g., fruit, nuts, honey, and more) and double the money from the first trip (Gen. 43:12). They are brought to Joseph's house, and they speak to his Egyptian servant. They explain what happened with the money during the first trip, that they have returned that money, and have also brought more money to buy more grain. When Joseph sees Benjamin with his brothers, he asks the steward of his house to prepare a meal. The story continues:

> The man did as Joseph told him and brought the men to Joseph's house. And the men were afraid because they were brought to Joseph's house, and they said, "It is because of the money, which was replaced in our sacks the first time, that we are brought in, so that he may assault us and fall upon us to make us servants and seize our donkeys." So they went up to the steward of Joseph's house and spoke with him at the door of the house, and said, "Oh, my lord, we came down the first time to buy food. And when we came to the lodging place we opened our sacks, and there was each man's money in the mouth of his sack, our money in full weight. So we have brought it again with us, and we have brought other money down with us to buy food. We do not know who put our money in our sacks." He replied, "Peace to you, do not be afraid. Your God and the God of your father has put treasure in your sacks for you. I received your money." Then he brought Simeon out to them. (Gen. 43:17–23)

We see here a vast contrast between Israel's apparent human response to this situation and the spiritual/theological response of Joseph's servant. Israel tells his sons to take gifts and double the amount of money they took on their first trip in order to assuage any doubts or hard feelings about what happened on their previous visit. Even the brothers' comments to Joseph's servant focus on the money issue. Obviously, in his humanness, Israel prepared to rectify the problem that he anticipates has arisen. Neither he nor his sons acknowledge any thought that God may have had a hand in the events that had transpired during the previous visit. Then the servant of Joseph tells them, "*Your God* and the *God of your father* has put treasure in your sacks for you" (v. 23, italics added). This comment is no coincidence. We do not know how the servant knows that the God of Abraham and Isaac is involved in the events that have transpired. God uses the Egyptian servant to point out God's involvement, from which we may infer that Israel and his sons have not yet considered God's active involvement.

In Genesis 44, Joseph tests the brothers once again, doing the same thing again, putting their money back in the mouth of their sacks when he sends them on their way. However, he makes one change: he places his chalice in Benjamin's sack. When they get outside the city, Joseph sends his servant after them with specific instructions of what he is to do and say (vv. 1–5). When confronted by Joseph's servant, the brothers deny having done anything wrong. When they open their sacks, they discover their money as well as Joseph's chalice. The servant brings them back before Joseph to answer for what they have done (vv. 6–13).

While interrogating his brothers about the chalice incident, Joseph can no longer keep up his pretense in front of his brothers and orders everyone out of the room except his brothers. Once they are alone, Joseph reveals himself to his brothers (Gen. 45:1–4). Then he tells them that he will give them enough grain to return to Canaan and instructs them to gather all their families, flocks, and herds and return to Egypt, bringing his father with them (vv. 5–15). Joseph reports to Pharaoh what has happened, and Pharaoh commands that he send wagons and more supplies with his brothers to bring all their families and possessions to Egypt (vv. 19–20).[14]

The brothers do as Joseph instructs them; they return to Canaan to reveal to Israel that Joseph is alive.

> So they went up out of Egypt and came to the land of Canaan to their father Jacob. And they told him, "Joseph is still alive, and he is ruler over all the land of Egypt." And his heart became numb, for he did not believe them. But when they told him all the words of Joseph, which he had said to them, and when he saw the wagons that Joseph had sent to carry him, the spirit of their father Jacob revived. And Israel said, "It is enough; Joseph my son is still alive. I will go and see him before I die." (Gen. 45:25–28)

Notice that when Israel finds out twenty years later that Joseph is alive, there is still no apparent recognition on his part of God's involvement in this surprising turn of events. Instead, his reaction indicates that he is satisfied that he will be able to see Joseph before he dies, a very human response to these events.

We finally see God entering into Israel's thoughts as his entire family, with all of his assets, depart for Egypt:

> So Israel took his journey with all that he had and came to Beersheba, and offered sacrifices to the God of his father Isaac. And God spoke to Israel in visions of the night and said, "Jacob, Jacob." And he said, "Here am I." Then he said, "I am God, the God of your father. Do not be afraid to go down to Egypt, for there I will make you into a great nation. I myself will go down with

---

[14] This instruction from Pharaoh to Joseph about his family will be examined in greater detail in the story of Joseph, chapter 4.

you to Egypt, and I will also bring you up again,
and Joseph's hand shall close your eyes." (Gen.
46:1–4)

We have seen this pattern before. In Israel's response to what his
sons told him, he does not attribute what has happened to God. Still,
he does stop at Beersheba on his way to Egypt to worship by offering "sacrifices to the God of his father Isaac" (v. 1). Based upon the
prayer that he offered before the brothers returned to Egypt, most
likely this is a prayer of thanksgiving for God's mercy—not for the
grain that they went to buy, but that his son Joseph is alive. We will
soon see, based on what happens next, that these events have not yet
succeeded in causing Jacob to *trust* God.

God Renews Promise

In Genesis 46:2, God again speaks to Jacob in visions of the
night. Jacob fears going to Egypt, but God comes to him in a dream
and says, "Do not be afraid" (v. 3). Jacob's fear demonstrates his continuing lack of trust in the covenant promises made to him by God.
It seems that God is still not personal enough to Jacob for him to
trust God *amid life circumstances* to uphold his promises to Jacob. So,
God comes to him again and renews the promises. He even goes a
step further and promises, "I myself will go down with you to Egypt,
and I will also bring you up again" (v. 4). This promise is intended to
deepen and strengthen Jacob's faith, to continue the work of transformation in Jacob's life.

Interestingly, the remainder of Genesis 46 is a genealogy of
Jacob's offspring who are going into Egypt with him. Here is a strange
place for such a genealogy to occur, leaving us to ask why it is placed
here. The seemingly apparent reason is that one of two elements of
the covenant promise to Jacob is offspring. Jacob had no wives or
children when the promise was received originally. Now he is leaving
Canaan to go to Egypt along with sixty-one members of his family.
They are not a great nation yet, but the fulfillment of the covenant
promise has begun, evidenced by the placement of this genealogy in

Jacob's story. Even if Jacob, at this time in his life, is still not entirely convinced of God's ability and willingness to fulfill his promises to Jacob, it seems the author of the book of Genesis wants his readers to see clearly that, at this time in Jacob's life, God has been at work fulfilling his promise of offspring. The purpose of the genealogical summary is not just to point out how God has been working in Jacob's life, but to also encourage and affirm for us that God is in the process of fulfilling his promises to us throughout our lifetimes as well.

Israel and Joseph Reunited

At the end of Genesis 46:29–30, Israel sees his son for the first time in over twenty years; they weep with each other. Israel then says, "Now let me die, since I have seen your face and know that you are still alive" (v. 30). There is no worship, no prayer to God, or any mention of God by Israel. He merely indicates his readiness to die. Here we again see the inconsistent movement toward transformation of Israel's faith.

The process of transformation in Israel is often one step forward and two steps back. May we not be quick to judge Israel for this, as we all experience such inconsistent forward movement in our process of spiritual transformation. God does not judge us for our inconsistent progress. Instead, he continues to gradually, with much grace, move us toward genuine faith, to that place where we trust God's faithfulness to the point of unconditional obedience. As Jacob's story continues, we will see more of that gradual movement toward genuine faith in him.

Emergence of Genuine Faith

In Genesis 47, Jacob and his family settle in the land of Goshen, the choicest land in all of Egypt. Seventeen years pass until we see Jacob again. He is now 147 years old, and the end of his life is near. He calls Joseph to come and see him. In the interchange between them, we see an indication of where Israel's faith is at this time in his life:

> And when the time drew near that Israel must die, he called his son Joseph and said to him, "If now I have found favor in your sight, put your hand under my thigh and promise to deal kindly and truly with me. Do not bury me in Egypt, but let me lie with my fathers. Carry me out of Egypt and bury me in their burying place." He answered, "I will do as you have said." And he said, "Swear to me," and he swore to him. Then Israel bowed himself upon the head of his bed. (Gen. 47:29–31)

This text is another example of Israel's continuing lack of complete trust in God's promise. He feels compelled to evoke an oath from Joseph to not bury him in Egypt but to return his body to the land of Canaan. When he asks, Joseph agrees to do so, but Israel is not satisfied and makes Joseph swear an oath. His actions stand in stark contrast to what God promised him at Beersheba on the way into Egypt, "I myself will go down with you to Egypt, and I will also bring you up again" (Gen. 46:4). God promised that *he* would bring Israel up out of Egypt again. However, that was not good enough for Israel; his trust in God's faithfulness to fulfill His promises is still insufficient for this level of faith. Yes, God made the promise seventeen years earlier and has seemingly been silent since giving that promise, but does that justify failing to trust the promise made? What does God's silence for some time indicate? At this point in Jacob's life, it is a test of whether or not Jacob will remember the promise and trust in it when the proper time arrives, despite current circumstances or how long it takes God to act. Even near the end of his life, Jacob's faith is not yet strong enough to result in extended trust over time. Even now, there is still a continuing need for the transformation of his faith.

The faith lesson here is that God is not obligated to fulfill his promises to us in our expected timeframe. God will do what he will do in his time. Additionally, his seeming silence or inaction for some time does not negate his promises made to us. Instead, the story of Jacob's evolving faith, as well as Abraham's story, teaches us that regardless of how long it takes, God *will be faithful* to his promises to us. Our step of faith is to trust in His faithfulness, even when he seems to be silent, or when he takes a long time to fulfill his promises to us.

God's Faithfulness Remembered

A critical milestone occurs at the end of Jacob's life when he sees Joseph's two sons for the first time:

> After this, Joseph was told, "Behold, your father is ill." So he took with him his two sons, Manasseh and Ephraim. And it was told to Jacob, "Your son Joseph has come to you." Then Israel summoned his strength and sat up in bed. And Jacob said to Joseph, "God Almighty appeared to me at Luz in the land of Canaan and blessed me, and said to me, 'Behold, I will make you fruitful and multiply you, and I will make of you a company of peoples and will give this land to your offspring after you for an everlasting possession.' And now your two sons, who were born to you in the land of Egypt before I came to you in Egypt, are mine; Ephraim and Manasseh shall be mine, as Reuben and Simeon are. And the children that you fathered after them shall be yours. They shall be called by the name of their brothers in their inheritance." (Gen. 48:1–6)

Notice that Jacob *now* remembers God's faithfulness and can recount God's promises to him. Also, notice that he refers to God as

"God Almighty" (v. 3). That seems to indicate that God is now quite real to him *personally*. The climax of Jacob's life is approaching, and all of the experiences of God throughout his life seem to be coming together. He recognizes God's hand at work throughout his lifetime. That part of God's transforming work is now complete in him.

We can see even more transformation of Jacob's faith in the next interchange between Israel and Joseph:

> When Israel saw Joseph's sons, he said, "Who are these?" Joseph said to his father, "They are my sons, whom God has given me here." And he said, "Bring them to me, please, that I may bless them." Now the eyes of Israel were dim with age, so that he could not see. So Joseph brought them near him, and he kissed them and embraced them. And Israel said to Joseph, "I never expected to see your face; and behold, God has let me see your offspring also." Then Joseph removed them from his knees, and he bowed himself with his face to the earth. (Gen. 48:8–12)

In this text, Israel recounts God's providence to him, what God has done for him. It seems God has finally become experientially real and personal for Jacob: he can now testify to God's involvement in *his* life—it is *God* who has given *him* his sons, thus fulfilling a part of God's promises to him. It took over one hundred years, a lifetime, to reach this point of faith. What encouragement can Jacob's journey of transforming faith provide to us! We can learn from his life to trust God's faithfulness to complete his work of transforming our faith over the full extent of our lifetime.

Blessings Passed On

Israel then acknowledges God's providence to him as he prepares to pass along the blessings of God to the next generation:

> And Israel stretched out his right hand and laid
> it on the head of Ephraim, who was the younger,
> and his left hand on the head of Manasseh, cross-
> ing his hands (for Manasseh was the firstborn).
> And he blessed Joseph and said,
>
> "The God before whom my fathers Abraham and Isaac walked,
> the God who has been my shepherd all my life long to this day,
> the angel who has redeemed me from all evil, bless the boys;
> and in them let my name be carried on, and the name of
> my fathers Abraham and Isaac;
> and let them grow into a multitude in the midst of the
> earth." (Gen. 48:14–16)

Here, Israel takes another step of faith. He acknowledges *who God is*. God, whom Jacob identified for so long as "the God of Abraham and Isaac his father," is now *his* God, for Jacob identifies him as "the God who has been *my* shepherd all my life long to this day" (v. 15b, italics added). Here is a clear statement that Jacob, looking back over the years of his life, recognizes that God has guided him like a shepherd through all that has happened in his life. Then he refers to God as "the angel who has redeemed me from all evil" (v. 16). He has finally arrived at the point of faith where God has indeed become real and personal to him.

Also, notice the entry of the element of trust. Both trust and acceptance are finally present in Jacob's faith. God has been his shepherd, guiding and directing him, and as an angel protecting him. There is no recounting of trouble, no note of what God did not do. Instead, God did all of these things in his providence, and now Jacob trusts that God will fulfill his covenant promise to future generations as well.

At this point, it is appropriate to ask once again "Where is God in this?" Here we see that transformation of Jacob's faith has progressed to the point of embracing God's sovereignty over all of his life. Note that seventeen years have passed since God last spoke to Jacob in a vision. No significant events in his life occur during this time that would have affected the transformation of his faith other than the passage of time itself. From these texts it is apparent that God used these seventeen years to allow Jacob sufficient time to reflect on his life and God's part in it. As a result of God's patience, trust and acceptance have blossomed in Jacob. He always acknowledged that God was with Abraham and Isaac, but now he acknowledges that God has also been *with him* as well. Genuine faith in its entirety—*belief, trust, and acceptance* of God's sovereignty—has blossomed into genuine faith, marking the success of the work of transformation in him.

Thus, we reach the completion of the story of Jacob/Israel. However, notice what it took to get him to have genuine faith. The process spanned over one hundred years; the promises and covenants were given and repeatedly renewed over those years. His faith was formed and strengthened in a lifetime of testing, pain, suffering, and loss. As we continually asked the question "Where is God in this?" we have seen the subtle indicators of growing and waning faith throughout Jacob's lifetime. Still, God did, indeed, transform Jacob into the man who to this day is a great patriarch of our faith.

Lessons Learned from the Story of Jacob

1. God transforms our faith so that we fulfill our life's purpose according to his plan for our lives and his world. A significant component of our life's purpose is to live life daily in complete trust in God's faithfulness, willing to obey whatever he commands. It is God who does the transforming work in us through the unfolding of life's circumstances. Jacob did not realize where the events of his life were leading. He did not understand that the ultimate purpose of his life, and life's circumstances, was for *God to become real and*

personal to him, no longer only thinking of God as the God of Abraham, or of Isaac, his father. In his dying declaration, he reveals that God did finally become *God Almighty, the God of Jacob*. This transformation of faith required Jacob to move beyond simple belief in the God of his father, to genuine faith exhibited by complete trust and acceptance of the will of God for his own life.

Consider: What challenges is life presenting to you right now? How might God be working in and through those circumstances to transform your faith? In what ways might God want to become more experientially real to you during these circumstances? How are you responding to his invitation to trust him more?

2. God transforms our faith throughout our lifetime so that we come to the point of openly acknowledging him as sovereign in all things, enabling us to obey him. Remember, obedience to what God asks us to do is a sign of trust and is a mark of transformed faith. However, the complete fulfillment of God's promises to us may not occur in our lifetime. Jacob did not see the fulfillment of the covenant promises of God for most of his life. He only experienced the beginning of their fulfillment. His trust in God to bring them to completion in future generations is evident in the final declarations of his life.

    Consider: What promises has God given you that you are still waiting and trusting God to fulfill? How is God drawing you into deeper surrender to his sovereignty and will for your life as you wait for the fulfillment of his promises to you? In what ways do you see your trust deepening as you wait? In what areas of your life are you doing what God has invited you to do?

3. God often leaves us to our foolish ways without intervening to stop us. His apparent silence is instrumental in fulfilling his purposes in our lives. The struggles we go through in life are designed by God, in His sovereignty, to lead us to the place of complete surrender to his will for our lives, surrender that he accomplishes in us as we struggle through those challenging circumstances.

Consider: As you reflect on your life up to this point in time, where do you see God's silence or lack of intervention that seemingly left you to your own devices? Did you eventually surrender to what seemed to be God's plan, in effect letting go of your plan for your life? Consider asking God, "Where are you in this situation?" Look for God's hand at work, intentionally orchestrating circumstances over time in order to transform your faith. Look for how your personal experience of God might eventually have become more tangible and personal as a result of those times of God's silence.

As you reflect on these lessons from the story of Jacob and add them to the lessons learned from Abraham, it will become increasingly apparent that God does not deal with each of us in the same way as he transforms our faith. But we hope you will begin to see parallels from the lives of these biblical characters in your own life, to help you see how God is transforming your faith throughout your lifetime.

CHAPTER 4

Joseph

Overview

Joseph's story is a story of how God takes a spoiled seventeen-year old, the favorite son of Jacob's old age, and transforms him into a man who recognizes God's hand at work in his life, blessing whatever he does. This is a journey from being a youthful dreamer, through unjust slavery, isolation, and imprisonment, to becoming the second most important man in Egypt, second only to Pharaoh. His life's challenges were intended not just for his own sake but for the benefit of the sixty-six people in Jacob's family, who eventually come to Egypt due to a famine, as well as for all those from the surrounding nations who will come to Egypt to buy grain during the famine. Through Joseph's life events, God keeps his covenant promise to Abraham: "I will make of you a great nation…in you all the families of the earth shall be blessed" (Gen. 12:2–3), and his promises to Jacob, Joseph's father, that his "offspring shall be like the dust of the earth … and in you and your offspring shall all the families of the earth be blessed" (Gen. 28:14).

In this chapter we examine the life of Joseph, who—like his father Jacob and his great-grandfather Abraham—is also mentioned in the honor roll of faith in Hebrews 11: "By faith Joseph, at the end of his life, made mention of the exodus of the Israelites and gave directions concerning his bones" (Heb. 11:22). The text makes no further comment about Joseph. So why is he mentioned in this passage in Hebrews? To understand the vital place Joseph holds in this list of faithful servants of God, we must look at the differences in Joseph between his youth and who he becomes later in life. It is an exciting story. We will ask again and again the question "Where is God in this?" as his story unfolds. We seek to understand more fully the unique path God takes him on throughout his life to transform his faith, from an immature faith rooted in pride to a faith that recognizes God's intentional hand at work in his life, even in harsh and unjust circumstances.

Background

In order to understand the context for this story, we must look back briefly to Joseph's father, Jacob, and how, through some significant life events, God transformed his faith, which we discussed in detail in chapter 3. Near the end of his father's life, Jacob fled to Haran, to his mother's brother (Laban) for fear that his life might be in danger at the hand of his brother, Esau. Jacob immediately fell in love with Rachel, the younger daughter of Laban.

> Jacob loved Rachel. And he said [to Laban], "I will serve you seven years for your younger daughter Rachel." Laban said, "It is better that I give her to you than that I should give her to any other man; stay with me." So Jacob served seven years for Rachel, and they seemed to him but a few days because of the love he had for her. (Gen. 29:18–20)

Jacob commits to working seven years for Laban in exchange for Rachel, but ends up being deceived into first marrying Leah, Laban's firstborn daughter. He then discovers he has to work for Laban an additional seven years before he is permitted to marry Rachel (Gen. 29:22–28).

We saw in chapter 3 that Leah feels unloved in her marriage to Jacob. Thus, in order to win her husband's love, Leah begins to focus on bearing sons for Jacob, convincing herself that by doing so, Jacob will love her. Showing mercy on her situation, God grants her wish, and she bears four sons for Jacob, but there is no evidence that his feelings for her change. At the same time, Rachel remains barren and, in desperation, gives her handmaiden to Jacob, who bears him two sons. Leah responds by also giving her handmaiden to Jacob, who likewise bears him two sons. Leah then again conceives and bears Jacob two more sons and a daughter. Finally, God opens Rachel's womb; she conceives and gives Jacob a son, saying, "God has taken away my reproach." She calls his name *Joseph*, saying, "May the LORD add to me another son!" (Gen. 29:1–30:24).[1] We need to understand this broader context of Joseph's family story in order to understand everything else that happens from this point forward.

Favored Son

Our study of Joseph begins in Genesis 37, where, by this point, Rachel has died while giving birth to her second son Benjamin. Joseph is seventeen years old at this time.

> Joseph, being seventeen years old, was pasturing the flock with his brothers. He was a boy with the sons of Bilhah and Zilpah, his father's wives. And Joseph brought a bad report of them to their father. Now Israel loved Joseph more than any other of his sons, because he was the son of his old age. And he made him a robe of many colors. But when his brothers saw that their father loved him more than all his brothers, they hated him and could not speak peacefully to him. (Gen. 37:2b–4)

Here we see Joseph's exalted status in the eyes of his father. Jacob's love for Rachel spills over onto her first son, Joseph, following her death. He becomes the favorite son even though he is the eleventh son born to Jacob by his wives and their handmaidens. Jacob

---

[1] An accepted meaning of *Joseph* is "he (God) adds."

reflects his bias toward Joseph, not only in his attitude for Joseph but also by his actions, by giving only Joseph the distinctive coat of many colors. This elevated status in his father's eyes resulted in his other brothers hating him.

We get a good indication of the impact on Joseph of being the favorite son, and how this affects his brothers' attitude toward him in the following verses:

> Now Joseph had a dream, and when he told it to his brothers they hated him even more. He said to them, "Hear this dream that I have dreamed: Behold, we were binding sheaves in the field, and behold, my sheaf arose and stood upright. And behold, your sheaves gathered around it and bowed down to my sheaf." His brothers said to him, "Are you indeed to reign over us? Or are you indeed to rule over us?" So they hated him even more for his dreams and for his words.
>
> Then he dreamed another dream and told it to his brothers and said, "Behold, I have dreamed another dream. Behold, the sun, the moon, and eleven stars were bowing down to me." But when he told it to his father and to his brothers, his father rebuked him and said to him, "What is this dream that you have dreamed? Shall I and your mother and your brothers indeed come to bow ourselves to the ground before you?" And his brothers were jealous of him, but his father kept the saying in mind. (Gen. 37:5–11)

Joseph, the seventeen-year-old favorite son, has two dreams. Both dreams indicate the same result: he is going to increase, and his family is going to bow down to him. Notice that Joseph does not keep the dreams to himself but tells them to his brothers and his father, even though his brothers' hatred and jealousy of him are blatant because his father treats him differently than the rest of them.

This text indicates that after hearing just the first dream, his brothers "hated him even more" (v. 8). In this exchange, Joseph exercises poor judgment because of his favored position in the family. This issue is a chief cause of the events that will follow in Joseph's life.

Jacob's rebuke of Joseph following the telling of the second dream does little to assuage his brothers' feelings of hatred toward him. Then Jacob makes a mistake. One day he sends Joseph out to check on his brothers who are tending the flocks:

> They saw him from afar, and before he came near to them they conspired against him to kill him. They said to one another, "Here comes this dreamer. Come now, let us kill him and throw him into one of the pits. Then we will say that a fierce animal has devoured him, and we will see what will become of his dreams." But when Reuben heard it, he rescued him out of their hands, saying, "Let us not take his life." And Reuben said to them, "Shed no blood; throw him into this pit here in the wilderness, but do not lay a hand on him"—that he might rescue him out of their hand to restore him to his father. (Gen. 37:18–22)

In this text, the ten older brothers see Joseph coming and conspire to kill him. However, Reuben stops them. It is important to note that Reuben is Jacob's firstborn son and, as such, is preeminent in the family according to the cultural practices of the day. The first-born son becomes the patriarch of the family upon the death of the father. Reuben demonstrates his understanding of his position and responsibility within the family with his response to the plans of the brothers. He seeks to protect the life of Joseph, asking that they not shed his blood (v. 21). Even so, he goes along with the brothers' plot to put Joseph into a pit, take his distinctive coat and drench it in blood and take it to his father. This plan is intended to deceive Jacob into believing that Joseph is dead. Their actions also reflect a desire to get back at their father for his exclusive treatment and love for Joseph. Reuben acquiesces to the amended plan and makes a plan of his own to eventually rescue Joseph from the pit and restore him to his father unharmed.

God's Purposes

It is appropriate to ask at this point "Where is God in this?" We must likewise ask: what would the ramifications have been if the brothers had been able to carry out their original plan to kill Joseph? If Reuben is not successful and Joseph dies as a teen, as a result of his brothers' jealousy and hatred, what events will *not* happen? To find answers to these questions, we need to look ahead to the later part of Joseph's life. It is sufficient at this point to state that many significant events that do ultimately take place, all of which play a huge role in God's higher purposes, would not have taken place. Keep in mind as we work through Joseph's story that the actions of his brothers are critical in fulfilling the larger covenant promises God made to both Abraham and Jacob—promises of offspring, of "a multitude of nations" (Gen. 17:5) and that they "shall be like the dust of the earth" (Gen. 28:14). Thus, the early death of Joseph as a teen would quite possibly prevent God's covenant promises from being fulfilled. So, we see here in Genesis 37 that God is at work guiding and directing not just Joseph's actions, but also those of his ten brothers, to move the course of events forward toward the fulfillment of his covenant promises. It will take another twenty years to begin to see how all of this plays out.

In Joseph's life, God's active involvement in these circumstances is evident in Reuben's attempt to save Joseph's life and his desire to return him unharmed to his father. God is working his will in all events that occur in Joseph's life; those events are not coincidences.

Remember, at this point, Joseph's brothers have put him in a pit. God's continuing active involvement in Joseph's life events, and his working through Judah, another of Joseph's brothers, can be seen in the following passage:

> Then they sat down to eat. And looking up they saw a caravan of Ishmaelites coming from Gilead, with their camels bearing gum, balm, and myrrh, on their way to carry it down to Egypt. Then Judah said to his brothers, "What profit is it if we kill our brother and conceal his blood? Come, let us sell him to the Ishmaelites, and let not our hand be upon him, for he is our brother, our own flesh." And his brothers listened to him. Then Midianite traders passed by. And they drew Joseph up and lifted him out of the pit, and sold him to the Ishmaelites for twenty shekels of silver. They took Joseph to Egypt. (Gen. 37:25–28)

The emergence of Joseph's brother Judah as an influential character is likewise no coincidence. Judah is part of the Davidic line that ultimately leads to Jesus Christ. Reuben is out of the picture for the moment (Gen. 37:29) and thus cannot influence what the brothers do next. Judah steps forward to convince his brothers to sell Joseph to the Ishmaelites rather than allowing him to languish and die in the pit. This action not only saves Joseph's life but further advances God's plan for him. Moreover, it takes place while Reuben is not with them.

It is also interesting that Joseph is sold to *Ishmaelites*, for they originated from Abraham's son that Sarah's handmaiden Hagar bore to him (Gen. 16:1–12); the son that came from human effort to bring about that which God had promised to do. Thus, Jacob's family and the Ishmaelites are distant relatives. God uses them to bring about his purposes in Joseph's life. Genesis 37:36 confirms what happens to Joseph once he arrives in Egypt: "the Midianites had sold him in Egypt to Potiphar, an officer of Pharaoh, the captain of the guard." Joseph was sold into slavery.

137

When Reuben returns to the group, he discovers what his brothers have done and anguishes over the absence of Joseph. In his grief he agrees to continue with the remainder of the current deceptive plan: to cover the coat in goat blood, return home, and take the bloody coat to Jacob for identification (Gen. 37:29–32).

Consider the impact that this series of events must have had on Joseph, a seventeen-year-old youth. He had been raised as the favorite son of his father, who has shielded him from his older brothers. As a result, they increasingly dislike him as the years pass. By the time he reveals two dreams to them, which foreshadow his ultimate position of dominance over them, they have grown to hate Joseph. Out of their hate and jealousy, they seize upon the opportunity to eliminate him by plotting to kill him, but they finally choose instead to sell him into slavery in Egypt. Anger and hatred toward his brothers would not be unreasonable emotions on Joseph's part. Later, we will see in his story, in his comments to Pharaoh's cupbearer (Gen. 40:9–13) and his reasoning for his choice of names for his first son (Gen. 41:51), that he does now experience negative emotions toward his brothers. This situation and Joseph's emotions toward his brothers will eventually play an important role in revealing God's work of transforming his faith.

God's Active Involvement

As the story of Joseph continues in Genesis 39, we discover what happens to Joseph once he arrives in Egypt, and how God is actively orchestrating events in his life.

> Now Joseph had been brought down to Egypt, and Potiphar, an officer of Pharaoh, the captain of the guard, an Egyptian, had bought him from the Ishmaelites who had brought him down there. The LORD was with Joseph, and he became a successful man, and he was in the house of his Egyptian master. His master saw that the LORD was with him and that the LORD caused

all that he did to succeed in his hands. So Joseph found favor in his sight and attended him, and he made him overseer of his house and put him in charge of all that he had. From the time that he made him overseer in his house and over all that he had, the LORD blessed the Egyptian's house for Joseph's sake; the blessing of the LORD was on all that he had, in house and field. So he left all that he had in Joseph's charge, and because of him he had no concern about anything but the food he ate. (Gen. 39:1–6)

This text is critical in helping us understand how God works in different ways in the lives of different individuals to accomplish the work of transforming their faith. In the lives of Abraham and Jacob, we saw that God appeared to both of them at various times to reveal his presence with them, and to reveal his plans for them, as a means of transforming and strengthening their faith. Over time we saw their initial simple, objective belief become personal, subjective, transformed faith. God became real to them personally through those revelatory events.

However, we do not see this self-revelation process occur with Joseph. Instead, God gives him two dreams at the age of seventeen, but he neither appears in nor speaks directly to Joseph in those dreams as he did with both Abraham and Jacob. We must look for other indications of God transforming Joseph's simple belief into genuine faith. We will see that God is, indeed, doing the work of transformation differently with him than he did with Abraham or Jacob.

In the Genesis 39 passage above, and through the rest of Joseph's story, we see God blessing him and giving him success in everything he does, from the minute he enters Potiphar's house until the end of his life. We have already seen God "speak" to Joseph by giving him dreams and the interpretation of those dreams. Also, we have just seen how the actions of two of his brothers spared his life. We must wonder if Joseph, at this time, recognizes God's active involvement in his life through the dreams and the messages of those dreams, along with the fact that his brothers did not kill him as they had planned. These are much more subtle processes of transformation than that experienced by Abraham and Jacob, whose individual faith was transformed through *personal encounters with God*. The process that God uses in Joseph's life to reveal his active presence and involvement in Joseph's life circumstances seems to be unique to him, that of *giving dreams and their interpretation, sparing his life*, and *making him successful* in all he does. These are the ways God uses to transform Joseph's faith.

So then the question naturally arises, how does Joseph come to realize that it is *God* who is guiding his life's events and prospering all that he does? We have to look further down the road of Joseph's life to see that later, he does recognize that he could not have accomplished all that he will eventually accomplish by himself. As his story progresses, we will see small but significant indications that he does, indeed, see God's involvement *now* in the events unfolding in his life.

One of the problems we encounter as we try to identify with and relate to the stories of Abraham and Jacob is that, for many of us, God does not appear to us or speak directly to us to reveal how he is working in our lives. Understanding that God will reveal his active involvement in our lives in different ways is a significant point that we can glean from the story of Joseph. It is essential to accept that we often do not see or understand God's *current* action and involvement in our lives. They become understandable to us only later upon reflection; only then do we see how God has been orchestrating and guiding daily events to accomplish his higher purposes. Thus, we, like Joseph, must learn to discern God's hand at work in our lives, in our daily circumstances, so that he becomes real to us. We can then point to various events in our lives and say, "God did that." This ability to notice what God is doing, and has done, in our lives does develop over time if we continually ask the question "Where is God in this situation?" This kind of question reveals our intention to find God amid all life's circumstances.

Falsely Accused

We can see evidence that the work of transformation is taking place in Joseph, and we glean an understanding of Joseph's faith at this time in his life by looking at how he responds to the events that occur in Genesis 39.

> And after a time his master's wife cast her eyes on Joseph and said, "Lie with me." But he refused and said to his master's wife, "Behold, because of me my master has no concern about anything in the house, and he has put everything that he has in my charge. He is not greater in this house than I am, nor has he kept back anything from me except you, because you are his wife. How then can I do this great wickedness and sin against God?" And as she spoke to Joseph day after day, he would not listen to her, to lie beside her or to be with her. (Gen. 39:7–10)

The first thing to notice is Joseph's contentment with his position in Potiphar's household. In his response to Potiphar's wife's advances, Joseph states that even Potiphar himself is not greater than Joseph in his household, as Joseph is responsible for all things in Potiphar's house except that which pertain to his wife (v. 9). That reveals a high level of contentment with his current position in life. It also reveals the degree of respect that Potiphar has for Joseph. Joseph intends to do nothing that might jeopardize his current position. Additionally, his response reveals the strength of his character, the degree of honesty and integrity in Joseph: to sleep with Potiphar's wife would betray Potiphar's trust that he has placed in Joseph.

The next thing to notice that reveals some measure of the ongoing effect of transformation in Joseph is this: he acknowledges that for him to lie with Potiphar's wife would be to "sin against God" (v. 9). Joseph holds no resentment toward God for being taken from his homeland by his brothers and sold into slavery in Egypt. Instead, he attributes to God his success and the attendant blessings received while in Egypt. Thus, to lie with Potiphar's wife would be a betrayal against God and what he has done for Joseph. He expresses these feelings in the strongest possible terms by categorizing such action as a sin. But not just sin against people; he views it as a sin against *God*. It is evident in this statement that God has become real for Joseph to such a degree that he actively seeks to live a holy life, intentionally choosing to not sin against God. We can see this as evidence of the extent of the transformation of Joseph's faith, which has taken place to this point.

Here is a critical turning point in Joseph's life. Joseph's rejection of the sexual advances of Potiphar's wife is necessary if God's covenant promises are to be fulfilled, which we will see as Joseph's story unfolds. However, we have no evidence that Joseph understands this truth at this time.

Next, we see Potiphar's reaction to the lie about Joseph that his wife tells him:

> As soon as his master heard the words that his wife spoke to him, "This is the way your servant treated me," his anger was kindled. And Joseph's master took him and put him into the prison, the place where the king's prisoners were confined, and he was there in prison. (Gen. 39:19–20)

Notice that despite Joseph's prior success and the complete confidence that Potiphar had previously placed in him, he accepts his wife's statement without question and condemns Joseph to prison. Yet, at the same time, Potiphar could have condemned him to death. Once again God protects Joseph from being killed. Both of these factors are important indications of God continuing to guide and direct the events of Joseph's life to ensure God's bigger purposes will eventually be fulfilled.

And once again, Joseph is being treated unfairly, even though his actions were without sin. If he had acted with a more human response, he could have derailed the continuing work of God to fulfill his covenant promises to the patriarchs. If his refusal had not led Potiphar's wife to lie about Joseph, charging him unjustly with making sexual advances toward her, he would not have ended up in prison. Potiphar would likely have retained Joseph as head of his household, and the future events that we will see emerge in Joseph's life (as result of the false accusation) would not come to pass. Thus, it is essential to keep asking, "Where is God in this?" with respect to both the good and the bad that occurs in Joseph's life.

It is important to ask this question in our own life circumstances as well. When we accept God's sovereignty over all of creation, we must be willing to also accept his sovereignty over the good *and* the bad events that occur in our lives. In God's sovereignty, he is always working to fulfill his promises to each of us, and he will use all events in our lives to bring about the fulfillment of those promises. What seems to us from a human perspective as "wrong" or unjust can be the very avenue that God uses to fulfill his promises to us. Additionally, God is at work in the circumstances of *our* lives to fulfill his bigger purposes in the lives of *others*.

Rather than allowing Joseph to be confined in chains, once again God places Joseph in a position where he can succeed. We see the writer of Genesis presenting the following perspective:

> But the LORD was with Joseph and showed him steadfast love and gave him favor in the sight of the keeper of the prison. And the keeper of the prison put Joseph in charge of all the prisoners who were in the prison. Whatever was done there, he was the one who did it. The keeper of the prison paid no attention to anything that was in Joseph's charge, because the LORD was with him. And whatever he did, the LORD made it succeed. (Gen. 39:21–23)

Remember that Moses wrote the book of Genesis, but he was not alive in the time of Joseph. So how did he know that *God was with Joseph* in prison, and *as a result* he gained favor with the overseer of the prison? He learned the stories that comprise the book of Genesis from the oral tradition passed down from one generation to the next, as was the custom of that time. Therefore, we need to also ask "Where did the oral story of Joseph begin?" The most obvious answer is from Joseph himself, telling the story to his offspring after him, which was then passed on to each future generation. Thus, the conclusion that God enabled Joseph to succeed in all he did likely comes from Joseph's own understanding of God's sovereignty and active involvement in all that was occurring in his life. This is an indication that God is indeed real for Joseph: he recognizes God's hand at work in his life circumstances. This awareness of God's active involvement even in the hard, difficult, or "bad" times in life reflects a measure of genuine faith. Thus, we can conclude from this passage that God is continuing the work of transforming Joseph's faith as life events unfold. Confirmation of this will become evident at the naming of Joseph's two sons in a future text.

Indications of Genuine Faith

As the story continues, Joseph is successfully running the prison, allowed to do so by the keepers of the prison. Two of Pharaoh's officers, his cupbearer and chief baker, were confined in the prison because they had committed an offense against Pharaoh. Because of his position over all the prisoners, Joseph interacts with Pharaoh's former officers.

> And one night they both dreamed—the cupbearer and the baker of the king of Egypt, who were confined in the prison—each his own dream, and each dream with its own interpretation. When Joseph came to them in the morning, he saw that they were troubled. So he asked Pharaoh's officers who were with him in custody in his master's house, "Why are your faces downcast today?" They said to him, "We have had dreams, and there is no one to interpret them."

And Joseph said to them, "Do not interpretations belong to God? Please tell them to me."
(Gen. 40:5–8)

In this text, Pharaoh's cupbearer and chief baker have dreams,
and there is no one to interpret them. Joseph immediately responds,
"Do not interpretations belong to God?" (v. 8). His immediate
response reveals the measure of genuine faith that he possesses at
this time. He knows that the interpretation of dreams *belongs to God*
and that it does not come from his wisdom. He also seems to be
confident that *he* will provide accurate interpretations of the dreams.
However, before doing so, he gives full credit to God. He is aware
in that moment that *God will act through him*, that he will, indeed,
be able to give *God's* interpretation of those dreams and not his own.
That is an indicator of Joseph's increasingly transformed faith compared to how he handled himself at age seventeen when he seemed
to believe that the dreams and the interpretation of those dreams
were his own. Obviously, during the intervening ten years, God has
become real for Joseph; it is now more important to him to first give
credit to God, to acknowledge the sovereignty and power of God,
than to take credit himself by immediately interpreting the dreams
of others. In his response to the cupbearer and the baker, he reveals
the progress of the transforming work of God in his life. God has
allowed Joseph ten years of living in a foreign land away from his
family to consider the significance of the dreams that he had at age
seventeen, and to consider who it was that gave him the dreams and
their interpretation.

Note that once he has given credit to God for the dreams and
their interpretation, he then immediately asks that they tell him
their dreams. We see here that God is using the same method of
"speaking" to Joseph that he used ten years before. Thus, dreams and
the interpretation of dreams are beginning to emerge as a consistent way in which God speaks to Joseph and through him to others.
Joseph's faith is maturing in the process, to the point where he *knows*
God gives and interprets dreams, and he *knows* that God will speak
through him to others in the process. His confidence comes from

experientially knowing that God speaks to him personally and works through him to encourage others.

What we see here in Joseph's story is that his faith has been transformed during the past ten years to the point where Joseph is willing to let God work through him as he chooses. This is a very different experience of God's self-revelation from what we have seen in the stories of Abraham and Jacob, whom God "spoke" to and had conversations with throughout their lives. Moreover, it is a different form of obedience to God. Abraham and Jacob were asked by God to do certain things, and ultimately, they did so, revealing the extent of their transforming faith. Here, Joseph makes himself available *to be used by God*, for God to work through him to bring about God's intended outcome in this situation. Thus, we see that "obedience to God" comes in different forms. Again, we learn from Joseph's life that God works in different ways to reveal himself to us and to actively work in life's situations. We must remain open to how God might choose to speak to each of us or to work through us to accomplish his bigger plans.

After he hears the dreams, Joseph goes ahead and accurately interprets the cupbearer's dream, which reveals that God will release him from prison and restore him to his former position with Pharaoh. Joseph then pleads with Pharaoh's cupbearer:

> "Only remember me, when it is well with you, and please do me the kindness to mention me to Pharaoh, and so get me out of this house. For I was indeed stolen out of the land of the Hebrews, and here also I have done nothing that they should put me into the pit." (Gen. 40:14–15)

Joseph feels unjustly treated because of what has occurred up to this point in his life. Then we discover that, despite his plea to the cupbearer, Joseph remains in prison for an additional two years (see Gen. 41:1, 14). Why did the cupbearer not remember his promise to Joseph for two years? We need to ask again "Where is God in this?" We will not understand God's reasons and purposes for this two-year delay until we read further in Joseph's story. Only then will we see from God's perspective the reason for this prolonged unjust imprisonment.

Interpreting Pharaoh's Dreams

The two years pass; Joseph is now age thirty. Pharaoh dreams two dreams: the first is about seven attractive and plump cows and seven ugly and thin cows; the second is about seven plump and good ears of grain and seven thin and blighted ears of grain. Pharaoh can find no one in Egypt to interpret his dreams until finally, his cup-bearer remembers Joseph and how he interpreted the cupbearer's dreams two years before and mentions this to Pharaoh (Gen. 41:1–13). Then we read:

> Then Pharaoh sent and called Joseph, and they quickly brought him out of the pit. And when he had shaved himself and changed his clothes, he came in before Pharaoh. And Pharaoh said to Joseph, "I have had a dream, and there is no one who can interpret it. I have heard it said of you that when you hear a dream you can interpret it." Joseph answered Pharaoh, "It is not in me; God will give Pharaoh a favorable answer." (Gen. 41:14–16)

Notice that in this text, as in the text with Pharaoh's cupbearer and chief baker, Joseph's initial response to Pharaoh's request is to credit God with the ability to interpret the dreams. Here he is, standing before Pharaoh, taking no credit whatsoever for what he is about to do. That further reveals the extent of transformation God has accomplished in Joseph. In humility, he openly acknowledges God's sovereignty and power over human events.

Further, note that Joseph tells Pharaoh before he hears the dreams, "God will give Pharaoh a favorable answer" (v. 16). Again, he makes this statement as "a matter of fact," which again reveals confidence rooted in *experiential knowing* what God is about to do through him. We can view this confidence as evidence of a spirit of discernment that God is developing in Joseph as part of the spiritual transformation occurring in him.

Continuing in Genesis 41, Joseph interprets Pharaoh's dreams. Notice that his interpretation focuses upon God:

> Then Joseph said to Pharaoh, "The dreams of Pharaoh are one; God has revealed to Pharaoh what he is about to do. The seven good cows are seven years, and the seven good ears are seven years; the dreams are one. The seven lean and ugly cows that came up after them are seven years, and the seven empty ears blighted by the east wind are also seven years of famine. It is as I told Pharaoh; God has shown to Pharaoh what he is about to do. There will come seven years of great plenty throughout all the land of Egypt, but after them there will arise seven years of famine, and all the plenty will be forgotten in the land of Egypt. The famine will consume the land, and the plenty will be unknown in the land by reason of the famine that will follow, for it will be very severe. And the doubling of Pharaoh's dream means that the thing is fixed by God, and God will shortly bring it about." (Gen. 41:25–32)

It is evident from how Joseph interprets Pharaoh's dreams that he recognizes and accepts that he is the means God uses to interpret the dreams. He is merely giving a human voice to God's words for Pharaoh. His interpretation is very matter-of-fact, including the comments that "the doubling of Pharaoh's dream means that the thing is fixed by God" and that "God will shortly bring it about" (v. 32). At this point in Joseph's story, unlike the stories of Abraham and Jacob, we see God developing prophetic gifting; Joseph's comments reveal what God *is about to do*. As such, they reveal the continuing work of transformation in Joseph as God works through him to speak to Pharaoh, just as he did to the cupbearer.

In light of the seeming impending fulfillment of Pharaoh's dreams, it is easy to imagine that Joseph must be thinking back to his dreams that have not yet come true. Moreover, he must still be wondering why it took the cupbearer so long to mention him to Pharaoh. In contrast to the faith struggles that both Abraham and Jacob experienced concerning trusting God to be faithful to his word (promises) to each of them, Joseph exhibits no hesitation to make such strong, confident statements about what God plans to do and soon will do. Thus, even as God delays fulfilling the dreams he gave Joseph personally, he still trusts the word God is giving him for others and God's faithfulness to fulfill his promises.

The important lesson for us is this: it takes time for God to fulfill his promises to us, and it takes genuine faith to stand with confidence amid delayed fulfillment of those promises. We can learn from the progression of Joseph's transforming faith how we too can walk with confidence in the promises God has made, trusting him to be faithful, in His perfect time, and in His perfect way, regardless of how long he might take to fulfill them.

God's Bigger Purposes

Now we must return to the questions about why the cupbearer did not talk to Pharaoh about Joseph and why Joseph had to endure another two years of unjust imprisonment. From our current perspective of what God has been doing during the two-year delay, it is clear that Joseph had to remain in prison because Pharaoh was not going to receive the dreams about the seven years of plenty and the seven years of famine until now. If Joseph was released previously, *as he desired*, who knows where he would have been two years later when he was needed to interpret Pharaoh's dreams? He could have returned home to his family in the land of Canaan, possibly to seek revenge against his brothers for having sold him into slavery. However, God is guiding and directing the sequence of each event for his higher purposes. Thus, Joseph cannot be released from prison for an additional two years after interpreting the cupbearer's dream.

It is quite helpful in difficult circumstances, in those times when it seems God has forgotten us, to continue to ask the question "Where is God in this?" or "What is God doing in this situation?" Continuing to ask such questions keeps us from falling into deep despair; we keep our eyes focused on God, his sovereignty, and his higher plans and purposes for our lives and the lives of others. We can quickly lose sight of those bigger plans when our immediate circumstances seem to be extremely difficult or unjust. Indeed, being willing to ask such questions reveals a measure of genuine faith; such questions are rooted in deep, abiding belief and trust in the goodness and faithfulness of God to do what he has said he will do.

Genesis 41 continues with Joseph humbly laying out a recommended course of action to Pharaoh to ensure that there will be sufficient food for the people during the seven years of famine. Once again, Joseph speaks of the proposal with no indication of self-serving motivation on his part. He does it with humility. Here too we see indications of the ongoing transformation of his faith, which God is working in him through the difficult circumstances of his life. Again we see that Joseph continues to act in confidence of what he "knows," but he also acts in humility because he knows God is giving him the understanding. It is not his understanding or intellect that has enabled him to know and speak such things.

The impact of Joseph's statements on Pharaoh becomes immediately evident as the story continues:

> This proposal pleased Pharaoh and all his servants. And Pharaoh said to his servants, "Can we find a man like this, in whom is the Spirit of God?" Then Pharaoh said to Joseph, "Since God has shown you all this, there is none so discerning and wise as you are. You shall be over my house, and all my people shall order themselves as you command. Only as regards the throne will I be greater than you." And Pharaoh said to Joseph,

"See, I have set you over all the land of Egypt."
(Gen. 41:37–41)

After hearing all that Joseph had to say, Pharaoh immediately recognizes the authority with which Joseph speaks, which is impressive since Joseph had to be summoned from prison where he was for more than two years. The text does not tell us whether Pharaoh knew Joseph was in prison before the comment made to him by his cupbearer (it was Potiphar who put him in prison). Also, there was nothing to give credibility to the statements made to Pharaoh about Joseph's abilities. Nonetheless, he immediately calls Joseph out of prison and gives Joseph command over his household and all the inhabitants of Egypt. That is a rather remarkable turn of events.

Once again, it is necessary to ask the question "Where is God in this?" What is God doing in this situation? Pharaoh provides the answer for us when he says, "Since God has shown you all this, there is none so discerning and wise as you are" (v. 39). Pharaoh recognizes and accepts the *power of God at work through Joseph* and attributes it to him as wisdom. It seems that Pharaoh is willing to entrust much power and authority to Joseph because he recognizes God's wisdom in and through him.

Here we can also see what God is up to from a different perspective. God is acting through others (at times, through "unbelievers") to ensure his plans and purposes for his people will come to pass. For example, we have seen in the stories of Abraham and Jacob various ways in which God saved their lives by acting through another or speaking ("revealing") truth through another:

-   In Abram's story (before God changed his name to *Abraham*), God revealed to Pharaoh that the affliction that came upon him was the result of Abram's lie about Sarai being his sister, not his wife. God's revelation to Pharaoh kept him from defiling Sarai. Pharaoh then sent Abram and Sarai on their way with all of their possessions (Gen. 12:17–20). Abram's life was spared.

- God spoke to Abram through Melchizedek, stating that it was God who enabled him to defeat his enemies when he went to rescue Lot, his family, and his possessions (Gen. 14:19–20). Melchizedek's words of knowledge and understanding to Abram reveal that it was God's empowerment in threatening circumstances that preserved his life.

- God spoke to Laban in a dream about how to act toward Jacob when he, his family, and all his possessions left Laban in secret and headed back to Canaan. This visitation by God resulted in Laban's eventual willingness to let Jacob continue his journey home after establishing a covenant of peace between them, rather than doing him harm, which he initially wanted to do (Gen. 31:22–55). God's intervention through a dream potentially spared Jacob's life and ensured God's plans for Jacob would continue to be fulfilled.

So too, in Genesis 41, Pharaoh reveals that it is *God* who has made Joseph very wise and discerning. God has somehow "revealed" this truth to Pharaoh. As a result, Joseph is released from prison and established as Pharaoh's "second-in-command" over all of Egypt (Gen. 41:39–41). Again, God has worked through another person (in this case, an "unbeliever") to further his intentions for Joseph's life.

Through these biblical stories, we can see that God sometimes speaks to us through unbelievers as he continues to guide our steps and the direction of our lives *so that* he will eventually fulfill his plans and purposes for our lives. In this, we see God's faithfulness and sovereignty at work to accomplish plans and intentions that are bigger than the events in our own lives. We must remain open to "hearing God's voice" speaking to us, regardless of the source or how God chooses to "speak." How many times might we have missed God "speaking" to us, or acting on our behalf, because we did not have the eyes to see, or the ears to hear, God acting or speaking through those whom we might least expect him to use? Because God is sovereign, he can work to transform us in any way he chooses, through any person or situation, to achieve his divine purposes in our lives.

Years of Plenty

Joseph's story continues in Genesis 41:

> Joseph was thirty years old when he entered the
> service of Pharaoh king of Egypt. And Joseph
> went out from the presence of Pharaoh and went
> through all the land of Egypt. During the seven
> plentiful years the earth produced abundantly,
> and he gathered up all the food of these seven
> years, which occurred in the land of Egypt, and
> put the food in the cities. He put in every city the
> food from the fields around it. And Joseph stored
> up grain in great abundance, like the sand of the
> sea, until he ceased to measure it, for it could not
> be measured. (Gen. 41:46–49)

Remember that when Joseph was in the household of Potiphar,
God made him successful. While he was in prison, God made him
successful. So now working for Pharaoh, God makes Joseph successful again, although others do not yet realize it. After all, the seven
years of abundance are not yet complete. Without a doubt, many
must have scratched their heads wondering why Joseph was doing
what he was doing in a time of plenty. Apparently, no one grumbled
or openly questioned his actions, likely because of his position of
authority.

Joseph was only thirty at this time, quite a young man to suddenly hold such a position. Given Joseph's arrogance and pride from
his early years, we might not be surprised to see such attitudes in
him now, given the position of power and authority he now holds.
However, we do not see them. In this text, there is no evidence of an
attitude of superiority. Instead, we see one who is carrying out wise
actions with confidence for the sake of others, planning for the years
of famine that he knows are coming. This wisdom and the lack of a
superior attitude are evidence of the ongoing work of transformation
in Joseph.

We can see the extent of ongoing transformation in Joseph in the next passage in Genesis 41, in his reasons for choosing specific names for his first two sons.

> Before the year of famine came, two sons were born to Joseph. Asenath, the daughter of Potiphera priest of On, bore them to him. Joseph called the name of the firstborn Manasseh. "For," he said, "God has made me forget all my hardship and all my father's house." The name of the second he called Ephraim, "For God has made me fruitful in the land of my affliction." (Gen. 41:50–52)

Here we see the first major *personal* milestone in Joseph's life of faith. Throughout his story, we have seen how he credits God when good things occur to him. However, here he memorializes his testimony in the naming of his two sons. He names the first *Manasseh* because, despite what his brothers did to him and the resulting hardships he endured, "God has made me forget all my hardship and all my father's house" (v. 51). Joseph's righteous anger, regarding what has transpired, could become a bitter stronghold in him. Here he testifies that God has made him forget all that has occurred. The result is that there is no anger or resentment toward his brothers.

Joseph names his second son *Ephraim*, "for God has made me fruitful in the land of my affliction" (v. 52), an apparent reference to now having two sons. There is no reference here to his success as a powerful man in Egypt or to any wealth and possessions he may have accumulated as a result of working for Pharaoh. Instead, he praises God for blessing him with two sons. The word *affliction* (v. 52) reveals his attitude toward his life in Egypt: life has been challenging and unfair. He has been "afflicted." In light of this, his understanding of what God has done for him during those difficult years reveals the extent of the transformation God has been working in him *through* those difficult years.

Joseph acknowledges God's active involvement in removing understandable negative attitudes toward his brothers for their
actions toward him. Remember, we stated at the beginning of this
chapter that God would eventually transform Joseph's faith to the
point where he would recognize God's intentional hand at work in
his life, even in harsh and unjust circumstances. Moreover, here, at
about the age of thirty, we see clear indications that Joseph is demonstrating an increasing level of genuine faith. Later, it will be essential
to remember this milestone, and Joseph's acknowledgment of God's
active involvement in his life, when he is tested—as he comes face-
to-face with his brothers.

Years of Famine

According to God's interpretation of Pharaoh's dreams through
Joseph (Gen. 41:29–30), seven years of abundance come to an end,
and seven years of famine begin. We see now the beginning of those
years of famine:

> So when the famine had spread over all the land,
> Joseph opened all the storehouses and sold to the
> Egyptians, for the famine was severe in the land
> of Egypt. Moreover, all the earth came to Egypt
> to Joseph to buy grain, because the famine was
> severe over all the earth. (Gen. 41:56–57)

This text tells us that "all the earth" comes to Egypt, ultimately
to Joseph, to buy grain because of the famine (v. 57). That is possible
only because God has planned it that way. God has been working
through all of the various events of Joseph's life, explicitly orchestrating them, so that Joseph would be in God's appointed place at God's
appointed time, with all the necessary grain to sell to all who would
come to him. God's sovereignty and faithfulness have been demonstrated *to Joseph personally* as his life has taken twists and turns, from
being sold as a slave, working in a trusted position, only to then be
unjustly accused and thrown in prison and forgotten for two years.

However, God's faithfulness toward the masses of people is apparent in his actions in Joseph's life. He has brought Joseph out of prison and established him as the second most powerful man in Egypt. God has given him a vision of what the future will hold, and direction about how to walk through times of abundance and famine, *all for the sake of the people throughout "all the land"* (Gen. 42:6, italics added), which, as we will eventually see, includes his own family.

The abundance that God has provided through Joseph is so plentiful that Joseph quit counting it; it was "beyond measure" (Gen. 41:49). There is not just sufficient grain; the grain is abundant in the storehouses. There is more grain than what Egypt needs, which is what Pharaoh expected. Also, we will soon see that there is more than what Egypt and Canaan need, which means that there is enough, ultimately, for Joseph's family.

Deception Begins

As we examined in Jacob's story, "ten of Joseph's brothers went down to buy grain in Egypt.[2] However, Jacob did not send Benjamin, Joseph's brother, with his brothers, for he feared that harm might happen to him" (Gen. 42:3–4). When the brothers arrive in Egypt, they meet with Joseph.

> Now Joseph was governor over the land. He was the one who sold to all the people of the land. And Joseph's brothers came and bowed themselves before him with their faces to the ground. Joseph saw his brothers and recognized them, but he treated them like strangers and spoke roughly to them. "Where do you come from?" he said. They said, "From the land of Canaan, to buy food." And Joseph recognized his brothers, but they did not recognize him. And Joseph remembered the dreams that he had dreamed of them.

---

2   For a deeper discussion of this part of Joseph's life, see chapter 3.

And he said to them, "You are spies; you have
come to see the nakedness of the land." They said
to him, "No, my lord, your servants have come
to buy food. We are all sons of one man. We are
honest men. Your servants have never been spies."
(Gen. 42:6–11)

Here we see at the beginning of the brothers' visit with Joseph
that they do not recognize him, but he knows who they are. In their
arrival in Egypt, we see that they fulfill the first dream that Joseph
had at age seventeen: his brothers bow down to him (Gen. 37:7). At
this point, Joseph undergoes a test of his transformed faith, which
God has been building in him during the previous twenty years.
Some struggle with understandable human emotions (anger, possibly
resentment) is evident within him since he does not identify himself
to his brothers, even though he recognizes them.

Joseph begins a path of deceit and treats them harshly, accusing them of being spies in the land (v. 9). He learns from them that
their younger brother (Benjamin) is not with them, but still at home
with their father (Gen. 42:13). Joseph declares that he will test the
truthfulness of their claim that they are not spies. He instructs that
one of them should go home and bring their younger brother back
to Egypt; in doing so, they will prove their innocence to him. Joseph
plans to keep the rest of the brothers in prison until the one brother
returns with the younger brother. He then puts them all in prison for
three days (Gen. 42:15–17), presumably to decide among themselves
who will be the one to return home. Is this a power play, possibly
with retribution or revenge mixed in, on Joseph's part? If so, we have
to ask, what happened to his conviction that God has removed such
emotions from his heart toward his brothers? If he, indeed, is no
longer angry or resentful toward them, then why this deception and
harsh behavior toward those whom he knows are his brothers? We
must wait for the answers to these questions as events continue to
unfold.

It is interesting that, although Joseph recognizes his brothers,
they do not recognize him, probably because they do not expect him

to be second-in-command in Egypt. After twenty years, they must have thought that if alive, he would still be living as a slave. At times we do not see what we are not seeking. Moreover, God has his reasons for not enabling them to see at this time that the man they are talking to is their brother Joseph.

Joseph plays out his deception well, speaking only Egyptian to them and using an interpreter. He continues the deception beginning in Genesis 42, verse 18:

> On the third day Joseph said to them, "Do this and you will live, for I fear God: if you are honest men, let one of your brothers remain confined where you are in custody, and let the rest go and carry grain for the famine of your households, and bring your youngest brother to me. So your words will be verified, and you shall not die." And they did so. Then they said to one another, "In truth we are guilty concerning our brother, in that we saw the distress of his soul, when he begged us and we did not listen. That is why this distress has come upon us." And Reuben answered them, "Did I not tell you not to sin against the boy? But you did not listen. So now there comes a reckoning for his blood." They did not know that Joseph understood them, for there was an interpreter between them. Then he turned away from them and wept. And he returned to them and spoke to them. And he took Simeon from them and bound him before their eyes. And Joseph gave orders to fill their bags with grain, and to replace every man's money in his sack, and to give them provisions for the journey. This was done for them. (Gen. 42:18–25)

Joseph again accuses his brothers of being spies, for which the usual penalty is death. Then he changes his mind. Instead of sending only one brother home to retrieve the youngest brother, he tells them that he will allow *all* of them to return home, except one (vv. 18–20), so that they may take grain home to their families *and* to bring their youngest brother to him as proof that what they're saying is true, that they are not spies. Why the shift from sending only one brother home to sending all but one? We might consider that during the three days of imprisonment of his brothers, he also had time to reflect, and changed his mind. It seems possible that his heart of forgiveness may have surfaced and, in mercy, decides to send most of his brothers home with grain for the sake of their families. He does bind Simeon and keep him in prison and warns the rest of them that they will confirm their assertion that they are not spies and will not die if they return with their younger brother (v. 20). In this text, we possibly see a mixture of a desire to get retribution for their past action toward him and mercy toward them in light of the reality of the famine.

Joseph effectively maintains his deception before them until they acknowledge their guilt within his hearing. At that moment he "turned away from them and wept" (v. 24). The old Joseph appears gone; in place of righteous anger and possible revenge, Joseph weeps. By doing so, he lives out his declaration of faith in the naming of Manasseh; at this moment, it seems he has forgotten the pain and suffering for which these ten brothers were responsible. Moreover, this applies not just to what has happened to Joseph since they threw him into the pit. It also applies to the initial seventeen years of his life, during which time they could not speak kindly to him because of their hatred toward him (Gen. 37:4).

So Joseph is overcome with emotion and weeps, seemingly revealing a change of heart toward them, and then is generous to them. Note that at the same time that he is *selling* grain to the rest of the world, Joseph *gives* grain to his brothers and generously returns their money to them in their sacks (Gen. 42:25). These actions show some progress from being an arrogant teenager; there *is* an element of payback toward his brothers, but it is not to *their* detriment. Nothing that he does to them now compares with what his brothers did to him. Thus, Joseph's orders, to return their money to them and to give them sufficient provision for their journey home, are very generous acts.

A critical point of this part of Joseph's story is this: transformation of faith comes in little steps over time. Years have passed at this point. We are now seeing further evidence of the transformation process that God has been working in him during these intervening years, transformation from simple belief to genuine faith. However, there is still need for more transformation to occur.

Remember, the brothers' trip to Egypt occurs at the end of the first year of the famine. Joseph knows that the famine will last another six years and that his brothers will be forced to return for more grain. He could legitimately keep their money, knowing he would see them again. What is transpiring here is more than a business deal. There are more significant issues at stake. Remember too Joseph's two dreams: one was that he would have dominion over his brothers, the other that his entire family would bow down to him. The first dream seems to have been fulfilled, in that at this time, Joseph does have power over his brothers. However the second dream has not yet been fulfilled; the entire family is not yet in Egypt. That is why he places specific conditions on them, requiring that they bring their little brother the next time they come to Egypt, or they will not see Simeon again.

During their journey home, when they reach a lodging place, one of the brothers opens his sack to give his donkey fodder and sees his money in the mouth of his sack (v. 27). When he tells his brothers about what he has found, they are all afraid, saying, "What is this that God has done to us?" (v. 28). Here is the first acknowledgment by the brothers that God is actively involved in what is happening. They continue on their journey without checking the other sacks or questioning whether they should return to Egypt in order to return the money.

As we previously examined in Jacob's story, the brothers return home and tell Jacob everything that has transpired in Egypt. Jacob responds in disbelief, lamenting that he previously lost one son (Joseph) and has now just lost another (Simeon). Despite what his sons have told him concerning Simeon, Jacob is willing to write him off as dead. The brothers want to return immediately to Egypt with Benjamin for more grain and to redeem Simeon, but Jacob categorically refuses (Gen. 42:29–38).

Time passes, and Jacob continues to refuse to allow Benjamin to accompany his brothers to Egypt to buy more grain and rescue Simeon, until they finally run out of grain. Only then does Jacob instruct the brothers to go to Egypt again to buy grain. The brothers remind him of what the man (Joseph) had said to them; they refuse to go unless Benjamin goes with them. Reuben personally guarantees Benjamin's safety. Jacob finally relents and allows Benjamin to go (Gen. 43:1–11), rather than watching his whole family die of starvation.

Thus, the ten brothers, with Benjamin, return to Egypt carrying the original money to pay for the grain they previously received, new money to buy more grain, and gifts for the man (Gen. 43:11–15). Once they arrive, Joseph sees them and invites them to his home to eat a meal with him (Gen. 43:16). They are so concerned about the money issues from their first trip that they immediately speak to Joseph's servant, explaining what happened during their last visit.

And the men were afraid because they were brought to Joseph's house, and they said, "It is because of the money, which was replaced in our sacks the first time, that we are brought in, so that he may assault us and fall upon us to make us servants and seize our donkeys." So they went up to the steward of Joseph's house and spoke with him at the door of the house, and said, "Oh, my lord, we came down the first time to buy food. And when we came to the lodging place we opened our sacks, and there was each man's money in the mouth of his sack, our money in full weight. So we have brought it again with us, and we have brought other money down with us to buy food. We do not know who put our money in our sacks." He replied, "Peace to you,

do not be afraid. Your God and the God of your
father has put treasure in your sacks for you. I
received your money." Then he brought Simeon
out to them. (Gen. 43:18–23)

Here the steward of Joseph's household credits *their* God, the
God of their father (Jacob), as having put the money in their sacks
(v. 23). We must ask why an Egyptian servant would give such an
explanation. A possible answer may be that God does not work on
just one individual's faith at a time. And as we have previously mentioned, he does not work only through his people. It seems that the
ongoing work of transformation in Joseph affected the steward of his
household; it seems to have had an impact on him.

Here is an essential point about the transformation process: our
transformation process can and does "speak" to others about who
our God is. We need to know this truth. We are often quite unaware
of how our faith is revealing to others who God is through how we
live our daily lives and how we handle life's challenges. Previously
we mentioned that we could miss what God may be saying to us
through others, even nonbelievers. It is also important to note that
God can be acting through us to speak to others, to reveal himself to
them, without our knowing it.

Deception Continues

After this exchange with Joseph's steward, we discover what
happens when Joseph sees his brother Benjamin for the first time:

When Joseph came home, they brought into the
house to him the present that they had with them
and bowed down to him to the ground. And he
inquired about their welfare and said, "Is your
father well, the old man of whom you spoke? Is
he still alive?" They said, "Your servant our father
is well; he is still alive." And they bowed their
heads and prostrated themselves. And he lifted

up his eyes and saw his brother Benjamin, his
mother's son, and said, "Is this your youngest
brother, of whom you spoke to me? God be gracious to you, my son!" Then Joseph hurried out,
for his compassion grew warm for his brother,
and he sought a place to weep. And he entered
his chamber and wept there. Then he washed his
face and came out. And controlling himself he
said, "Serve the food." (Gen. 43:26–31)

In this situation, Joseph's eleven brothers prostrate themselves
before him. We might infer that this scene finally fulfilled his second
prophetic dream. However, his father and the rest of his extended
family are not yet part of this group that has bowed down to him. So
the second dream has not yet been fulfilled.

After inquiring about their father, he sees Benjamin for the first
time in approximately twenty-one years. Notice that the very first
thing he does is to pronounce a blessing over Benjamin: "God be gracious to you, my son!" (v. 29), and then he quickly leaves the room,
overcome with emotion (v. 30). God is at the forefront of Joseph's
thinking in this situation, as we have seen many times in past events.
We can view this as a reflection of the ongoing work of transformation in Joseph's life; he naturally reacts to life events from a "God
perspective." Further, note that this demonstration of such faith in
Joseph stands in stark contrast to his brothers, who have rarely shown
evidence of such thinking.

Even after seeing Benjamin, Joseph continues to maintain his
deception, which started during the brothers' first trip to Egypt. He
still does not reveal himself to them. The reason for this will become
evident shortly. Returning after composing himself, he orders his servants to serve a meal:

They served him by himself, and them by themselves, and the Egyptians who ate with him by
themselves, because the Egyptians could not eat
with the Hebrews, for that is an abomination to

the Egyptians. And they sat before him, the firstborn according to his birthright and the youngest
according to his youth. And the men looked at
one another in amazement. Portions were taken
to them from Joseph's table, but Benjamin's portion was five times as much as any of theirs. And
they drank and were merry with him. (Gen.
43:32–34)

It is reasonable to assume that Joseph's brothers were very confused at this point. The text notes that they were amazed (v. 33).
This second encounter with the man was going so differently than
their first encounter. Remember, at that time, Joseph accused them
of being spies, and he spoke harshly to them (Gen. 42:14–15). He
kept one brother (Simeon) in bondage as security, to ensure that they
would return with their little brother (Gen. 42:14–20, 24). Now,
having returned with Benjamin as they promised, they are sitting
down to eat a meal with the man who is second in power only to
Pharaoh. They must be asking why this is happening when they only
came to buy grain. However, here they are eating with the man and
eating the same food that he is eating. Surprisingly, the youngest son
(Benjamin) is served five times the amount of food as each of the
other brothers (Gen. 43:34). That must have been incredibly confus-
ing for all of them, perhaps most notably for Benjamin.

In Genesis 44, we find Joseph continuing to deceive his brothers. He does the same thing as he did during their first trip to Egypt:
as they were preparing to return home, he instructs his steward to
place all their money in the mouth of their sacks. However, this
time he instructs the steward to also place his chalice in the sack of
Benjamin (Gen. 44:1–2). There is no reason to think that the brothers suspect anything terrible is going to happen to them as they start
their return trip home. After all, they have just eaten with the man
in his own home! Moreover, they are all allowed to leave and return
home with the grain that they came to purchase, including Simeon.

So, the brothers depart, and soon after that, Joseph instructs his
steward to go after them. He gives the steward the exact words to say

to them once he catches up with them (Gen. 44:4–5). The steward finally catches up with them and does as he was instructed, accusing them of stealing from the man. Surprised by this turn of events, they strenuously protest their innocence, confidently stating, "Whichever of your servants is found with it shall die, and we also will be my lord's servants" (v. 9). However, the steward has a better idea. He counters with "he who is found with it shall be my servant, and the rest of you shall be innocent" (v. 10). So, the steward instructs them to open their sacks and discovers the money in each man's sack, along with the chalice in Benjamin's sack. Everything plays out exactly as Joseph has planned. At this point, there is nothing for them to do but to return to face the man (Gen. 44:11–13).

When Judah and his brothers arrive again at Joseph's house, he immediately confronts them, thereby maintaining his deception:

> Joseph said to them, "What deed is this that you have done? Do you not know that a man like me can indeed practice divination?" And Judah said, "What shall we say to my lord? What shall we speak? Or how can we clear ourselves? God has found out the guilt of your servants; behold, we are my lord's servants, both we and he also in whose hand the cup has been found." But he said, "Far be it from me that I should do so! Only the man in whose hand the cup was found shall be my servant. But as for you, go up in peace to your father." (Gen. 44:15–17)

Notice that Judah also attributes what has happened to the work of God, similar to the comment made previously by the steward of Joseph's household (v. 16). Here is a clear indication of some measure of faith in Judah; the idea that God is involved in what is going on is not foreign to him. In this situation, we see again that God's transforming work in one individual's life can, and often does, affect the faith of other individuals as they share life situations. Neither the comment previously made by Joseph's steward nor that made by Judah now constitutes a confession of faith by either of them. However, their comments do reveal that they have some understanding of God's active involvement in the unfolding situation. Here is an example of simple belief: having eyes to see and the willingness to acknowledge God's active involvement in life events.

We also see in this text that Judah's comment allows Joseph to satisfy any desire for revenge that he might have harbored; Judah's comment could serve to enslave the rest of the brothers (v. 16). However, Joseph does not take advantage of this opportunity. Instead, he declares that only the guilty person (Benjamin) will be his slave. This decision does not speak of revenge toward his brothers, who were responsible for his enslavement, but rather mercy. We can view this episode as another indication of the progress of ongoing transformation taking place in Joseph.

In the next passage, we can see how Judah's faith is different from that of Joseph:

> "Now therefore, as soon as I come to your servant my father, and the boy is not with us, then, as his life is bound up in the boy's life, as soon as he sees that the boy is not with us, he will die, and your servants will bring down the gray hairs of your servant our father with sorrow to Sheol. For your servant became a pledge of safety for the boy to my father, saying, 'If I do not bring him back to you, then I shall bear the blame before my father all my life.' Now therefore, please let your servant remain instead of the boy as a servant to my lord, and let the boy go back with his brothers. For how can I go back to my father if the boy is not with me? I fear to see the evil that would find my father." (Gen. 44:30–34)

Here, Judah steps forward to offer himself in place of Benjamin. We might like to think he is demonstrating care and concern for his father as well as striving to protect the life of Benjamin. We might even like to think that this action on his part demonstrates some measure of genuine faith. However, it seems he is merely trying to avoid feeling responsible for his father's absolute despair if something happens to Benjamin. In comparison to Joseph's tendency to see God actively involved in these unfolding events, we do not see in Judah the same level of faith. Yes, Judah has previously admitted that God is involved in what is happening now, that these events are the result of their guilt for their treatment of Joseph twenty-one years earlier. However, in this text, there is no mention of God.

God is indeed sovereign over all of the events taking place; he is actively involved in what is transpiring. Joseph's continuing deception, his delay in revealing himself to his brothers until the right time, is according to God's plan for everyone involved. Here is a critical point to understand regarding God's transforming work: he may be working in the lives of multiple individuals at the same time through one series of related events, as we see here in Joseph's story. We need to keep in mind that God may delay the ultimate resolution of a situation so that he can accomplish his intended transformation in the lives of others as well as in our own life.

Deception Ends

Returning to our story, we see in Genesis 45 that Joseph can no longer restrain himself from revealing who he is:

> Then Joseph could not control himself before all those who stood by him. He cried, "Make everyone go out from me." So no one stayed with him when Joseph made himself known to his brothers. And he wept aloud, so that the Egyptians heard it, and the household of Pharaoh heard it. And Joseph said to his brothers, "I am Joseph! Is my father still alive?" But his brothers could not answer him, for they were dismayed at his presence.

So Joseph said to his brothers, "Come near to me, please." And they came near. And he said, "I am your brother, Joseph, whom you sold into Egypt. And now do not be distressed or angry with yourselves because you sold me here, for God sent me before you to preserve life." (Gen. 45:1–5)

We previously saw Joseph lose his composure when he saw his brothers for the first time during their initial trip to Egypt, but he then recovered (Gen. 42:24). We saw Joseph weep when he saw Benjamin, his little brother, for the first time in twenty-one years; he again regained his composure (Gen. 43:30–31). In this text, however, he can no longer maintain the deception; he finally breaks down and reveals himself to his brothers.

Now we see the genuine concern in Joseph's brothers, for they "were dismayed at his presence" (Gen. 45:3). Obviously, upon discovering that "the man" is their brother, they are quite afraid. Joseph's self-revelation completely surprises them, so much so that he has to convince them of the truth of what he is saying (v. 4). We can imagine that their fear is rooted in their guilt about what they had done to Joseph in his youth. Now, twenty-one years after they put him in the pit, there is no sign of any anger or desire for revenge in Joseph, which confirms the degree of transformation God has accomplished in his life. Joseph says to them, "Do not be distressed or angry with yourselves because you sold me here, for God sent me before you to preserve life" (v. 5). They need not fear because Joseph understands and accepts God's purpose in their actions against him. God's bigger purpose is that he was preparing to preserve life through their actions. God's purpose was not just for Joseph's sake, although he certainly benefited by becoming second-in-command in Egypt. Nor was it solely for the benefit of the sixty-six persons in Jacob's family, who eventually come to Egypt because of the famine. It is essential to see that even the famine is used by God to keep his covenant promise to Israel of numerous offspring (Gen. 32:12). God's purpose was also to preserve the life of all those from the nations who came to Egypt to buy grain during the famine (Gen. 41:53–57).

Notice that Joseph came to realize all this without any biblical evidence that God spoke with him in any way other than through the two initial dreams when he was seventeen years of age. We certainly have evidence that Joseph has, indeed, become aware throughout his life of how God has blessed him and how God has worked through him to accomplish higher purposes. What then is the primary manner through which God brought about such understanding in Joseph? It is likely the passage of time and having the opportunity to reflect upon what has happened to him and why. Over time, God became real (personal) for Joseph through such events as being thrown into the pit and sold into slavery. Despite having done so, God blesses him; everything he did succeeded. Joseph's life contains a series of successful milestones—being the head of Potiphar's household, being in charge of the prison, becoming second only to Pharaoh in Egypt, successfully executing his plan to save lives throughout the years of famine. We can imagine how the time in between each milestone allowed Joseph to consider God's active involvement in all that has taken place in his life. Such reflection enables him to understand where and how God has been at work in his life, and the life of others, through times of good and evil.

Joseph instructs his brothers to return to Canaan to get his father Jacob and their wives and children (Gen. 45:9–10). When Pharaoh hears that Joseph's brothers have arrived in Egypt, he commands Joseph to send his brothers back to get the rest of their family and bring them to Egypt and provides wagons to transport them all (Gen. 45:17–19). Pharaoh's generosity enables Joseph's family to come to Egypt and to settle in the best land in Egypt (Gen. 45:20–47:11).

The brothers return to Canaan to do as Joseph and Pharaoh have instructed them. However, Jacob is reticent to believe them until he sees the wagons and provisions that they have brought with them (Gen. 45:25–27). He knows that they went to Egypt with sufficient money to buy food, but it was not sufficient for all the provision that he now sees. He finally accepts what they are telling him as real (v. 28). However, doubt still lingers. In his heart, there is still no trust that what he sees *has come from God*. After all, in the brothers' account of what has occurred, they have made no mention of God.

As Jacob and all his family begin their journey to Egypt, God speaks once again to him. God reassures him, saying, "I myself will go down with you to Egypt, and I will also bring you up again" (Gen. 46:4). That is God's guarantee to Jacob, presumably to counteract his doubt and thus strengthen his faith. So Jacob's entire family, sixty-six people, now travel to Egypt (Gen. 46:26).

Why does the biblical text include such details as the number of people in Jacob's family that go to Egypt? Such details are essential when we look ahead to the exodus of the Israelites from Egypt, 430 years later (Exod. 12:40). Numbers 1 tells us from the first census of Israel taken in the wilderness that 603,550 people twenty years old or older who were "able to go to war" (warriors) eventually come out of Egypt (Num. 1:45–46). These figures did not include men not able to go to war, and women and children under the age of twenty. So, a great multitude emerges out of this group of sixty-six that travel to Egypt because of the famine. Details such as these become important when we remember the covenant promises made by God to Abraham, Isaac, and Jacob—promises to make their offspring too numerous to count (Gen. 15:5, 28:14). They help us remember that *God keeps his promises*, thereby helping to build our trust in him when we read these texts, and when he makes promises to us.

When Jacob's family arrives in Egypt, they appear before Pharaoh, who directs that they should reside in the land of Goshen, in "the best part of the land" (Gen. 47:4–6). Additionally, he instructs Joseph to assign some of them to care for Pharaoh's flocks and herds (v. 6). Here we see that Joseph is not the only one who is blessed while living in Egypt. The famine is quite severe; everyone is eating the grain that Joseph stored in warehouses in every city. They could plant no crops. Therefore, at Pharaoh's instruction, Joseph sends his family to an area where there are still pasture lands because they are shepherds (Gen. 47:11). Thus, Joseph's brothers and their herds and flocks can also prosper during the famine.

There are two crucial points to notice from this part of the story. First, although the text is not explicit, we can view the arrival of the rest of Joseph's family and his authority over them as an implied fulfillment of Joseph's second dream. Second, Joseph *provides* his family with food and other provisions (Gen. 47:12) without payment, which is an act of love and grace that he is free to perform because he is in a position of authority. Here is an indication of the degree of transformation God has completed in Joseph's life. He could make his family buy food as everyone else, but he does not.

As the seven years of famine continue, that is what the Egyptians are required to do. The text makes note that everyone else, including Egyptians, are coming to *buy* food during this time (Gen. 47:14). First, they purchase grain with the money they have. When their money runs out, they purchase grain with their flocks, herds, and other livestock. When those are all gone, they sell themselves and their land to Pharaoh as servants (Gen. 47:15–17). As a result, Pharaoh controls all the wealth, the flocks, herds, livestock, and land in Egypt. Then, Joseph gives all the people seed to plant and requires in return that they give one-fifth of the harvest to Pharaoh in perpetuity. Only the land of the priests is exempt from this requirement. The people are glad to do this since Joseph has saved their lives (Gen. 7:23–24). Pharaoh benefits from Joseph's plan as well as the people.

Role of Isolation

We now move ahead seventeen years. In Genesis 47, we read, "Thus Israel settled in the land of Egypt, in the land of Goshen. And they gained possessions in it, and were fruitful and multiplied greatly. And Jacob lived in the land of Egypt seventeen years. So the days of Jacob, the years of his life, were 147 years" (Gen. 47:27–28). This short text takes us on a bit of a side road into what God is doing in Jacob's life at this time and sets up what will soon occur.

This passage can best be understood in light of what Jacob said when he first saw Joseph in Egypt: "Now let me die, since I have seen your face and know that you are still alive" (Gen. 46:30). Here Jacob declares that he is ready to die once having seen Joseph's face.

However, seventeen years have passed since that time, no doubt a time of isolation for Jacob similar to the years experienced by Joseph. During those years, Jacob has been in a foreign country, not the land his God had promised to him and his offspring (Gen. 28:13, 35:12). By using the famine, God moved him out of the land promised to him and into Egypt. He has been a sojourner in a foreign land, and not by his choosing. God has taken him there for his higher purposes.

What are those higher purposes of God? In Joseph's story, we learn this: none of these events could have come to fruition if God had not undertaken the work of transformation in *Joseph's* life. Through many unjustified and challenging situations, we have seen God transform Joseph and his faith, but not just for Joseph's benefit. The work of transformation occurs in the individual, but *it is for the higher purpose of and benefit to others.*

As we continue to ask the question "Where is God in this part of *Jacob's* life?" we see—as we did in Joseph's life—that God uses times of isolation to continue the ongoing work of transformation.[3] Part of God's purpose in taking individuals through wilderness experiences is to place them in isolation *so that* they have time to ponder and think about that very question—what *is* God doing in the current situation? It seems Jacob is still not quite ready to fully trust God's word to him. God spoke to Jacob seventeen years earlier, as he was setting out on his journey to Egypt: "I am God, the God of your father. Do not be afraid to go down to Egypt, for there I will make you into a great nation. I myself will go down with you to Egypt, and I will also bring you up again, and Joseph's hand shall close your eyes" (Gen. 46:3–4). Thus, at the very beginning of his trek to Egypt, God not only promised to go with Jacob into Egypt *but also* to bring him out again. Even after receiving these promises from God, seventeen years later, Jacob makes *Joseph* swear to take his body back to Mamre for burial. Without knowing what God previously promised Jacob, Joseph swears to him to honor his request (Gen. 47:29–31).

---

[3] See chapter 3 for a full discussion of the development of Jacob's faith throughout his lifetime.

The story of Jacob continues from Genesis 48 into the beginning of chapter 50. We have examined in the previous chapter the events in Jacob's faith journey, so we will not repeat them here. What *is* essential to see is that God's process of transforming Joseph's faith is now intertwined with Jacob's transformation process; the two cannot be separated. Here is another clear example of God doing the work of transformation in the lives of multiple individuals at the same time, a theme we have seen several times in Joseph's story. As we undergo God's process to transform us, it is helpful to remember that as God is doing his work in us to transform *our* faith, he is also at work in the lives of others around us to transform *their* faith. If we know God has higher purposes in mind beyond our life situation, if we know that God transforms the faith of others through *our* life circumstances, then we can more readily accept the difficult circumstances in our own lives. It is not for us to explain to others; but as we are being transformed, it is helpful to know that God is working *through us* and our circumstances to transform the faith of others. Moreover, it is helpful to know that God uses his transforming work in others to do his work *in us*.

Genuine Faith

Beginning in Genesis 50:15, the focus of the story returns once again to Joseph following the burial of Jacob at Mamre and Joseph's return to his position in Egypt. As Joseph does so, his brothers are uncertain about what their future holds.

> When Joseph's brothers saw that their father was dead, they said, "It may be that Joseph will hate us and pay us back for all the evil that we did to him." So they sent a message to Joseph, saying, "Your father gave this command before he died: 'Say to Joseph, "Please forgive the transgression of your brothers and their sin, because they did evil to you."' And now, please forgive the transgression of the servants of the God of your

father." Joseph wept when they spoke to him. His brothers also came and fell down before him and said, "Behold, we are your servants." But Joseph said to them, "Do not fear, for am I in the place of God? As for you, you meant evil against me, but God meant it for good, to bring it about that many people should be kept alive, as they are today. So do not fear; I will provide for you and your little ones." Thus he comforted them and spoke kindly to them. (Gen. 50:15–21)

Notice that Joseph's brothers are afraid of what he might do to them now that their father is dead. There is minimal evidence of transformation of their faith over time. We saw in chapter 3 that by the time of Jacob's death, the work of transformation in him was complete. By this, we mean that he had finally come to see God's hand at work throughout his life and that God had become *his* God through personal experience, no longer just the God of Abraham and Isaac.

In the text above we can see the degree to which God has already transformed Joseph's faith. God is personal to Joseph now and has been for some time. For example, we have seen that he has given credit to God multiple times for the interpretation of dreams (e.g., Gen. 41:16–28). We first saw some evidence of transforming faith when Joseph first revealed himself to his brothers when he said, "It was not you who send me here, but God" (Gen. 45:8). Joseph has been able to see God's active involvement in his life, beyond his own needs. We see it again in this text. Joseph reveals that he knows God has been at work through all that has transpired when he says to them, "As for you, you meant evil against me, but God meant it for good, to bring it about that many people should be kept alive" (Gen. 50:20). This statement provides evidence of genuine transformed faith.

We can also see the degree to which God has changed Joseph's heart over time: he weeps when his brothers ask him to forgive them for their previous actions against him (v. 17). We see compassion and mercy in his kind speech and willingness to comfort them in their current fear (v. 21). These actions reveal and confirm the depth of transformation in Joseph that God has accomplished. A heart so changed is a core element of God's transforming work in his people.

We do not see the same transformation evidenced in his brothers that we have previously seen in the lives of Abraham and Jacob, and that we see here in Joseph. The contrast is rather stark. Although the brothers are humbled enough by current events to ask for Joseph's forgiveness, their faith is still more objective than subjective. They still refer to God as "the God of *your* father" (v. 17, italics added), sounding very much like Jacob did early in his life and immature faith. Joseph's brothers have some understanding and respect for God, but they show no evidence of having genuine faith as Joseph does.

As we reflect upon the work of transformation in Joseph's life, we learn to ask again and again "Where is God?" in our own life circumstances. When evil occurs in our lives, can we say with Joseph, "You meant evil against me, but God meant it for good"? During our pain and suffering, can we stop and seek to find God's higher purpose in what is happening? When we can do so, it will be evidence of God's ongoing work in our hearts to transform and strengthen our faith. This point becomes evident at the end of Joseph's life.

> And Joseph said to his brothers, "I am about to die, but God will visit you and bring you up out of this land to the land that he swore to Abraham, to Isaac, and to Jacob." Then Joseph made the sons of Israel swear, saying, "God will surely visit you, and you shall carry up my bones from here." So Joseph died, being 110 years old. They embalmed him, and he was put in a coffin in Egypt. (Gen. 50:24–26)

Here we see one more indicator of the work of transformation of Joseph's faith. In his final words to his brothers, he says, in essence, that through his brothers God will fulfill his covenant promises given to their ancestors. His statement reveals a deep conviction of his faith and trust in God to fulfill his promises. For Joseph, God is faithful, not only to his ancestors and to himself, but he believes that God will continue to be faithful to his brothers as the sons of Israel.

Lessons Learned from the Story of Joseph

We have discussed many different and essential points about how God worked his transformation process differently in Joseph's life when compared to the way God "spoke" to Abraham and Jacob. However, there is one more vital point to consider in more detail, which we touched upon early in Joseph's life: what happens if he dies at the hands of his brothers because of their hatred and jealousy toward him? What would have been the result if Reuben had not been able to stop his brothers from killing Joseph?

The following essential events would not have occurred: Joseph would not have gone to Egypt; therefore, he would not have been available to interpret the dreams of Pharaoh's cupbearer and baker. He would not have the opportunity to interpret the dreams of Pharaoh; therefore, he would not become the second most important person in Egypt. If his brothers' original plan had been successful, Joseph would not be able to implement God's plan to feed people from many nations through seven years of famine, which ultimately ensured the continued fulfillment of God's promises to Abraham, Isaac, and Jacob, promises of land and progeny (offspring). It is evident at the end of Joseph's life that all of the events of his life, the good and the bad, including the "natural disaster" of famine, are tied inextricably to those covenant promises. These various events of Joseph's life all come together under the sovereignty of God to accomplish his bigger plans that reach far beyond Joseph's life.

Joseph's story is our story. God is at work in various ways in our lives to accomplish his higher purposes, not just for us but for countless others as well. We encourage you to take some time to reflect further on how Joseph's story might affect the transformation of your faith.

1. God transforms our faith so that we fulfill our role according to his higher and perfect plan and purpose. Life is not about us, about the singular events in our lives, or our own goals and dreams. Instead, it is about whom God created us to be and how he goes about the work of transforming our faith in order to accomplish *his* purposes for our lives. Joseph did not celebrate the exalted position he held in Egypt. Instead, he was humble throughout all those years in his position as second only to Pharaoh in Egypt. We see his continual confession that all of his success occurred according to God's will, according to God's plan and purposes. In this case, God is sovereign over all that transpires in Joseph's life to (1) save Israel, (2) save the line of Judah (through which Jesus Christ will be born), and (3) save the nations of the earth.

   Consider: As you reflect on your life's twists and turns, look for a thread of God's active involvement in saving your life, ordering life events, and/or giving you success. How has reading about the transformation of Joseph's faith challenged or changed your perspective about God's intentional involvement in and through your life's various circumstances?

2. God transforms us in order to demolish strongholds in our lives by building our belief, trust, and acceptance of him through life's events and circumstances. Genuine belief and faith go beyond simple mental assent. Even demons *believe* that Jesus is the Son of God, but they do not *trust* him as LORD. We can see in Joseph's life that God's work in transforming his faith demolished the strongholds of (1) being spoiled and precocious and (2) destructive emotions such as anger and resentment.

Consider: In what ways has God been working through your life's circumstances to free you from strongholds of destructive emotions and attitudes? In what ways can you see God gradually *changing your heart* toward others who have hurt you in the past or treated you unfairly? What is God's expectation of you now toward those people?

3. God transforms our faith using a variety of means. How God transformed Joseph's faith is different from how he transformed Abraham's and Jacob's faith. Unlike them, God never appeared to or spoke with Joseph directly—at least we have no evidence from Scripture that he did. Instead, God acted through various life events, and orchestrated long periods of isolation for him, to give Joseph time to think about God's active involvement in his life. Through those times of isolation, and presumed reflection, Joseph's belief, trust, and acceptance of God as sovereign over all aspects of his life grew strong. He was then able to see God's higher purposes during his life's circumstances. That perspective enabled him to forgive others for their unjust treatment of him. The same will be valid for any individual who examines God's work of transformation in their own life. There may be many similarities in our lives to Joseph's story of transformation. However, there will also be differences. It is not one-size-fits-all when God undertakes the work of transforming our faith.

Consider: As you read through Joseph's story, what did you notice in your own transformation process that is similar to, or different from, that of Joseph? How does God "speak" to you? In what way does understanding how God uses seasons of isolation in the process of transforming our faith change your perspective of those times in your life? What has God done in your life to further develop your understanding and acceptance of his sovereignty over *all aspects* of your life?

Our prayer is that Joseph's story will inspire and challenge you to search for God's active involvement in your life's circumstances. We encourage you to see what is happening at any given moment as part of God's bigger plan to transform and strengthen your faith *so that* you might partner with him as he works through you to accomplish his plans and purposes for others.

CHAPTER 5
Moses

In this chapter we examine the life of Moses. We begin with his birth and then move quickly through his early years in order to understand the condition of his early faith, which becomes the foundation for his faith journey through the rest of his life. As we follow his story, our main focus will be the formative forty years of his life, through God's call and the subsequent process of faith development that enables him to obey God. We will see that the development of his faith transforms him into the man God intends for him to be, in order to fulfill God's call on his life, and ultimately God's broader purposes for the people of Israel.

In order to see the significance of what transpires throughout the life of Moses, we need to keep one eye on the end of the story, the *purpose* of all that transpires in the life of Moses. Thus, unlike the previous chapters where we let the story unfold through the pertinent Scripture texts, here we need to keep looking to the "future" in order to see the significance of events in the "present." We will see that *his personal transformation* is necessary for fulfilling God's bigger plans and purposes for the people of Israel. We will also see clearly in the life of Moses God's sovereignty over all that takes place: God knows exactly what he is going to do—and when, why, and how he will do it.

Unlike Abraham and Jacob, the process of transformation in Moses is not needed to bring him to a point of simple belief in God *as God*. He shared the common faith of Israel, which had been handed down from the patriarchs. However, when God reveals himself to Moses in the burning bush event and calls him to lead the

Israelites out of slavery, Moses questions his own ability to do what God wants him to do. This is the situation that reveals the need for God to transform his simple belief into genuine faith that enables him to obey God.

In Moses, we see clearly the issue of self-doubt, which is common in many people, even people of faith. In this regard, he is no different from Abraham and Jacob in the early years of their faith journey. Through the story of Moses, we will see how God transforms this self-doubting individual from one who runs into the wilderness because of his fear of Pharaoh, into the person who eventually confronts Pharaoh directly several times, demanding (on behalf of God), "Let my people go!" We will see how God uses the process of bringing ten plagues on Egypt to accomplish the work of transformation in Moses. Thus, as these events unfold, we will continue to ask the question "Where is God in this?" in order to see God orchestrating the events in Moses's life for the purpose of transforming and maturing his faith.

Background

The story of Moses has roots in Joseph's story. Remember that Joseph dies at the end of the book of Genesis. A new Pharaoh now reigns in Egypt who perhaps doesn't know Joseph, doesn't know what he did for the previous Pharaoh or for the people of Egypt during the seven years of famine and the years before that famine.[1] This Pharaoh does not have a positive perspective on the Israelites living in his country. Rather, he is actually afraid of the number and might of the people of Israel, as seen in his words in Exodus 1:9–10: "And he said to his people, 'Behold, the people of Israel are too many and too mighty for us. Come, let us deal shrewdly with them, lest they multiply, and, if war breaks out, they join our enemies and fight against us and escape from the land.'"

His fear causes him to throw the Hebrews into slavery. He then seeks to implement a plan to eliminate future growth of the people of

---

[1] See chapter 4 on Joseph for details on these events.

Israel. He instructs the Hebrew midwives to kill all male babies born to Hebrew women (Exod. 1:16). But his plan does not work, because "the midwives feared God and did not do as the king of Egypt commanded them, but let the male children live" (Exod. 1:17). The midwives ignore the command of Pharaoh, and even make up an excuse for their lack of obedience to Pharaoh's command, claiming that the Israelite mothers give birth before they arrive (Exod. 1:19), which is a blatant lie. They lie because they fear God more than they fear Pharaoh (Exod. 1:17).

At this point we must remember that in God's first covenant to Abraham, there was a promise of a great number of Abraham's descendants. As we saw in Joseph's story, only seventy persons came into Egypt with the household of Jacob, but more than six hundred thousand people will eventually depart Egypt at the beginning of the exodus (Exod. 12:37). To accomplish this growth of the people of Israel, it is necessary to ensure that Pharaoh's plan to kill the Hebrew newborn male children does not succeed. If we ask where God is in this situation, we can see that it is God himself who causes the midwives to fear him more than they fear Pharaoh. This is a sovereign act by God to confirm that he is, indeed, actively at work ensuring his promises to Abraham will be fulfilled.

Moses's Early Years

The story of Moses begins with his birth, which is recounted in Exodus 2:

> Now a man from the house of Levi went and took as his wife a Levite woman. The woman conceived and bore a son, and when she saw that he was a fine child, she hid him three months. When she could hide him no longer, she took for him a basket made of bulrushes and daubed it with bitumen and pitch. She put the child in it and placed it among the reeds by the river bank. And his sister stood at a distance to know what

would be done to him. Now the daughter of
Pharaoh came down to bathe at the river, while
her young women walked beside the river. She
saw the basket among the reeds and sent her servant woman, and she took it. (Exod. 2:1–5)

After hiding Moses for three months from the authorities, his
mother hides him in a basket on a riverbank. When Moses's sister
sees Pharaoh's daughter rescue Moses from the river, a plan for his
care emerges that includes his mother:

Then his sister said to Pharaoh's daughter, "Shall I
go and call you a nurse from the Hebrew women
to nurse the child for you?" And Pharaoh's
daughter said to her, "Go." So the girl went and
called the child's mother. And Pharaoh's daughter said to her, "Take this child away and nurse
him for me, and I will give you your wages."
So the woman took the child and nursed him.
When the child grew older, she brought him to
Pharaoh's daughter, and he became her son. She
named him Moses, "Because," she said, "I drew
him out of the water." (Exod. 2:7–10)

Obviously, Pharaoh's daughter would need a wet nurse for the
baby, and Moses's sister just happens to know of one that is available:
Moses's own mother. Here we see that God is actively orchestrating events to keep Moses alive, by enabling his mother to raise him
until "the child grew older" (v. 10). The text does not tell us how
long Moses was raised by his mother. However, it was long enough
for Moses to later identify himself with the people of Israel rather
than with the Egyptians, as Exodus 2:11–12 reveals: "One day, when
Moses had grown up, he went out to *his people* and looked on their
burdens, and he saw an Egyptian beating a Hebrew, *one of his people*"
(italics added).

Moses so thoroughly identifies with the Hebrews as "his people" that he becomes enraged at what he considers to be an unjust beating. He takes action that then threatens his life:

> He looked this way and that, and seeing no one, he struck down the Egyptian and hid him in the sand. When he went out the next day, behold, two Hebrews were struggling together. And he said to the man in the wrong, "Why do you strike your companion?" He answered, "Who made you a prince and a judge over us? Do you mean to kill me as you killed the Egyptian?" Then Moses was afraid, and thought, "Surely the thing is known." When Pharaoh heard of it, he sought to kill Moses. But Moses fled from Pharaoh and stayed in the land of Midian. (Exod. 2:12–15)

This is a major milestone event in Moses's life; it is critical that we not miss the importance of the role it plays in the process of transforming his faith. This situation did not "just occur." Rather, we see that God is again actively orchestrating the events in Moses's life for the purpose of transforming his faith, so that God's broader purposes for the people of Israel can be fulfilled. If Moses does not get out of Egypt, will he ever be able to stand up to Pharaoh in the future, as God will require him to do? The answer to this question will become evident as the story of Moses continues.

Wilderness Years

Fearing for his life, Moses flees to the wilderness and ends up in Midian. There he helps the daughters of Jethro, the priest of Midian (Exod. 3:1), water their flock at the well in town when the local shepherds seek to prevent them from doing so (Exod. 2:17). In return, Moses is invited to stay with the family. "Moses was content to dwell with the man, and he gave Moses his daughter Zipporah" in marriage (Exod. 2:21). Notice that Moses flees from the only life he knows, ends up in a country he does not know, and becomes content to live there.

After Moses settles in Midian, God begins to put his plan in motion for Israel's redemption from slavery. In the next passage, we read:

> During those many days the king of Egypt died, and the people of Israel groaned because of their slavery and cried out for help. Their cry for rescue from slavery came up to God. And God heard their groaning, and God remembered his covenant with Abraham, with Isaac, and with Jacob. God saw the people of Israel—and God knew. (Exod. 2:23–25)

Notice that the text says that God "heard their groaning" and "remembered his covenant" (v. 24). Did God not know that this time would come? Yes, he did, for the text says, "God saw the people of Israel—and God knew" (Exod. 2:25). He saw the plight of the people of Israel; he knew they were suffering. This suffering of the people of Israel is in sharp contrast to the contentment Moses is experiencing as he lives in Midian.

God Has a Plan

Next, we see Moses's first encounter with God:

> Now Moses was keeping the flock of his father-in-law, Jethro, the priest of Midian, and he led his flock to the west side of the wilderness and came to Horeb, the mountain of God. And the angel of the LORD appeared to him in a flame of fire out of the midst of a bush. He looked, and behold, the bush was burning, yet it was not consumed. And Moses said, "I will turn aside to see this great sight, why the bush is not burned."

When the LORD saw that he turned aside to
see, God called to him out of the bush, "Moses,
Moses!" And he said, "Here I am." (Exod. 3:1–4)

This is the second major milestone in Moses's life. God calls to
him out of a burning bush, and he responds, "Here I am" (v. 4). This
is the moment of conversion for Moses, the moment when his faith
moves from simple belief in God to God becoming real for him. God
is no longer an objective idea or concept because he is now experiencing the reality of God. God is talking to Moses, and Moses responds.
Communication between God and Moses begins, and therefore, an
intimate relationship begins, which continues for the remainder of
Moses's life. There is never a point in his life when there is a break in
communication or relationship between Moses and God.

Yet that fact does not negate the need for the work of transformation to occur in Moses. Although God has now become real for
him, and although they are communicating with each other, Moses is
not yet ready to do the work that God asks of him. Thus, as we have
seen before in the lives of Abraham, Jacob, and Joseph, the process of
transformation in Moses will focus on building his trust in God and
acceptance of God's purposes for his life. From this initial experience
with God, Moses begins a life of obedience to God.

God Calls Moses

This interaction between God and Moses continues, as God
speaks to him again:

Then he said, "Do not come near; take your sandals off your feet, for the place on which you are
standing is holy ground." And he said, "I am the
God of your father, the God of Abraham, the
God of Isaac, and the God of Jacob." And Moses
hid his face, for he was afraid to look at God.
(Exod. 3:5–6)

From a biblical standpoint, *holy* means "set apart." Thus, this ground is now set apart from the other ground all around and beyond the tree because of God's presence. Notice that God identifies himself as the same God that his own father worshiped, as well as being "the God of Abraham, the God of Isaac, and the God of Jacob" (v. 6). And Moses immediately responds by hiding his face (v. 6). He has no doubt who is speaking to him; his response to hearing God speaking to him indicates that he has developed at this point in his life some measure of reverence toward God.

After clearly identifying himself, God succinctly lays out to Moses his reason for calling to him:

> Then the LORD said, "I have surely seen the affliction of my people who are in Egypt and have heard their cry because of their taskmasters. I know their sufferings, and I have come down to deliver them out of the hand of the Egyptians and to bring them up out of that land to a good and broad land, a land flowing with milk and honey, to the place of the Canaanites, the Hittites, the Amorites, the Perizzites, the Hivites, and the Jebusites. And now, behold, the cry of the people of Israel has come to me, and I have also seen the oppression with which the Egyptians oppress them. Come, I will send you to Pharaoh that you may bring my people, the children of Israel, out of Egypt." (Exod. 3:7–10)

Notice that God's approach for revealing his purposes to Moses is very different from those he used with Abraham or Jacob. God gave them promises that revealed his purposes, and then he repeated those promises again and again to build their trust in him as their personal God. It took most, if not all, of their lifetimes to finally experience God as *their* God. But after only one encounter, God gives Moses a call to do something for him, revealing God's broader purposes for his people. He does not need to take time to build Moses's faith to bring him to a place of knowing God personally. This is a clear indication that God became real for Moses from the very first moment of their encounter. It is a unique point in Moses's transformation process.

Notice Moses's response to God's revelation:

> But Moses said to God, "Who am I that I should go to Pharaoh and bring the children of Israel out of Egypt?" He said, "But I will be with you, and this shall be the sign for you, that I have sent you: when you have brought the people out of Egypt, you shall serve God on this mountain." (Exod. 3:11–12)

Moses immediately exposes his self-doubt by asking God, "Who am I that I should go to Pharaoh and bring the children of Israel out of Egypt?" (v. 11). Yet God very gently and lovingly responds, as he did with Abraham, seeking to reassure Moses by saying, "I will be with you" (v. 12). God is saying that he does not intend to send Moses up against Pharaoh by himself. God understands Moses's personality; he understands what he is thinking before he thinks it. That is why God tells Moses that he will be with him, to further build his trust in God.

But God does not stop there. He goes on to say, "When you have brought the people out of Egypt, you shall serve God on this mountain" (v. 12). The mountain was Mount Horeb, the mountain from which God will speak to the whole nation of Israel after their exodus from Egypt. And as we shall see, what God says to Moses now does come to pass. Notice the assurance with which God speaks to Moses: "When you have brought the people out of Egypt" (v. 12), not *if* but *when*. This interchange around Moses's self-doubt and God's assurance to be with him begins in earnest the process of transforming Moses's faith.

As the story continues, we find a very significant text:

> Then Moses said to God, "If I come to the people of Israel and say to them, 'The God of your fathers has sent me to you,' and they ask me,

'What is his name?' what shall I say to them?" God said to Moses, "I AM WHO I AM." And he said, "Say this to the people of Israel: 'I AM has sent me to you.'" God also said to Moses, "Say this to the people of Israel: 'The LORD, the God of your fathers, the God of Abraham, the God of Isaac, and the God of Jacob, has sent me to you.' This is my name forever, and thus I am to be remembered throughout all generations. Go and gather the elders of Israel together and say to them, 'The LORD, the God of your fathers, the God of Abraham, of Isaac, and of Jacob, has appeared to me, saying, "I have observed you and what has been done to you in Egypt, and I promise that I will bring you up out of the afflic-tion of Egypt to the land of the Canaanites, the Hittites, the Amorites, the Perizzites, the Hivites, and the Jebusites, a land flowing with milk and honey."' And they will listen to your voice, and you and the elders of Israel shall go to the king of Egypt and say to him, 'The LORD, the God of the Hebrews, has met with us; and now, please let us go a three days' journey into the wilderness, that we may sacrifice to the LORD our God.'" (Exod. 3:13–18)

Here, for the first time in Scripture, God identifies himself as "I AM" (v. 14), which is encompassed in the name *Yahweh*, the name by which God will be known to the people of Israel through-out time. Notice that right after he reveals his name to Moses, he continues telling Moses what to do: "Say this to the people of Israel: 'The LORD, the God of your fathers, the God of Abraham, the God of Isaac, and the God of Jacob, has sent me to you'" (v. 15). God is very careful and intentional in doing this; he has to create credibility for Moses with the people. He knows that he cannot just have Moses identify him with a new name to the people; they do not yet know who Yahweh is. But they do know "the LORD, the God of Abraham, Isaac and Jacob" (v. 16), since their stories would have been passed down through the generations. So God identifies himself as "I am" *and* as the God of their fathers. This particular interchange between God and Moses reveals his unique relationship with Moses, one of intimacy and trust.

This is a critical moment in the story of Moses for all of us. It reveals something of how God works to transform *our* faith. Consider how gently God deals with him. God appears to Moses and immediately tells him what he is going to have him do. Moses's self-doubt causes him to question God. And God gently responds with additional information to encourage and reassure him. Moses continues to question and doubt—the same pattern that we saw with Abraham. The difference here is that this doubting, questioning, and assurance occurs in one conversation, as opposed to multiple conversations, like those God had with Abraham over a number of years. And, Abraham's faith was originally in himself, not in God. So God had to build Abraham's faith *in God* so that he would trust God *rather than himself.* In our current passage, God is building Moses's faith, his trust in God and acceptance of God's will, to *counteract his self-doubt.* God is working to grow his faith until it becomes greater than his self-doubt.

What we see here is a way for anyone to overcome self-doubt. God confronts this very human issue through his work of transforming our faith, so that our trust in God *as God,* and acceptance of his will for our lives, becomes greater than our self-doubt. Thus, he can do in us today exactly what he was doing on the mountain with Moses to transform our faith.

To provide further reassurance to Moses, God then foretells what is going to happen—that Moses *will* do as God has asked, and the events that will happen when he does obey God.

> But I know that the king of Egypt will not let
> you go unless compelled by a mighty hand. So
> I will stretch out my hand and strike Egypt with
> all the wonders that I will do in it; after that he

> will let you go. And I will give this people favor
> in the sight of the Egyptians; and when you go,
> you shall not go empty, but each woman shall ask
> of her neighbor, and any woman who lives in her
> house, for silver and gold jewelry, and for cloth-
> ing. You shall put them on your sons and on your
> daughters. So you shall plunder the Egyptians."
> (Exod. 3:19–22)

Notice that God adds the detail "when you go" (v. 21). This text is still part of the initial conversation between God and Moses on Mount Horeb. Moses is still swimming in his self-doubt, and yet God is telling Moses explicitly what *he will do*, even though Moses has not yet agreed to go to Egypt. Even in his self-doubt, God knows that Moses will obey. By telling Moses now what will happen in the future, he will later be able to recall this first encounter with God and see how God told him at this time what would come true in the future. This process will eventually serve to further build Moses's trust in God at critical moments in the future as God's process of bringing the people of Israel out of Egypt unfolds.

Despite all that God has said to this point, Moses continues to doubt:

> Then Moses answered, "But behold, they will
> not believe me or listen to my voice, for they will
> say, 'The LORD did not appear to you.'" The
> LORD said to him, "What is that in your hand?"
> He said, "A staff." And he said, "Throw it on the
> ground." So he threw it on the ground, and it
> became a serpent, and Moses ran from it. But
> the LORD said to Moses, "Put out your hand
> and catch it by the tail"—so he put out his hand
> and caught it, and it became a staff in his hand—
> "that they may believe that the LORD, the God
> of their fathers, the God of Abraham, the God
> of Isaac, and the God of Jacob, has appeared to

you." Again, the LORD said to him, "Put your hand inside your cloak." And he put his hand inside his cloak, and when he took it out, behold, his hand was leprous like snow. Then God said, "Put your hand back inside your cloak." So he put his hand back inside his cloak, and when he took it out, behold, it was restored like the rest of his flesh. "If they will not believe you," God said, "or listen to the first sign, they may believe the latter sign. If they will not believe even these two signs or listen to your voice, you shall take some water from the Nile and pour it on the dry ground, and the water that you shall take from the Nile will become blood on the dry ground." (Exod. 4:1–9)

Notice that Moses has not expressed doubt *in God*; rather, he continues to doubt whether the people of Israel will believe what *he* tells them (v. 1). After all, who is Moses to the people? A murderer who fled to the wilderness. Obviously, Moses does not want to do what God is telling him to do, despite all the reassurance and details that God has provided. So God gives him three signs and wonders to perform in the sight of the people (vv. 2–9). Each sign is more powerful than the one before. Here, before speaking to the people, God takes Moses through a "practice" session with the signs, in God's presence alone, that God will later perform in front of the people. Amazing! Through this process, God is working to build his trust in God. He continues to seek to reassure Moses that he will be with Moses and that it is God's power at work, not Moses's own effort or abilities, that will accomplish all that God says will occur. God knows that Moses must trust that *he*, Moses, will indeed be able to do what God is asking *him* to do because God is capable of making it happen. He has just proven that to Moses. In this situation, God is not only working to further the work of transformation in Moses's life, he is also preparing to begin to transform the faith of the people of Israel.

Despite the fact that God gave Moses powerful signs to perform, Moses continues to doubt, and thus resist, God's call.

> But Moses said to the LORD, "Oh, my Lord, I am not eloquent, either in the past or since you have spoken to your servant, but I am slow of speech and of tongue." Then the LORD said to him, "Who has made man's mouth? Who makes him mute, or deaf, or seeing, or blind? Is it not I, the LORD? Now therefore go, and I will be with your mouth and teach you what you shall speak." (Exod. 4:10–12)

Moses argues that he is slow of speech (v. 10). He continues to insist that his lack of capabilities must somehow disqualify him from doing what God is asking him to do. In response to Moses's ongoing moaning about his insufficiency, God is saying in essence, "Stop doubting and get moving!" Amazingly, even after all of the reassurance God has given Moses to this point, he continues to argue with God; he is still unwilling to face Pharaoh.

As we have said, God is real to Moses; he does not seem to doubt that God *is God.* However, there is still something in Moses's belief about *who God is* that needs to be transformed. God is asking him to do as commanded, even in the face of his own doubts about his ability to do what God has asked him to do. This is all part of the process of transformation that God is working in Moses.

Moses's ongoing self-doubt is a good example of how God disciplines individuals who resist obeying God's call based on perceived lack of qualifications. So, in one final effort to convince Moses that he (God) is able to bring about all that he has said he will do, he challenges Moses's thinking about who God is by asking, "Who makes man's mouth?" (v. 11). He then declares, "I will be with your mouth and teach you what you shall speak" (v. 12). No longer does God use logic or words or signs to reassure Moses. God basically says, "I myself will control your mouth and teach you exactly what to say."

God is revealing to Moses just how powerful he is—he can control what people say and, more specifically, what Moses will say. Amazingly, after all this, Moses still does not relent.

> But he said, "Oh, my Lord, please send some-one else." Then the anger of the LORD was kindled against Moses and he said, "Is there not Aaron, your brother, the Levite? I know that he can speak well. Behold, he is coming out to meet you, and when he sees you, he will be glad in his heart. You shall speak to him and put the words in his mouth, and I will be with your mouth and with his mouth and will teach you both what to do. He shall speak for you to the people, and he shall be your mouth, and you shall be as God to him. And take in your hand this staff, with which you shall do the signs." (Exod. 4:13–17)

Moses is so desperate that he pleads with God to send some-one else, which triggers God's anger. But notice how God responds. He relents and agrees to choose another, Moses's brother Aaron, to speak for Moses to the people. Notice that God did not say that Aaron will also speak to Pharaoh, just to the people. Then he goes on to say, "And he shall be your mouth, and you shall be as God to him. And take in your hand this staff, with which you shall do the signs" (vv. 16–17). In essence, Moses will now be the voice of God to Aaron. And, God still expects Moses to perform miracles with the staff. Therefore, we have to ask, did God really do as Moses asked? He wanted to be released altogether from what God had commanded him to do, but God did not do that. He did not really let Moses off the hook. God is clear: Moses has to go, and speak … just not to Pharaoh, yet. And, he will still perform miracles with the staff. In this text, God only partially deals with Moses's continuing reluctance to obey.

So, it appears that God has released some of the pressure on self-doubting Moses, thereby continuing the work of transformation in Moses, continuing in a gentle and loving manner to get him to move forward toward being willing to obey God's will. We will eventually see that Moses will be the one that God uses to confront Pharaoh. However, Moses is not yet ready to do so.

In these last few passages of Moses's story, we can see that God understands individuals and their concerns, and at times *fears*, about their ability to do what God is asking them to do. He uses the process of transformation, moving them step by step to exactly where he wants them to be, to that place where they are willing to obey his call and command. Transformation of simple belief into saving faith can occur in an instant; it does happen for some people. But most often it occurs slowly over time, as we have seen in the stories of Abraham, Jacob, and Joseph, and we now see in Moses. God meets us where we are, in some way revealing himself to us, and then he incrementally moves us forward through trust to obedience. Interestingly, the work of transformation often goes unnoticed in us until a new milestone is reached, and God reveals to us what he has already accomplished in transforming our faith.

Moses Accepts

Finally, Moses surrenders to God's will:

> Moses went back to Jethro his father-in-law and said to him, "Please let me go back to my brothers in Egypt to see whether they are still alive." And Jethro said to Moses, "Go in peace." And the LORD said to Moses in Midian, "Go back to Egypt, for all the men who were seeking your life are dead." So Moses took his wife and his sons and had them ride on a donkey, and went back to the land of Egypt. And Moses took the staff of God in his hand. (Exod. 4:18–20)

Moses becomes obedient to the command of God—having run out of excuses and arguments to the contrary. So he goes and asks permission of his father-in-law, Jethro, to return to Egypt. And Jethro simply says to him, "Go in peace" (v. 18). Then notice what God immediately does. Once again, he demonstrates his loving-kindness and patience toward Moses by reassuring him, saying, "All the men who were seeking your life are dead" (v. 19). God did not say that in their first encounter, although he could have. Instead, God saves this piece of information until a point in time when Moses finally obeys what God has commanded him to do. Moses had to get to the point of being obedient, actually taking action to begin to go to Egypt, and then God reassures him. We can take comfort from knowing through Moses's story that God is with us all along the way as we choose to obey what he calls us to do, encouraging us, and therefore revealing that he is, indeed, with us.

The Journey Begins

Having moved Moses to the point of initial obedience, God now tells him what will occur once he returns to Egypt:

> And the LORD said to Moses, "When you go back to Egypt, see that you do before Pharaoh all the miracles that I have put in your power. But I will harden his heart, so that he will not let the people go. Then you shall say to Pharaoh, 'Thus says the LORD, Israel is my firstborn son, and I say to you, "Let my son go that he may serve me. If you refuse to let him go, behold, I will kill your firstborn son."'" (Exod. 4:21–23)

This is a key point in the story of Moses. God tells him that God will harden Pharaoh's heart; therefore, he will not agree to let the people leave Egypt (v. 21). When we read through the texts that follow Moses's multiple encounters with Pharaoh, each time demanding that he let the Israelites go, it is easy to miss the fact that in many of the instances it is *God* who hardens Pharaoh's heart. That is not to say that Pharaoh is devoid of responsibility for the plagues that will afflict Egypt, but the responsibility for what happens is not his alone. Notice too that God has reaffirmed to Moses that *he* will speak to Pharaoh *and* that God has given *him* the power necessary to do the signs God is calling him to do (v. 21). Already we see that God is leading Moses to fully obey that which God originally called him to do, and that God has equipped him to do so.

In this text, God reveals that all he plans to do in the process of freeing the people of Israel from slavery *must take place*. We can infer this from his command to Moses to "do all the miracles" (v. 21). There will be several miracles, and God will be actively involved in causing Pharaoh to resist letting the people leave Egypt after each one. The way in which God will ensure that all of his plans actually take place is to continue to harden Pharaoh's heart (v. 21). God reveals just how far he will go before Pharaoh will finally relent and let the people go. God tells Moses that *he* will eventually say to Pharaoh, "If you refuse to let him go, behold, I will kill your firstborn son" (v. 23). Only at that point will God have achieved his purposes in afflicting Egypt with the coming plagues. And as a sidenote, we have to wonder how Moses reacted when he realized that he will not only *talk* to Pharaoh, but he will say something quite strong and threatening to him, that Pharaoh's firstborn son will die. Without anything in Scripture to tell us of Moses's response to this revelation by God, we can imagine that Moses's trust in God has already deepened to the point where he was not significantly rocked by it.

We must ask at this point, what are those purposes of God? Why would God plan to harden the heart of Pharaoh multiple times? The most important answer is to get to the Passover.[2] According to God's will, all that God has planned to do must occur; nothing can be left undone. If Pharaoh releases Israel before the final plague occurs, then there is no need for the Passover event. And if the Passover does not occur, is God's bigger purpose undermined? Perhaps, although we know God can orchestrate any combination of events to fulfill

---

[2] The Passover event does not emerge in the story until Exodus 12. At this point we must look ahead in the story to see what God is pushing toward, what he ultimately intends to accomplish, in order to make sense of the need for many plagues and the repeated hardening of Pharaoh's heart.

his purposes. It seems that all of the events God has planned must occur in order to demonstrate the indisputable power and authority of God, not only to Pharaoh, but also to Moses, to the people of Israel, and to future generations. The faith of everyone involved in this situation will not be left untouched.

There is another noteworthy point: from God's command to do *all* the miracles (v. 21), we get a sense that God is preparing Moses for a possible lengthy *process*; all events must occur according to God's plan. This is going to take some time. Without this preliminary indication that some time will pass before Pharaoh finally agrees to let the people leave Egypt, Moses might give up in frustration, as Pharaoh will again and again refuse to let the people go. Without having some idea that what he is walking into may be a prolonged process, Moses might be tempted to refuse to do *all* that God commands him to do.

What God is doing here seems designed to build trust in Moses, trust that God will, indeed, bring about all that he has planned. This is a critical part of God's transforming work in Moses. He must stay the course and not walk away frustrated before God's entire plan is accomplished. And the same is true for us today. When we do not understand God's purposes in a particular situation, especially when a solution to a situation seems delayed, it is critical to trust in God's sovereign will, to accept that he has the greatest good in mind and knows the best way to accomplish it. This is the ultimate challenge of the life of a genuine believer: do we believe that God is greater than we are? Are we going to trust him completely? In the case of Moses, that means being willing to stand in front of Pharaoh again and again, to say and do what God tells him to say and do.

As soon as Moses and his family, his wife, Zipporah, and sons, Gershom and Eliezar, start their journey back to Egypt, God seeks to do a surprising thing:

> At a lodging place on the way the LORD met him and sought to put him to death. Then Zipporah took a flint and cut off her son's foreskin and touched Moses' feet with it and said, "Surely you are a bridegroom of blood to me!"

> So he let him alone. It was then that she said, "A
> bridegroom of blood," because of the circumci-
> sion. (Exod. 4:24–26)

The question must be asked, why does God seek to put Moses to death? Because he failed to circumcise one of his sons (which one is not known), and thus failed to follow God's initial command to Abraham that was to be followed by all of his descendants: the circumcision of *all* offspring. This situation reveals a stumbling point in Moses's faith. His failed actions may demonstrate that he may be careless in following all of God's laws. If this is so, then how can Moses be allowed to become the instrument God will use to deliver his law to the people of Israel during the exodus? This is an issue of faith and an issue of personal integrity. God is right to pass judgment on him for violating this command. And yet God is merciful and delivers Moses from his wrath through his wife's actions.

But here we also have to ask, how does she know what to do? She is a Midianite, not part of the people of Israel. However, Zipporah's father, Jethro, is an offspring of Abraham and his wife Keturah (Gen. 25:1–2). So, even though he is not in the line of Isaac and Jacob, he still worships God just as Abraham had. Thus, we can assume his family, including Zipporah, knows about God's command to Abraham to circumcise all offspring.

In this passage we see that God is just, but he is also merciful. And, the fact that this episode in Moses's life occurs while he is on the way back to Egypt, demonstrates to Moses that God will be with him throughout all that he will go through. Additionally, we see in this passage that God does work in our lives through others, believers and nonbelievers alike.

The story continues in Exodus, chapter 4. God tells Aaron to go into the wilderness and find Moses, which he does. Moses tells Aaron all that God had told him, including the signs (Exod. 4:27–28) that are to be performed in front of the people, which are intended to convince them that God has, indeed, sent Moses to lead them out of slavery, out of Egypt. Moses and Aaron then go to the people together. Aaron speaks the words that God has given to Moses and performs the signs in front of the people. The people believe Aaron. When they hear that the LORD has seen their affliction, they bow their heads and worship God (Exod. 4:29–31).

Notice that the response Moses feared he would get from the people does not occur. Rather than responding in disbelief, they actually believe, and the result of that belief is worship. In addition to moving Moses from absolute resistance to obedience, God has also done a work in the hearts of the people, so that when they hear God's word to them through Aaron and see the signs, they do, indeed, believe. We can imagine that this unexpected response from the people toward Moses and Aaron served to strengthen Moses's trust that God is, indeed, with him, working to bring about the outcome that God intends to achieve.

The Work Begins

Moses's and Aaron's encounters with Pharaoh begin in Exodus, chapter 5:

> Afterward Moses and Aaron went and said to Pharaoh, "Thus says the LORD, the God of Israel, 'Let my people go, that they may hold a feast to me in the wilderness.'" But Pharaoh said, "Who is the LORD, that I should obey his voice and let Israel go? I do not know the LORD, and moreover, I will not let Israel go." Then they said, "The God of the Hebrews has met with us. Please let us go a three days' journey into the wilderness that we may sacrifice to the LORD our God, lest he fall upon us with pestilence or with the sword." But the king of Egypt said to them, "Moses and Aaron, why do you take the people away from their work? Get back to your burdens." And Pharaoh said, "Behold, the people of the land are now many, and you make them rest from their burdens!" (Exod. 5:1–5)

Given what God previously told Moses, that he would harden Pharaoh's heart (Exod. 4:21), this first encounter with Pharaoh ends in an expected way: Pharaoh does not agree to let the people leave Egypt. Why should he let them go? *He* does not know "the LORD"; thus, he has no reason to obey God's command (Exod. 5:2). The Hebrews are a very large and thus an important workforce for Pharaoh; *he* has power and authority over them, and *he* has no need to release them. Not only will he not let them go, he also does not want them to rest! The only thing that comes out of this first encounter with Pharaoh is a renewal of his command that they do their work.

However, Pharaoh quickly decides to increase their work by no longer providing the straw they need to make bricks. Now, they must gather the straw themselves in addition to doing a full day's work (Exod. 5:6–8). Things have just become more unbearable for the Hebrews. When the supervisors appeal to Pharaoh for relief from the increased burden, he accuses all the people of Israel of being lazy, which he believes is the reason they want to go into the wilderness to offer a sacrifice to God (v. 8). The supervisors then blame Moses and Aaron for this turn of events (Exod. 5:19–21). Rather than being set free, their bondage has become more severe. The people's trust in God to free them from slavery has been challenged, and they quickly turn on Moses and Aaron. Rather than trusting that God will be faithful to his word, they can only see that their burden of work has become even more unbearable. It seems they expect God to immediately fulfill his promise to free them, which he has not done.

And what is Moses's response to this situation? He questions God:

> Then Moses turned to the LORD and said, "O Lord, why have you done evil to this people? Why did you ever send me? For since I came to Pharaoh to speak in your name, he has done evil to this people, and you have not delivered your people at all." (Exod. 5:22–23)

When God does not immediately fulfill his promise, when things do not go as expected based on God's word, it seems everyone's trust in God falters. The people blame Moses and Aaron for the additional work, and Moses accuses *God* of mistreating the people (v. 22) and not doing what he said he would do (v. 23). It is interesting that Moses sees God as somehow involved in what is happening, and he is angry about what has transpired. But then he complains, "Why did you ever send me?" (v. 22). Moses is feeling sorry for himself! Here we see Moses still wrestling with doubt: even though he knows God is involved, he also seems afraid that God will not be faithful to his word, so he again fears for his own reputation.

So we have to ask the question again, where is God in this? What is his purpose with regard to Moses in this situation? What about the people's faith? Their response is a complete turnaround from just a short time before when they heard that God was going to free them from slavery, and they worshiped *because they believed* (Exod. 4:30–31). And it seems Moses's faith is wavering as well in the face of an unexpected outcome; things have not gone as he apparently thought they would, and he is despairing over his own predicament.

This situation demonstrates an important part of the transformation process: we can be easily discouraged, and our trust in God can falter, when we *think we know* what God is going to do, and then he does not fulfill those expectations. We must be careful to not hold God accountable to what *we think he should do or how he should act* on our behalf. God is God; he is sovereign over all things. Thus, when our expectations are not met, it is important to stop and ask again, "God, where are you in this situation? What are you trying to accomplish? What are you doing?" Such situations can serve to strengthen our trust if we let them do this work in us, or they can weaken our trust if we choose to doubt God's faithfulness.

Now let's look at this passage again. There are actually two important indicators in this text that reveal the work of transformation in Moses is proceeding. The first indicator is that he does not break communication with God; rather, Moses cries out to God. Notice that Moses is comfortable speaking to God in an uncensored way; he is brutally honest and direct, even though he is not yet ready to be so direct and bold with Pharaoh. The second indication of the ongoing work of transformation in Moses is seen in that his first concern is for the people of Israel. He does not seem to understand why these things are happening, and he is deeply concerned for what the people are experiencing.

Yet it also seems Moses has already forgotten what God previously said to him: "*When you have brought the people out of Egypt,* you shall serve God on this mountain" (Exod. 3:12, italics added). God previously told him what was going to happen, and now he is working to build Moses's trust and his willingness to accept that what God has said will actually happen, *but not in the way Moses thinks.* It will happen only in God's time and according to God's plan. God is working to teach Moses that he is sovereign *and* faithful, which will further build and strengthen Moses's faith, transform it beyond simple belief into genuine trust in God and acceptance of God's will.

God responds to Moses:

> But the LORD said to Moses, "Now you shall see what I will do to Pharaoh; for with a strong hand he will send them out, and with a strong hand he will drive them out of his land."
>
> God spoke to Moses and said to him, "I am the LORD. I appeared to Abraham, to Isaac, and to Jacob, as God Almighty, but by my name the LORD I did not make myself known to them. I also established my covenant with them to give them the land of Canaan, the land in which they lived as sojourners. Moreover, I have heard the groaning of the people of Israel whom the Egyptians hold as slaves, and I have remembered my covenant. Say therefore to the people of Israel, 'I am the LORD, and I will bring you out from under the burdens of the Egyptians, and I will deliver you from slavery to them, and I will redeem you with an outstretched arm and with great acts of judgment. I will take you to be my

people, and I will be your God, and you shall
know that I am the LORD your God, who has
brought you out from under the burdens of the
Egyptians. I will bring you into the land that I
swore to give to Abraham, to Isaac, and to Jacob.
I will give it to you for a possession. I am the
LORD.'" (Exod. 6:1–8)

Once again, God responds to Moses's continuing lack of trust
and acceptance with gentleness and patience. First, he tells Moses
that it is now time for action and that *he* will now see God do what
he has previously told Moses he would do (v. 1). We have to conclude
that what God is about to do is, partially, for the sake of further
transforming Moses's faith.

Then, God reminds Moses of who he is, "I am the LORD"
(v. 2), and goes on to provide Moses with the words to say to the
people of Israel (vv. 6–8). What God asks him to say is a reminder
to the people of God's covenant promises to Abraham: that God will
give his descendants (the people who are now in slavery) the land of
Canaan.

The other portion of the covenant promise, that Abraham's offspring would be more numerous than the stars (Gen. 15:5), is being
fulfilled in their lifetime. The people of Israel have grown in number
from the original seventy persons who went into Egypt with Jacob and
his family (Gen. 46:27); they now total over six hundred thousand
persons (see Exod. 12:37). Even Pharaoh is afraid of how numerous
they have become.[3] That is why the Egyptians are so upset. As we
have previously mentioned, if they were to leave Egypt, the economy
could fall apart, for the Israelites are the main workforce for Pharaoh.

So God is reassuring the people of Israel through Moses that
he will also keep that portion of the covenant promise regarding the
land, and that includes bringing Abraham's descendants out of an
alien land where they would be enslaved for four hundred years (Gen.

---

[3] Exodus 5:5: Pharaoh describes them as being "more numerous than the people
of the land" (i.e., the Egyptians).

15:13–14). In essence, he is saying that just because they have not yet seen the entirety of his word fulfilled, and just because Moses's first confrontation with Pharaoh did not result in the people being freed, does not mean that the covenant promises are invalid. This underscores the need for the people to both trust God and accept his sovereign control over the timing of how and when those promises are fulfilled.

After God reaffirms all that he has promised to do for the people of Israel, we find that they do not listen to Moses, because of their broken spirit and harsh slavery conditions (Exod. 6:9). The people are scared; they do not trust either Moses or God. Their daily reality overshadows what little faith they may have gained when Moses and Aaron first spoke to them.

The people's lack of trust in Moses continues to negatively affect him, as we see in the following two passages:

> So the LORD said to Moses, "Go in, tell Pharaoh king of Egypt to let the people of Israel go out of his land." But Moses said to the LORD, "Behold, the people of Israel have not listened to me. How then shall Pharaoh listen to me, for I am of uncircumcised lips?" But the LORD spoke to Moses and Aaron and gave them a charge about the people of Israel and about Pharaoh king of Egypt: to bring the people of Israel out of the land of Egypt. (Exod. 6:10–12)

> On the day when the LORD spoke to Moses in the land of Egypt, the LORD said to Moses, in the land of Egypt, "I am the LORD; tell Pharaoh king of Egypt all that I say to you." But Moses said to the LORD, "Behold, I am of uncircumcised lips. How will Pharaoh listen to me?" (Exod. 6:28–30)

We can see in these two passages indications that, although the work of transformation is underway in Moses, more transformation is needed. Moses still doubts his own abilities, and as a result, he also questions Pharaoh's willingness to listen to him. After all, if the people are not willing to trust what Moses is saying to them, why would he expect Pharaoh to listen? Yet God simply and directly responds to his doubt by charging Moses and Aaron to do what he is asking them to do.[4] He does so because he knows that Moses does not doubt God, but rather he still doubts his own ability to do what God instructs him to do. Additionally, Pharaoh has already refused once to listen to what Moses said to him; why would Moses expect him to listen now? And yet God gives Moses and Aaron a simple, direct command (Exod. 6:11, 29), confident that Moses will obey his command. But even a simple, direct command by God, telling him exactly what to say, does not overcome his doubt about his own abilities to speak effectively to Pharaoh, nor does it seem to reassure him that Pharaoh will actually listen to him.

It is obvious that God sees this continuing internal struggle in Moses, so he makes his command to Moses as simple as possible, saying, "I am the LORD, tell Pharaoh king of Egypt all that I say to you" (Exod. 6:29). There is nothing elaborate here. God is simply stating to *Moses* who it is that is speaking to him and then tells him what he is to say. Thus, the main faith question for Moses at this point is this: what is more important to him, God's word to him or his own self-doubt? And who is greater in Moses's eyes, God or Pharaoh? Even though some time has passed since God first spoke to Moses on Mount Horeb, and God has spoken to him several times, has told him exactly what to do and what the outcome will be, Moses continues to doubt *his* ability to do as God asks.

---

4   As the story of Moses continues, it is important to observe Aaron's role in the unfolding events. In response to Moses's initial lack of confidence in his ability to do what God is asking him to do, God agrees that Aaron can be the spokesperson (Exod. 4:13–16). As Moses's trust and acceptance of God's presence with him enables him to do all that he is commanded to do, his trust in his own abilities also grows. As a result, Aaron's role in the story diminishes, which indicates transformation is taking place in *Moses's* faith.

As the story continues and we continue to examine God's process for transforming Moses's faith, it will be important to keep in mind that Moses still doubts himself and his ability to do what God instructs him to do, even after all the reassurance God has given him. In essence he is saying, "I can't do it." Note that he is not saying, "I *won't* do it." It is not a question of his will but of his confidence in his own ability to do what God has asked him to do. He really is afraid that he will not get the desired outcome because he does not believe *he is able* to bring it about.

Once again, however, God gently and patiently responds to Moses's deep concerns:

> And the LORD said to Moses, "See, I have made you like God to Pharaoh, and your brother Aaron shall be your prophet. You shall speak all that I command you, and your brother Aaron shall tell Pharaoh to let the people of Israel go out of his land. But I will harden Pharaoh's heart, and though I multiply my signs and wonders in the land of Egypt, Pharaoh will not listen to you. Then I will lay my hand on Egypt and bring my hosts, my people the children of Israel, out of the land of Egypt by great acts of judgment. The Egyptians shall know that I am the LORD, when I stretch out my hand against Egypt and bring out the people of Israel from among them." (Exod. 7:1–5)

Notice that God no longer seeks to persuade Moses in order to build his trust. Instead, God provides simple direct instructions that he knows Moses will obey (v. 2). This does not mean that Moses has abandoned his self-doubt. But it does indicate God's confidence that Moses will be obedient even in the face of his self-doubt.

Also, it is important to notice the subtle changes that occur in what God says to Moses in this passage. First, God previously told Moses that he would "be as God" to Aaron (Exod. 4:16), but here he says that Moses will "be as God" *to Pharaoh* (v. 1). This change is actually moving Moses a step closer to being able to do what God ultimately wants him to do. Notice also that God has changed Aaron's role at this point to be that of prophet: *he* will be the one to tell Pharaoh to let the people of Israel go out of his land (v. 2). Then God seeks to reassure Moses by telling him what will happen as he does what God tells him to do: God will harden Pharaoh's heart, and Pharaoh will not let the people go (vv. 3–4).

So Moses and Aaron go to Pharaoh and do just as the LORD commanded (Exod. 7:6). Aaron then throws down his staff before Pharaoh and his servants, and it becomes a serpent. Pharaoh summons the wise men and the sorcerers of Egypt, and each of them cast down his staff, and they also become serpents. But Aaron's staff swallows up their staffs (Exod. 7:10–12). And just as God had said, Pharaoh's heart is hardened; he does not listen to them. Notice that Moses and Aaron do exactly what God told them to do. From this point on, everything will occur exactly as God has said.

We will see this pattern again and again as the story of Moses continues: God tells Moses what to say and do; he and Aaron go to Pharaoh and say and do what God has commanded; Pharaoh' heart is hardened, and he resists releasing the people of Israel; and Moses and Aaron leave his presence. We will see that each time events unfold as God has ordained them. And as this pattern continues, we will see indications that Moses's faith is strengthening in this process. Through it all, he will be transformed into the man God intends for him to be.

Plagues

First plague: water turned to blood

And so the plagues begin. Moses announces the first plague on Egypt:

> Then the LORD said to Moses, "Pharaoh's heart is hardened; he refuses to let the people go. Go

to Pharaoh in the morning, as he is going out to the water. Stand on the bank of the Nile to meet him, and take in your hand the staff that turned into a serpent. And you shall say to him, 'The LORD, the God of the Hebrews, sent me to you, saying, "Let my people go, that they may serve me in the wilderness." But so far, you have not obeyed. Thus says the LORD, "By this you shall know that I am the LORD: behold, with the staff that is in my hand I will strike the water that is in the Nile, and it shall turn into blood. The fish in the Nile shall die, and the Nile will stink, and the Egyptians will grow weary of drinking water from the Nile."'" And the LORD said to Moses, "Say to Aaron, 'Take your staff and stretch out your hand over the waters of Egypt, over their rivers, their canals, and their ponds, and all their pools of water, so that they may become blood, and there shall be blood throughout all the land of Egypt, even in vessels of wood and in vessels of stone.'" (Exod. 7:14–19)

Notice that what must occur next, the water in Egypt turning into blood and the fish dying, is because "Pharaoh's heart is hardened," and he therefore refuses to release the Israelites (v. 14). Also note that the purpose of what will occur is so that Pharaoh "shall know that I am the LORD" (v. 17). God is working to convince Pharaoh that he, alone, is God. So, God tells Moses what is going to take place, what he and Aaron will do.

So Moses and Aaron do exactly as God has commanded. In the sight of Pharaoh and his servants, Moses instructs Aaron what to do according to the word of God. Aaron lifts up the staff and strikes the water in the Nile, and all the water turns into blood (Exod. 7:20). Everything that God said would happen does, indeed, happen. The water turns to blood; all of the fish die, and the water becomes undrinkable (v. 21). But again, the magicians of Egypt do exactly has Aaron has done (v. 22), so Pharaoh's heart remains hardened. He goes into his house seemingly unaffected by all that has happened (v. 23).

Here we do not see any struggle in Moses; he does not seem to question what God has told him to do or resist doing it based on self-doubt. Nor does the text say that he is in any way concerned about the outcome that God has ordained. Moses seems to be learning that God does, indeed, cause events to unfold as he has said they will.

Second plague: frogs

In Exodus, chapter 8, we see that seven days have passed, and God again instructs Moses about the second plague that will come:

> Then the LORD said to Moses, "Go in to Pharaoh and say to him, 'Thus says the LORD, "Let my people go, that they may serve me. But if you refuse to let them go, behold, I will plague all your country with frogs. The Nile shall swarm with frogs that shall come up into your house and into your bedroom and on your bed and into the houses of your servants and your people, and into your ovens and your kneading bowls. The frogs shall come up on you and on your people and on all your servants."'" And the LORD said to Moses, "Say to Aaron, 'Stretch out your hand with your staff over the rivers, over the canals and over the pools, and make frogs come up on the land of Egypt!'" (Exod. 8:1–5)

Once again Moses does exactly as God has directed him: he tells Aaron what to do. And everything happens exactly as God said it would. And once again, the magicians in service to Pharaoh perform the same acts by their secret arts; they too make frogs come up on the land.

The next passage of text reveals that a change occurs at this point in the predetermined pattern of events that we have seen so far:

> Then Pharaoh called Moses and Aaron and said, "Plead with the LORD to take away the frogs from me and from my people, and I will let the people go to sacrifice to the LORD." Moses said to Pharaoh, "Be pleased to command me when I am to plead for you and for your servants and for your people, that the frogs be cut off from you and your houses and be left only in the Nile." And he said, "Tomorrow." Moses said, "Be it as you say, so that you may know that there is no one like the LORD our God. The frogs shall go away from you and your houses and your servants and your people. They shall be left only in the Nile." So Moses and Aaron went out from Pharaoh, and Moses cried to the LORD about the frogs, as he had agreed with Pharaoh. And the LORD did according to the word of Moses. The frogs died out in the houses, the courtyards, and the fields. (Exod. 8:8–13)

In this instance, Pharaoh calls Moses back into his presence and for the first time asks Moses to plead with God to take away the frogs from the land. It seems that Pharaoh is beginning to be personally affected by the plagues that are taking place. Moses responds without needing God to tell him what to say. And he does so in a God-honoring manner. He asks Pharaoh when he would like the frogs to be removed. And when Pharaoh responds, "Tomorrow," Moses replies, "Be it as you say, so that you may know that there is no one like the LORD our God" (v. 10).

This is a significant indicator of the progress being accomplished in the ongoing work of transformation in Moses's life. God has not told Moses what to say in response to Pharaoh; nor has he told him if, how, or when the frogs will be removed. Yet at this point, Moses's trust has grown to such a level that he can respond to Pharaoh with complete confidence. And notice that the text says, "The LORD did according to the word of Moses" (v. 13).

This is a huge step forward in the work of transformation in Moses. For the first time he speaks to Pharaoh, in the moment, without being told by God exactly what to say and do. Further, he makes a promise to Pharaoh, committing God to do something, and Moses does not know if he will do it or not. Then God does exactly what Moses has said he would do. As a result, Moses's level of confidence in his own ability to do as God asks him to do must have grown significantly. This indication of growing trust in Moses demonstrates significant progress in the work of transformation in his life.

At this point we need to look ahead in the story of Moses to understand that the purpose of God's transforming work in Moses's life extends beyond simply getting Pharaoh to release the people of Israel from slavery in Egypt. Once that occurs, we will see that Moses will then be responsible for leading the people from Egypt to the promised land of Canaan. We have already seen that the people of Israel can be difficult, untrusting people. To get them through what will eventually be forty years in the wilderness will be a far greater test of Moses's faith—his trust in God and acceptance of his will. Therefore, a significant amount of transformation of his faith must occur before he is prepared to lead the people out of Egypt, before the exodus journey can begin. We can see at this point that the necessary transforming work is indeed in process.

Third plague: gnats

The second plague is immediately followed by a third plague:

> Then the LORD said to Moses, "Say to Aaron, 'Stretch out your staff and strike the dust of the earth, so that it may become gnats in all the land of Egypt.'" And they did so. Aaron stretched out his hand with his staff and struck the dust of the earth, and there were gnats on man and beast. All

the dust of the earth became gnats in all the land
of Egypt. (Exod. 8:16–17)

Once again, the initial pattern set forth by God is repeated: God
instructs Moses what to do, and Moses and Aaron comply. And again,
for the fourth time, the magicians try by their secret arts to produce
gnats, but this time they cannot do so (v. 18). Then the magicians
say to Pharaoh, "This is the finger of God" (v. 19). But Pharaoh's
heart is still hardened, and he will not listen to them (v. 19). Notice
that the magicians come to see God's hand in what is happening, but
only when they reach the end of their own ability, infused with some
unknown power, to do as Moses has done. But consistent with God's
word to Moses, Pharaoh's heart remains hardened.

Fourth plague: flies

Immediately after this, God tells Moses to rise up early in the
morning and once again say to Pharaoh, "Thus says the LORD, 'Let
my people go, that they may serve me'" (Exod. 8:20), warning him
that if he does not, God will send swarms of flies on him and his
servants and the people and that the houses of the Egyptians shall be
filled with swarms of flies (v. 21). This time, however, God says that
he will set apart the land of Goshen, where the people of Israel dwell,
so that they will not be affected by what is coming. This is to show
the Egyptians that God "is in the midst of the earth" (v. 22). God
continues to take action against Pharaoh and the people so that they
will know that he, alone, is God. His actions will also demonstrate
to the people of Israel that God is protecting them. In doing so, God
will distinguish between his people and the Egyptians (v. 23).

The next day, God does as he said he would do: a great swarm
of flies goes into all of the houses throughout all the land of Egypt.
As a result, the land was ruined (v. 24). After this, we see for a second
time that Pharaoh calls Moses back into his presence:

Then Pharaoh called Moses and Aaron and said,
"Go, sacrifice to your God within the land." But

Moses said, "It would not be right to do so, for the offerings we shall sacrifice to the LORD our God are an abomination to the Egyptians. If we sacrifice offerings abominable to the Egyptians before their eyes, will they not stone us? We must go three days' journey into the wilderness and sacrifice to the LORD our God as he tells us." So Pharaoh said, "I will let you go to sacrifice to the LORD your God in the wilderness; only you must not go very far away. Plead for me." Then Moses said, "Behold, I am going out from you and I will plead with the LORD that the swarms of flies may depart from Pharaoh, from his servants, and from his people, tomorrow. Only let not Pharaoh cheat again by not letting the people go to sacrifice to the LORD." So Moses went out from Pharaoh and prayed to the LORD. (Exod. 8:25–30)

Once again Moses returns to Pharaoh, who says to him, "Go, sacrifice to your God within the land" (v. 25). And once again Moses responds without God having to tell him what to say. He tries to get Pharaoh to allow them to go three days into the wilderness in order to sacrifice to God, because to do so within Egyptian land would be an abomination to the Egyptians (v. 26). Evidently, Moses is correct in making this comment, because Pharaoh accepts his argument. However, he adds a single restriction, saying, "Only you must not go very far away" (v. 28). He then asks Moses, "Plead for me" (v. 28). And Moses agrees to do as Pharaoh asks. But then Moses confronts Pharaoh, saying, "Only let not Pharaoh cheat again by not letting the people go to sacrifice to the LORD" (v. 29).

This interchange is another key indicator of the continuing work of transformation in Moses's life: he dares to challenge the integrity of Pharaoh to his face. This act demonstrates a significant increase in confidence in Moses. He is not just acting in obedience to God's word without resistance; he is now boldly speaking truth to Pharaoh, truth that we have not seen God give him directly. It seems to emerge out of his personal integrity before God and reflects components of his character that God is developing in him: courage and truth.

Then, apparently without waiting for a reply from Pharaoh, Moses leaves his presence and prays to God, as he said he would (v. 30). In God's continuing effort to reassure Moses and thus continue to build his trust and acceptance of him as God, he does as Moses asks, removing all the swarms of flies from Pharaoh and his people (v. 30). And again, according to what God has previously told Moses would happen, Pharaoh hardens his heart once again and does not let the people go (v. 32).

Fifth plague: Egyptian livestock die

The story continues in Exodus, chapter 9. God tells Moses to once again tell Pharaoh, "Let my people go, that they may serve me" (v. 1). He is then to warn Pharaoh that if he refuses to do so, the next day a very severe plague from God will fall upon the Egyptian livestock, one that will affect all Egyptian horses, donkeys, camels—all herds and flocks (v. 3). Moses is then instructed to also say that this will not affect the livestock of Israel, that all of their livestock will be spared (v. 4). And the next day, God does as he said he would do. All the livestock of the Egyptians die, but the livestock of the people of Israel is spared (v. 6).

Once again God's action demonstrates to Moses that God does all that he says he will do. Pharaoh sends someone to verify if what Moses had said has occurred. Upon hearing that this was so, Pharaoh's heart is hardened again, and he does not let the people go (v. 7). All of this has occurred just as God said it would.

Sixth plague: boils

Continuing on in Exodus, chapter 9, God tells Moses and Aaron to take handfuls of soot from the kiln and throw them in the air in the sight of Pharaoh. When they do, the soot will become fine dust over all of Egypt, causing boils to break out in sores on all living things (v. 8–9). So Moses and Aaron obey; they do as instructed (v. 10). This time the Egyptian magicians cannot stand before Moses because of the boils (v. 11). God hardens the heart of Pharaoh once again, and he does not listen (v. 12). Again, this is exactly what God said would happen.

In this text, God gives no warning to Pharaoh; he does not give him an opportunity to change his heart before the plague is released. He simply directs Moses what to do, and he does it. This is a bold manifestation of God's power, directed at Pharaoh. We can imagine that it is also a reminder to Moses as well of just how powerful God is.

Before moving further in the story, it is important to note that in Exodus 9:12, the text says, "The LORD hardened the heart of Pharaoh." In other places the text says that "Pharaoh hardened his heart." And in still other cases, the text says, "Pharaoh's heart was hardened," indicating the hardening was caused by an unnamed outside influence (but presumably by God). So, an important question arises, why would *God* harden Pharaoh's heart? We must look ahead in the story to answer that question. God's broader plan must come to fulfillment, and that will only occur when the angel of death kills all the firstborn in Egypt (see Exod. 12). The Passover must occur according to God's plan and purpose, not only for the people of Israel currently in bondage in Egypt, but for all future generations of God's people. Remember, God knows all that he is doing in the hearts of the Egyptians, Pharaoh, Moses, Aaron, and the people of Israel as these plagues continue. Thus, Pharaoh cannot accede to God's demands too early, before the tenth plague on Egypt occurs.

This is an important lesson for us today. The events of our lives must proceed according to God's plan and purpose, according to his sovereign will for all who are involved in the events of our lives. God knows that our personal need is not the only need he is working to meet; he is working in the lives of everyone who is somehow involved in the events of our daily lives. And we too are being touched and transformed in some way as God works to meet the needs of others that we know.

Seventh plague: hail

God tells Moses to go to Pharaoh early the next morning, and if he will not let the people of Israel go, he is to say to him that this time God will send plagues on Pharaoh himself, his servants, and all the people of Egypt (vv. 13–14). Even in the face of God's words, Pharaoh does not fear God; instead, he continues to exalt himself against God's people (v. 17). Thus, Moses is instructed to tell Pharaoh that the next morning, God is going to cause "very heavy hail to fall, such as never has been in Egypt" (v. 18). Moses then instructs the Egyptians to get their livestock, everything in the field, into a safe place. The hail that is coming will be so severe that any creature, slave or animal, left in the fields will die when the hail falls (v. 19). The text tells us that every one of the Egyptians who "feared the word of the LORD" did as Moses instructed, but whoever did not left the slaves and animals in the field (v. 20–21).

In this passage, God reveals that if he had wanted to, he could have already cut off Pharaoh and his people from the face of the earth (v. 15). But he explains that he has not done so, "*so that* you may know that there is none like me in all the earth" (v. 14b, italics added). This explanation clearly indicates that God's purpose extends beyond redeeming the people of Israel out of slavery in Egypt; it extends to the glorification of God as unequaled in all the earth. As we have just read, it seems this is beginning to happen in some of the Egyptians, for those who "feared the word of the LORD" took action before the hail started (v. 20).

And again, as Moses is speaking to Pharaoh, what he is saying is no doubt a further lesson for him personally. Moses is also learning the extent of God's power as God acts to demonstrate his power to Pharaoh, and thus he is no doubt gaining a holy fear of the LORD. As we read this story in our own day, it should remind us as well about who God really is, about his power, but also about his mercy, the extent he will go to in order to turn the hearts of people toward him and acknowledge him as God.

In Exodus 9:22–26, God then tells Moses to stretch out his hand toward heaven so that hail will begin to fall. And Moses does

as he is instructed, causing thunder, hail, and fire to fall to the earth
from the hand of God, striking down every living thing that was in
the field. Only the land of Goshen where the people of Israel dwell
is spared.

Once again, the plague is severe enough to capture Pharaoh's
attention:

> Then Pharaoh sent and called Moses and Aaron
> and said to them, "This time I have sinned; the
> LORD is in the right, and I and my people are in
> the wrong. Plead with the LORD, for there has
> been enough of God's thunder and hail. I will
> let you go, and you shall stay no longer." Moses
> said to him, "As soon as I have gone out of the
> city, I will stretch out my hands to the LORD.
> The thunder will cease, and there will be no
> more hail, so that you may know that the earth is
> the LORD's. But as for you and your servants, I
> know that you do not yet fear the LORD God."
> (Exod. 9:27–30)

This time, Pharaoh admits to Moses that "the LORD is in the
right, and I and my people are in the wrong" (v. 27). He asks Moses
to plead with God to stop the thunder and hail. Then he states that
he will let the people of Israel go without delay or any other stipula-
tions. Moses responds that he will do as requested as soon as he leaves
the city. But then he adds, "But as for you and your servants, I know
that you do not yet fear the LORD God" (v. 30).

This is the strongest indicator yet of the increasing progress of
the work of transformation in Moses's life. Here, without instructions from God, he in essence tells Pharaoh that he still does not
meet God's requirements for ending the plagues. If Pharaoh and his
servants do not yet fear God, then God's purposes have not yet been
fulfilled, and the plagues cannot come to an end.

God's bigger purposes continue to be at the center of what God asks Moses to do:

> Then the LORD said to Moses, "Go in to Pharaoh, for I have hardened his heart and the heart of his servants, that I may show these signs of mine among them, and that you may tell in the hearing of your son and of your grandson how I have dealt harshly with the Egyptians and what signs I have done among them, that you may know that I am the LORD." (Exod. 10:1–2)

In this text, God reveals that another purpose of his is for this story of what is now occurring in Egypt to be told to future generations. Notice that God specifically states that he intends for his harsh actions against the Egyptians, the signs he has performed in their midst, to be told to Moses's future generations. Here we see the importance of Scripture and how it has been preserved down through the centuries so that the story can continue to be told accurately for the benefit of future generations.

Eighth plague: locusts

Without further instruction from God, Moses and Aaron go to speak to Pharaoh:

> So Moses and Aaron went in to Pharaoh and said to him, "Thus says the LORD, the God of the Hebrews, 'How long will you refuse to humble yourself before me? Let my people go, that they may serve me. For if you refuse to let my people go, behold, tomorrow I will bring locusts into your country, and they shall cover the face of the land, so that no one can see the land. And they shall eat what is left to you after the hail, and they shall eat every tree of yours

that grows in the field, and they shall fill your houses and the houses of all your servants and of all the Egyptians, as neither your fathers nor your grandfathers have seen, from the day they came on earth to this day.'" Then he turned and went out from Pharaoh. (Exod. 10:3–6)

Clearly, Pharaoh did not let the people go after he pleaded with Moses to pray to God to stop the hail. Notice that in this next section, God tells Moses to go in and speak to Pharaoh but does not give him the words to say. So we have to ask, does Moses discern that the next plague will be locusts, or does he decide this himself? The text does not give us an answer. But clearly, unlike in previous instances, there is no specific direction from God about what Moses is to say. It seems God now trusts Moses to say what God would have him say in the moment, without receiving previous instruction from God. This is another important indication that the work of transformation continues to progress in Moses's life; it indicates that Moses is tuned in to God and is aware of what God is working to accomplish. An increasing measure of intimacy has developed in his relationship with God.

By this time, desperation is setting in among Pharaoh's servants, for they understand that Egypt is ruined, but Pharaoh does not yet fully understand the consequences of what has been happening (v. 7). At the urging of his servants, Moses and Aaron are brought back to Pharaoh, and he tells them, "Go, serve the LORD your God" (v. 8). But he then asks who Moses intends to take into the wilderness to worship God (v. 8). In his strongest response yet to Pharaoh, Moses replies, "We will go with our young and our old. We will go with our sons and daughters and with our flocks and herds, for we must hold a feast to the LORD" (v. 9). He is extremely specific about what will happen. But Pharaoh only allows the men to go; he will not allow anyone else to leave (v. 11).

There is no longer any self-doubt or hesitancy in Moses when he answers Pharaoh's question. His trust in God has been built up through the work of transformation in him; he no longer fears Pharaoh, and thus speaks with confidence and authority. This reveals that the work of transformation in Moses that is necessary to prepare him to lead the Israelites out of Egypt is nearing its completion. He is now prepared to do what God charged him to do, to lead the people out (Exod. 3:10).

But God's other purposes, to actually free the people, and for God to be glorified to Pharaoh and the Egyptians, have not yet been accomplished. We see this in the next verses: "But he said to them, 'The LORD be with you, if ever I let you and your little ones go! Look, you have some evil purpose in mind. No! Go, the men among you, and serve the LORD, for that is what you are asking.' And they were driven out from Pharaoh's presence" (Exod. 10:10–11). In his strongest refusal yet, Pharaoh threatens Moses, accusing him of having some evil purpose in mind. This is a clear indication that Pharaoh was not convinced that Moses was speaking for God. He remains steadfast in saying that only the men can go.

In Exodus 10:12–20, we see that God then tells Moses to stretch out his hand over the land so that the locusts may come and devour everything not destroyed by hail (v. 12). Moses does so, and God brings an east wind that blows in the locusts (v. 13). They cover the entire land and eat all the plants that still remain (vv. 14–15). Then Pharaoh hastily calls Moses and Aaron and says, "I have sinned against the LORD your God, and against you. Now therefore, forgive my sin, please, only this once, and plead with the LORD your God only to remove this death from me" (vv. 16–17). Moses does as Pharaoh has asked and pleads with God on Pharaoh's behalf (v. 18). God responds by changing the direction of the wind so that it drives the locusts west into the Red Sea (v. 19). But once again God hardens Pharaoh's heart, and he does not let the people of Israel go (v. 20). Clearly these last two plagues, hail and locusts, have taken their toll on Pharaoh; but according to God's plan, the time is not right yet for him to accede to God's demands. So once again God hardens Pharaoh's heart.

Ninth plague: darkness

After this, we see in Exodus 10:21–23 that God tells Moses to stretch out his hand toward heaven so that there may be darkness over the land. Moses does as God instructs him, and "pitch darkness" covers the land for three days (v. 22). No one leaves their homes for three days because they cannot see, yet the people of Israel have light where they live (v. 23).

Pharaoh responds to this ninth plague:

> Then Pharaoh called Moses and said, "Go, serve the LORD; your little ones also may go with you; only let your flocks and your herds remain behind." But Moses said, "You must also let us have sacrifices and burnt offerings, that we may sacrifice to the LORD our God. Our livestock also must go with us; not a hoof shall be left behind, for we must take of them to serve the LORD our God, and we do not know with what we must serve the LORD until we arrive there." But the LORD hardened Pharaoh's heart, and he would not let them go. Then Pharaoh said to him, "Get away from me; take care never to see my face again, for on the day you see my face you shall die." Moses said, "As you say! I will not see your face again." (Exod. 10:24–29)

In this text, Pharaoh tries to retain some degree of control over what the people of Israel will do. But Moses is not willing to negotiate, further demonstrating the progress of the work of transformation in his life. At this point, he is strong enough in his faith to stand firm and oppose Pharaoh, in essence saying to him, "No, *this* is what we must do." He knows that God wants *all* of their possessions to leave Egypt with them, and Pharaoh has not yet agreed to this. Moses is now so confident in his ability to handle the responsibility that God has given him that he stands firmly before Pharaoh and demands that everything that belongs to the Israelites go with them. Then, once again God hardens Pharaoh's heart, pushing him to the point of utter frustration, and he threatens Moses's life. Obviously, Moses knows that the critical point in time has been reached, and his final comment, that he will not see Pharaoh again, indicates that he has insight as to what is coming and what it will mean for Pharaoh.

Tenth plague: death of the firstborn

The process of bringing the tenth and final plague now begins:

> The LORD said to Moses, "Yet one plague more I will bring upon Pharaoh and upon Egypt. Afterward he will let you go from here. When he lets you go, he will drive you away completely. Speak now in the hearing of the people, that they ask, every man of his neighbor and every woman of her neighbor, for silver and gold jewelry." And the LORD gave the people favor in the sight of the Egyptians. Moreover, the man Moses was very great in the land of Egypt, in the sight of Pharaoh's servants and in the sight of the people. (Exod. 11:1–3)

Notice that the only instruction that God gives Moses at this time is to speak "in the hearing of the people" (v. 2). There is no mention of speaking to Pharaoh. We see here, as in previous texts, that as the work of transformation progresses in Moses, he requires fewer and fewer instructions from God to accomplish what God wants him to do. God has gradually moved from telling Moses exactly what to say and do to no longer telling Moses what to say to Pharaoh. And now, as God threatens one more plague, he does not even tell Moses to speak to Pharaoh. Instead, he asks him to tell the people of Israel what they are to do.

Also notice in this text that there is no resistance from the people, either from Israel or the Egyptians. Moses speaks to the people as instructed by God, telling them to ask every neighbor for gold and silver jewelry (v. 2). And God moves on the hearts of the Egyptians, giving the people of Israel favor in their eyes (v. 3), so that they give up their valuable possessions without question or complaint.

Why do the Egyptians do such a thing when the people of Israel are slaves in Egypt? Why does God tell Moses to have the people of Israel ask the Egyptians for gold and silver jewelry and clothing? First, remember that God told Moses during their first encounter at the burning bush that God, through Moses, would bring the people out of slavery, out of Egypt (Exod. 3:17), and that they would not go empty-handed (Exod. 3:21), that they would "plunder the Egyptians" (Exod. 3:22). Also, we need to look forward approximately two years, to the time when God will appear to the people of Israel on Mount Horeb. At that time, God will instruct them to give this gold and silver jewelry and any other things of great value for the building of the tabernacle.[5] It is important to see here, at this time, that God is preparing for that future event, which will create a place for God to dwell among his people.

Also notice that this text says, in addition to the people having favor with the Egyptians, "The man Moses was very great in the land of Egypt" (v. 3). What is it that the Egyptians witness that causes Moses to have favor with the people? Is it due to the plagues and his role in how they have unfolded? Probably. And, it is this favor that the Egyptian people have for Moses that God now uses to plunder the Egyptians of their valuable commodities in preparation for freeing his people from slavery. God's bigger purposes are being fulfilled.

After this, Moses speaks once again to Pharaoh:

> So Moses said, "Thus says the LORD: 'About midnight I will go out in the midst of Egypt, and every firstborn in the land of Egypt shall die, from the firstborn of Pharaoh who sits on his throne, even to the firstborn of the slave girl who

---

[5] For details on the items God asks the people to bring to him in order to build a sanctuary (tabernacle), see Exodus 25:1–8.

is behind the handmill, and all the firstborn of the cattle. There shall be a great cry throughout all the land of Egypt, such as there has never been, nor ever will be again. But not a dog shall growl against any of the people of Israel, either man or beast, that you may know that the LORD makes a distinction between Egypt and Israel.' And all these your servants shall come down to me and bow down to me, saying, 'Get out, you and all the people who follow you.' And after that I will go out." And he went out from Pharaoh in hot anger. Then the LORD said to Moses, "Pharaoh will not listen to you, that my wonders may be multiplied in the land of Egypt." (Exod. 11:4–9)

By this point in time it would be reasonable for Pharaoh to acquiesce to Moses's demands. After all, we have seen hints during the past few plagues that he may be on the verge of doing so, but God continues to harden his heart in each case. In this text God finally reveals his bigger purpose: so that his "wonders may be multiplied in the land of Egypt" (v. 9). God intends for his greatness and power to be known to Pharaoh and all of Egypt, but this has not yet happened. So the plagues continue, and God continues to harden Pharaoh's heart (v. 10).

Also notice in this text that Moses himself decides what to say to Pharaoh, seemingly without any instruction from God. It appears that through discernment, Moses knows exactly what is about to happen, and he speaks to Pharaoh accordingly. This is a critical point in Moses's personal journey of faith. The man that Moses was when he fled Egypt after killing an Egyptian, and the man he was when he first encountered God at the burning bush, could not have done what this text says he now does. He boldly declares on behalf of God that the firstborn of all Egyptians, slaves and cattle, will die.

Through all that Moses has experienced and observed during the plagues, his trust in and acceptance of God's will has grown. He now stands firmly in front of Pharaoh without any reluctance, confidently speaking the word of God to him, declaring an unimaginable event is about to occur. In his actions here we can see that the transformation of his faith that was needed for him to be ready and able to do what God will soon ask him to do, is fairly complete.

It is important that we learn from what has transpired in the transformation of Moses's faith. We need to look for parallels in Moses's faith development process to our own transformation process. As the events of our lives progress, can we identify where the knowledge and understanding, the trust and acceptance of God's will has grown and continues to increase? Can we see points at which God has become real to us, followed by an increasing desire to do God's will? And if we are living a lifestyle of obedience to God's will for us, is our discernment, our ability to know what God would want done in any given situation, continuing to grow?

Passover

Remember that during the plagues, God has protected his people. They have not suffered as the Egyptians have suffered. Now God needs to protect his people once again from the death that is coming to the Egyptians. So, in Exodus 12, God gives Moses very detailed instructions for the people of Israel regarding the Passover, what they are to do so that death will "pass over" their home and family. These instructions are not only for the people in Egypt at this time, but for all future generations. We can see the main point of God's instructions in the next passage in Exodus 12:

> "Then they shall take some of the blood and put it on the two doorposts and the lintel of the houses in which they eat it. They shall eat the flesh that night, roasted on the fire; with unleavened bread and bitter herbs they shall eat it. Do not eat any of it raw or boiled in water, but roasted, its head with its legs and its inner parts. And you shall let none of it remain until the morning; anything that remains until the morning you shall burn.

In this manner you shall eat it: with your belt fastened, your sandals on your feet, and your staff in your hand. And you shall eat it in haste. It is the LORD's Passover. For I will pass through the land of Egypt that night, and I will strike all the firstborn in the land of Egypt, both man and beast; and on all the gods of Egypt I will execute judgments: I am the LORD. The blood shall be a sign for you, on the houses where you are. And when I see the blood, I will pass over you, and no plague will befall you to destroy you, when I strike the land of Egypt." (Exod. 12:7–13)

In this part of the text, the process that the people are to follow and the purpose of the Passover are revealed. The spreading of blood on the two doorposts and lintel of each house is to be done for all houses occupied by the people of Israel, as a sign for God to see and thus pass over the occupants of that house, so that this final plague of death does not strike them.

At this point it is important to look again at who Moses was when God first spoke to him from the burning bush on Mt. Horeb. At that time, he resisted God's directions, arguing that the people of Israel would not listen to him, firmly believing that he could not do what God was asking him to do. That which God originally asked him to say was simple compared to telling the people of Israel now that if they sacrifice a lamb, including putting blood on the two doorposts and lintel of their houses, that the angel of death will pass over them and not strike down the first born of their family. His initial fear was that the people would not believe him. How will the people respond now to what God is asking him to say to them?

After God tells Moses what to say, he gathers the elders of Israel to do as God has told him to do. He says to them:

"Go and select lambs for yourselves according to your clans, and kill the Passover lamb. Take a bunch of hyssop and dip it in the blood that is in

the basin, and touch the lintel and the two doorposts with the blood that is in the basin. None
of you shall go out of the door of his house until
the morning. For the LORD will pass through
to strike the Egyptians, and when he sees the
blood on the lintel and on the two doorposts,
the LORD will pass over the door and will not
allow the destroyer to enter your houses to strike
you. You shall observe this rite as a statute for you
and for your sons forever. And when you come to
the land that the LORD will give you, as he has
promised, you shall keep this service. And when
your children say to you, 'What do you mean by
this service?' you shall say, 'It is the sacrifice of the
LORD's Passover, for he passed over the houses
of the people of Israel in Egypt, when he struck
the Egyptians but spared our houses.'" And the
people bowed their heads and worshiped. (Exod.
12:21–27)

How do the people respond now to Moses's instructions? They
listen to him and do as he instructs them to do. Clearly Moses has
gained stature and favor in the eyes of the Israelites during the season of plagues, for now they do as he instructs, seemingly without
question. Additionally, they seem to know that Moses is God's voice
to them, for after he tells them what to do, and what is coming, they
worship God (Exod. 12:27).

It is important to note that if the people do not listen to Moses's
instructions, the firstborn in each Israelite house will be struck down
just as in the houses of the Egyptians. This time the people of Israel
are not excluded from the effects of this plague because of who they
are. This time they will be excluded only when they do as Moses
instructs them, only when they obey God's will. This indicates that
the work of transformation has not been limited to Moses. God has
also been preparing the people of Israel for this moment in time.
And, just as we have seen in the stories of Abraham and Jacob, the

response of the people to the instructions of God is an act of worship, which reveals that they do, indeed, have some measure of faith in God as their God.

The tenth plague strikes

In Exodus 12:29–32, we see that God strikes down all the first-born children in Egypt, including all the firstborn of the livestock (v. 29). This results in a great outcry from Pharaoh and all of the Egyptians, for no house is spared this death (v. 30). Pharaoh then summons Moses and Aaron in the night and tells them and the people of Israel to leave Egypt to worship God and to take everything they own with them (vv. 31–32). Pharaoh finally acknowledges in the face of extreme loss the power of God, and he finally accedes to God's will; he also asks for a blessing for himself (v. 32). It takes all that has come before and this last drastic act of God to bring Pharaoh to the point of being willing to let the people of Israel leave Egypt in the way God originally intended—with all that they possessed. Clearly, when they leave, they are not coming back.

As a result of this last plague, the Egyptians are now quite desperate for the people of Israel to depart, fearful that they all may die. The people of Israel have already done what Moses told them to do: they have asked the Egyptians for silver and gold jewelry and for clothing (Exod. 12:33, 35). As we have previously said, the people are able to plunder the Egyptians because God has given them favor in the sight of the Egyptians (Exod. 12:36). They are ready to leave Egypt.

After this, the people of Israel "journeyed from Ramses to Succoth, more than six hundred thousand men plus women and children, and their flocks and herds" (Exod. 12:37). Leaving Egypt was no easy matter and certainly could not have been done quietly or unnoticed. This was a massive effort, and it was one that Pharaoh finally agreed to.

The people of Israel lived in Egypt for 430 years, from the time when Jacob and his family first entered Egypt during the famine to the day when the Israelites—all of Jacob's descendants—left Egypt and began the exodus (Exod. 12:40–41). This is a fulfillment of God's promise to Abraham, that his descendants would be "sojourners … servants … and they will be afflicted for four hundred years. But I will bring judgment on the nation that they serve, and afterward they shall come out with great possessions" (Gen. 15:13–14). And as they leave Egypt, God is keeping watch over his people; it is "a night of watching by the LORD, to bring them out of the land of Egypt" (Exod. 12:42).

Why does the text say that God kept vigil, watching over his people? Why is this important? He was watching the fulfillment of his promise that he made to the people of Israel, through Moses, to do this very thing, to bring them out of Egypt (Exod. 3:17). The reason God appeared to Moses in the burning bush on Mount Horeb was to begin to accomplish what eventually occurred at the Passover. Moses's first encounter with God was the beginning of the exodus, the beginning of God's intentional action to bring the people of Israel out of slavery in Egypt.

The Work Is Done

At this point, the transformation work in Moses that was needed to enable him to fulfill God's command is complete. That does not mean that he will not have difficulties during the coming forty years in the wilderness. But he is now prepared to lead the people of Israel through what lies ahead. Nor does it mean that he will not make mistakes—he will. And one of those mistakes will prevent him from personally entering the promised land of Canaan. But those issues do not raise questions for us about the *genuineness* of Moses's faith at this time in his life. The fact that God is ready to work through Moses to lead the people out of Egypt means that God has determined Moses is ready for that next milestone in his life: leading the people of Israel out of the land of Egypt and getting them to the promised land of Canaan.

Lessons from the Story of Moses

One of the main themes of this chapter, which is different from the previous chapters, is that we see clearly from Moses's first experience with God that God knows exactly what he is going to do, and he knows how he is going to do it. God is obviously orchestrating events, from the various plagues to the continued hardening of Pharaoh's heart. He knows he is moving toward the Passover event. He knows *why* all that transpires *must* come to pass—to fulfill his bigger purposes. God does not just want to free the people of Israel from slavery; he wants to establish them as *his people*, and he wants to be *their God*. God knows what it is going to take to accomplish all of this. And he knows what is needed to move Moses from his initial place of resistance to doing God's will, to the place where he begins to speak confidently on God's behalf, seemingly without direct instruction from God. God knows what it will take to gradually transform Moses's simple, reluctant faith that is mired in self-doubt into faith that enables Moses to obey God's command, and eventually confidently speak for God.

What was true for Moses is true for us today. All that occurs in our daily lives is according to God's plan and purposes for us personally, and also for his broader purposes for his world. This is all rooted in God's sovereignty. From the story of Moses we learn we can trust that God knows what he is doing and that he is actively bringing about the transformation he desires in each of us through those daily circumstances. *Trusting the faithfulness and power of God to transform our faith, and thus transform us,* is the heart of the transformation process. That trust is necessary *so that* we are willing and able to surrender to God's will for our lives, *so that* we can accomplish God's purposes for our lives and for his world.

Below are some things to ponder from the story of Moses:

1. God transforms our faith, and thus transforms us, *so that* we fulfill our role and his purpose according to his perfect plan for our lives. When Moses was in Midian, the text says that he was "content" (Exod. 2:21). When God first spoke

to him on Mount Horeb, he displayed no desire to leave where he was. He gave every excuse he could possibly think of to not agree to or accept God's call on his life because of his own self-doubt. And God had only laid out in broad terms his plan and purposes for Moses. Yet he continually resisted accepting what God was telling him. What he seemed to miss is that God promised to go with him (Exod. 3:12), and that presumably meant that God was going to *enable him* to do the work God was asking him to do. Thus the work of transformation in Moses was necessary in order for him to fulfill his role in God's bigger plan. He had to learn that God was *with him*, that God would work in various ways to ensure his own plans and purposes would be fulfilled. He had to learn that God would be faithful to his word, to accomplish that which he declared he would do.

Consider: Like Moses, we all have excuses for why we resist surrendering to God's will for our lives. What excuses have you used, or are you currently using, to avoid accepting the call on your life? Are you content where you are, and thus resisting change? Do you swim in self-doubt, as Moses did? Or is it something else that is getting in the way of you trusting God to enable you to do what he is calling you to do?

2. The process of God's work of transformation in us is accomplished with great patience and gentleness. Despite all of Moses's ongoing resistance to doing what God was calling him to do, God proceeded to transform him with gentleness and patience over time. He did not reveal the details of his plan all at one time. Instead he revealed his intentions in a way that enabled Moses to grow increasingly comfortable with what God was telling him to do. Step by step he gently moved Moses into a position where he was actually doing what God wanted him to do. Moses eventually moved beyond what God told him to do and say to

speaking on behalf of God without prompting. Ultimately, despite all of Moses's resistance, God continued to deal with him with patience and gentleness, gradually proving to Moses that God was actively involved in all that was going on and that God would, indeed, bring about that which he said he would do.

Consider: Look back over your journey with God. Can you see times when his gentle and patient hand was at work guiding you forward into the call he has given you? And as he did so, can you see your trust in him growing? Can you see that you have moved over time into a place of more confidence in God's ability and willingness to enable you to do what he is calling you to do? If not, what is hindering your willingness to trust God?

3. God transforms our faith, and therefore transforms us, in order to demolish strongholds in our lives. He does this by building our belief, trust, and acceptance of him over time. For Moses, the main stronghold in his life was actually a lack of trust that God would enable him to do what God was calling him to do. That lack of trust manifested itself as self-doubt: he had no confidence in his own ability to do what God was asking him to do. Most often strongholds are considered to be things such as anger or addictions. In reality, a stronghold is anything that prevents us from being all that God has created us to be and from doing all that he calls us to do. Thus, strongholds work to prevent us from fulfilling God's plan and purpose for our lives. God's transformation process serves to break those strongholds by developing and strengthening our faith in God *as God*, and he uses a variety of means and techniques to do so in each of us. There is nothing that is not at God's disposal to accomplish this transforming work. Only God, through the power of the Holy Spirit, can accomplish this work of transformation.

Consider: What might be currently interfering with your willingness to trust God to the point of obedience? What strongholds might be at work keeping you from surrendering fully to God's will for your life? How might God be working right now to transform your faith *so that* you are able to trust him as your God and obey his will for your life?

CHAPTER 6
Saul

In this chapter, we will examine the story of Saul as found in the book of 1 Samuel 8–31. Samuel is the last judge over Israel, so a great deal of time has passed since Moses led the people of Israel to the Promised Land. As a prophet, Samuel walked in the ways of God and obeyed his statutes and commandments throughout his life. When Samuel was old, he made his two sons, Joel and Abijah, judges over Israel (1 Sam. 8:1–2). However, his sons did not walk in his ways (i.e., in the ways of God), but instead took bribes and perverted justice. In response, all the elders gathered together and demanded that Samuel appoint a king to judge them like all the nations—in place of Samuel's two sons (1 Sam. 8:3–5).

God responds to the desire of the people to have a king over them "like all the nations" (1 Sam. 8:5) by selecting a young man, Saul, to be king.[1] Outwardly he looks to be a perfect choice—he is tall and good-looking, which sets him apart from all the people (1 Sam. 9:2, 10:24). As Saul's story unfolds, his words and actions appear to indicate that God became real for him, to some degree, early in life. He continually tries to say and do what he thinks both Samuel and, more importantly, God would accept as expressions of genuine faith. There seems to be in young Saul a measure of humility,

---

[1] See 1 Samuel 9 for the details on how Saul is identified as God's choice to be king over Israel.

honest concern for others, and reluctance to function in a prominent role, as can be seen in the following episodes from young Saul's life:

- One day Saul does as his father asks and goes with another young man to look for lost donkeys. This takes more time than expected, and three days later, not having found the donkeys, he expresses his concern that his father will be worried because they have not yet returned home (1 Sam. 9:3–5).
- When Samuel comes to announce Saul as king publicly, he is hiding "in the baggage" (1 Sam. 10:22).
- Even after being anointed king by Samuel, Saul is again working in his father's fields when news arrives about the Philistine attack on Jabesh (1 Sam. 11:5).

As the story unfolds, we will see that Saul moves away from this humility, becoming inward-directed and self-centered. God continually seeks to become real to him. Yet to the very end, Saul is self-centered, seeking his own welfare, not wanting to be abused by his enemies. Nothing that Saul does or says reveals that his *heart* is being transformed. Thus, God's judgment will be carried out against him.

Background

It is interesting to note from the outset that the people of Israel feel that they have good reason to demand that Samuel appoint a king over them rather than leaving his two sons as judges. They already know of the evil of Samuel's sons, who are taking bribes and perverting justice (1 Sam. 8:3). Therefore, the people do not want to give them additional authority as judges over them.

However, their demand for a king displeases Samuel, so he prays to the LORD (1 Sam. 8:6). And God responds to Samuel's prayer:

> And the LORD said to Samuel, "Obey the voice of the people in all that they say to you, for they have not rejected you, but they have rejected

me from being king over them. According to all the deeds that they have done, from the day I brought them up out of Egypt even to this day, forsaking me and serving other gods, so they are also doing to you. Now then, obey their voice; only you shall solemnly warn them and show them the ways of the king who shall reign over them." (1 Sam. 8:7–9)

God's response to Samuel's displeasure is to tell him that this demand for a king is no different from the people's behavior ever since they entered the Promised Land. Their demand does not reflect upon Samuel's behavior, but instead is a clear indication of their attitude toward God: they do not want him as king over them. Rather, they desire to have a person be their king so that they might be like all the other nations (1 Sam. 8:5). God knew this day was coming, having told Moses about it: "When you come to the land that the LORD your God is giving you, and you possess it and dwell in it and then say, 'I will set a king over me, like all the nations that are around me,' you may indeed set a king over you whom the LORD your God will choose" (Deut. 17:14–15). This clearly explains why God agrees now to choose a king to rule over them; he previously said that he would do so. However, he instructs Samuel to warn people of the consequences of rebelling against God by rejecting him as king over them:

So Samuel told all the words of the LORD to the people who were asking for a king from him. He said, "These will be the ways of the king who will reign over you: he will take your sons and appoint them to his chariots and to be his horsemen and to run before his chariots. And he will appoint for himself commanders of thousands and commanders of fifties, and some to plow his ground and to reap his harvest, and to make his implements of war and the equipment of his chariots.

He will take your daughters to be perfumers and cooks and bakers. He will take the best of your fields and vineyards and olive orchards and give them to his servants. He will take the tenth of your grain and of your vineyards and give it to his officers and to his servants. He will take your male servants and female servants and the best of your young men and your donkeys, and put them to his work. He will take the tenth of your flocks, and you shall be his slaves. And in that day you will cry out because of your king, whom you have chosen for yourselves, but the LORD will not answer you in that day." (1 Sam. 8:10–18)

God's declaration about what a human king will do is rather clear: he will *take from the people*. This warning about the future actions of a king stands in stark contrast to how Samuel conducted himself as judge over Israel. He tries to point this out to the people in 1 Samuel 12 during his final words to them, stating that *he* has taken nothing from the people (vv. 3–5). However, the people refuse to heed God's warning and continue to demand that Samuel appoint a king over them. They are determined to be like the other nations; they want a king that will serve as judge and who will lead them in battle. Samuel inquires of God, who responds, "Obey their voice and make them a king" (1 Sam. 8:19–22). The sin here is that, in wanting to be like the other nations, the people are rejecting God *as their God*. God knows what is going to happen because of this choice, yet he remains in control of the process. Samuel is distressed because he knows that this is a sign of further rebellion by the people of Israel against God. And in their rebellion and sin, they do not take God's warnings seriously. They are insistent on having a king rule over them.

Saul Chosen to Be King

At this point, Saul is introduced in the story in 1 Samuel, chapter 9:

> There was a man of Benjamin whose name
> was Kish, the son of Abiel, son of Zeror, son of
> Becorath, son of Aphiah, a Benjaminite, a man of
> wealth. And he had a son whose name was Saul,
> a handsome young man. There was not a man
> among the people of Israel more handsome than
> he. From his shoulders upward, he was taller than
> any of the people. (1 Sam. 9:1–2)

From this initial description, two things become apparent about Saul. First is that he comes from a wealthy family. Second, as we have previously mentioned, he is tall and good-looking; he looks just like one would expect a king to look. With this simple introduction, the story then shifts to the process God uses to reveal that Saul will be king.

Next we read the story about his father's lost donkeys (1 Sam. 9:3–5). When Saul is ready to return home, not having found the donkeys, his servant suggests instead that they visit the "man of God" who lives nearby to seek his guidance before giving up and returning home (v. 6). Saul agrees to do so (vv. 7–10).

So, they walk up the hill to the nearby town. As they enter the town, they see Samuel coming out toward them on his way up to the high place (vv. 11–14). The day before, God had revealed to Samuel what would happen this day, telling him to anoint Saul to be prince over Israel for the purpose of saving God's people from the Philistines (vv. 15–16). Now, as Saul approaches, God tells Samuel, "Here is the man of whom I spoke to you! He it is who shall restrain my people" (v. 17). Saul and Samuel then speak with each other:

> Then Saul approached Samuel in the gate and
> said, "Tell me where is the house of the seer?"
> Samuel answered Saul, "I am the seer. Go up

before me to the high place, for today you shall eat with me, and in the morning I will let you go and will tell you all that is on your mind. As for your donkeys that were lost three days ago, do not set your mind on them, for they have been found. And for whom is all that is desirable in Israel? Is it not for you and for all your father's house?" Saul answered, "Am I not a Benjaminite, from the least of the tribes of Israel? And is not my clan the humblest of all the clans of the tribe of Benjamin? Why then have you spoken to me in this way?" (1 Sam. 9:18–21)

It is interesting to note the flow of the exchange between Samuel and Saul. Samuel has the complete picture given to him by God, so he does not need to ask Saul why he and his companion are seeking him. Instead, he immediately invites them to eat with him at the feast that is occurring, intending that they spend the night. Then Samuel says that in the morning he will address their concerns (v. 19). All of this occurs before he tells Saul that his father's donkeys have been found.

Then Samuel asks a provocative question that finally elicits a response from Saul: "And for whom is all that is desirable in Israel? Is it not for you and for all your father's house?" (v. 20). The question gets Saul's attention, who just a moment before must have been relaxed, anticipating an excellent meal and a good night's sleep. Confused, Saul asks Samuel why he would say such a thing to him, given that he is from the humblest clan of the smallest tribe in Israel (v. 21). This reveals the level of humility in Saul at this time.

As further evidence that Samuel knew in advance of Saul's visit, he has already set aside a select portion of the meal, the whole leg of lamb, just for Saul. So they eat together. Then Saul and his servant spend the night with Samuel (1 Sam. 9:23–24).

Samuel awakens Saul early the next morning. As he accompanies Saul and his servant to the outskirts of the city, he instructs Saul to tell the servant to go ahead of them. This creates an opportunity for Samuel to make known to Saul the word of God (v. 27). We then read:

> Then Samuel took a flask of oil and poured it on his head and kissed him and said, "Has not the LORD anointed you to be prince over his people Israel? And you shall reign over the people of the LORD and you will save them from the hand of their surrounding enemies. And this shall be the sign to you that the LORD has anointed you to be prince over his heritage. When you depart from me today, you will meet two men by Rachel's tomb in the territory of Benjamin at Zelzah, and they will say to you, 'The donkeys that you went to seek are found, and now your father has ceased to care about the donkeys and is anxious about you, saying, "What shall I do about my son?"' Then you shall go on from there farther and come to the oak of Tabor. Three men going up to God at Bethel will meet you there, one carrying three young goats, another carrying three loaves of bread, and another carrying a skin of wine. And they will greet you and give you two loaves of bread, which you shall accept from their hand. After that you shall come to Gibeath-elohim, where there is a garrison of the Philistines. And there, as soon as you come to the city, you will meet a group of prophets coming down from the high place with harp, tambourine, flute, and lyre before them, prophesying. Then the Spirit of the LORD will rush upon you, and you will prophesy with them and be turned into another man. Now when these signs meet you, do what your hand finds to do, for God is with you." (1 Sam. 10:1–7)

This entire sequence of events is exceedingly stimulating and describes yet another way in which God undertakes the work of transformation in individuals. He first removes Saul from his comfort zone at home with his family and sends him out to unknown parts. Saul never achieves the purpose of his trip—to find the lost donkeys. But God uses Saul's servant to make sure that he reaches God's desired destination for him: to meet Samuel. Once there, while appearing perfectly relaxed, Samuel makes a series of statements to Saul designed to get his attention. He first tells him that his father's donkeys are safe; then to pique his interest, he asks Saul a very provocative question, which he does not answer.

The next morning, after anointing Saul's head with oil, Samuel kisses him and then asks him another provocative question, "Has not the LORD anointed you to be prince over his people Israel? And you shall reign over the people of the LORD and you will save them from the hand of their surrounding enemies" (1 Sam. 10:1). Samuel provides no further explanation; he merely moves on to tell Saul what will happen during his journey home. Those events shall be the sign that the LORD has anointed him to be prince over his people (1 Sam. 10:2–6).

The question naturally arises, "Why did God choose this method to prepare Saul to be king?" We have seen in previous chapters that God told some individuals he was calling for his purposes what was expected of them, taking the time to convince the individual that what God was saying was true. In other instances, God patiently waited up to forty years for Abraham or Moses to be ready to fulfill their calling. Here, God tells Samuel to privately anoint Saul and tell him that, if he doubts that God has commanded Samuel's actions, he should wait to see if the three events about which he tells Saul actually do occur on his way home. On the surface, it appears that time is of the essence; apparently God cannot wait whatever time it might take to convince Saul by other more time-consuming means. Israel's enemies, the Philistines, are gathering to engage in battle against them. However, we have to ask, does God need Saul to defeat the Philistines?

Notice that Saul (according to the text) has not said anything since early the night before. Since that time, it seems Saul has been silent about what Samuel has said, and compliant, doing whatever Samuel instructs him to do. Why does God give Saul evidence that Samuel is indeed a prophet (1 Sam. 9:19–20)? It seems this is what Saul needs to get him to do as Samuel tells him to do. Samuel gives Saul direct, straightforward instructions that he never questions. This is an important example of how God uses various means to accomplish the transformation of our faith, depending upon the circumstances and personality of each individual. Even though his approach varies with Saul from what we have seen in previous chapters, God continues to do the work of transformation in a kind and loving manner. At this point, Saul is compliant and trusting; he does what is expected of him. But is compliance and trust real evidence that the work of transformation is actually occurring in Saul's life?

The interaction between Samuel and Saul ends as Samuel sends him on his way:

> "Then go down before me to Gilgal. And behold, I am coming down to you to offer burnt offerings and to sacrifice peace offerings. Seven days you shall wait, until I come to you and show you what you shall do."
>
> When he turned his back to leave Samuel, God gave him another heart. And all these signs came to pass that day. (1 Sam. 10:8–9)

Here is a deceptively short, yet critical, text in the entire story of Saul. On the surface, Samuel instructs him to go on ahead to Gilgal and to wait for him there, presumably so that Samuel can undertake the public activities appropriate for appointing Saul as king, which would include making different types of sacrifices. So he tells Saul to wait seven days for him there. Based on Saul's compliant nature exhibited so far, there is no reason to believe that this text contains anything more than a simple continuation of the story; we might easily expect Saul to simply comply with Samuel's instructions.

However, we will see that this is not so. Therefore, this becomes a pivotal point in the story of Saul.

Also, upon closer examination, verse 9 reveals a significant change in Saul's story. It says that when Saul turned his back to leave Samuel, God gave him another heart. We have to ask, what kind of heart did God give him? This text holds the key to understanding what will transpire throughout the rest of Saul's story. We will see that eventually God rejects him and removes him as king over Israel. Therefore, as we continue with the story of Saul, it will be essential to return to the question "Where is God in this process of selecting him as king?" and to further ask, "Did God's work of transformation fail with Saul?" The key to answering these questions lies in the text above. We will return to it later to give these questions further consideration.

We also see in verse 9 that, as Saul and his servant approach Gilgal, all that Samuel told him would occur, has occurred. This fact teaches Saul that he can trust what Samuel says and that Samuel does, indeed, speak on behalf of God. Seeing Samuel as a prophet will play an important part in how Saul relates to Samuel in the future.

In the next significant passage, 1 Samuel 10:17–24, we see that the process for choosing a king is done by lot in a public forum. Samuel calls the people together at Mizpah (v. 17) and instructs them to present themselves before the LORD by their tribes (v. 19). The tribe of Benjamin is chosen by lot, then the clan of the Matrites; and finally Saul, the son of Kish, is chosen by lot (v. 21). When they look for Saul, they cannot find him until God reveals that he is hiding among the baggage (v. 22). Then as he stands among the people, he is found to be head and shoulders taller than any of the people (v. 23). Samuel then says, "Do you see him whom the LORD has chosen? There is none like him among all the people." And with that, the people accept Saul as king by declaring, "Long live the king!" (v. 24).

We have to ask, why is Saul hiding? This does seem to be questionable behavior. Is it an indication of the humility that we have previously seen; is he reluctant to become king? Or does it indicate something altogether different? Things were happening just as Samuel had said they would, so why does he feel compelled to hide?

We have no immediate answers to these questions from the text, but the best evidence is that his behavior is, indeed, an act of humility.

Next, we read in 1 Samuel 10:25–27 that Samuel tells the people about "the rights and duties of the kingship," and he "wrote them in a book." Then he instructs the people to return to their homes (v. 25). Saul also goes back to his home in Gibeah (v. 26). He is accompanied by "men of valor whose hearts God had touched" (v. 26); apparently these men supported Saul as king. However, other men question his leadership capability and despise him; yet Saul maintains his peace (v. 27). It seems Saul shows no visible reaction to the disrespect shown him by those who question his leadership capabilities. Notice, however, that he also shows no visible response to being accompanied by men of valor who do not question his ability to lead. Thus, it is appropriate to ask why Saul does not react in either instance. We could reasonably think that being chosen king would elicit some kind of emotional response from Saul, but we see none. This text does not provide an answer to that question. But, based on what we have already seen, it is reasonable to conclude that his lack of response is likely rooted in humility.

Saul Made King

Our story continues in 1 Samuel 11:1–5. Soon after Saul is chosen to be king of the Israelites, the Ammonites come and besiege Jabesh-gilead. The men of Jabesh try to make a treaty with them in order to avoid destruction by becoming their servants (v. 1). However, the leader of the Ammonites responds to their request, saying that they will do so only if they are allowed to gouge out all the men's right eyes in order to bring disgrace on all Israel (v. 2). The elders ask for seven days' respite in order to send messengers throughout Israel to determine who might come to save them. If no one comes, they will agree to the conditions of the treaty (v. 3). When the messengers come with this news to Saul's town of Gibeah, all the people are distressed, and they weep (v. 4).

At the same time that the messengers arrive in Gibeah, Saul is coming in from the field with the oxen. Seeing the people weeping, he asks what has happened (v. 5). The people tell him the news about the Ammonite siege and potential treaty (v. 5). We then see how Saul responds to this threat:

> And the Spirit of God rushed upon Saul when he heard these words, and his anger was greatly kindled. He took a yoke of oxen and cut them in pieces and sent them throughout all the territory of Israel by the hand of the messengers, saying, "Whoever does not come out after Saul and Samuel, so shall it be done to his oxen!" Then the dread of the LORD fell upon the people, and they came out as one man. When he mustered them at Bezek, the people of Israel were three hundred thousand, and the men of Judah thirty thousand. And they said to the messengers who had come, "Thus shall you say to the men of Jabesh-gilead: 'Tomorrow, by the time the sun is hot, you shall have salvation.'" When the messengers came and told the men of Jabesh, they were glad. Therefore the men of Jabesh said, "Tomorrow we will give ourselves up to you, and you may do to us whatever seems good to you." And the next day Saul put the people in three companies. And they came into the midst of the camp in the morning watch and struck down the Ammonites until the heat of the day. And those who survived were scattered, so that no two of them were left together. (1 Sam. 11:6–11)

Remember that Saul has recently returned home from Gilgal, where he was chosen to be king. From this text we can see that he has resumed his normal activities, working in his father's fields. Life has returned to normal for Saul. Then, when news comes of the crisis at Jabesh, the text says that his anger erupts when "the Spirit of God rushed upon" him (v. 6), which moves Saul to swift and decisive action. His actions result in a victory for Israel over the Ammonites. The subsequent comments recorded in 1 Samuel 11:12–13 emphasize this point: "Then the people said to Samuel, 'Who is it that said, "Shall Saul reign over us?" Bring the men, that we may put them to death.' But Saul said, 'Not a man shall be put to death this day, for today the LORD has worked salvation in Israel.'"

Notice that this is the first time we see Saul openly acknowledge God. We have no previous indication that he has ever done so through acts of worship or by what he has said. Here he acknowledges God, not only by what he says but also by the fact that he is not willing to take revenge upon those who oppose him as king. This is a critical moment in Saul's story, this acknowledgement of God's role in the victory just achieved. It is further emphasized by what occurs next:

> Then Samuel said to the people, "Come, let us go to Gilgal and there renew the kingdom." So all the people went to Gilgal, and there they made Saul king before the LORD in Gilgal. There they sacrificed peace offerings before the LORD, and there Saul and all the men of Israel rejoiced greatly. (1 Sam. 11:14–15)

Let's look at these events from a broader context. Previously while at Gilgal, Saul was chosen to be king by lot in front of all the people of Israel, who then proclaimed, "Long live the king!" (1 Sam. 10:24). Samuel took time to explain to the people the rules and duties of kingship. Then he immediately sent them home without doing anything further.

Now, in light of the threat to the Israelites in Jabesh-gilead, Saul is finally willing to lead the fight against the Ammonites, and then lead the people back to Gilgal to "renew the kingdom" (v. 14). It is at this time that the people finally make Saul king of Israel, before the LORD, sacrificing peace offerings; and everyone greatly rejoices (v. 15).

Several questions naturally arise at this point: Why is Saul *now* made king? Why was this not done when he was first revealed as God's choice to be king? Has something different occurred that reveals Samuel is now prepared to complete the process of making Saul king? If so, what has changed?

From this last series of texts, it appears that transformation of Saul's faith has begun, so that he is now able to say, "For today the LORD has worked salvation in Israel" (v. 13). As we have noted, this is his first acknowledgment of any kind that God is real to him. It appears he believes God has been at work to bring victory in the conflict with the Ammonites. What we don't know is if he truly believes in his heart what he has said or if his words reflect a cultural way of speaking and thinking. After all, the Israelites are the people of God; they have a history of centering daily life around their religious beliefs. So it would not be unusual for someone like Saul to attribute the outcome of a battle to God.

Samuel seems to agree that God has been involved in this victory, which can be seen in the following passage:

> And he said to them, "The LORD is witness, who appointed Moses and Aaron and brought your fathers up out of the land of Egypt. Now therefore stand still that I may plead with you before the LORD concerning all the righteous deeds of the LORD that he performed for you and for your fathers." (1 Sam. 12:6–7)

Samuel recounts what God has done for the people of Israel since he called Moses to lead the people out of Egypt. But then he makes a dramatic shift to deliver a warning:

> "And when you saw that Nahash the king of the Ammonites came against you, you said to me, 'No, but a king shall reign over us,' when the LORD your God was your king. And now behold the king whom you have chosen, for

whom you have asked; behold, the LORD has
set a king over you. If you will fear the LORD
and serve him and obey his voice and not rebel
against the commandment of the LORD, and if
both you and the king who reigns over you will
follow the LORD your God, it will be well. But
if you will not obey the voice of the LORD, but
rebel against the commandment of the LORD,
then the hand of the LORD will be against you
and your king." (1 Sam. 12:12–15)

The people are excited that they finally have a king over them
(they are finally like all the other nations around them), especially
following Saul's initial victory over the Ammonites. However, Samuel
tries to remind them that whether a judge or a king rules over them,
the essential element in either situation is that they must follow God:
only if both they and their king follow the LORD their God, and not
"rebel against the commandment of the LORD," will it go well for
them (v. 14). Moreover, if they do not follow in God's ways, it will
not go well for them (v. 15). As king, Saul will play an important role
in whether things go well or badly for the people of Israel. Samuel is
very clear that even though there is now a king in Israel, God is still
the sovereign one.

Samuel continues to admonish the people:

"Do not be afraid; you have done all this evil.
Yet do not turn aside from following the LORD,
but serve the LORD with all your heart. And
do not turn aside after empty things that cannot profit or deliver, for they are empty. For the
LORD will not forsake his people, for his great
name's sake, because it has pleased the LORD to
make you a people for himself. Moreover, as for
me, far be it from me that I should sin against
the LORD by ceasing to pray for you, and I will
instruct you in the good and the right way. Only

fear the LORD and serve him faithfully with all your heart. For consider what great things he has done for you. But if you still do wickedly, you shall be swept away, both you and your king." (1 Sam. 12:20–25)

These are grave and severe warnings to deliver at a coronation celebration. It should be a joyous and festive occasion; indeed, we've just seen that when Saul was made king, he and all the people "rejoiced greatly" (1 Sam. 11:15). So, we must ask, did Samuel not feel the same way as the people? If not, why not? We've previously said that Saul's comments about the LORD bringing deliverance to Israel from the Ammonites seems to indicate that God has become real for Saul to some degree. But it seems Samuel, being a prophet, perhaps knows that Saul's faith is not what it appears to be. This may be the reason he makes an emphatic point about the importance of the people *and the king* following God.

Saul Tested

We now pick up Saul's story in 1 Samuel, chapter 13. Remember that Samuel instructed Saul to go to Gilgal and wait seven days for him (see 1 Sam. 10:8):

[Saul] waited seven days, the time appointed by Samuel. But Samuel did not come to Gilgal, and the people were scattering from him. So Saul said, "Bring the burnt offering here to me, and the peace offerings." And he offered the burnt offering. As soon as he had finished offering the burnt offering, behold, Samuel came. And Saul went out to meet him and greet him. Samuel said, "What have you done?" And Saul said, "When I saw that the people were scattering from me, and that you did not come within the days appointed, and that the Philistines had mustered at Michmash, I said, 'Now the Philistines will come against me at Gilgal, and I have not sought the favor of the LORD.' So I forced myself, and offered the burnt offering." And Samuel said to Saul, "You have done foolishly. You have not kept the command of the LORD your God, with which he commanded you. For then the LORD would have established your kingdom over Israel forever. But now your kingdom shall not continue. The LORD has sought out a man after his own heart, and the LORD has commanded him to be prince over his people, because you have not kept what the LORD commanded you." (1 Sam. 13:8–14)

This is the watershed moment in the story of Saul. As previously instructed by Samuel, Saul waits seven days for him at Gilgal, because Samuel had said *he* would offer sacrifices and offerings to God (1 Sam. 10:8). Saul does wait seven days. But now, when Saul realizes the Philistines are gathering for an attack at Michmash, which is causing the people to flee to places of safety (1 Sam. 13:5–7), Saul decides he needs to seek the LORD's favor (v. 12) before taking any action against the Philistines. Even though Samuel instructed him to wait for him, and Samuel has not yet arrived, Saul proceeds to offer the burnt offerings and sacrifices on his own, rather than having a priest do so in compliance with God's laws.[2] At that very moment, Samuel appears on the scene as if waiting nearby to see how Saul will react to his late arrival.

Upon arriving, Samuel immediately rebukes Saul for what he has done, causing Saul to attempt to defend his actions by first blaming the people and then Samuel himself. He tries to explain that the situation

---

[2] God selects who may offer sacrifices to him. He appointed the descendants of Aaron to be his priests; thus, their authority came from God (Num. 3). At times God told others to offer sacrifices, so they too operated under *the order of God.* Saul, however, decided on his own to make an offering to God and, as a result, was condemned for it.

became so bad that he finally had to *force himself* to offer the burnt offerings because he had not yet "sought the favor of the LORD" (v. 12). Saul is working hard to justify his actions. We might think that Saul has done a good thing, realizing that he cannot go up against the Philistine army without seeking God's favor. But this may not be the case.

Not persuaded in the least by Saul's attempts at self-justification, Samuel responds that Saul has acted foolishly. He further states that the consequence of his foolish actions, which were against the commandment of God, is that his kingdom will not continue. God has already selected a replacement; "a man after his own heart" (v. 14). From the beginning, Samuel makes very clear the importance of the people *and the king* following God's commands. By offering sacrifices himself, Saul has broken God's law about who has the authority to offer sacrifices. Saul's faith has been tested, and he has failed.

Appearance of Transformation

And now we must question, has God really undertaken the work of transformation in Saul and it has failed (i.e., has not taken root in Saul), or has the true work of transformation never really begun in him? The answer to this question is exceedingly significant for understanding God's process of transforming faith in people. If God has indeed begun the work of transformation in Saul and it has failed, then what does that failure say about God and his sovereignty? Can God fail at anything he undertakes? If so, is God truly God? The answer is obvious: God cannot and does not fail at anything that he undertakes. Therefore, we must conclude that true work of transformation in Saul has not really begun.

Given that, the question then is why does the work of transformation *appear* to have begun in Saul in these texts from 1 Samuel? For example:

- Samuel took a flask of oil and poured it on his (Saul's) head and kissed him and said, "Has not the LORD anointed you to be prince over his people Israel?" (10:1)

- When he (Saul) turned his back to leave Samuel, God gave him another heart. And all these signs came to pass that day. (10:9)
- And the Spirit of God rushed upon Saul when he heard these words, and his anger was greatly kindled. (11:6)
- But Saul said, "Not a man shall be put to death this day, for today the LORD has worked salvation in Israel." (11:13)

Doesn't the pattern of the story of Saul to this point, as revealed in these verses, give evidence of ongoing work of transformation in Saul? On initial examination, the answer appears to be *yes*. But in light of what occurred in the previous text, that God has rejected Saul for his actions and has selected another to be king, "a man after his own heart" (1 Sam. 13:14), the answer cannot be *yes*. Therefore, let's look again at these four texts to discover what they reveal about the work of transformation in Saul.

In 1 Samuel 10:1, the key word to focus on is the word *prince*. Since most Christians are generally familiar with the story of Saul, it would not be unlikely for them to overlook the significance of the difference between a prince and a king. A *prince* has not yet *inherited* the throne, but is waiting to do so. And until that happens, a grave failure of some kind could result in the prince being stripped of position and status, as we see in the case of Saul. Thus, merely becoming a prince (or in our case, profess to be a Christian) is not a guarantee that one will receive their inheritance. As Samuel's comments in 1 Samuel 13:14 reveal, God is very interested in the status of our *hearts*. And it seems Saul's heart is not committed to following God's commandments. Rather he is willing to do what he thinks needs to be done, even if his action is not in accordance with God's commands.

In 1 Samuel 10:9, the key phrase to focus on is "another heart." (Think a "different" heart.) If read with "New Testament eyes," it would not be unlikely for someone to overlook the significance between "another heart" and "a new heart." From that perspective, we could easily conclude that this verse indicates that Saul experienced conversion at that moment in time. Here, however, the use of "another heart" is not being used in a moral or spiritual sense as "a new heart" would be used. Further, it does not indicate that Saul received "a new spirit" as would have been the case in conversion. Instead, "another heart" is used in a civil sense, a right heart—a heart fit for governing the people of Israel—one filled with wisdom, prudence, strength, and courage to protect and defend the people against their enemies. So the other heart God gave Saul was one of governance.

In light of the preceding information, we need to ask a question concerning 1 Samuel 11:6, whether the Spirit of God can and does move on individuals who have not been converted—and therefore are not being transformed by God. We only need to think back to the stories of Abraham or Moses to know that the answer to that question is *yes*. And now, it seems we see the same situation in Saul.

Thus, the critical lesson to learn here is that an individual can *appear* to have experienced conversion, hence beginning the process of transformation in their life, without actually having done so. The genuineness of one's conversion, whether the process of transformation is actually occurring, may not be evident from a single event or statement at one point in time. However, evidence of genuine transformation will become apparent over time in the way the person lives daily life, in a variety of situations, which will reveal that the transformation is, indeed, genuine.

Saul's True Heart Revealed

The evidence of this truth in Saul is demonstrated by what happens next:

> Samuel arose and went up from Gilgal. The rest of the people went up after Saul to meet the army; they went up from Gilgal to Gibeah of Benjamin.
>
> And Saul numbered the people who were present with him, about six hundred men. And Saul and Jonathan his son and the people

who were present with them stayed in Geba of Benjamin, but the Philistines encamped in Michmash. (1 Sam. 13:15–16)

Samuel has just told Saul that he has acted foolishly by not following the law of the LORD; as a result, his reign will not continue. Saul does not react to this news as we might expect. He demonstrates no shame or guilt, no contrition or repentance or seeking forgiveness for having broken God's laws. Instead, he allows Samuel to depart and then turns to count the number of people with him. Counting the number of people is a sign that he is relying on the "strength of numbers" rather than on God himself to protect him and fight the battle. This is clear evidence that God is not real for Saul. His actions reflect his true belief, that whatever God says or does can have little or no real impact on him or his kingdom. So long as the people follow him, as long as he has sufficient military might behind him, he will continue to rule over them as their king.

Soon after that, Saul's son Jonathan decides to spy on the Philistine garrison without telling his father. None of the people with Saul know that Jonathan has left the encampment. Within the mountain pass, by which Jonathan sought to go over to the Philistine garrison, are two rocky crags. What is lacking in Saul's faith is emphasized by the contrast of Jonathan's actions:

> Jonathan said to the young man who carried his armor, "Come, let us go over to the garrison of these uncircumcised. It may be that the LORD will work for us, for nothing can hinder the LORD from saving by many or by few." And his armor-bearer said to him, "Do all that is in your heart. Do as you wish. Behold, I am with you heart and soul." Then Jonathan said, "Behold, we will cross over to the men, and we will show ourselves to them. If they say to us, 'Wait until we come to you,' then we will stand still in our place, and we will not go up to them. But if they

say, 'Come up to us,' then we will go up, for the LORD has given them into our hand. And this shall be the sign to us." So both of them showed themselves to the garrison of the Philistines. And the Philistines said, "Look, Hebrews are coming out of the holes where they have hidden themselves." And the men of the garrison hailed Jonathan and his armor-bearer and said, "Come up to us, and we will show you a thing." And Jonathan said to his armor-bearer, "Come up after me, for the LORD has given them into the hand of Israel." (1 Sam. 14:6–12)

In distinct contrast to the attitude of Saul reflected in the previous texts, it is clear by Jonathan's remarks that God is real for him. He entrusts his life to God in going up against the Philistine garrison. His trust is expressed in his simple declaration that "nothing can hinder the LORD from saving by many or by a few" (v. 6). In confronting the Philistines, Jonathan does not depend upon his strength or that of the army of Israel. Instead, he seeks to know the will of God and trusts that it will be revealed to him based on how the sentries in the Philistine garrison respond when they see Jonathan and his armor-bearer appear. While Saul counts the number of people who are with him, Jonathan goes forth seeking after the will of God.

Notice that in response to Jonathan's act of genuine faith and trust, God creates a panic among the Philistines. When Saul and the people take note of what is happening, they finally get motivated to join in the action:

So Saul said to Ahijah, "Bring the ark of God here." For the ark of God went at that time with the people of Israel. Now while Saul was talking to the priest, the tumult in the camp of the Philistines increased more and more. So Saul said to the priest, "Withdraw your hand." Then Saul and all the people who were with him rallied and went into the battle. And behold, every Philistine's sword was against his fellow, and there was very great confusion. Now the Hebrews who had been with the Philistines before that time and who had gone up with them into the camp, even they also turned to be with the Israelites who were with Saul and Jonathan. Likewise, when all the men of Israel who had hidden themselves in the hill country of Ephraim heard that the Philistines were fleeing, they too followed hard after them in the battle. So the LORD saved Israel that day. And the battle passed beyond Beth-aven. (1 Sam. 14:18–23)

The flow of this text reveals a great deal about Saul. Before he realizes what is happening in the camp of the Philistines, Saul is preparing to go into battle with the ark of God carried before the people. Once he hears the growing confusion in the Philistines' camp, he no longer feels the need for God's participation in the battle. In addition to Saul and the people with him, even people who had previously surrendered to the Philistines, or had been in hiding from them, came forth to join in the battle with Israel (vv. 21–22). The text makes clear that Saul and the people contribute too little too late to the victory. Instead, it is God who saves Israel from the Philistines that day.

As the story continues, it becomes apparent that Saul is oblivious to what was happening. The battle was hard that day, so Saul laid an oath on the people, forbidding them to eat food until the evening, and "I am avenged on my enemies" (1 Sam. 14:24). So, none of the people eat any food that day. When they come to the forest, honey is found on the ground; but no one tastes it because of the oath. However, Jonathan, not having heard his father charge the people to not eat, puts out the tip of his staff, dips it in the honeycomb, and tastes it (vv. 26–27). Then someone tells him about the oath. Seeing that the people are faint from the lack of eating, Jonathan says:

> "My father has troubled the land. See how my eyes have become bright because I tasted a little

of this honey. How much better if the people had eaten freely today of the spoil of their enemies that they found. For now, the defeat among the Philistines has not been great." (1 Sam. 14:29–30)

Notice that the critical priority from Saul's perspective is that "I am avenged on my enemies" (v. 24). Even though he had been given another heart by God, a heart needed to serve as king, Saul is more interested in defeating his enemies than in the condition of those who serve under his leadership. Again, by contrast, Jonathan is more concerned about the people, even if it means that he speaks out against his father. He goes on to conclude that because the people have not been allowed to eat that day, the victory is not as big as it could have been (v. 30).

The real condition of Saul's heart is disclosed further in the next passage:

They struck down the Philistines that day from Michmash to Aijalon. And the people were very faint. The people pounced on the spoil and took sheep and oxen and calves and slaughtered them on the ground. And the people ate them with the blood. Then they told Saul, "Behold, the people are sinning against the LORD by eating with the blood." And he said, "You have dealt treacherously; roll a great stone to me here." And Saul said, "Disperse yourselves among the people and say to them, 'Let every man bring his ox or his sheep and slaughter them here and eat, and do not sin against the LORD by eating with the blood.'" So every one of the people brought his ox with him that night and they slaughtered them there. And Saul built an altar to the LORD; it was the first altar that he built to the LORD. (1 Sam. 14:31–35)

The foolishness of Saul's vow ultimately causes the people to sin. Once the big victory is over, the people are so famished from not having eaten all day that they quickly slaughter the animals from the spoils of war and eat the meat that still contains blood.[3] Their hunger is so great that they forget the commandments of God. When notified of the people's actions, Saul accuses the people of acting "treacherously" (v. 33), thereby failing to recognize that it was *his* *oath* that caused the people to act in this way. Thus, without showing any remorse, he instructs them on how to correct the error (v. 34). Then, as if that resolves the problem entirely, the text says that Saul builds an altar to the LORD (v. 35). Without recognizing his responsibility in what has just transpired, Saul acts as if this act of worship makes everything all right once again.

Saul's Real Concern

But we will see that everything is not all right, as the story continues:

> Then Saul said, "Let us go down after the Philistines by night and plunder them until the morning light; let us not leave a man of them." And they said, "Do whatever seems good to you." But the priest said, "Let us draw near to God here." And Saul inquired of God, "Shall I go down after the Philistines? Will you give them into the hand of Israel?" But he did not answer him that day. (1 Sam. 14:36–37)

---

[3] The LORD had previously instructed Moses about this issue of eating blood: "For every person who eats of the fat of an animal of which a food offering may be made to the LORD shall be cut off from his people. Moreover, you shall eat no blood whatever, whether of fowl or of animal, in any of your dwelling places. Whoever eats any blood, that person shall be cut off from his people" (Lev. 7:25–27).

Finally, for the first time, Saul inquires of the LORD, but he receives no answer. Once again unwilling to wait, and concluding that sin is the cause of God's silence, Saul calls together the leaders of the people, declaring that whoever has sinned will surely die (v. 38). Therefore, in order to discern who has sinned, Saul instructs all the people to be on one side while he and Jonathan stand on the other. Ultimately, Jonathan is chosen as the responsible party (v. 40–42).

Saul then confronts Jonathan with wrongdoing:

> Then Saul said to Jonathan, "Tell me what you have done." And Jonathan told him, "I tasted a little honey with the tip of the staff that was in my hand. Here I am; I will die." And Saul said, "God do so to me and more also; you shall surely die, Jonathan." Then the people said to Saul, "Shall Jonathan die, who has worked this great salvation in Israel? Far from it! As the LORD lives, there shall not one hair of his head fall to the ground, for he has worked with God this day." So, the people ransomed Jonathan, so that he did not die. Then Saul went up from pursuing the Philistines, and the Philistines went to their own place. (1 Sam. 14:43–46)

At this point, the question arises, why would Saul condemn Jonathan to death, condemn his son for tasting some honey to restore his strength during battle? Yes, King Saul had every right to do so; Jonathan even acknowledges this in his response to Saul (v. 43). The only logical explanation is that, at this point, Saul considers going back on his word a sign of weakness and thus a threat to his kingship, likely fearing that the people will turn their allegiance to Jonathan instead of continuing to follow Saul. His actions demonstrate that remaining firm and steadfast to his vow in front of the people is more important to him than the life of his son. His real concern is for his reputation, his position as king, and whether or not the people will continue to respect him as king.

Such an attitude on the part of Saul causes a turning point in his relationship with the people. Up to this point, whatever Saul has suggested, the people have responded with, "Do whatever seems good to you" (e.g., 1 Sam. 14:36). This time, however, the people oppose Saul's condemnation of Jonathan, acknowledging that he has saved Israel from the Philistines. What is more, he has done so by working with God (v. 45). So, it is the people's turn to save Jonathan.

It is interesting that the text notes that Saul stops pursuing his enemies, the Philistines. This is an unusual action for Saul at this time, or for any king in a similar situation. As if highlighting this observation, the text immediately notes:

> When Saul had taken the kingship over Israel, he fought against all his enemies on every side, against Moab, against the Ammonites, against Edom, against the kings of Zobah, and against the Philistines. Wherever he turned he routed them. And he did valiantly and struck the Amalekites and delivered Israel out of the hands of those who plundered them. (1 Sam. 14:47–48)

Once he became king, Saul was busy fighting enemies on all sides. In this, it is essential to note the text continues to lack any indication that credit has been given to God throughout these descriptions of Saul's action as king. Remember, in 1 Samuel 14:24, Saul made it clear that his most important priority was to "avenge his enemies," which is further highlighted in 1 Samuel 14:52, "There was hard fighting against the Philistines all the days of Saul. And when Saul saw any strong man, or any valiant man, he attached him to himself." For Saul, the most important thing for him as king is to gather strong and valiant men to follow him and fight for him. Thus, it becomes increasingly apparent that, throughout his kingship, Saul consistently places his desires above any thought of following the ways of God or obeying his statutes and commandments, which he was instructed to do from the beginning by Samuel.

Saul's Failure of Faith

Despite Saul's self-centered attitude, God once again reaches out to Saul through Samuel:

> And Samuel said to Saul, "The LORD sent me to anoint you king over his people Israel; now there-fore listen to the words of the LORD. Thus says the LORD of hosts, 'I have noted what Amalek did to Israel in opposing them on the way when they came up out of Egypt. Now go and strike Amalek and devote to destruction all that they have. Do not spare them, but kill both man and woman, child and infant, ox and sheep, camel and donkey.'" (1 Sam. 15:1–3)

As we have just seen, Saul has demonstrated self-centeredness. God, through Samuel, is testing the genuineness of Saul's faith by seeing if he will now be obedient to God's commands.

We then read, "So, Saul summoned the people and numbered them in Telaim, two hundred thousand men on foot, and ten thousand men of Judah" (1 Sam. 15:4). Then he defeats the Amalekites, keeping King Agag alive, while destroying all the people by the sword. However, they keep what seems to be of value, sparing the best of the flocks and herds (vv. 7–9), rather than utterly destroying them as Samuel had instructed. Once again, Saul is not obedient to the command of God.

God Rejects Saul

Next, we discover the ramifications of Saul's disobedience and willful heart:

> The word of the LORD came to Samuel: "I regret that I have made Saul king, for he has turned back from following me and has not per-

formed my commandments." And Samuel was angry, and he cried to the LORD all night. (1 Sam. 15:10–11)

These verses reveal a great deal about the heart of God and how he relates to individuals who do not walk in his ways or obey his statutes and commandments. From the beginning, God knew that the kings of Israel would not walk in his ways, yet he has given Saul every chance to do so. Even after declaring to Saul that his kingdom will not last forever and that his successor has already been chosen, God gives Saul another chance to be obedient, demonstrating ongoing patience and kindness toward him. God continues to act the same way toward Saul, even as he continues to sin against God:

> And Samuel rose early to meet Saul in the morning. And it was told Samuel, "Saul came to Carmel, and behold, he set up a monument for himself and turned and passed on and went down to Gilgal." And Samuel came to Saul, and Saul said to him, "Blessed be you to the LORD. I have performed the commandment of the LORD." And Samuel said, "What then is this bleating of the sheep in my ears and the lowing of the oxen that I hear?" Saul said, "They have brought them from the Amalekites, for the people spared the best of the sheep and of the oxen to sacrifice to the LORD your God, and the rest we have devoted to destruction." Then Samuel said to Saul, "Stop! I will tell you what the LORD said to me this night." And he said to him, "Speak." (1 Sam. 15:12–16)

Is it any wonder that God now regrets having made Saul king? Not only does he not obey God's commands, he now builds a monument to himself to commemorate his victory over the Amalekites. Thus, God sends Samuel to confront him.

Upon seeing him, Saul tries to take control of the conversation, declaring that he has "performed the commandment of the LORD" (v. 13). However, when Samuel immediately challenges his statement, Saul tries to deflect responsibility for what has occurred by saying, "The *people* spared the best of the sheep and the oxen to sacrifice to the LORD your God" (v. 15, italics added). He then tries to justify their disobedience by claiming that they intend to engage in an act of worship (which wasn't true). Saul's statement, however, reveals the core of his problem: he tells Samuel that the sacrifice was to be made "to the LORD *your* God" (v. 15, italics added). This is clear evidence that God has not become real for Saul; he does not see God as *his* God, but as Samuel's God.

Their confrontation continues:

> And Samuel said, "Though you are little in your own eyes, are you not the head of the tribes of Israel? The LORD anointed you king over Israel. And the LORD sent you on a mission and said, 'Go, devote to destruction the sinners, the Amalekites, and fight against them until they are consumed.' Why then did you not obey the voice of the LORD? Why did you pounce on the spoil and do what was evil in the sight of the LORD?" And Saul said to Samuel, "I have obeyed the voice of the LORD. I have gone on the mission on which the LORD sent me. I have brought Agag the king of Amalek, and I have devoted the Amalekites to destruction. But the people took of the spoil, sheep and oxen, the best of the things devoted to destruction, to sacrifice to the LORD your God in Gilgal." (1 Sam. 15:17–21)

Even as Samuel continues to challenge Saul's defense of his actions, he fails to understand what he has done to cause such criticism. He genuinely believes that he has done what God asked him to do (v. 20). He then goes on to argue as though the people's actions in preserving the best of the sheep and oxen to sacrifice to the LORD is a good thing, while simultaneously reminding Samuel that if that was wrong, then the responsibility for doing so rests on the people and not on him (v. 21).

As has been evident from various texts, God is not real for Saul personally. Yet, by what he says, he tries to convince Samuel that the motivation for what has happened was to worship God with burnt offerings and sacrifices. As is typical of many nonbelievers or nominal believers, Saul uses righteous-sounding words and religious activities to justify his actions, trying to sound and appear as if he has obeyed God's command. But his heart is not, and has not been, genuinely surrendered to God.

However, God has revealed the truth to Samuel, so he continues to challenge Saul:

And Samuel said:

> "Has the LORD as great delight in burnt offerings and
>   sacrifices,
>   as in obeying the voice of the LORD?
> Behold, to obey is better than sacrifice,
>   and to listen than the fat of rams.
> For rebellion is as the sin of divination,
>   and presumption is as iniquity and idolatry.
> Because you have rejected the word of the LORD,
>   he has also rejected you from being king." (1 Sam.
>   15:22–23)

Samuel exposes Saul's excuses to justify his actions as having no value in the eyes of God (v. 22), which is far more critical than mere acts of worship. He characterizes Saul's failure to obey God's commands as rebellion and presuming that God would accept his words of self-justification as evil (v. 23). Samuel then declares the consequences of Saul's actions are that God has again rejected him from being king (v. 23). Saul does not get away with excuses and attempts at self-justification. Yet it is crucial to notice that although

God again rejects him from being king, he does not act immediately to remove and replace him.

Thus, we have to ask why God delays replacing Saul as king. God's great patience and long-suffering are evident throughout Scripture, and can be seen in this instance as well. However, there is a more significant, overarching reason for God's delay: God's reputation and glory among the people of Israel and the surrounding nations. God chose Saul himself and had Samuel anoint him as king. So, did God made a mistake by choosing Saul as king? Or, if God acts to remove him so soon, will it be seen as a flaw in the fundamental character of God? Again, this situation and these questions are rooted in God's sovereignty. God does not make mistakes; he knows what he is doing and why he is doing it. Therefore, as the story of Saul continues, notice how God accomplishes his bigger purposes.

At last, Saul appears to realize the seriousness of his situation:

> Saul said to Samuel, "I have sinned, for I have transgressed the commandment of the LORD and your words, because I feared the people and obeyed their voice. Now therefore, please pardon my sin and return with me that I may bow before the LORD." And Samuel said to Saul, "I will not return with you. For you have rejected the word of the LORD, and the LORD has rejected you from being king over Israel." As Samuel turned to go away, Saul seized the skirt of his robe, and it tore. And Samuel said to him, "The LORD has torn the kingdom of Israel from you this day and has given it to a neighbor of yours, who is better than you. And also the Glory of Israel will not lie or have regret, for he is not a man, that he should have regret." Then he said, "I have sinned; yet honor me now before the elders of my people and before Israel, and return with me, that I may bow before the LORD your God." So Samuel

turned back after Saul, and Saul bowed before
the LORD. (1 Sam. 15:24–31)

The text begins with Saul acknowledging his sin and disobedience against God, but he rapidly returns to seeking to justify his
actions by stating that he fears the people and thus obeyed their voice
(v. 24). Samuel repeats the judgment that God has rejected Saul from
being king (v. 26) and then turns to leave. In desperation, Saul grabs at
his robe, tearing it (v. 27). Samuel then uses that action to repeat that
God has likewise torn the kingdom from Saul (v. 28), who then shifts
direction once again. He pleads with Samuel to honor him before the
elders and all Israel by accompanying him as he goes to worship God
(v. 30). Note that again Saul refers to God as "*your* God" (v. 30, italics
added). God is still not real to Saul; he still relates to God as an objective other who must be pacified by confession of sin. God is still not
real to Saul's *heart*; God is not yet his *personal God.*

Saul's Ongoing Failure

It appears that Saul's change in direction and pleading are effective, because Samuel agrees to go with him. Saul's appeal to Samuel
reveals his real motivation: he wants to be honored before the elders
and all the people of Israel (v. 30). He wants Samuel to accompany
him so that it appears to the people that he has restored his relationship with Samuel and, by inference, with God. Saul is most concerned about his image in the eyes of the people so that they will
continue to support him as king. This reveals the true attitude of
Saul's heart, that the people's opinion is more important to him than
God's opinion or God's commands. This is the second time Saul has
responded with such an attitude. We saw that the first time Samuel
rebuked him, Saul immediately turned and numbered the people
who followed him (1 Sam. 13:15), which revealed his trust in people, in the might of his men, rather than God. This time when he is
rebuked by Samuel, Saul shows no sign of genuine repentance, but
rather concern for his image. This is another indicator that no genuine transformation has occurred in Saul.

Following this, Samuel commands that Agag, the king of the Amalekites, be brought to him, who "came to him cheerfully" (1 Sam. 15:32), possibly expecting to be released and not killed. Instead, Samuel hacks Agag to pieces before the LORD in Gilgal. By this act, Samuel completes the work that God had originally commanded, that all the Amalekites be killed (1 Sam. 15:3). Then Samuel goes to Ramah, and Saul returns to his house in Gibeah of Saul. Samuel does not see Saul again until the day of his death (vv. 34–35).

New King Anointed

God immediately instructs Samuel to go to Jesse prepared to anoint the next king to replace Saul. However, Samuel is hesitant to do so because of his fear of how Saul will react (1 Sam. 16:1–2). God ignores his concern and continues giving instructions, and Samuel obeys (v. 4). He gathers together Jesse's family:

> When they came, he looked on Eliab and thought, "Surely the LORD's anointed is before him." But the LORD said to Samuel, "Do not look on his appearance or on the height of his stature, because I have rejected him. For the LORD sees not as man sees: man looks on the outward appearance, but the LORD looks on the heart." (1 Sam. 16:6–7)

This passage reveals another critical point in Saul's story, and an important point for understanding God's work of transformation. It is clear from the text that Samuel thinks Eliab is the obvious choice to be anointed as king, apparently because of his appearance and stature (v. 7). Those were the most apparent characteristics of Saul. Did they serve Saul well? From a human perspective, yes; he was successful leading the people in defeating the enemies of Israel. However, was he successful in leading the people to walk in the ways of God? No. Here God corrects Samuel's thinking, pointing out that God looks not on outward appearance but on the heart (v. 7). Saul's heart has never changed during his rule over the people. God has been focused on the true state of Saul's heart all along. This lesson is still applicable today: do not judge an individual's ability to lead merely by their appearance or their words. Instead, seek to discern if they strive to walk in the ways of God.

After this, Jesse makes seven of his sons pass before Samuel, but the LORD does not choose any of them (1 Sam. 16:8–10). Then Samuel asks if Jesse has any more sons. He indicates he has one more, the youngest, who is tending the sheep (v. 11). Samuel instructs Jesse to send and get him. He is described as "ruddy and had beautiful eyes and was handsome" (v. 12). God then tells Samuel to anoint him (v. 12). Samuel does so, anointing him in front of his brothers (v. 13). Then "the Spirit of the LORD rushed upon David from that day forward" (v. 13).

With the anointing of David, God begins to bring about what he said he would do, replace Saul with a successor. First Samuel 16:13 records the immediate impact on Saul: "Now the Spirit of the LORD departed from Saul, and a harmful spirit from the LORD tormented him." Notice, however, that until this point in time, God has been seeking to become real to him, but never does. Thus, the beginning of the end for Saul starts as a harmful spirit from God torments him (v. 14). This spirit will continue to torment him for the remainder of his life.

At this point, the story of David begins to interconnect with the story of Saul and continues to do so until the death of Saul. In the next chapter, we will take a closer look at the nature of the interaction between Saul and David, as reported in 1 Samuel, chapters 16–27, and their different responses to God's actions in each of their lives.

Saul Seeks Guidance

For now, we pick up the story of Saul once again in 1 Samuel, chapter 28. At this time, we learn that Samuel has died and was mourned by all Israel. The Philistines again come out to make war against Israel. When Saul sees the army of the Philistines, he is terrified. His fear causes him to inquire of the LORD, but God does not answer him, "either by dreams, by Urim, or by prophets" (v. 6), which were the approved methods for determining the will of God. Then, even though Saul had put the mediums and necromancers out of the land, Saul tells his servants to seek out a medium so that he might use her to inquire of Samuel (see 1 Sam. 28:2–11).

Notice in this series of events that Saul is so terrified about engaging in battle with the Philistines that he tries to inquire of the LORD himself, which we have seen has not been his habit. When God does not answer him, he decides to inquire of a medium, even though he had previously banished them all from the land. In his desperation, he resorts to using unholy methods to obtain some guidance that he can trust. And he does so to contact Samuel, who has died. We then see their last encounter with each other:

> Then Samuel said to Saul, "Why have you dis-turbed me by bringing me up?" Saul answered, "I am in great distress, for the Philistines are war-ring against me, and God has turned away from me and answers me no more, either by prophets or by dreams. Therefore I have summoned you to tell me what I shall do." And Samuel said, "Why then do you ask me since the LORD has turned from you and become your enemy? The LORD has done to you as he spoke by me, for the LORD has torn the kingdom out of your hand and given it to your neighbor, David. Because you did not obey the voice of the LORD and did not carry out his fierce wrath against Amalek, therefore the LORD has done this thing to you this day. Moreover, the LORD will give Israel also with you into the hand of the Philistines, and tomor-row you and your sons shall be with me. The LORD will give the army of Israel also into the hand of the Philistines." (1 Sam. 28:15–19)

In light of God's silence, Saul seeks guidance through unholy means. Even in his desperation, Saul is still only worried about himself, explaining in this exchange with Samuel that the Philistines have come up against "me," that he has cried out to God, but he has turned away from "me" and does not answer "me" (v. 15). To the very end of his life, Saul is weak; his chief concern is still only about himself, rather than being outward-oriented toward God or the people of Israel.

In response to Saul's request, Samuel repeats what he previously told Saul, once again setting forth the reasons for God's actions. Finally, Samuel pronounces Saul's death sentence, telling him that the next day both he and his two sons will die at the hands of the Philistines (v. 19).

Here is a crucial lesson for both nominal believers and nonbelievers alike. As Saul's story has unfolded, his words and actions could have been interpreted to indicate that God had indeed become or was becoming real for him. It is apparent from this recent series of texts that he increasingly tries to say and do what he thinks both Samuel and, more importantly, God would accept as expressions of genuine faith. However, the texts also make clear that nothing that Saul does or says convinces either of them that genuine transformation has occurred in him. Thus, God's judgment will be carried out. In Saul's story it is clear that God reads the heart's motivations and is not fooled by words or actions that do not emerge out of a genuinely transformed heart. In this story we see that God is interested in our obedience that comes from a heart that genuinely embraces him as God, not empty words and actions.

God's Judgment

The beginning of 1 Samuel 31 reveals the fulfillment of God's judgment on Saul:

> Now the Philistines were fighting against Israel, and the men of Israel fled before the Philistines and fell slain on Mount Gilboa. And the Philistines

overtook Saul and his sons, and the Philistines struck down Jonathan and Abinadab and Malchi-shua, the sons of Saul. The battle pressed hard against Saul, and the archers found him, and he was wounded by the archers. Then Saul said to his armor-bearer, "Draw your sword and thrust me through with it, lest these uncircumcised come and thrust me through, and mistreat me." But his armor-bearer would not, for he feared greatly. Therefore, Saul took his own sword and fell upon it. And when his armor-bearer saw that Saul was dead, he also fell upon his sword and died. Thus Saul died, and his three sons, and his armor-bearer, and all his men, on the same day together. And when the men of Israel who were on the other side of the valley and those beyond the Jordan saw that the men of Israel had fled and that Saul and his sons were dead, they abandoned their cities and fled. And the Philistines came and lived in them. (1 Sam. 31:1–7)

To the very end, Saul is inward-directed and self-centered, not wanting to be abused by his enemies. Thus, he instructs his armor-bearer to kill him, which would have caused that young man to sin in the eyes of God.

Still, the saddest part of this story is that Saul was not always this way. Remember, when he was young, he did as his father had asked and went to look for the lost donkeys, later expressing concern that his father would be worried when they had not returned after three days. Even after being anointed by Samuel, Saul was out in his father's fields working when the news arrived about the Philistine attack on Jabesh-gilead. When Samuel came to announce Saul publicly as king, he was hiding in the baggage. It is reasonable to conclude that part of the reason God chose Saul to be king was his evident humility at that time in his life. But his failure to remain humble upon becoming king is the reason God later regretted having done so. It seems Saul eventually loved the prestige that being king gave him in the eyes of the people. Additionally, it became clear that Saul's heart was not open to God, for he consistently referred to God as Samuel's God or as "the LORD," but never as his own. Moreover, Saul continues to be inward-directed and self-centered, as we will see in the next chapter.

Lessons from the Story of Saul

1. Impatience leads to taking matters into our own hands rather than waiting upon the LORD. This was evident when Saul was instructed to wait for Samuel at Gilgal. Saul had a choice to make—which was more important: making sure that the people continued to follow his leadership, being prepared to engage the Philistines in battle whenever they attacked, or waiting as instructed for God's spokesman Samuel? The third alternative, waiting, was the least important to Saul. Taking prompt action was more critical for him than obeying the command of God, regardless of the outcome. We learn from this that the impatient individual reflects an attitude that they are as capable of making the right decision as is God. This infers that they expect God to act according to their timeline and expectations.

    Consider: In what types of circumstances do you believe that you are as capable as God of making the right decision? Do you struggle with waiting and trusting God to communicate his will to you regarding decisions you need to make? How is God drawing you into deeper surrender to his sovereignty and will for your life by making you wait? In what ways do you see your ability to understand how God communicates to you is growing as you wait? In what areas of your life are you impatient for God to communicate what he wants you to do or for God to take action in a situation on your behalf?

2. The individual in whom transformation has not or is not occurring manifests no repentance when rebuked for their unholy attitudes and actions. Instead, they seek to deflect responsibility to others or to justify their actions. Saul repeatedly did both whenever confronted by Samuel. He consistently demonstrated an attitude that revealed he believed in his own mind he could do no wrong. If an error was made, either the people of Israel or his enemies were responsible. This type of self-centered attitude is a common characteristic of the individual in whom transformation is not taking place.

   Consider: As you reflect on your life up to this point in time, are there actions and attitudes that have led to a sense of rebuke by God? Have you repented of these actions and attitudes? Or, has God seemingly left you to your own devices so that you feel that repentance is no longer necessary? Do you believe that God has forgiven you, even though you have not asked for his forgiveness? Is God at work, intentionally orchestrating circumstances over time, in order to deepen your faith? Or, are you at risk of being rejected as Saul was?

3. The individual in whom transformation is not taking place tries to use the right words or do the right things to convince others of their genuine faith. But the story of Saul shows us that God knows the true status of our heart, and that God judges the heart. As Saul realized that God might be real, when he realized that Samuel might be speaking the truth about God's opinion of him as king, and he finally realized the possibility of losing his kingship, he began to change the way he spoke to and acted in the presence of Samuel. However, his words and actions were inconsistent with his underlying, yet overt, attitudes and opinions. Such inconsistency is a critical indicator that transformation is not occurring in an individual, or that more transformation is needed.

Consider: As you continue to reflect on your life up to this point in time, do you see that you try to use the right words or do the right things to convince others of your genuine faith, or is your faith readily apparent in everything you say and do? Has God become real for you? Are your words and actions consistent with your core attitudes and opinions, or are they just a façade to try to fool other people and God? What is the *true* attitude of your heart toward God? As you reflect, remember that God is long-suffering and patient and will continue to work to draw you to himself, to transform your belief into genuine faith.

CHAPTER 7
Saul and David

In this chapter, we will continue to examine the story of Saul, as well as look at the story of David before he ascends to the throne as king of Israel, as found in 1 Samuel 16–31. In these chapters, their lives intertwine, so it gives us a great view of the differences between Saul and David. By comparing and contrasting their respective stories, we can examine more clearly how and why God's work of transformation succeeds in one and not the other.

As we saw in the last chapter, when Samuel instructs Saul (on God's behalf) to destroy the Amalekites and all they own, he disobeys and does not do as instructed. He spares King Agag and destroys only the worthless things. In response, God regrets that he has made Saul king, instructing Samuel that he has thus rejected Saul as king over Israel (1 Sam. 15:10–24), and he sends Samuel to anoint a new king in his place (1 Sam. 16). When informed by Samuel of God's judgment, Saul pleads with him to worship God with him, trying to get Samuel's assistance in saving his reputation and image before the people, and perhaps God will change his mind. But Samuel knows that God's decision will not change. Thus, he acquiesces and worships with Saul. But then Samuel turns away and does not see Saul again until the day of his death (see 1 Sam. 15:25–35).

After these things occurred, Samuel mourns for Saul until God snatches him from his grief:

> The LORD said to Samuel, "How long will you grieve over Saul, since I have rejected him from being king over Israel? Fill your horn with oil, and

> go. I will send you to Jesse the Bethlehemite, for I
> have provided for myself a king among his sons."
> And Samuel said, "How can I go? If Saul hears
> it, he will kill me." And the LORD said, "Take a
> heifer with you and say, 'I have come to sacrifice
> to the LORD.' And invite Jesse to the sacrifice,
> and I will show you what you shall do. And you
> shall anoint for me him whom I declare to you."
> Samuel did what the LORD commanded and
> came to Bethlehem. (1 Sam. 16:1–4)

Even though Samuel is being sent to anoint David here in chapter 16 of 1 Samuel, remember that Saul does not lose his kingship and his life until years later (see 1 Sam. 28). Thus, those intervening twelve chapters of Scripture allow us to examine both Saul and David, who were both chosen and anointed by God to be king over Israel, and compare them to each other in order to see how and why God's work of transformation succeeds in one but not the other.

Even at this point, Samuel knows how Saul will react when he finds out that Samuel is going to anoint the individual chosen by God to replace him as king over Israel (1 Sam. 16:2). Samuel has seen how determined Saul has been to retain his kingship despite what God has revealed to Samuel. Thus, it is evident that God is not real for Saul; he does not fear God's word or follow God's commandments and laws.

David Anointed King

Even though Samuel fears what Saul might do, he obeys God and goes to seek out Jesse's family as instructed. We pick up the story of David in 1 Samuel, chapter 16:

> When they came, he looked on Eliab and
> thought, "Surely the LORD's anointed is before
> him." But the LORD said to Samuel, "Do not
> look on his appearance or on the height of his

stature, because I have rejected him. For the
LORD sees not as man sees: man looks on the
outward appearance, but the LORD looks on the
heart." (1 Sam. 16:6–7)

This text contains a valuable lesson. Once Samuel arrives, he
sees Eliab, Jesse's firstborn son, and concludes that he must be the
one to be anointed. The text does not indicate why he would think
this way, but it is clear that this is what he thinks. However, God
corrects him, saying, "For the LORD sees not as man sees: man looks
on the outward appearance, but the LORD looks on the heart" (v. 7).
From the outset of David's story, God reveals the critical difference
between Saul and David. When chosen as king, Saul was handsome,
much taller than all the people; in terms of outward appearance,
he looked like one would expect a king to look. However, God has
rejected him as king because he does not obey God; he does not
walk in God's ways or keep his statutes and commandments. Saul has
become the kind of king about whom God had warned the people
(see 1 Sam. 12:14–25). David, however, has already been described
by Samuel as "a man after [God's] own heart" (1 Sam. 13:14) and
who will later be described by God as one "who will do all my will"
(Acts 13:22).

So, Samuel rejects Eliab as God's choice for the new king. Jesse
makes all seven of his sons pass before him, but God does not choose
any of them.

Then Samuel said to Jesse, "Are all your sons
here?" And he said, "There remains yet the
youngest, but behold, he is keeping the sheep."
And Samuel said to Jesse, "Send and get him, for
we will not sit down till he comes here." And he
sent and brought him in. Now he was ruddy and
had beautiful eyes and was handsome. And the
LORD said, "Arise, anoint him, for this is he."
Then Samuel took the horn of oil and anointed
him in the midst of his brothers. And the Spirit

of the LORD rushed upon David from that day forward. And Samuel rose up and went to Ramah. (1 Sam. 16:11–13)

As soon as David arrives, God identifies him as the one to choose and instructs Samuel to anoint him in front of all his family. No doubt they were surprised that he would anoint the youngest of all the brothers. After all, in their minds, he was not even important enough to have been invited to dinner. He was handsome with beautiful eyes, but God saw more in David than his outward appearance.

Notice that the text says that once David is anointed king, the Spirit of God rushes upon him and will stay with him throughout his life (v. 13). This description of what happens to David upon being anointed king stands in stark contrast to what happened to Saul following his anointing: that God gave Saul "another heart" (see 1 Sam. 10:9). In that text we saw that this was the first time Scripture describes the Spirit of God coming upon Saul, and that it was to kindle his anger upon hearing news of the Philistines' attack on Jabeshgilead (see 1 Sam. 11:5–8). By way of further contrast, there was no comment indicating that the Spirit of God would remain with Saul from that day forward, as we have read about David.

Given the statement about the different heart that God has given David, should we consider this a moment of conversion for David? Has God been real for David before this moment? The text does not provide an answer to that question. However, it will become evident as the story of David unfolds that God became quite real to David at some point in his early life. Moreover, that answer will be essential to understand God's work of transformation in David.

David Serves Saul

The stories of Saul and David draw even closer together:

Now the Spirit of the LORD departed from Saul, and a harmful spirit from the LORD tormented him. And Saul's servants said to him,

"Behold now, a harmful spirit from God is tormenting you. Let our lord now command your
servants who are before you to seek out a man
who is skillful in playing the lyre, and when the
harmful spirit from God is upon you, he will play
it, and you will be well." So Saul said to his servants, "Provide for me a man who can play well
and bring him to me." One of the young men
answered, "Behold, I have seen a son of Jesse the
Bethlehemite, who is skillful in playing, a man
of valor, a man of war, prudent in speech, and
a man of good presence, and the LORD is with
him." Therefore Saul sent messengers to Jesse and
said, "Send me David your son, who is with the
sheep." (1 Sam. 16:14–19)

Notice the progression of what is occurring. In the preceding passage, we saw that the Spirit of God rushed upon David and
will stay with him throughout his life. That event is followed by a
description in this passage of how the Spirit of God immediately
departs from Saul, only to be replaced by a harmful spirit that torments him. In response, his servants tell Saul that they know someone who can play the lyre, which will cause the tormenting spirits to
leave him. The servants immediately identify David as such a man,
so Saul sends for him.

It is appropriate to ask at this point "Where is God in this?"
There is a great deal of evidence in this text of God working to effect
his desired outcome, starting with God's Spirit departing from Saul.
Then, while being tormented by the harmful spirit *sent from God,*
Saul's servants decide that a man who can play the lyre well could
cause the harmful spirit to stop tormenting him. So of course, it is no
coincidence that the servants happen to know that David, the son of
Jesse, is able to do so. Saul's torment is so severe that he instructs his
servants to send for David. The only reasonable explanation for how
these things occur is that God is at work guiding and directing these
circumstances for his greater purposes.

Further evidence of God's active involvement in the unfolding events surfaces:

> And Jesse took a donkey laden with bread and a skin of wine and a young goat and sent them by David his son to Saul. And David came to Saul and entered his service. And Saul loved him greatly, and he became his armor-bearer. And Saul sent to Jesse, saying, "Let David remain in my service, for he has found favor in my sight." And whenever the harmful spirit from God was upon Saul, David took the lyre and played it with his hand. So Saul was refreshed and was well, and the harmful spirit departed from him. (1 Sam. 16:20–23)

The important point in this text is that, when David plays the lyre, Saul is refreshed and becomes well. We have to ask, how is that possible? The answer lies not in the playing of the lyre, but instead in the one who is playing it. Previous texts indicated that the Spirit of God is now upon David; thus, it is appropriate to conclude that when David plays, God's Spirit is at work driving out the harmful spirit from Saul.

Notice that, in response to the relief that Saul receives when the harmful spirit departs from him, the text says that he "loved" David. He does so because David is useful to him, not for any other reason. As the story continues, we will see evidence that Saul loves those who are useful to him and that the focal point of Saul's life is Saul; he is not capable of loving anyone except himself, including God. Eventually his self-centeredness leads to disobedience, which will cause him to lose his kingship.

One other significant element contained in this text is what it says about David's character. He has recently been anointed by Samuel to be the next king over Israel; he will replace Saul as king. Still, in this text, he humbles himself to serve the very one whose kingship he will take over. As the story of David continues, it will become further evident that his attitude toward Saul never changes. David never raises his hand against "the LORD's anointed," regardless of what Saul does.

David Confronts Goliath

At this time, the Philistines gather their armies for battle against Israel. As Saul and the men of Israel position themselves for battle, out from the camp of the Philistines comes a champion named Goliath, who is over nine feet tall. He stands and taunts Israel, challenging them to choose a man to come down to fight with him. Whoever loses, their people will become servants of the victor. When Saul and all Israel hear Goliath's words, they become dismayed and afraid. For forty days, Goliath continues to taunt and challenge the army of Israel (see 1 Sam. 17:1–11).

The three eldest sons of Jesse have followed Saul into this impending battle. However, during this time, David goes back and forth from Saul to tend to his father's sheep. One day, Jesse tells David to take provisions to his brothers and their commander, and to see if they are well. The next day, David rises early, leaves the sheep, and takes the provisions to the encampment. He arrives just as both armies prepare for battle. He leaves the provisions with the keeper of the baggage and runs to greet his brothers. As he talks with them, Goliath comes up out of the ranks of the Philistines and again taunts and challenges the army of Israel (see 1 Sam. 17:17–23).

It is important to point out that the timing of these events cannot be mere coincidence. After all, Goliath has been taunting and challenging Israel for forty days without a response from them. Then this young shepherd arrives on the scene to deliver provisions to his brothers and happens to arrive just in time to hear Goliath's taunts. Clearly, God is actively involved once again orchestrating events, and the timing of those events, for his greater purposes.

David's reaction to this is recorded in the next passage in 1 Samuel 17:

> All the men of Israel, when they saw the man, fled from him and were much afraid. And the men of Israel said, "Have you seen this man who has come up? Surely he has come up to defy Israel. And the king will enrich the man who kills him with great riches and will give him his daughter and make his father's house free in Israel." And David said to the men who stood by him, "What shall be done for the man who kills this Philistine and takes away the reproach from Israel? For who is this uncircumcised Philistine, that he should defy the armies of the living God?" And the people answered him in the same way, "So shall it be done to the man who kills him." (1 Sam. 17:24–27)

Note the contrast between Saul and David, as revealed in this text. On the one hand, Saul is highly concerned about losing to the Philistines' champion, Goliath. His men reveal that he promises to give great riches, his daughter in marriage, and to cancel any levies and taxes against his father's house for the man who can defeat him. Clearly, he is hoping this will motivate someone to take on this giant. On the other hand, David cannot believe that it will require such a pricey reward to entice a man to kill Goliath and thus take away the reproach from Israel. He cannot believe that, regardless of his size, this uncircumcised Philistine is still standing there defying the armies of the living God. Here we see that Saul's intent is to depend upon a rational, human solution, while David intends to depend upon God to provide a victory.

When David's brothers hear what he has said, they deride him, accusing him of wrongdoing by coming to watch the battle rather than tending his father's sheep. However, when Saul hears from his

men what David has said, his reaction is quite different, no doubt
due to his desperation:

> When the words that David spoke were heard,
> they repeated them before Saul, and he sent for
> him. And David said to Saul, "Let no man's heart
> fail because of him. Your servant will go and fight
> with this Philistine." And Saul said to David,
> "You are not able to go against this Philistine to
> fight with him, for you are but a youth, and he
> has been a man of war from his youth." But David
> said to Saul, "Your servant used to keep sheep for
> his father. And when there came a lion, or a bear,
> and took a lamb from the flock, I went after him
> and struck him and delivered it out of his mouth.
> And if he arose against me, I caught him by his
> beard and struck him and killed him. Your ser-
> vant has struck down both lions and bears, and
> this uncircumcised Philistine shall be like one of
> them, for he has defied the armies of the living
> God." And David said, "The LORD who deliv-
> ered me from the paw of the lion and from the
> paw of the bear will deliver me from the hand
> of this Philistine." And Saul said to David, "Go,
> and the LORD be with you!" (1 Sam. 17:31–37)

This is a critical text in the first part of David's story. It is evident from what he says that God is real for David. But notice that
his testimony in this text refers to an earlier time in his life. God
became real to David when, at some earlier time, while keeping his
father's sheep, God delivered him when attacked by bears and lions.
Thus, because he has experienced God's saving grace and mercy at
those times, he is confident now that God will do the same for him
against Goliath. Because of his earlier life experiences that taught
him something about God's presence and power, David is now will-

ing to confront this giant that threatens his people. He trusts God, so he is unafraid.

This is a crucial lesson concerning the work of transformation. On the one hand, Saul knows *about* God, having been raised in an Israelite home and later instructed by Samuel about how to walk in his ways and obey his statutes and commandments. However, as was evident in the previous chapter, none of those things caused God *to become real* for him. On the other hand, David has *experienced* God's power and protection from a young age, as described in this text. In the process of transformation, there is a vast difference between *knowing about* God and *intimately knowing* him by experiencing him. David's reference to God as "the living God" further highlights this difference, especially when we have seen few references to God by Saul, and those references do not indicate that he knows God personally. Rather, while talking to Samuel, he has referred to God in an objective manner, as "the LORD" and "your God" (e.g., 1 Sam. 15:13, 15, and 24). We see here, early in David's story, the foundation for everything that he does and does not do for the remainder of his life.

Then Saul puts his armor on David, but it is too much for him to manage, so he takes it off. Then he takes his staff, picks up five smooth stones from the brook and puts them in his pouch, and puts his sling in his hand. He then approaches Goliath (see 1 Sam. 17:38–40). The confrontation between David and Goliath now begins:

> And the Philistine moved forward and came near to David, with his shield-bearer in front of him. And when the Philistine looked and saw David, he disdained him, for he was but a youth, ruddy and handsome in appearance. And the Philistine said to David, "Am I a dog, that you come to me with sticks?" And the Philistine cursed David by his gods. The Philistine said to David, "Come to me, and I will give your flesh to the birds of the air and to the beasts of the field." Then David said to the Philistine, "You come to me with a

sword and with a spear and with a javelin, but I come to you in the name of the LORD of hosts, the God of the armies of Israel, whom you have defied. This day the LORD will deliver you into my hand, and I will strike you down and cut off your head. And I will give the dead bodies of the host of the Philistines this day to the birds of the air and to the wild beasts of the earth, that all the earth may know that there is a God in Israel, and that all this assembly may know that the LORD saves not with sword and spear. For the battle is the LORD's, and he will give you into our hand." (1 Sam. 17:41–47)

The disparity between David and Goliath is monumental, not just in terms of size and physical strength, or experience in battle … or lack of it, but also in terms of Goliath being heavily armored and David wearing no armor at all. From a human perspective, there is no comparison. Goliath comes equipped with human tools of war, with a sword, spear, and javelin, deriding David and confident of victory. David is also confident of victory, because he comes in the name of the LORD, the God of the armies of Israel. Goliath's purpose in the battle is to kill one man, one *youth*, so that the army of Israel will be forced to become servants of the Philistines. David's purpose in the battle is also to kill one man. However, his desired outcome is different—that by doing so, "all the earth may know that there is a God in Israel" and that "the LORD saves not with sword and spear" (1 Sam. 17:46–47). Goliath has come to this battle depending upon his power and human-made weapons that he carries into this confrontation, but David comes solely depending upon the living God, instead of himself.

Here is clear evidence that even despite his youth, God's work of transformation is progressing in David. What he says to Goliath testifies to his genuine belief and trust in God. His willingness to step forward to fight Goliath when no one else will do so testifies to his acceptance that God has sovereign control over the outcome of his fight with Goliath. This is a lesson for us: when we genuinely believe in, trust, and accept all that God is, the totality of his character, we are moved beyond mere words of belief to action based on that trust, which is evidence that God is real in our life. This is what we see in David.

David prevails against Goliath with his sling and a stone, killing him. Then he uses Goliath's own sword to cut off his head. When the Philistines see that their champion is dead, they flee; and the army of Israel pursues them (see 1 Sam. 17:48–52). Thus, David's actions not only cause the Philistines to flee in fear, but they also inspire the fearful men of Israel to action.

Without a doubt, David's desire for all the earth to know that there is a God in Israel was accomplished on the battlefield that day. There is no doubt that his goal, his heart's desire, was also God's desire in this situation. Thus, we have seen that God's work of transformation can occur at any age, even in young people; it can change the gentle lyre player and poet into one who can strike down the enemies of God, in trusting obedience to God.

Saul Fears David

Following David's victory over Goliath, the people rejoice in his, and thus Saul's, success:

> As they were coming home, when David returned from striking down the Philistine, the women came out of all the cities of Israel, singing and dancing, to meet King Saul, with tambourines, with songs of joy, and with musical instruments. And the women sang to one another as they celebrated,

> "Saul has struck down his thousands, and David his ten thousands." (1 Sam. 18:6–7)

Notice that the people give a more glorious statement about David than Saul. Saul becomes very angry upon hearing this praise of David, displeased that they ascribe to David ten thousands of kills while ascribing only thousands of kills to him. He fears that he is beginning to lose the allegiance of the people, that they might make David king in his place. Thus, Saul becomes suspicious of David, even though David has done nothing to breach Saul's trust. We will see that Saul's fear of David never leaves him, and that it is the root of all that follows in the rest of the story.

The next day, a harmful spirit from God rushes upon Saul; he raves within his house. Yet David continues playing the lyre for him daily. One day while David is playing for Saul, he holds his spear in his hand. At one point he hurls it at David, trying to pin him against the wall. Yet David evades him twice (see 1 Sam. 18:8–11).

By this point in time, David has already been anointed by Samuel to be the next king over Israel. He has defeated Goliath and the Philistines. Yet we see that he continues to play the lyre daily to ease the tormented Saul. This is clear evidence of the ongoing transformation process in David; he retains a humble servant's heart despite the success he has already experienced in his life. In sharp contrast, Saul is afraid of David because he realizes that the LORD is with him in a way that he is not with Saul. So, he removes David from his presence by establishing him as a commander of a thousand men in the Israel army. In this new role, David continues to have success in everything he does. Thus, when Saul sees that David has great success, he stands in fearful awe of him. However, all of Israel and Judah[1] love David (see 1 Sam. 18:12–16).

Instead of being afraid of David, Saul should stand in fearful awe of the one to whom David gives credit for his success—the living God, the God of Israel. However, he still does not understand, even

---

[1] In our discussion of 1 Samuel 16:18 (above), David's father was identified as a Bethlehemite. Bethlehem was located in the land given to the tribe of Judah when the people entered the Promised Land. Thus, David was from the tribe of Judah. It would be natural for the people of Judah to love David, as he was part of them. However, this statement indicates that David was universally loved by all the people of Israel, not just the tribe of Judah.

though he recognizes that the spirit of God had departed from him and now rests upon David. As this story continues, we will see that Saul repeatedly seeks to protect his kingship by devising situations in which David might die—instead of repenting and seeking God's forgiveness. It will become increasingly apparent that this is a significant difference between David's genuine belief, trust, and acceptance of God and Saul's complete lack of genuine faith.

Saul Turns against David

In the next passage, we can see Saul's fear of David taking root and ruling his actions:

> Now Saul's daughter Michal loved David. And they told Saul, and the thing pleased him. Saul thought, "Let me give her to him, that she may be a snare for him and that the hand of the Philistines may be against him." Therefore Saul said to David a second time, "You shall now be my son-in-law." And Saul commanded his servants, "Speak to David in private and say, 'Behold, the king has delight in you, and all his servants love you. Now then become the king's son-in-law.'" And Saul's servants spoke those words in the ears of David. And David said, "Does it seem to you a little thing to become the king's son-in-law, since I am a poor man and have no reputation?" And the servants of Saul told him, "Thus and so did David speak." Then Saul said, "Thus shall you say to David, 'The king desires no bride-price except a hundred foreskins of the Philistines, that he may be avenged of the king's enemies.'" Now Saul thought to make David fall by the hand of the Philistines. And when his servants told David these words, it pleased David well to be the king's son-in-law. (1 Sam. 18:20–26)

Note that previously Saul had placed David as a commander over a thousand men, which on the surface, and at this point in time, appeared to be a smart strategic military move due to his victory over the Philistines. However, in this text it becomes apparent that Saul's objective is something different; he is scheming to bring about David's death. He is hoping that his daughter Michal might become "a snare" for him (v. 21), and thus, by having a wife, David might be distracted during an upcoming battle. Saul is manipulating circumstances in hope that the Philistines will kill him. Saul continues his manipulation of this situation as he sets the bride-price for marrying Michal. In order to meet his price, David must kill Philistines. Yet Saul says that the bride-price is tied to being avenged from his enemies. This price does not seem to faze David; he is confident that it is a price he can provide. In his self-centeredness, pride, and fear of David, Saul is hoping that David will die trying.

Before the set time has expired to achieve this task, David goes with his men and kills two hundred of the Philistines and brings their foreskins to the king, so that he might become the king's son-in-law. Saul kept his word and gave him his daughter Michal for a wife, but Saul's real feelings are reported in 1 Sam. 18:28–29, "But when Saul saw and knew that the LORD was with David, and that Michal, Saul's daughter, loved him, Saul was even more afraid of David. So Saul was David's enemy continually."

Not only did David not die at the hands of the Philistines, he and his men killed two hundred of them, twice the agreed-upon amount. Once again, Saul realizes that God is with David and thus becomes more afraid of him. We see here that Saul's fear of David continues to escalate over time, and it reveals noticeable differences in their faith. Instead of realizing his foolishness and seeking to change his attitude and behavior, this text says that "Saul was David's enemy continually" (1 Sam. 18:29). Thus, we will see that Saul seeks diligently to kill David so that his kingship might endure. Saul is clearly most interested in remaining king, regardless of what it might take to ensure that this happens.

As if to underscore the foolishness of Saul's continuing conduct, the commanders of the Philistines come out to battle; when they do,

David has more success than all of Saul's servants, and his name is highly esteemed (1 Sam. 18:30). At this point, the question naturally arises, will all of David's success cause a change in him? Will he eventually become like Saul—depend upon his own human strength and that of his mighty men and forget God, the one who has given him success from his youth? The answer to this question will reveal whether or not God's work of transformation is ongoing in him.

As the story of David continues, Saul's attitude toward him continues to deteriorate to the point that he commands his son Jonathan and his servants to kill David. Jonathan tries to change his father's feelings about David, stating that David has not sinned in any way against Saul, so there is no justification for his attempts to kill David, who is an innocent man. Saul seems to take Jonathan's words to heart; he declares that he will not seek David's death. Jonathan is convinced by Saul's oath, so he reports to David what Saul has said. Jonathan then brings David to Saul, and he stands in Saul's presence once again (see 1 Sam. 19:1–7). However, we will soon see that Saul's oath is a lie.

The relationship between Saul and David immediately reaches a crisis point in the next passage:

> And there was war again. And David went out and fought with the Philistines and struck them with a great blow, so that they fled before him. Then a harmful spirit from the LORD came upon Saul, as he sat in his house with his spear in his hand. And David was playing the lyre. And Saul sought to pin David to the wall with the spear, but he eluded Saul, so that he struck the spear into the wall. And David fled and escaped that night. (1 Sam. 19:8–10)

This text again highlights the significant difference between David, as God's work of transformation continues in him, and Saul, who has been rejected by God. It begins by recounting another victory for David over the Philistines, from which he immediately returns. Next, we see that David is again playing the lyre for Saul, as another harmful spirit from the LORD torments him. In contrast, Saul tries to pin David to the wall with his spear, intending once again to kill him. In his humanness, Saul is so focused on David's perceived threat to his kingship that he is unable to see David for the humble servant he continues to be. God is clearly with David as he evades the attack and once again flees from Saul.

Saul does not relent; he sends messengers to David's house to watch him, because he intends to kill David the next morning. Michal, David's wife, tells him to either escape that night or he will be killed the next day. She helps David escape through the window (see 1 Sam. 19:11–12), giving further evidence of God's hand at work in David's life. God continues to protect David, this time through the word and actions of his wife. Thus David successfully escapes and goes to Samuel at Ramah and tells him all that Saul has done.

Saul's campaign to kill David continues. David and Samuel go to Naioth and decide to live there, presumably to find a safe place. When Saul finds out where David is, he sends messengers to capture David; however, he has to do so three times because each time he sends his messengers, the Spirit of God comes upon them and produces a prophetic frenzy. Then Saul himself goes to Ramah, and the Spirit of God comes upon him as well, and he also comes under the influence of the prophetic spirit of God, lying naked all day and night (see 1 Sam. 19:18–24). However, even such a direct manifestation of God's power could not persuade Saul not to kill David, which reveals the intensity of his determination to kill David.

David Flees

This story continues with a series of passages from Scripture that reveal just how determined Saul is to kill David. After the prophetic frenzy mentioned above occurs, David flees from Ramah and asks Jonathan what he had done to cause Saul to desire to kill him. Jonathan has no answer; thus, David suspects that Saul has been lying to his son, including his previous oath to not kill David. So David and Jonathan devise a plan to reveal Saul's true feelings:

> David said to Jonathan, "Behold, tomorrow is the new moon, and I should not fail to sit at table with the king. But let me go, that I may hide myself in the field till the third day at evening. If your father misses me at all, then say, 'David earnestly asked leave of me to run to Bethlehem his city, for there is a yearly sacrifice there for all the clan.' If he says, 'Good!' it will be well with your servant, but if he is angry, then know that harm is determined by him." (1 Sam. 20:5–7)

They then devise a plan that will enable Jonathan to notify David about what happens at the feast:

> Then Jonathan said to him, "Tomorrow is the new moon, and you will be missed, because your seat will be empty. On the third day go down quickly to the place where you hid yourself when the matter was in hand, and remain beside the stone heap. And I will shoot three arrows to the side of it, as though I shot at a mark. And behold, I will send the boy, saying, 'Go, find the arrows.' If I say to the boy, 'Look, the arrows are on this side of you, take them,' then you are to come, for, as the LORD lives, it is safe for you and there is no danger. But if I say to the youth, 'Look, the arrows are beyond you,' then go, for the LORD has sent you away. And as for the matter of which you and I have spoken, behold, the LORD is between you and me forever." (1 Sam. 20:18–23)

When the day of the new moon arrives, the king sits on his seat by the wall, Jonathan sits opposite him, and Abner sits by Saul's side—as is their custom; but David is not present. Saul does not say anything that day, thinking that something has happened to cause him to be unclean. On the second day when David is still absent, Saul inquires of Jonathan about David's absence. Jonathan answers that he had earnestly asked leave to go to sacrifice in the city, and to which his brother had commanded his attendance (see 1 Sam. 20:24–29).

In response, Saul's anger turns against Jonathan, hurling insults and accusations at his son. This is followed by ordering him to bring David to him so that he can kill him. When Jonathan questions Saul's orders, he hurls his spear at Jonathan to strike him. As a result, Jonathan now knows that his father is determined to put David to death, thus revealing that his earlier oath was a lie. Jonathan leaves the table in fierce anger and grieves for David (see 1 Sam. 20:30–34).

As prearranged, Jonathan goes to the field the next day to warn David:

> And as soon as the boy had gone, David rose from beside the stone heap and fell on his face to the ground and bowed three times. And they kissed one another and wept with one another, David weeping the most. Then Jonathan said to David, "Go in peace, because we have sworn both of us in the name of the LORD, saying, 'The LORD shall be between me and you, and between my offspring and your offspring, forever.'" And he rose and departed, and Jonathan went into the city. (1 Sam. 20:41–42)

This text recounts the final encounter between David and Jonathan. We see that they reaffirm their relationship and the covenant they had previously entered into in the name of the LORD. They commit each other forever into the hands of God. Then they depart from each other.

In this passage we see further evidence of transformation taking place in David as they reconfirm their relationship and covenant, a covenant that David has previously made with Jonathan, the son of the man who is determined to kill him. Later, when Saul and Jonathan perish in battle, David will keep the covenant they have just reaffirmed with each other.

Test of Faith and Character

The story of David now continues in 1 Samuel 21—23, where Saul undertakes a more determined campaign to capture and kill David, ruthlessly killing anyone who helps David in any way. Saul presses the campaign, continually chasing David in the wilderness, until the Philistines once again come out to battle against Israel. He presses his campaign against David's perceived threat to him, until this actual threat from the Philistines appears and temporarily diverts his attention. However, once he obtains victory over them, Saul returns to his pursuit of David:

> When Saul returned from following the Philistines, he was told, "Behold, David is in the wilderness of Engedi." Then Saul took three thousand chosen men out of all Israel and went to seek David and his men in front of the Wildgoats' Rocks. And he came to the sheepfolds by the way, where there was a cave, and Saul went in to relieve himself. Now David and his men were sitting in the innermost parts of the cave. And the men of David said to him, "Here is the day of which the LORD said to you, 'Behold, I will give your enemy into your hand, and you shall do to him as it shall seem good to you.'" Then David arose and stealthily cut off a corner of Saul's robe. And afterward David's heart struck him, because he had cut off a corner of Saul's robe. He said to his men, "The LORD forbid that I should do this thing to my LORD, the LORD's anointed, to put out my hand against him, seeing he is the

LORD's anointed." So David persuaded his men with these words and did not permit them to attack Saul. And Saul rose up and left the cave and went on his way. (1 Sam. 24:1–7)

At this point, Saul has been pursuing David for years, trying to kill him. In this passage, he presents David with the perfect opportunity to take revenge against him and end his life when he enters a cave to relieve himself, a cave in which, unknown to Saul, David and his men are hiding. David does not take advantage of the opportunity, even though he is encouraged to do so by the men who are hiding in the cave with him. Instead, he cuts off only a corner of Saul's robe, to prove just how close he is to Saul. Even doing this minor act troubles David; he considers even such a small act, cutting off a corner of his robe, as lifting his hand against the LORD's anointed, and thus sees it as an act of disobedience. This is a critical indication of the transformation process taking place in David: he chooses to not pursue revenge against the man who continually tries to kill him. Instead of doing what seems to be reasonable from a human perspective, he places a higher value upon honoring and respecting God's anointed ruler. The *condition of his heart* is seen clearly after he takes a small piece of Saul's robe; apparently, he feels guilty about doing even a very small act of possible revenge against the king.

This close encounter between David and Saul is no coincidence. So, we have to ask the question again, where is God in this situation? Saul has no idea that David and his men are in the area, much less in the cave that he enters. It seems God's purpose in this encounter is to test David, to reveal what is fundamentally most important to him: taking revenge against Saul for his unjust campaign to kill him, or walking in the ways of God and keeping his statutes and commandments—which in this case is to not take any action against God's anointed king, regardless of Saul's actions toward him.

It is important that we understand that, at various times during the process of transformation, God tests us to determine whether our actions validate our words; we prove our words are true by following them up with congruent actions. In this case, David has the perfect opportunity to kill Saul and stop the threats to his life, but that is not as important to him as living obediently to God's commandments.

David's encounter with Saul at the cave continues, as he follows Saul out of the cave and, calling to him, says,

> "My lord the king!" And when Saul looked behind him, David bowed with his face to the earth and paid homage. And David said to Saul, "Why do you listen to the words of men who say, 'Behold, David seeks your harm'? Behold, this day your eyes have seen how the LORD gave you today into my hand in the cave. And some told me to kill you, but I spared you. I said, 'I will not put out my hand against my lord, for he is the LORD's anointed.' See, my father, see the corner of your robe in my hand. For by the fact that I cut off the corner of your robe and did not kill you, you may know and see that there is no wrong or treason in my hands. I have not sinned against you, though you hunt my life to take it. May the LORD judge between me and you, may the LORD avenge me against you, but my hand shall not be against you. As the proverb of the ancients says, 'Out of the wicked comes wickedness.' But my hand shall not be against you. After whom has the king of Israel come out? After whom do you pursue? After a dead dog! After a flea! May the LORD therefore be judge and give sentence between me and you, and see to it and plead my cause and deliver me from your hand." (1 Sam. 24:8–15)

Notice here that David could be satisfied with what he has done and why, but he is not. Instead, he comes out of the cave, behind Saul and confronts him, seeking to prove to Saul that he is no threat to him. David tries to persuade Saul that he is not going to lift his hand against him as the LORD's anointed one (v. 6). So he shows Saul the corner of his robe as evidence of the truth of his words. Notice that David's previous actions alone, by humbly serving Saul for some time, have not succeeded in proving to Saul that David is no threat to his kingship. So David takes the opportunity now to reveal himself to Saul, in close proximity to him, talking to him face-to-face, asserting his innocence.

It is important to also note that David does this in the face of Saul's army of three thousand men who are with him in his search for David[2] (1 Sam. 24:2). This underscores what has been evident from the beginning, that David relies solely upon God to protect him in all circumstances. This too reveals how strong his faith is, how much transformation has taken place in him through his life to this point. His dependence upon God for his safety was clearly evident when he confronted Goliath, and is still evident here in this situation, years later.

Further, in this text, David reveals that his trust in God extends to trusting him to judge between him and Saul and to avenge David against Saul because of his innocence. David's trust in God leaves him feeling no need to take revenge against Saul. Rather, he submits to the will of God, trusting God to do what is right on his behalf—not from David's perspective, or Saul's, but based on what is truly right in the eyes of God. Such a level of trust in God means David is free from having to consider how to defend or justify himself. He has no need to consider raising his hand against Saul in any manner.

David's words and actions stand in sharp contrast to those of Saul, providing further evidence of the extent of God's work of transformation in him. David's faith is strong; he is courageous in the face of the ongoing threat of death, and still he does not desire to harm the one who seeks to kill him.

---

[2] In 1 Samuel 24, we are not told how many men David has with him, only that there are men with him in the cave when Saul comes in (1 Sam. 24:3).

Next, we see Saul's response to David's actions and words:

> As soon as David had finished speaking these
> words to Saul, Saul said, "Is this your voice, my
> son David?" And Saul lifted up his voice and
> wept. He said to David, "You are more righteous
> than I, for you have repaid me good, whereas I
> have repaid you evil. And you have declared this
> day how you have dealt well with me, in that you
> did not kill me when the LORD put me into
> your hands. For if a man finds his enemy, will he
> let him go away safe? So may the LORD reward
> you with good for what you have done to me
> this day. And now, behold, I know that you shall
> surely be king, and that the kingdom of Israel
> shall be established in your hand. Swear to me
> therefore by the LORD that you will not cut
> off my offspring after me, and that you will not
> destroy my name out of my father's house." And
> David swore this to Saul. Then Saul went home,
> but David and his men went up to the strong-
> hold. (1 Sam. 24:16–22)

David's words and actions finally get Saul's attention. On the
surface, Saul's response appears to be an honest, heartfelt reaction to
David's righteous actions. He appears to see his own actions clearly
and honestly, when compared to the honor of David's integrity.
Additionally, he appears to accept what Samuel told him long ago,
that David will one day be king of Israel. The words Saul uses here
appear to indicate that perhaps his heart is changing.

However, we immediately see that his real concern, even in the
midst of these words, is for his own family and future offspring. This
self-centeredness causes him to plead with David to swear an oath
that he will not cut off Saul's offspring after his death or destroy his
legacy. So, ultimately, his self-centeredness drives him to pursue a
guarantee for the sake of *his* name and *his* legacy. Even here we see

that Saul's self-centeredness continues to dominate his heart. So we see that, in reality, his words were not sincere. Rather, they continue to be self-serving.

Notice that Saul seeks to protect his offspring and his name by depending upon a rational solution. Rather than appealing to God on his own, he pleads with David to swear to him *in the name of the LORD* to not do these things. This text makes clear that even though Saul wants to kill David, Saul believes him to be an honorable man, a man of his word.

Again, we see here the degree of transformation that has taken place in David's heart throughout his life to this point: he is willing to swear an oath, in the name of the LORD, to do as Saul has asked. He believes that David will keep this oath; otherwise, he would not have pressed to get it from David. This stands in sharp contrast to Saul's heart, as he is self-consumed; he is more concerned with his future reputation, the lasting value of his name through his descendants, than with doing what is right in the eyes of God. Clearly, Saul's heart still is not turned toward God.

David Seeks Revenge

At this point, the story of David diverges from recounting the ongoing campaign by Saul to seek out and kill David, to relate an encounter between David and a prosperous man named Nabal and his wife, Abigail. In 1 Samuel 25:2–11, we find that, following his separation from the encounter with Saul and while still in the wilderness, David hears that Nabal is shearing his sheep. David and his men had previously protected Nabal's men and their sheep, keeping them safe while they were in the wilderness. Since it was a feast day, David sent some of his men to ask Nabal to give whatever he has at hand to David and his men, that they might celebrate the feast day, as a way of thanking them for safeguarding his sheep and shepherds while they were with David in the wilderness. Not only had David and his men protected them from others, it is evident that they did not take anything from them for their own consumption during that time. Nabal defiantly refuses to give any of his own provisions to

David and his men. David is unknown to him, so he feels no compulsion to do as David asks.

We then read about David's reaction to Nabal's rebuff:

> Now David had said, "Surely in vain have I guarded all that this fellow has in the wilderness, so that nothing was missed of all that belonged to him, and he has returned me evil for good. God do so to the enemies of David and more also, if by morning I leave so much as one male of all who belong to him." (1 Sam. 25:21–22)

Clearly David is mad—mad enough that he intends to wipe out all that belongs to Nabal. He does not intend to go in and just take enough to provide a feast for his men. Rather, he is going to avenge Nabal's rebuff. However, as the encounter continues, it is appropriate to ask the question "Where is God in this?"

Continuing on with this episode in 1 Samuel, chapter 25, we see that Nabal's wife, Abigail, sees David and hurries to him. She takes her husband's guilt upon herself for being ungracious; she calls his actions "folly" (v. 25). She then seeks to calm David's emotions and to keep him from taking vengeance by his own hand by, in essence, praying that his enemies will become like Nabal (v. 26). She then continues speaking to David:

> "And now let this present that your servant has brought to my lord be given to the young men who follow my lord. Please forgive the trespass of your servant. For the LORD will certainly make my lord a sure house, because my lord is fighting the battles of the LORD, and evil shall not be found in you so long as you live. If men rise up to pursue you and to seek your life, the life of my lord shall be bound in the bundle of the living in the care of the LORD your God. And the lives of your enemies he shall sling out as from the

hollow of a sling. And when the LORD has done to my lord according to all the good that he has spoken concerning you and has appointed you prince over Israel, my lord shall have no cause of grief or pangs of conscience for having shed blood without cause or for my lord working salvation himself. And when the LORD has dealt well with my lord, then remember your servant." (1 Sam. 25:27–31)

Abigail reminds David that God will surely take care of him, even when his life is threatened. Her words and actions stop him from taking matters into his own hands, from shedding blood without cause, rather than trusting in God to do what is right. Notice that God uses Abigail to restrain David from personally seeking revenge against Nabal, and thus committing sin against God.

The critical point here is that his desire to do these very things stands in stark contrast to his complete constraint in the past from taking revenge against Saul in response to the king's continuing campaign to seek him out and kill him. In that case, his fear of God continues to restrain him from striking back at the one committed to killing him, because he is the LORD's anointed. Yet this time he shows no such fear of taking revenge against one who has rebuffed his request for enough provisions to have a feast with his men. Here we see God protecting David from sin through the words of another person. This is another critical lesson in how God accomplishes his work of transformation in those whose hearts are turned toward the LORD. God will intervene in our circumstances, at times through the words of another, to keep us from engaging in sin.

We then see David's response to Abigail:

And David said to Abigail, "Blessed be the LORD, the God of Israel, who sent you this day to meet me! Blessed be your discretion, and blessed be you, who have kept me this day from bloodguilt and from working salvation with my own hand! For as surely as the LORD, the God of Israel, lives, who has restrained me from hurting you, unless you had hurried and come to meet me, truly by morning there had not been left to Nabal so much as one male." Then David received from her hand what she had brought him. And he said to her, "Go up in peace to your house. See, I have obeyed your voice, and I have granted your petition." (1 Sam. 25:32–35)

Upon hearing Abigail's words, David immediately acknowledges God's hand in sending her to keep him "from bloodguilt and working salvation" to gain revenge by his own power (v. 33). His response is evidence of the continuing progress of God's transforming work in him. He is immediately aware that God is actively at work in his daily life events, protecting, confronting, and teaching him, even as he is seeking to solve this affront in ways that were no doubt culturally acceptable and expected, but unacceptable to God. Notice that he blesses Abigail, a woman, for intervening as God directed, thus stopping him before he could act in a sinful manner.

This is an important indication of the ongoing work of transformation in our lives—that *we are able to see*, and *willing to acknowledge*, that God is active in the events of our daily life. An additional indicator of this transforming work is the ability to discern when God is guiding and directing us *through the words and actions of others*. Thus, it is essential to note that if we do not look for God's hand guiding and directing the events of our life, we are likely to take things in our own hands, as David was about to do, to bring about the end result that *we* desire, which may not be God's desire for us.

Abigail returns home to find her husband holding a great feast, and she notices that he is very drunk. So, she waits until the next morning to tell him what she has done. Upon hearing her words, "his heart died within him, he became like a stone" (v. 37). About ten days later, God strikes Nabal, and he dies. God has acted to take revenge on David's behalf, once again validating David's trust in and obedience to God (see 1 Sam. 25:36–38).

Another Test of Faith

In 1 Samuel, chapter 26, the story of David now returns to Saul's continuing pursuit of him. David hides on a hill, and Saul is informed about his location. So Saul goes into the wilderness with a large contingent of his men, and they set up camp near where David is hiding. David quietly approaches where Saul and his men are encamped and discovers that Saul is asleep in the middle of the camp, surrounded by his three thousand-man army (see 1 Sam. 26:1–6). The story continues:

> So David and Abishai went to the army by night. And there lay Saul sleeping within the encampment, with his spear stuck in the ground at his head, and Abner and the army lay around him. Then Abishai said to David, "God has given your enemy into your hand this day. Now please let me pin him to the earth with one stroke of the spear, and I will not strike him twice." But David said to Abishai, "Do not destroy him, for who can put out his hand against the LORD's anointed and be guiltless?" And David said, "As the LORD lives, the LORD will strike him, or his day will come to die, or he will go down into battle and perish. The LORD forbid that I should put out my hand against the LORD's anointed. But take now the spear that is at his head and the jar of water and let us go." So David took the spear and the jar of water from Saul's head, and they went away. No man saw it or knew it, nor did any awake, for they were all asleep, because a deep sleep from the LORD had fallen upon them. (1 Sam. 26:7–12)

Upon discovering that Saul is indeed right in front of him, Abishai (one of David's military leaders) encourages David to kill

Saul in his sleep, stating that "God has given your enemy into your hand this day" (v. 8). This seems to be the perfect opportunity for David to take revenge against Saul by killing him. However, God has set up another test of the genuineness of David's faith. And once again he refuses to take the obvious action from a human perspective, even in the face of seeming righteous encouragement from Abishai. David responds, "Who can put out his hand against the LORD's anointed *and be guiltless?*" (v. 9, italics added). David is acutely aware of God's preferred action here; he knows what God wants him to do, and not do. So he refuses to take revenge against Saul.

Notice that the text states that the LORD causes a deep sleep to fall upon Saul and his army. This seems to explain why Abishai thinks David can do whatever he wishes to Saul. And yet David chooses instead to only take evidence that will prove he has been close enough to Saul to kill him, and yet did not do so.

What is behind this decision and action from David? It seems he learned an important lesson from the episode with Nabal and Abigail. He is convinced that God can take *his revenge* against Saul in some other way—the LORD could strike him down, or he could die in battle, or he could simply die at God's appointed time (v. 10). Clearly David believes that God will certainly pay Saul back in some way for his ongoing campaign to kill David. His statement reveals that his trust in God has reached a new level; he is trusting God to bring about the desired revenge *in his way and in his time.* He is willing to leave it all up to God. This confirms a greater degree of transformation of faith that God has accomplished in David's life, especially when compared to Saul's conduct toward David and his lack of trust in God.

Notice, however, that David does not forgo an opportunity to point out his righteous conduct regarding Saul. David goes to the top of a far-off hill and calls to the army, particularly Abner, and ridicules Abner in front of the king and the army—in essence, accusing him of not keeping successful watch over the king, the LORD's anointed. This implies that he has failed at his duty to protect the king; therefore, he deserves to die. As evidence that what he is saying is true, he asks Abner to look and see where the king's spear is and the jar of water that was at his head (see 1 Sam. 26:13–16).

David's accusations get the attention of those within the camp; Saul responds to him:

> Then Saul said, "I have sinned. Return, my son David, for I will no more do you harm, because my life was precious in your eyes this day. Behold, I have acted foolishly, and have made a great mistake." And David answered and said, "Here is the spear, O king! Let one of the young men come over and take it. The LORD rewards every man for his righteousness and his faithfulness, for the LORD gave you into my hand today, and I would not put out my hand against the LORD's anointed. Behold, as your life was precious this day in my sight, so may my life be precious in the sight of the LORD, and may he deliver me out of all tribulation." Then Saul said to David, "Blessed be you, my son David! You will do many things and will succeed in them." So David went his way, and Saul returned to his place. (1 Sam. 26:21–25)

In this text, David's own words provide clear evidence that the work of transformation has reached its pinnacle in his life. This is the second time he has had the opportunity to end Saul's life and his relentless campaign to kill him. Yet David's words and actions reveal his complete trust in and acceptance of God's will in this ongoing situation. To be seen as righteous and faithful by God is more important to David than taking revenge upon Saul (v. 23). Apparently, David considers this situation as a test by God to see whether or not he will lift his hand against the LORD's anointed, and in so doing against God himself. David goes on to reveal that his genuine concern is not for Saul to cease his efforts to kill him, but that his own life would be precious in the sight of God, just as Saul's life is precious enough to David to spare his life. David hopes that God will deliver him not just from Saul but from all tribulation (vv. 24–25).

David Flees to the Philistines

After this encounter with Saul, David realizes that Saul is not going to abandon his ongoing campaign to kill David until he is dead. He realizes that all his efforts to change Saul's attitude toward him have been in vain. Thus, since David cannot convince Saul to stop his campaign to kill him, he decides it is in his best interest to withdraw and go to the land of the Philistines, where Saul will no longer pursue him. So David goes to Gath along with his six hundred men, together with all their families and possessions. When Saul hears this, he no longer pursues David (see 1 Sam. 27:1–4). So it seems David's logic has worked.

David and his men, along with their households, stay in the land of the Philistines for one year and four months. But neither the Philistines nor Saul understand what his real purpose is:

> Now David and his men went up and made raids against the Geshurites, the Girzites, and the Amalekites, for these were the inhabitants of the land from of old, as far as Shur, to the land of Egypt. And David would strike the land and would leave neither man nor woman alive, but would take away the sheep, the oxen, the donkeys, the camels, and the garments, and come back to Achish. When Achish asked, "Where have you made a raid today?" David would say, "Against the Negeb of Judah," or, "Against the Negeb of the Jerahmeelites," or, "Against the Negeb of the Kenites." And David would leave neither man nor woman alive to bring news to Gath, thinking, "lest they should tell about us and say, 'So David has done.'" Such was his custom all the while he lived in the country of the Philistines. And Achish trusted David, thinking, "He has made himself an utter stench to his people Israel; therefore he shall always be my servant." (1 Sam. 27:8–12)

Here we see David's strategic retreat from Saul, knowing that he will not pursue David. However, as this text reveals, from the land of the Philistines, David performs raids against nations who are Israel's enemies, nations that God had instructed Israel (through Moses) to wipe out before them as they entered the Promised Land (Josh. 9:24). David and his men were not idle during this time of escaping Saul's pursuit. They were busy following God's commandment of old, which was left unfinished since the time when Israel first entered the land. Notice that David conceals these activities from the king of the Philistines. He lies to Achish, telling him he has taken action against other people groups that are enemies of the Philistines. This leads Achish to conclude that David has destroyed his reputation among the people of Israel, because news of the false action would suggest that David has finally sided with the Philistines, and thus become an enemy of Israel. Notice that while David knowingly deceives the Philistines, he takes no action against the Philistines that will harm them, only against their enemies. Once again, we see a high level of personal integrity in David's character, a further indicator of God's work of transformation in him.

The story continues in 1 Samuel, chapter 28. The Philistines again decided to come up to battle against Israel. Saul calls all the people of Israel together to fight the Philistines, but when he sees their army, he is very afraid. By this time, Samuel has died. As we saw in chapter 6, Saul previously banished mediums and necromancers from the land, so now there is no one he can go to for guidance and direction. Saul becomes desperate for guidance, so he seeks out one of the mediums who has remained in the land. He asks her to contact Samuel from beyond the grave to counsel Saul. Samuel reiterates what he has previously told him, that the LORD has torn the kingdom out of his hand and given it to David. Further, Saul is told that God will give Israel into the hand of the Philistines, and that the next day, he and his sons will die (see 1 Sam. 28:1–25).

As the time for battle approaches, David prepares to go into battle with the Philistines, but the commanders of the Philistines will not allow him to do so, fearing that in the battle, David will turn on them and become their adversary. They question how David can reconcile himself to his God if he fights against Israel. Thus, David and his men return to their homes in Ziklag (see 1 Sam. 29:1–11).

What were David's intentions in his willingness to go with the Philistines into battle against Israel? Would he have fought against Israel? Or would he have turned against the army of the Philistines during the battle? From David's words, he appears sincere in his willingness to fight with the Philistines against Israel. But because of what actually happens, it is appropriate to ask instead "Where is God in this?" Here God uses David's reputation to create fear of him in the minds of the Philistine commanders, which prevents him from going into battle with them against Israel. God intervenes to prevent him from having to make a decision about what to do. Thus, it remains unclear what David might have done, whether he would have fought against Israel or turned against the Philistines (see 1 Sam. 29:1–11).

As the story continues, it becomes apparent that God has purposes in mind for David other than engaging in the impending battle. When David and his men arrive in Ziklag three days later, they discover that the Amalekites have raided the broader area, including Ziklag. They have burned it and taken captive everyone in it and then left the area. David is greatly distressed, for his family who were living there, and because the people who are with him blame him for what has happened to their own families (see 1 Sam. 30:1–6).

David's Actions of Faith

In response to this devastating situation, David strengthens himself in the LORD, rather than responding in his humanness to this situation. He seeks God's direct instruction about what action he is to take:

> And David said to Abiathar the priest, the son of Ahimelech, "Bring me the ephod." So Abiathar brought the ephod to David. And David inquired of the LORD, "Shall I pursue after this band? Shall I overtake them?" He answered him, "Pursue, for you shall surely overtake and shall surely rescue." (1 Sam. 30:7–8)

In a situation such as this, the natural reaction would be for David and his men to immediately pursue the Amalekites in order to recover the family members and property seized in the raid. But David does not do that. Instead, he seeks direction from God. He is told to pursue the Amalekites and that he will overtake them. David's habit of seeking God's guidance and direction is confirmation that the work of transformation has succeeded in him, especially when his actions are compared to Saul; we have not seen him ask *God* for guidance and direction in similar situations. In fact he has sought guidance and advice from the dead through sorcerers. As we have seen and will continue to see, David consistently seeks God's guidance and council.

So David pursues the Amalekites as directed by God. He finds an Egyptian along the way who has been a servant to one of them; he knows where they were camped. When David and his men arrive at the Amalekite camp, they find the Amalekite army spread over all the land, eating, drinking, and dancing because of all the great spoil they have taken in raids in the land of the Philistines and Judah. David engages in battle, striking them down from dusk that day until the evening of the next day. He recovers all that the Amalekites took from them, including his two wives. No people and no possessions are missing. David also captures all the flocks and herds, so the people drive the livestock before him as they go back to their home in Ziklag (see 1 Sam. 30:8–20).

David's pursuit of the Amalekites succeeds just as God said it would, but the impact extends beyond merely recovering everything that was taken, as we read in the next passage:

> Then David came to the two hundred men who had been too exhausted to follow David, and who had been left at the brook Besor. And they went out to meet David and to meet the people who were with him. And when David came near to the people he greeted them. Then all the wicked and worthless fellows among the men who had gone with David said, "Because they did not go with us,

we will not give them any of the spoil that we have recovered, except that each man may lead away his wife and children, and depart." But David said, "You shall not do so, my brothers, with what the LORD has given us. He has preserved us and given into our hand the band that came against us. Who would listen to you in this matter? For as his share is who goes down into the battle, so shall his share be who stays by the baggage. They shall share alike." (1 Sam. 30:21–24)

Remember, David and his men had first gone out to prepare for battle against Israel, but they were forbidden to fight, so they returned to Ziklag after a total of six days of travel. Upon arrival and seeing what the Amalekites have done, they weep and moan until they are exhausted (1 Sam. 30:4). Immediately after expressing their deep sorrow, they depart in pursuit of the Amalekites. After an undisclosed number of days of additional travel, one-third of the men cannot continue, so they stay behind with the baggage.

Upon returning with family members and possessions that have been recovered, a number of the men do not want to share the spoils taken from the Amalekites with those who stayed behind. From a human perspective, their position has merit. In fact, the people whom they rescued from the Amalekites consider all of the spoil to belong to David personally (1 Sam. 30:20). However, notice David's response to their objections: he gives God all the credit for the victory, thereby nulli-fying any argument by these men about who should share in the spoils. Further, he declares that the share of those who went into battle will be the same as the share of those who stayed behind (v. 24). We then see that, upon returning to Ziklag, David begins to divide the spoils recov-ered from the Amalekites with the elders of the broad territory of Judah, and they had not even been out in the wilderness with him.

Here then is further confirmation of the successful work of transformation in David: he has a generous heart, a sign of godly character. It is revealed in his actions toward those who stayed behind because of exhaustion, and toward those who did not go with him to live in Philistine territory. He treats them the same as those who risked their lives when they went with him to recover possessions and family members. And that godly character is further revealed in his continued insistence to only give credit to God for this recent victory.

Transformation Complete

While David pursues the Amalekites, the Philistines fight against Israel. They overtake Saul and his sons, killing Jonathan and his two brothers, and then severely wound Saul. Afraid of what might happen if captured alive, Saul pleads with his armor-bearer to end his life; but ultimately, he takes his own sword and falls upon it. Thus, Samuel's prediction of Saul's death and that of his sons has been ful-filled.[3] When the men of Israel see that Saul and his sons are dead, they abandon their cities and flee, and the Philistines then come and live in the cities from which they have fled (see 1 Sam. 31:1–7).

We are now at an important point of transition in the story of David. The prophecy of Samuel has come true; Saul is dead. So David will soon become king, in fulfillment of Samuel's early prophecy. As we have seen, the work of transformation is complete in David: his faith and character have been tested, and he has remained faithful to God. In light of the ongoing comparisons between Saul and David in this chapter, we have to ask: will David be changed, as Saul was, once he ascends to the throne? In the next chapter, as we pick up David's story in 2 Samuel, we will examine whether such change occurs in him, or if his future words and actions remain consistent and thus confirm the successful work of transformation in him.

Lessons Learned from the Stories of Saul and David

1. One of the valuable lessons learned from the combined sto-ries of Saul and David is that the LORD sees not as man sees: man looks on "the outward appearance, but the LORD looks on the heart" (1 Sam. 16:7). From the outset, God

---

[3] See 1 Samuel 28:19 for Samuel's prediction about the death of Saul and his sons.

reveals the critical difference between Saul and David. Saul was physically handsome, head and shoulders taller than all the people; in terms of outward appearance, he looked like one would expect a king to look. However, God rejected him as king because he became the kind of king about whom God had warned the people: he refused to walk in God's ways or keep his statutes and commandments. David was also handsome with beautiful eyes (1 Sam. 16:12). Even the servants of Saul described him as "skillful in playing, a man of valor, a man of war, prudent in speech, and a man of good presence" (1 Sam. 16:14–19). But God saw more in David; God described him as "a man after my heart, who will do all my will" (Acts 13:22). When confronted by Israel's enemies, Saul depends upon the numbers of men who surround him and rational solutions to provide victory, while David depends upon God for victory. God became real for David, when early in his life while keeping his father's sheep, God delivered him from attacks by bears and lions. Because he had experienced God's saving grace and mercy in his youth, as an adult he trusted that God would do the same for him against Goliath and all his enemies, including Saul. Thus, from the outset, God knew why David would succeed where Saul had failed.

Consider: How does God view your heart? Like Saul, do you look and sound good outwardly, but inwardly refuse to walk in God's ways or keep his statutes and commandments? Or, will God see that you, like David, depend upon God for victory against your enemies and seek to do his will in all circumstances? As you contrast your story with David's, can you identify how and when God became real for you, when he became more than just an abstract concept read about in Scripture? Can you identify how and when you have experienced God's saving grace and mercy in such a way as to see your faith be transformed and strengthen over time?

2. Another valuable lesson to learn from the story of Saul and David is the difference between Saul's and David's *relationship with God*. On the one hand, Saul knew about God—having been raised in a Jewish home and later instructed by Samuel about how to walk in his ways and obey his statutes and commandments. However, none of those things caused God to become real for him. On the other hand, from a young age, David experienced God's power and protection, by which God became real for him. Thus, it is evident that there is a vast difference between *knowing about God* and intimately *knowing him by experiencing him*. David's reference to him as "the living God" (1 Sam. 17:26) further highlights this difference, especially when compared to Saul's few references to God. Remember that while talking to Samuel, he always referred to God as "your God." David's relationship with the "living God" is the foundation for everything that David does and does not do. Thus, despite his youth, God undertakes the process of transformation in him. David's willingness to step forward to fight Goliath when no one else would do so testifies to his trust in God's sovereign control over all things. Likewise, even after Samuel anoints him to be the next king over Israel, David continues to humble himself to serve the very one whose kingship he will take over. Genuine belief, trust, and acceptance move an individual beyond mere words of faith to actually living out that faith, giving clear evidence that God is real in one's life. God's process of transformation can occur even in young people like David; it can change the gentle lyre player and poet into one who can strike down the enemies of God.

Consider: As you reflect on your life up to this point in time, how do you view your relationship with God? How have your early attitudes and feelings about God affected your faith? Is he the God of your parents or grandparents or spouse, or is he the one true living God as he was for

David? Has God become real for you? Have you experienced his power and protection? If not, take some time now to ask him to reveal himself to you in a way that changes your heart toward him.

3. A final lesson to learn from the story of Saul and David occurs when, on a certain feast day, David sent some of his men to ask Nabal to give whatever he has at hand to David and his men, that they might celebrate the feast day, as a way of thanking them for safeguarding his sheep and shepherds while they were with David in the wilderness. When Nabal defiantly refuses to give any of his own provisions to David and his men, David becomes angry—mad enough that he intends to wipe out all that belongs to Nabal. But, Nabal's wife, Abigail, sees David and takes her husband's guilt upon herself for being ungracious. She then seeks to calm David's emotions and to keep him from taking vengeance by his own hand and thus sin against God. He is immediately aware that God is actively at work in his daily life events, even as he seeks to solve Nabal's affront in ways that are unacceptable to God. He blesses Abigail, a woman, for intervening as God directed, thus stopping him before he could act in a sinful manner.

Consider: As you reflect on this part of the story of Saul and David, ask yourself if you are able to discern when God is guiding and directing you through the words and actions of others. Do you consistently look for God's hand guiding and directing the events of your life? Or do you consistently take things in your own hands to bring about the end result that you desire, which may not be God's desire for you?

CHAPTER 8

David

In the last chapter we focused on comparing and contrasting the lives of both Saul and David. As we have seen in Moses, we see also in David that the work of transformation necessary for him to do the work God has called him to do has been completed well before the end of his life. In fact, it has been completed before he ascends to the throne and reigns as king.

In this chapter, we will examine the *genuineness* of David's transformed faith. The rest of his story is about testing God's work of transformation in him: Is it genuine? Is it sturdy? Will he live from a place of genuine faith, even in the face of the challenges he will face as king? Or like Saul, will he become more self-centered and choose to rely on human strength and wisdom?

We saw at the end of the last chapter that Saul and his three sons, including Jonathan, have died in yet another battle with the Philistines. We now pick up David's story in 2 Samuel 1 and follow it through 2 Samuel 24.

Saul and Jonathan Die

After David returns from striking down the Amalekites, a man comes from Saul's camp to tell him what has happened during the battle with the Philistines: the people have fled from the battle, and many have fallen and died—including Saul and his son Jonathan. When David asks how the young man knows that Saul and his son Jonathan are dead, he reveals that, at Saul's request, he stood beside him and killed him, because the young man was sure that Saul could not live after he was wounded. He then shows David that he has Saul's crown and armlet (see 2 Sam. 1:1–10). We see David respond to this news in the next passage:

> Then David took hold of his clothes and tore them, and so did all the men who were with him. And they mourned and wept and fasted until evening for Saul and for Jonathan his son and for the people of the LORD and for the house of Israel, because they had fallen by the sword. And David said to the young man who told him, "Where do you come from?" And he answered, "I am the son of a sojourner, an Amalekite." David said to him, "How is it you were not afraid to put out your hand to destroy the LORD's anointed?" Then David called one of the young men and said, "Go, execute him." And he struck him down so that he died. And David said to him, "Your blood be on your head, for your own mouth has testified against you, saying, 'I have killed the LORD's anointed.'" (2 Sam. 1:11–16)

This is a crucial text from which to begin to evaluate whether the work of transformation is genuinely fruitful in David's life. Here is a perfect opportunity for him to think: Saul is dead, and I have been anointed to replace him; thus, whatever feelings I have previously had toward Saul no longer matter. However, this is not what happens. Rather, from this text it is clear that David continues to be guided by the standard that *no one* raises their hand against the LORD's anointed. The young Amalekite man has no reason to think this way since he is a foreigner, not an Israelite. However, by his words and actions, David reveals that God's standards are sovereign over the conduct of all people, not just the people of Israel. Thus, David has the young man put to death.[1]

---

[1]   Most commentators believe that the account of the Amalekite is a lie told in the opportunistic hopes of gaining a reward from King David; they give a variety of

Then David greatly laments the death of Saul and his son Jonathan, which reveals the actual condition of his heart. It is easy to understand his lament over Jonathan, whom he loved more than any other. But we might expect that he would not lament over Saul, who relentlessly pursued him, who sought to kill him for years. However, we see in his actions that he also loved Saul simply because he was the LORD's anointed. For David, loving God's anointed is an act of love toward God himself (see 2 Sam. 1:17–27).

This is a crucial lesson about the lasting impact that God's work of transformation has upon us, and an indication that his work in us has taken root: we become able to truly love our enemies, because doing so becomes an act of loving God. Loving our enemies is an act of unconditional love that emerges out of a transformed heart.

Seeking God's Will

David's subsequent actions provide another critical indicator of the successful work of transformation in him:

> After this David inquired of the LORD, "Shall I go up into any of the cities of Judah?" And the LORD said to him, "Go up." David said, "To which shall I go up?" And he said, "To Hebron." So David went up there, and his two wives also, Ahinoam of Jezreel and Abigail the widow of Nabal of Carmel. And David brought up his men who were with him, everyone with his household, and they lived in the towns of Hebron. And the men of Judah came, and there they anointed David king over the house of Judah. (2 Sam. 2:1–4)

---

reasons for doing so. But the single reason David gives for killing him *in this text* is further underscored by his words in 2 Sam. 4:9–10, "As the LORD lives, who has redeemed my life out of every adversity, when one told me, 'Behold, Saul is dead,' and thought he was bringing good news, I seized him and killed him at Ziklag."

Following Saul's death, David is ready to move on. But before doing so, he asks the LORD where he should go. This is a simple request for guidance and direction. He does not *presume* to know what God wants him to do now that Saul is dead, neither about where to go nor about the timing of being crowned king. There is no indication that he is intent upon asserting his kingship at this time. Instead, he merely inquires of God about where he should go next and leaves the details to God. So, God directs him to go to Hebron. David obeys, taking two wives with him, along with his army and all their families and possessions. Take note, however, of what verse 4 says, "The men of Judah came, and there they anointed David king over the house of Judah." Once he arrives in the Hebron region, God moves the hearts of the men of Judah to anoint him king over them.[2]

We see in this passage that, in this critical transition point in David's life, he continues to live his life as a transformed individual, continuing to seek out God's guidance and direction before he acts, and then he obeys. It is interesting that, as David is obediently doing what God tells him to do, God prepares to do more than David expects, confirming his kingship by the actions of the men of Judah.

After this, David learns that the men of Jabesh-gilead have buried Saul. So, he sends messengers to them, relaying his desire that God will bless them and show them his steadfast love and faithfulness, because they have shown their loyalty to Saul by burying him. Further, he assures them that he will treat them well in light of their actions toward Saul. Finally, he encourages them to be strong and valiant, even though Saul is dead, because he has been anointed king over them (see 2 Sam. 2:5–7). Once again, David is not required to do these things. Yet, by doing so, he continues to reveal his unconditional love for Saul which demonstrates the successful work of transformation in his life.

Following this, there is a long war between the house of Saul and the house of David. The commander of Saul's army installs one of Saul's sons over Israel (excluding Judah), who reigns for two years.

---

[2] This action by the men of Judah is a limited action, as it does not establish David as king over all of Israel at this time, only over Judah.

During this time, David gradually grows stronger while the house of Saul becomes weaker (see 2 Sam. 2:8–3:1). And yet, through this time David does not seek to have himself established as the king of Israel. He continues to leave the outcome of this situation in the hands of God.

As the story continues, and in light of someone else acting as king over Israel, it is important to remember that David previously made two promises: one to Saul and the other to Jonathan. To Saul, he promised not to wipe out his offspring and thus his name from the land (1 Sam. 24:21–22). To Jonathan, he promised to take care of his descendants after him (1 Sam. 20:15). Thus, as this conflict between David and Saul's sons continues in the following texts, it is essential to notice whether David keeps his promises to Saul and Jonathan, even after they have died. Remember, no one knows about these promises except David and God. Therefore, whether or not he honors those promises will provide further evidence as to whether the work of transformation has genuinely succeeded in him.

Abner and Ish-bosheth

While this conflict between "the house of Saul and the house of David" (2 Sam. 3:1) continues, an internal conflict emerges in Saul's camp between Abner, the commander of Saul's army, and Ish-bosheth, Saul's son. Abner vows to transfer the kingdom from the house of Saul to David. So, he sends messengers to David, and they make a covenant with each other: Abner will gather all Israel to David as king. Notice that David still does not initiate any effort to become king over Israel; Abner initiates everything that is about to transpire.

This is a good point to ask, where is God in this? As commander of the army of Israel, Abner could attempt to become king himself. But he does not do so, even though he led Saul's relentless campaign to kill David. Additionally, this action that he initiates is startling because of his embarrassment by David during their last encounter.[3]

---

[3] See 1 Samuel 26:13–16 for the last encounter between David and Abner, when David accused him of failing in his duty to keep the king safe while he slept.

Through Abner's actions, his lack of seeking the kingship for himself, seeking instead to make David king over all of Israel, God continues to work on David's behalf to ensure that God's purposes become a reality (see 2 Sam. 3:12–21).

When Joab hears that David has let Abner leave and return home in peace, rather than keeping him with David as a potential spy, Joab sends messengers to bring Abner back without David's knowledge. Abner returns to Hebron and is then killed by Joab and his brother Abishai, in revenge for killing their brother Asahel during a battle at Gibeon. When David hears what has happened, he openly mourns for Abner, clearly placing responsibility for his death on Joab and his brother. But he refrains from taking action against them. Instead, he defers that right to the LORD to repay those who have done wrong. Again, we see confirmation that the work of transformation has succeeded in David's life; he resists seeking revenge himself and trusts that God will do so (see 2 Sam. 3:22–39).

In chapter 4 of 2 Samuel, we see that Ish-bosheth, king of Israel, loses his courage when he hears that Abner has died. In fact, all in Israel are dismayed. Two captains of his own raiding bands come into his house and kill Ish-bosheth in his sleep to avenge David against his enemies, and thus endear themselves to him. David, however, considers Ish-bosheth a righteous man, because of his covenant with Saul. Additionally, in the two years of his reign, he has not sought to kill David as his father had done. So, just as David had the man killed who killed Saul, he commands his men to kill these two captains. Then, David shows respect for Ish-bosheth when he has the head of Ish-bosheth buried in the tomb of Abner at Hebron. This action of respect shows that he will fulfill his promise to Saul to continue to honor his name. And it is further confirmation that the work of transformation endures in David (see 2 Sam. 4:1–12).

David Anointed King of Israel

After this, all the tribes of Israel come to David at Hebron, acknowledging to him that they know of his military leadership during the years of Saul's reign. They also acknowledge that God has said that *David* is to be king over his people Israel, so all of the elders of the tribes of Israel go to David in Hebron, where David makes a covenant with them before God. They then anoint him king over Israel (see 2 Sam. 5:1–12), which reunites all of Israel (Judah and the rest of Israel) under one king once again.

The following text describes two battles with the Philistines, which serve to challenge David as king:

> When the Philistines heard that David had been anointed king over Israel, all the Philistines went up to search for David. But David heard of it and went down to the stronghold. Now the Philistines had come and spread out in the Valley of Rephaim. And David inquired of the LORD, "Shall I go up against the Philistines? Will you give them into my hand?" And the LORD said to David, "Go up, for I will certainly give the Philistines into your hand." And David came to Baal-perazim, and David defeated them there. And he said, "The LORD has broken through my enemies before me like a breaking flood." Therefore, the name of that place is called Baal-perazim. And the Philistines left their idols there, and David and his men carried them away.
>
> And the Philistines came up yet again and spread out in the Valley of Rephaim. And when David inquired of the LORD, he said, "You shall not go up; go around to their rear, and come against them opposite the balsam trees. And when you hear the sound of marching in the tops of the balsam trees, then rouse yourself, for then the LORD has gone out before you to strike down the army of the Philistines." And David did as the LORD commanded him, and struck down the Philistines from Geba to Gezer. (2 Sam. 5:17–25)

This is a pivotal text in which to examine the genuineness of David's faith, to see what effect becoming king might have on his faith—his dependence upon and trust in God. He has just become king over both Israel and Judah. And the Philistines immediately prepare for battle against him and the people of Israel.

It is easy to see these two battles, one after the other, as some kind of test for David as king on a human level, and a test of the genuineness of his faith on a spiritual level. Since David has not yet lost a battle against the Philistines, he could become overly confident in his own strength and wisdom, as Saul had done. However, David responds to the Philistine threats differently. In his response, we can see several important points that clarify the condition of his faith and reveal what kind of king he really is.

First, notice that in the face of both battles, David seeks God's guidance and direction before determining how to respond to the Philistines' challenge to himself and his people. He does not question *if* he should seek guidance from God; *he simply does so.* This is the way he lives life. He knows God is sovereign in all things; he learned in his youth that God is with him, giving him guidance, direction, and protection.[4] Therefore, he automatically seeks God's wisdom about how to proceed in the face of the Philistine threat before he takes any action.

Next, notice that God is very specific about what David is to do. Also notice that he gives David different guidance for each situation. In the face of the first battle, David asks if he should do what he is thinking of doing, "go up against the Philistines" (v. 19), and God tells him to go. When the second confrontation emerges, David again asks if he should go up against the Philistines; God says no. Instead, God redirects David around his enemy and then commands him to wait until God is ready to go before him (vv. 22-24). In both situations, God reveals that if David obeys God's instructions, he will defeat the Philistines. David does obey God, and he does defeat them.

---

[4] See 1 Samuel 17:34–37.

The detail of this interaction reveals that, over time, a very intimate and trusting relationship has developed between David and God. We see the degree of David's trust in God, for he immediately seeks out God's guidance. God speaks freely to David about what he is to do and what the outcome of his actions will be—assuming he obeys God. David does not question what God has told him; he simply hears and obeys.

This response from David is the hallmark of genuine faith. When God has become real for a person, their trust in God is deep and unquestioning. It results in one seeking out God's guidance and wisdom in life situations, with a willingness to obey God's direction. The challenge for us today, as we go through our own transformation process, is to learn how to discern the way God communicates his guidance and wisdom to us. The broader lesson here is that we have clear evidence that God is, indeed, active in the lives of those whom he has called to provide genuine guidance and direction to his people.

Testing David's Faith

In 2 Samuel 6:1–7, following his dual victories over the Philistines, we see that David's heart returns to focus on God. In the exuberance of the recent victories, David gathers thirty thousand of his chosen men to bring the ark of God to Jerusalem. Thus, it appears that David and all of Israel are celebrating their victory over the Philistines before the LORD with lyres, harps, tambourines, castanets, and cymbals. At one point in the journey, the oxen stumble as they pull the cart that contains the ark. Uzzah puts his hand out to keep it from falling. God's anger is kindled against Uzzah and immediately strikes him down. He dies right there beside the ark of God. David responds to what has happened:

> And David was angry because the LORD had broken out against Uzzah. And that place is called Perez-uzzah to this day. And David was afraid of the LORD that day, and he said, "How can the

ark of the LORD come to me?" So David was not willing to take the ark of the LORD into the city of David. But David took it aside to the house of Obed-edom the Gittite. And the ark of the LORD remained in the house of Obed-edom the Gittite three months, and the LORD blessed Obed-edom and all his household. (2 Sam. 6:8–11)

Notice David's response to what happened. First, he is angry at God for striking Uzzah dead for what seems to be an innocent act, trying to keep the ark upright. He then becomes so afraid of God that he changes his plans. In light of what has just occurred, he decides to leave the ark where it is; he aborts the move of the ark to "the city of David" (v. 10).

Verse 3 notes that Uzzah died for "his error"—he touched the ark of God, which was forbidden by God's statutes on how to move the ark (see Exod. 25:13–14 and elsewhere). His intentions were understandable, a natural reaction to the possibility that the ark might fall to the ground. In that quick moment, God's statutes regarding the handling of the ark did not come to mind. Obviously, by God's reaction, we see that actions that stem from good intentions but are not in line with God's statues are not sufficient to avoid the serious consequences of breaking God's commands—especially in "holy" matters. Thus, Uzzah's death became a gruesome reminder for David of the "absoluteness" of God's statutes. It is no wonder that he now fears God (v. 9).

In reality, David was the one ultimately responsible for Uzzah's death. In his exuberance to bring the ark of God to Jerusalem, he forgot God's statutes and commandments about how the ark is supposed to be moved. Based on the text, David does not consult with the priests before moving the ark, nor do we see him ask God if he is to do so. In this case, he does not follow his habit of seeking God's direction and guidance before taking action. David must have quickly realized his errors as he looked upon the body of Uzzah, perhaps wondering what his own punishment might be. So he stops the procession, refusing to move the ark any further. And he leaves it there three months.

Eventually David is told that God has blessed the house of Obed-edom during the months that the ark as been there. David goes back and brings the ark of God to the city of David, rejoicing with a sacrifice and dancing before the LORD with "all his might" amid exuberant celebration (see 2 Sam. 6:12–15).

Notice that God does not directly speak to David throughout the time that this event is unfolding. However, it is clear that God has been present and is actively involved in what is going on because of the quick death of Uzzah. We can also see God's active involvement in this situation in the blessing of the house of Obed-edom while the ark has been lodged there. In this text, we can see God testing David, to determine if he will come to understand his errors without God specifically pointing them out to him. And David does so, which provides further confirmation of the continuing effect of the work of transformation in his life. He discovers his sin and immediately repents—changes direction to a path that is acceptable to God.

This effect of transformation becomes further evident by what happens next:

> And David returned to bless his household. But Michal the daughter of Saul came out to meet David and said, "How the king of Israel honored himself today, uncovering himself today before the eyes of his servants' female servants, as one of the vulgar fellows shamelessly uncovers himself!" And David said to Michal, "It was before the LORD, who chose me above your father and above all his house, to appoint me as prince over Israel, the people of the LORD—and I will celebrate before the LORD. I will make myself yet more contemptible than this, and I will be abased in your eyes. But by the female servants of whom you have spoken, by them I shall be held in honor." And Michal the daughter of Saul had no child to the day of her death. (2 Sam. 6:20–23)

To fully appreciate what happens in this text, it is essential to remember that Michal is David's first wife for whom he and his men killed two hundred Philistines as double the agreed-upon bride-price. She was also the one for whom David demanded of Abner and Ish-bosheth that they bring her to him before he would enter into covenant with them to become king of Israel (see 2 Sam. 3:13). Michal was the most important woman in his life up to this point. Yet when Michal criticizes him for dancing before the LORD in what she considers to be an inappropriate manner, he rebukes her. David is not interested in her feelings about how he chooses to celebrate before the LORD. He responds by saying that he will continue to celebrate, and in doing so, he will no doubt make himself even more contemptible (v. 22).

In this episode with the ark, we see David's actions as a failure to seek God's guidance, and he receives a correction. We also see that, regardless of how important Michal is to David, the only opinion that matters to David is God's opinion, which is further evidence of the continuing strength of the work of transformation in his life.

God's Rebuke

After this, God gives David rest from all his enemies, during which time he tells Nathan the Prophet of his desire to build a house of cedar in which the ark of God can dwell. Initially, Nathan tells him to do all that is in his heart. But then God gives Nathan different instructions for David:

> "Now, therefore, thus you shall say to my servant David, 'Thus says the LORD of hosts, I took you from the pasture, from following the sheep, that you should be prince over my people Israel. And I have been with you wherever you went and have cut off all your enemies from before you. And I will make for you a great name, like the name of the great ones of the earth. And I will appoint a place for my people Israel and will plant them,

so that they may dwell in their own place and be disturbed no more. And violent men shall afflict them no more, as formerly, from the time that I appointed judges over my people Israel. And I will give you rest from all your enemies. Moreover, the LORD declares to you that the LORD will make you a house. When your days are fulfilled and you lie down with your fathers, I will raise up your offspring after you, who shall come from your body, and I will establish his kingdom. He shall build a house for my name, and I will establish the throne of his kingdom forever. I will be to him a father, and he shall be to me a son. When he commits iniquity, I will discipline him with the rod of men, with the stripes of the sons of men, but my steadfast love will not depart from him, as I took it from Saul, whom I put away from before you. And your house and your kingdom shall be made sure forever before me. Your throne shall be established forever.'" In accordance with all these words, and in accordance with all this vision, Nathan spoke to David. (2 Sam. 7:8–17)

In this text, God has Nathan deliver a mild rebuke to David for desiring to build a house for God, which he never requested. David's failure is one of presuming that God would want such a thing done, without asking him. Thus, God proceeds to remind David of all that he has done, first for Israel and then for David himself. God then tells him what he intends to do in the future for Israel and for him and his offspring. Dwelling in a house of cedar such as David would build is not essential to God. Additionally, he does not intend for *David* to be the one to build a house for God. Rather, God has already decided that one of David's offspring will do so. Thus, God draws a clear distinction for David between the physical house that David could build and the spiritual one that only God will build through David and his offspring.

In David's response to the rebuke in 2 Samuel 7:18–24, we see the effects of the transformation process on his heart. He immediately goes before the LORD and prays, acknowledging that God is responsible for the promise that he has just made to David (to "establish his kingdom" of his offspring after him; 2 Sam. 7:12). His humility leads him to acknowledge God's greatness, that there is none like him, and that it is God himself who has established the people of Israel as God's own people. He then continues in prayer:

"And now, O LORD God, confirm forever the word that you have spoken concerning your servant and concerning his house, and do as you have spoken. And your name will be magnified forever, saying, 'The LORD of hosts is God over Israel,' and the house of your servant David will be established before you. For you, O LORD of hosts, the God of Israel, have made this revelation to your servant, saying, "I will build you a house." Therefore your servant has found courage to pray this prayer to you. And now, O LORD God, you are God, and your words are true, and you have promised this good thing to your servant. Now therefore may it please you to bless the house of your servant, so that it may continue forever before you. For you, O LORD God, have spoken, and with your blessing shall the house of your servant be blessed forever." (2 Sam. 7:25–29)

By his prayer of adoration, David reveals his understanding of what God was communicating to him through Nathan the Prophet, recognizing and attributing to God all that he has already done for Israel and for himself. He submits himself to God's will by saying, "Do as you have spoken" (v. 25). Notice that there is no self-justification, no effort to explain his motivation. Thus, David's response to God's word to him confirms his understanding of the supremacy of

God over all things. He has a right perspective about who *God* is and who *he* is. This is also evidence of the genuineness of his faith.

Fulfilling a Covenant

About this time, David seeks to know if there is anyone left of the house of Saul; he wants to carry out his covenantal promise to Jonathan, to show his kindness toward his descendants for Jonathan's sake. Ziba, a servant of the house of Saul, tells him that there is still a son of Jonathan named Mephibosheth, who is lame in both feet. David asks for Mephibosheth to be brought to him. When he arrives, David tells him that he desires to show him kindness for the sake of his father Jonathan; thus, he does not need to be afraid. David reveals that he will restore to him all the land of Saul and that he has decided that Mephibosheth will always have a place at David's table, to eat with him as one of his own sons. Then David declares to Ziba that all who once belonged to Saul, including Ziba and his sons, now belong to Mephibosheth (see 2 Sam. 9:1–13).

It is important to note that David's treatment of Mephibosheth exceeds the covenant he had made with Jonathan, which was to not to cut off his love from Jonathan's house forever (see 1 Sam. 20:15). Restoring Saul's land to Mephibosheth was a grand gesture of love. Ziba and his household were more than capable of providing for him, but David was not satisfied with just providing for him. So, he gave Mephibosheth a permanent seat at the king's table, which elevated him to a position of honor within his kingdom. This act of generosity, faithfulness, and love reveal more of David's true heart and the transforming work God has accomplished in him.

Conflict with Enemies

In chapter 10 of 2 Samuel, we see David take on the armies of neighboring countries. David learns that the king of the Ammonites has died. Since David has maintained good relations with him, he sends his servants to Hanun, who succeeded his father as king, to express his condolences to Hanun. However, Hanun is convinced by others that David's servants are there to spy out the city and to overthrow it. So Hanun takes actions against David's servants, greatly humiliating them, and then sends them away. When the Ammonites see that they have been wrong about David's intentions, they hire thousands of foot soldiers, along with a large number of men from other neighboring countries, to fight against David and his men who come out to avenge the shame committed against David's servants (see 2 Sam. 10:1–8).

Joab and the people who are with him position themselves to battle against the Syrians, who flee. When the Ammonites see that the Syrians have fled, they likewise flee before Israel. Then the Syrians gather together more reinforcements and join with other forces to again confront David. He gathers all of Israel's army together and defeats the opposing armies, whose leaders then make peace with Israel (see 2 Sam. 10:9–19).

Once again it is critical to ask, where is God in this situation? Notice that, unlike on previous occasions when David sought God's guidance and direction before taking action, he does not do so in these most recent texts—at least Scripture does not say that he does. And yet, the army of Israel continues to be victorious every time they go out to battle against their enemies. So we have to ask: does David now believe that the army of Israel can be victorious apart from God, as Saul did? Or does he still maintain his trust in and obedience to God? These texts do not provide the answer. Thus, it is essential to keep these questions in mind as the story of David continues, to see if the work of transformation has been genuinely fruitful in David's life.

Character Failure

One of the best-known parts of the story of David is how his relationship with Bathsheba begins, and that it ends with her becoming his wife and giving birth to a son. Because this period of David's life is so well-known, we only summarize it here, from 2 Samuel 11:1–12:14, including God's rebuke to David through Nathan.

While all of Israel's army is out on the battlefield to battle the Ammonites, David is in Jerusalem. Late one afternoon he takes a walk on the roof of his house, and he sees a beautiful woman bathing. Even after learning that she is married, David sends messengers to bring her to him, and he sleeps with her. She returns to her house, only to discover later that she is pregnant. Upon hearing this news, David sends word to Joab, his army commander, to send her husband, Uriah the Hittite, back from the battlefield. David is hoping that he will take the opportunity to go home and sleep with his wife, and thus provide a cover-up for his own mistake. Uriah does return from battle. In three different ways, David then tries to entice him to go home and lay with his wife so that what he has done might be concealed. But Uriah repeatedly refuses to do so (see 2 Sam. 11:1–13).

As the story continues, David then asks commander Joab to station Uriah in the forefront of the hardest fighting. David's hope is that Uriah might die in battle. Joab does as David has commanded, and Uriah dies in battle. He then sends a servant to David with the news about the battle, including the fact that Uriah is dead. David responds with apparent indifference, as a seasoned warrior would be expected to do; men die in battle. When Bathsheba hears that her husband is dead, she laments over him. When her mourning period ends, David sends for her, and she becomes his wife and bears him a son. For the moment, he no doubt believes all that he has done will remain a secret. However, the LORD is displeased with David's actions (see 2 Sam. 11:14–27).

Consequences of Sin

In 2 Samuel 12:1–10, we see that, in response to David's actions, God again sends Nathan to David to confront him about his sin. He does so by telling a story of how a rich man, who has large flocks and herds, is unwilling to take one of his animals to prepare a meal for a guest. Instead, he takes the poor man's only lamb and prepares it. Upon hearing this, David's anger is great, declaring that the man who has done this deserves to die. He even suggests that the man be required to restore the lamb fourfold to the poor man. Nathan tells David that *he* is that man. His rebuke is for despising the word of the LORD and doing what is evil in God's sight; he has taken another man's wife and has had Uriah killed by the sword. Nathan declares to him that, as a result of his sinful actions, "the sword would never depart from his house" (v. 10). Nathan continues:

> "Thus says the LORD, 'Behold, I will raise up evil against you out of your own house. And I will take your wives before your eyes and give them to your neighbor, and he shall lie with your wives in the sight of this sun. For you did it secretly, but I will do this thing before all Israel and before the sun.'" David said to Nathan, "I have sinned against the LORD." And Nathan said to David, "The LORD also has put away your sin; you shall not die. Nevertheless, because by this deed you have utterly scorned the LORD, the child who is born to you shall die." (2 Sam. 12:11–14)

This text reveals a great deal regarding the heart of David, the heart of a man in whom the work of transformation has succeeded. Nathan confronts him, laying bare all that David has done and his attempts at a cover-up. He declares what God's judgment will be. In response, David humbly replies that he has "sinned against the LORD" (v. 13). Notice that in sharp contrast to what Saul did when he was confronted by Samuel, David offers no excuse or justification for his actions when confronted by Nathan. Rather, he offers a simple word of confession.

Here we see further confirmation of the success of the work of transformation in David's life. We are all human; no one is perfect. Therefore, we *will* sin. Failure by sin does not diminish, remove, or undo the work of transformation that has already taken place. Rather, such events in our lives reveal that God does test our faith. Our *response* is what is most important, for it reveals the degree of transformation that has taken place and the genuineness of our faith. We see that David's response is one of stating the truth in humility, not providing justification for his actions. His response to Nathan's rebuke is what we would expect from a person whose faith has been transformed from simple belief into genuine faith.

Notice also God's response to David's simple act of contrition. First, Nathan says that God "has taken away your sin," indicating that forgiveness is complete. David will not die, although his actions show "utter contempt for the LORD" (v. 13). God shows great mercy for David himself, but he will still experience the consequences of his sin through the death of his child. What is true for David is also true for us. When we sin, our sins are forgiven when we confess in humble truth and repent. However, we will still experience the consequences of our actions.

In light of God's response to David's confession, we might question if he was sincere in what he spoke, or was he merely responding in a way that would satisfy Nathan, just as Saul did to Samuel? The answer to that question is apparent from David's words recorded in Psalm 51:1–12. There we see the heartfelt cry of one who knows his sin, the merciful character of God, and his own deep desire to be cleansed from his sin. He reveals that his sin is against God alone. He acknowledges that God is justified in his words and is thus blameless in his judgment on David. He knows that only God is able to cleanse his heart and give him a new and right spirit. He well knows that his sin can separate him from God, and he prays for cleansing that he might be restored to an intimate relationship with God once again.

David's words are the expression of his relationship with God. He acknowledges that he is ultimately accountable to God in all things, that what Nathan had said was right, that his sin was against God alone. By saying this, David accepts God's judgment—that the son born to him will die.

God's Judgment

His son becomes sick, and for seven days, David fasts and prays in the hope that God will change his mind. When his son does die, we again see David's true heart:

> Then David arose from the earth and washed and anointed himself and changed his clothes. And he went into the house of the LORD and

worshiped. He then went to his own house. And when he asked, they set food before him, and he ate. Then his servants said to him, "What is this thing that you have done? You fasted and wept for the child while he was alive; but when the child died, you arose and ate food." He said, "While the child was still alive, I fasted and wept, for I said, 'Who knows whether the LORD will be gracious to me, that the child may live?' But now he is dead. Why should I fast? Can I bring him back again? I shall go to him, but he will not return to me." (2 Sam. 12:20–23)

The sequence of events in these verses is critical for understanding God's work of transformation in David's life. It reveals that David's actions confirm the truth of his words. While the child is still alive, he fasts, prays, and weeps, hoping that God will be gracious and let the child live. In so doing, he humbly acknowledges the sovereignty of God in this matter. Then when the child dies, he cleans himself up and goes to worship God. He then goes home, asks for food, and eats once again. These actions further confirm his submission to the sovereignty of God; he has accepted God's judgment. Additionally, in the midst of his loss, he worships. This is a profound demonstration of his submission to the authority and sovereignty of God.

This series of texts regarding the relationship between David and Bathsheba, and the consequences of David's actions, provides two critical lessons regarding the work of transformation. The first lesson shows that even when the work of transformation is complete, our conduct will not be perfect. And when confronted with our sin, David's example shows us that our response is to be one of humble confession and repentance before God.

The second lesson shows that when the work of transformation has been successful, our actions will be consistent with the words we have spoken. In stark contrast to Saul, whose actions were rarely congruent with his words, David's actions in these texts confirm what he says to Nathan and God: he knows he has sinned, and he acts accordingly. The consistency between David's words and actions is confirmation of the genuineness of the transformation process that has taken place in him.

Kingship Threatened by Absalom

Another well-known part of the story of David, which reveals how God continues to test the genuineness of David's transformed faith, begins in 2 Samuel, chapter 13, with an internal family crisis. As this part of David's story continues to unfold, we learn about David's love for his son Absalom.

Absalom's sister, Tamar, is sexually assaulted by Amnon, another of David's sons. When David finds out what has happened, he is outraged; but he takes no action (2 Sam. 13:1–22). After two years, and still no action taken by David, Absalom takes revenge himself against Amnon and has him killed, which he has been determined to do from the day the event took place. Absalom then flees to another country where he stays for three years. During this time, David mourns for his son Absalom. Finally, having reconciled himself with Amnon's death, he longs to see Absalom (see 2 Sam. 13:23–38).

When challenged about his continuing estrangement from Absalom, David relents and sends Joab to bring Absalom back to Jerusalem (2 Sam. 14:1–24). Absalom returns and lives two years in Jerusalem without coming to see his father. Then Absalom forces Joab to go to his father to get permission for Absalom to go into the king's presence. He acknowledges that if David finds him guilty, he is willing to be put to death. As a result of Joab's report to David, he summons Absalom. When he arrives, Absalom bows his face to the ground before David. In response, David kisses Absalom (see 2 Sam. 14:28–33), an action that indicates he will not kill him.

However, Absalom is not satisfied with simply having his privileges as a son restored. He begins to seek to undermine David's kingship and steal the loyalty of the men of Israel. At the end of four years, Absalom sends secret messengers throughout all the tribes of Israel revealing his plan to have himself declared king. As a result, the

conspiracy grows strong, and the number of people with him continues to increase (see 2 Sam. 15:1–12).

When David learns what Absalom is doing, he leaves Jerusalem
with the people from his household, including Zadok, the priest.
The Levites, who are with him, carry the ark of the covenant of God.
David instructs Zadok:

> "Carry the ark of God back into the city. If I
> find favor in the eyes of the LORD, he will bring
> me back and let me see both it and his dwelling
> place. But if he says, 'I have no pleasure in you,'
> behold, here I am, let him do to me what seems
> good to him." (2 Sam. 15:25–26)

David's words demonstrate his complete trust in God and his
unwavering acceptance of God's will for his life. For David, it is God
who determines what will happen, and David will accept whatever he
does without question. By sending the ark of God back to Jerusalem
with the priests, his actions match his words; both his words and
actions demonstrate his trust and acceptance of God's sovereignty.

As the story of David continues, the consistency between David's
words and actions continues to confirm the success of the work of
transformation in his life. When David is told that Ahithophel, his
most respected counselor, is among the conspirators with Absalom,
he is bold enough to ask God to turn Ahithophel's counsel into foolishness (2 Sam. 15:30–31). Once again, David demonstrates his trust
in, and acceptance of, God's will when he is faced with the defection
of his top advisor. His only response to this situation is simply to
ask God to turn Ahithophel's counsel into foolishness. His heart is
rooted in God's compassion, along with the trust that knows God
will one day take care of this situation, in God's timing, in God's way.

Sometime later, David is cursed and called a murderer by
Shimei, who is from the same clan as Saul's family. He is angry that
David is reigning as king over Israel, and he sees God setting up
Absalom to reign in David's place. Instead of allowing his men to kill
Shimei, David tells them to let him curse. David believes God has

told Shimei to do so and that God will one day take revenge against Shimei because of the injustice of what has been done to David, God's anointed king (2 Sam. 16:5–12).

In these texts we see that David has fallen as low as a king can fall. His son has moved to take over his kingship. His top advisor has defected. And now, this man from Saul's household openly curses and accuses him of being a murderer, within the hearing of all the people who are with him. Such an offense against a king would typically result in death. But David accepts the man's great insults because "the LORD has told him to" (v. 11). Once again, David accepts even these insults as being God's will, without question or complaint. But at the same time, he believes God will look upon his misery and restore to him God's covenant blessing instead of his curse (v. 12). He is willing to be cursed at God's direction, hoping that it will lead to the restoration of his covenant relationship with God.

When David is informed that Absalom plans to pursue David and his men to kill them all, David gathers his men who are with him and sets up three commanders over them. He wants to go out with them, but his men will not let him. So instead, he stands at the side of the gate as they depart and tells them to handle Absalom gently, for David's sake (2 Sam. 16:15–18:5).

David's men go out against the men of Israel who are under the leadership of Absalom. The servants of David defeat the men of Israel, who sustain large losses. During the battle, while Absalom is riding his mule, his head becomes caught in the branches of a great oak tree, leaving him suspended off the ground. Seizing the opportunity, Joab thrusts his spears into Absalom, and Joab's young armor-bearers surround Absalom and kill him. Joab then blows the trumpet, and the troops come back from pursuing Israel. They take Absalom and bury him in a great pit (see 2 Sam. 18:6–18).

As David is about to receive news from the battlefield, he shows concern only for what has happened to his son Absalom. When he finally learns that Absalom is dead, David is deeply moved (see 2 Sam. 18:24–32). He weeps, saying, "O my son Absalom, my son, my son Absalom! Would I had died instead of you, O Absalom, my son, my son!" (v. 33). This response from David is startling, in light of what Absalom was attempting to do—to lead a coup to take over the kingship of Israel from his father.

What is at stake in this battle—for Absalom, the people of Israel, the commanders of David's army, and all the people following him— is who will be king over all of Israel. Once again, we see David's heart in contrast to Saul, for whom retaining his kingship was preeminent. David wins this battle. Yet in doing so, he holds no importance for himself when compared to the life of his son Absalom, whom he loves and has now lost.

Mourning Absalom's Death

Joab learns of the king's mourning for Absalom, which is so great that all the people mourn, but they mourn for different reasons. Joab comes to David and confronts him with how he has caused the people to feel ashamed, even though they saved his life. By his actions, he has made it clear that commanders and servants are nothing to him when compared to the life of Absalom. He instructed David to arise, go out, and speak kindly to his servants. Otherwise, David will lose the loyalty of all of his men, which Joab says will be worse than all the evil that he has experienced since his youth. David gets up and takes his seat in the gate, and all of David's army comes before the king (see 2 Sam. 19:1–8a).

Notice that, this time, after he gets up from his mourning, he does not stop to worship as he did after he stopped mourning for Bathsheba's son, since this rebuke is not from God. As a father, David is still grieving the loss of his son Absalom. But as king, he knows that he must do as Joab has directed. The consistency of David's words and actions continue to provide confirmation of the success of the work of transformation in him. We have just seen it in David's acceptance of God's outcome for the battle, the future of his kingship, and for his personal life. And now we see it in his acknowledgement of what he must do as king: leave his personal grieving behind for the sake of serving his people.

There are numerous additional examples in the rest of the story of David's life that continue to confirm the effectiveness of the process of transformation in him. However, we will only focus on two additional episodes of his life that are particularly worth discussing.

David's Testimony to God's Greatness

We pick up the story at a time near the end of David's life. Thus, it is appropriate to examine his thoughts and final words in 2 Samuel 22, beginning first with a Song of Deliverance, which reveals his belief in God at an early age:

> And David spoke to the LORD the words of this
> song on the day when the LORD delivered him
> from the hand of all his enemies, and from the
> hand of Saul. He said,

> "The LORD is my rock and my fortress and my deliverer,
> my God, my rock, in whom I take refuge,
> my shield, and the horn of my salvation,
> my stronghold and my refuge,
> my savior; you save me from violence. (2 Sam. 22:1–3)

David's Song of Deliverance continues for a total of fifty-one verses, all of which glorify God and credit to him everything that David had accomplished in his life to that point. An oracle of David, his last words, follows the Song of Deliverance in 2 Samuel 23:

> The oracle of David, the son of Jesse,
> the oracle of the man who was raised on high,
> the anointed of the God of Jacob,
> the sweet psalmist of Israel:

> "The Spirit of the LORD speaks by me;
> his word is on my tongue.
> The God of Israel has spoken;
> the Rock of Israel has said to me:
> When one rules justly over men,

ruling in the fear of God,
he dawns on them like the morning light,
    like the sun shining forth on a cloudless morning,
    like rain that makes grass to sprout from the earth.

"For does not my house stand so with God?
    For he has made with me an everlasting covenant,
    ordered in all things and secure.
For will he not cause to prosper
    all my help and my desire?
But worthless men are all like thorns that are thrown away,
    for they cannot be taken with the hand;
but the man who touches them
    arms himself with iron and the shaft of a spear,
    and they are utterly consumed with fire." (2 Sam.
23:1–7)

The theme of both texts is the same: whatever David achieved during his life, he attributes to God. This confirms that God's transforming work in him is genuine—he continues to be a humble man before God. However, the story of David, and thus his life of faith, does not end with this oracle.

Another Test of Faith

We read in 2 Samuel 24 that God's anger is stirred up against Israel once again, and he commands David to number Israel and Judah (i.e., to take a census). So, David obeys God, even when Joab and the commanders of his army know that doing so is wrong,[5] and they question him about it. David's unquestioning obedience to God's command provides explicit confirmation of the work of transformation in him: God commands, he obeys. Yet, as the numbering of

---

[5] When kings function from faith in a mighty army rather than in the mighty arm of God, they "number" the people. Thus, David knew that taking a census was a sin.

the people concludes, David realizes that what he has done is wrong, that it is a great sin, even though God himself commanded him to do it. Therefore, he confesses and repents before God. Moreover, he does so without trying to justify what he has done on the basis of obeying God's command. David accepts full responsibility for his actions, thereby providing further confirmation of the genuineness of the work of transformation in him (see 2 Sam. 24:1–14).

Then, when God decides to punish him, David does not choose one of the options God offers him as a consequence of his sin. Rather, he leaves the choice up to God because God's mercy is great. The only request that he makes is that he "not fall into the hand of man" (v. 14). In this request, David once again demonstrates his complete trust in and acceptance of God's will for his life.

As a consequence of David's sin, God chooses to send a pestilence on Israel. When seventy thousand men have died, David pleads with God that no more men should die, for he alone has sinned; he alone should be punished. In response to his pleas, God instructs David to build an altar on the threshing floor of Araunah the Jebusite. Araunah offers to give the king the threshing floor, along with his oxen for the burnt offering and wood for the fire. But David refuses to take these things as gifts. Rather, he determines that he will not offer burnt offerings to his God that do not cost him anything. David pays for what he needs, builds an altar to the LORD, and offers burnt offerings and peace offerings. Then the LORD responds to the plea for the land, and the plague was averted from Israel (see 2 Sam. 24:18–25).

Here, at the end of his life, David demonstrates an unprecedented level of integrity when fulfilling God's commands; he will offer to God only sacrifices that cost him something. This is the ultimate demonstration that David's actions confirm his words and reveal his personal integrity before God. Also notice that God continues to test the genuineness of David's faith to the end of his life. Both of these are vital lessons for us from the story of David's life of faith.

Lessons Learned from the Story of David

Following Saul's death and David's ascension to kingship, we asked if all of David's success as king would cause a change in him. Would he eventually become like Saul—depending upon human strength, his own and that of his mighty men? Would he forget God, the one who gave him success from his youth? Or, would he stay true to his faith that enabled him, even in his youth, to trust God's action and power in the midst of his daily life? Would his faith enable him to be obedient to God throughout his life? We have seen that, for the most part, David did remain faithful to God, trusting God's plans for his life and for the future of Israel.

1. Following Saul's death, David has the perfect opportunity to think, "Saul is dead, and I have been anointed to replace him; thus, whatever feelings I have previously had toward Saul no longer matter." However, David greatly laments the death of Saul and his son Jonathan, which reveals the actual condition of his heart. It is easy to understand his lament over Jonathan, whom he loved more than any other. But we might expect that he would not lament over Saul, who relentlessly pursued him, who sought to kill him for years. However, we see in his actions that he also loved Saul simply because he was the LORD's anointed. For David, loving God's anointed is an act of love toward God himself. This is a crucial lesson about the lasting impact that God's work of transformation has upon us, and an indication that his work in us has taken root: we become able to truly love our enemies, because doing so becomes an act of loving God. Loving our enemies is an act of unconditional love that emerges out of a transformed heart.

Consider: As you ponder the impact that God's work of transformation has had upon your life, can you identify ways in which it has changed how you view your enemies? Have you become able to truly love your enemies unconditionally? Have you begun to pray for them? Has loving your enemies become an act of loving God for you?

2. A pivotal moment in which to examine the genuineness of David's faith, to see what effect becoming king might have on his faith—his dependence upon and trust in God—occurs as soon as David becomes king over both Israel and Judah. The Philistines immediately prepare for battle against him and the people of Israel. Since David has not yet lost a battle against the Philistines, he could become overly confident in his own strength and wisdom, as Saul had done. However, David responds to the Philistine threats differently. Before both battles, he automatically seeks God's wisdom about how to proceed before he takes any action, which reveals that, over time, a very intimate and trusting relationship has developed between David and God. David does not question what God tells him; he simply hears and obeys. David's response is the hallmark of genuine faith. When God has become real for a person, their trust in God is deep and unquestioning. It results in one seeking out God's guidance and wisdom in life situations, with a willingness to obey God's direction. The challenge for us today is to learn to discern the way God communicates his guidance and wisdom to us. The broader lesson here is that we have clear evidence that God is, indeed, active in the lives of his people.

Consider: As you proceed through God's transforming work in your life, has God become real for you? Have you been able to discern how God communicates with you? Has your trust in God become so deep and unquestioning that you immediately seek out his guidance and wisdom as David does, and simply hear and obey? Over time, has an intimate and trusting relationship developed between you and God? If not, ask God to deepen your intimacy with him.

3. We have seen that following the completion of the work of transformation, God continued to test David's faith to determine whether his actions would continue to validate his words, and thereby confirm the genuineness of his faith. But David's response in times of testing did not always immediately reflect the results of the work of transformation in him; sometimes he failed, he sinned. But his *response* when confronted with his sin proved that his faith was, indeed, genuine. We are all human; no one is perfect. Therefore, we *will* sin. Failure by sin does not diminish, remove, or undo the work of transformation that has already taken place. Rather, such events in our lives reveal that God continues to test our faith. Our *response* when confronted with our sin is what is most important, for it reveals the degree of transformation that has taken place and the genuineness of our faith. Notice God's response to David's simple act of contrition when Nathan says that God "has put away your sin" (2 Sam. 12:13): forgiveness is complete; David will not die. God shows great mercy for David himself, but he will still experience the consequences of his sin through the death of his child. What is true for David is also true for us. When we sin, our sins are forgiven when we confess in humble truth and repent. However, we will still experience the consequences of our actions.

   Consider: As you reflect on your own faith transformation process, look for those times when God has tested your faith in the midst of daily circumstances. How did you respond? Were your actions rooted in an attempt to rely on human effort and wisdom, did you try to justify your actions, or did you choose to rely on God's presence, action, and power on your behalf? Do you accept God's word to you that your sins are forgiven? How does this truth change the way you move forward in relationship with God?

CHAPTER 9
Peter and the Other Apostles

The story of Peter is the only New Testament character we will examine in this work, but no single book of the Bible focuses explicitly on Peter. This is different from all of the biblical characters we have previously examined; each of their stories have been contained in a book of Scripture that was primarily about their lives. From that one book we have been able to glean God's work of transformation of their faith throughout their life story. This is not the case with Peter; his story spans the four gospels and the book of Acts. Thus, in order to compile the story of Peter, it is necessary to examine the four gospels in parallel, and then conclude with the early chapters of the book of Acts in order to see God's process of transformation in him.

Rather than following a chronological order of the unfolding of events as we have done in previous chapters, our focus in this chapter is on Jesus's teachings in the gospels to discover *the process he takes* as he seeks to teach, and thus prepare, his disciples to continue his work in the world after he has left the scene. We will also include observations about what is happening over time in the lives of the other disciples, of which Peter is one. We assume that if a passage of Scripture reveals that "the disciples," or even "the crowds," are present with Jesus as he is teaching, then Peter is also present.

In this study we will see a pattern unfold in which Jesus teaches the disciples a specific point about a number of important theological concepts that are significant, such as the kingdom of God, himself, his Father, and eternal life. He then follows his teachings with demonstrations of divine power, which may or may not be directly tied to the topic of the teaching he has just given. The important point is not whether his demonstration of power connects to the teaching point, but rather that the power he displays is *divine* power, thus revealing something about his nature, *about who he is.* But in every case, the one constant between the teaching moments and the demonstrations of divine power is Jesus himself.

Please note that Peter was chosen for inclusion in this study not just because he is the most prominent of the apostles through-out the gospels, but because he can serve as a prototypical apostle and disciple in the New Testament. Just as Peter and the disciples learn by observing Jesus as he teaches, we are observers as well—we observe both Jesus and Peter (and the others)—as we read Scripture. Therefore, what occurs in Peter's story is applicable to any post-res-urrection disciple of Jesus Christ, including us. The apostles were the first ones to be commanded to go and teach the gospel to others, and thus carry on the work of Jesus in the world. We are commanded to do the same. This is the work that Jesus was preparing Peter and the other disciples to do.

Peter Comes to See Jesus

To begin, we will look at Peter as he first appears in chapter 1 of John's gospel:

> The next day again John was standing with two of his disciples, and he looked at Jesus as he walked by and said, "Behold, the Lamb of God!" The two disciples heard him say this, and they fol-lowed Jesus. Jesus turned and saw them following and said to them, "What are you seeking?" And they said to him, "Rabbi" (which means Teacher), "where are you staying?" He said to them, "Come and you will see." So they came and saw where he was staying, and they stayed with him that day, for it was about the tenth hour. One of the two who heard John speak and followed Jesus was Andrew, Simon Peter's brother. He first found his

own brother Simon and said to him, "We have
found the Messiah" (which means Christ). He
brought him to Jesus. Jesus looked at him and
said, "You are Simon the son of John. You shall
be called Cephas" (which means Peter). (John
1:35–42)

Notice that it is Peter's brother, Andrew, who calls him to come
and see Jesus, explaining that he and the others have found the
Messiah. He says this because of what John the Baptist says when
Jesus walks by, that he is "the Lamb of God" (v. 36). Stating that they
have found the Messiah, Andrew indicates that he believes what John
has been preaching about the one who was still to come—the coming messiah (see John 1:19–28). Andrew accepts John's word about
Jesus and runs off to tell his brother Peter.[1]

The question naturally arises at this point, is Peter responding
to the call of God, or does he go with Andrew for some other reason?
Peter is Jewish and, therefore, like all young men of the Jewish faith,
would be steeped in the Hebrew Scriptures. Thus, he has a religious
foundation rooted in the Old Testament, which contains an expectation of a coming messiah. The problem is that the Jews expected
the Messiah would be a geopolitical messiah, one that would come to
free them from Roman domination. So, as Peter goes with Andrew
to see Jesus, he is likely expecting to see the one whom he hopes will
free Israel from that Roman domination, the one who will reestablish
Israel as an independent nation with a king, which is what existed
before the Roman conquest.[2] Thus, it is essential to note that who
Peter thinks Jesus is when they first meet is not the Christ whom he
will follow for the remainder of his life. Jesus is the same person, but
Peter will come to a different understanding of who Jesus is, as God's
work of transformation takes place in him.

---

[1] From the very beginning of this study, we use the name *Peter*, rather than *Simon*,
because at the very beginning of his encounter with Jesus, his name is changed,
and this is the name by which he is commonly known.

[2] *ElijahNet*, "The First Century Concept of Messiah: Governance,"
http://elijahnet.net/The%20First%20Century%20Concept.html.

It is also important to note another aspect of Peter's belief in God: he does not question Andrew's statement or hesitate to go with him. From his foundation of Jewish faith, God begins the work of transformation in him by immediately changing his name—from *Simon* to *Peter* (*Cephas*). As discussed previously in the chapter on Abraham, the one who names another declares authority over the one who has been named. In this instance, Jesus is already demonstrating to Peter that he has authority over him.

First Demonstration of Divine Power

In the next passage in the gospel of John, Jesus manifests his power for the first time:

> On the third day there was a wedding at Cana in Galilee, and the mother of Jesus was there. Jesus also was invited to the wedding with his disciples. When the wine ran out, the mother of Jesus said to him, "They have no wine." And Jesus said to her, "Woman, what does this have to do with me? My hour has not yet come." His mother said to the servants, "Do whatever he tells you."
> Now there were six stone water jars there for the Jewish rites of purification, each holding twenty or thirty gallons. Jesus said to the servants, "Fill the jars with water." And they filled them up to the brim. And he said to them, "Now draw some out and take it to the master of the feast." So they took it. When the master of the feast tasted the water now become wine, and did not know where it came from (though the servants who had drawn the water knew), the master of the feast called the bridegroom and said to him, "Everyone serves the good wine first, and when people have drunk freely, then the poor wine. But you have kept the good wine until now."

This, the first of his signs, Jesus did at Cana in
Galilee, and manifested his glory. And his disciples believed in him. (John 2:1–11)

From the perspective of examining God's work of transformation in Peter and the other disciples, we might ask why this first manifestation of Jesus's divine power occurs immediately after Peter and
other disciples begin to follow him, and that it concludes with the
statement, "And his disciples believed in him" (v. 11). Typically when
studying the Bible, people tend to focus on one incident or situation
at a time, without stepping back to notice the flow of a series of stories or incidents. To get a broader picture of what is happening, we
need to understand what the flow and pattern of multiple incidents
communicate that may not be apparent when focusing on only one
situation or event at a time.

Here at the outset of John's gospel, a pattern emerges that continues throughout the story of Peter. Jesus teaches or gives a series of
teachings (what we call "teaching moments"), which is followed by
one or more manifestations of his divine power. It is the manifestation of his power that affirms who he is, that he is more than a mere
human being, and thus he can be trusted. This pattern continues
throughout the parallel gospels and helps us see how God accomplishes his work of transformation in Peter and the disciples, who are
participants with Jesus in almost every event that occurs throughout
the gospels.

As we have said, when Jesus renames Simon to *Peter*, he is working to get the disciples' attention; he is demonstrating *who he is*—one
who has the *authority* to do so. This is his first step in laying the
foundation that will prove who he is over time, even though he has
not yet declared who he is in words. Rather, he is simply beginning
to demonstrate his divine authority.

We then see that the process of transformation has begun in the
disciples in the story of the Cana wedding. At the end of this text,
John adds, "And his disciples believed in him" (v. 11). This is the first
evidence that something is changing in the disciples' faith as a result
of Jesus's demonstration of divine power. As we have seen in all pre-

vious character studies in this work, the process of transformation is rooted in God becoming real for the individual. As a result of what Peter and the others have just observed, their faith is beginning to be transformed; they are beginning to believe in him.

It is important to note that the most common term his disciples use to address Jesus is *Rabbi*, or teacher (e.g., John 1:38). But merely believing in Jesus as a great teacher is not sufficient for genuine faith. Today, Jews continue to refer to Jesus as a "teacher." Even Muslims respect and revere Jesus as one of the greatest of God's messengers to mankind.[3] Nevertheless, *they fail to combine his teaching with the signs and miracles that are manifestations of his divine power*, so they fail to grasp the reality of who Jesus really is. As the story of Peter continues, it should become increasingly apparent that, as Jesus's teaching progresses, he gradually states more clearly who he is, who his father is, and the mission of his earthly life.

Begins Revealing Who He Is

Jesus's focus upon the Father first emerges when he travels to Jerusalem to celebrate Passover:

> The Passover of the Jews was at hand, and Jesus went up to Jerusalem. In the temple he found those who were selling oxen and sheep and pigeons, and the money-changers sitting there. And making a whip of cords, he drove them all out of the temple, with the sheep and oxen. And he poured out the coins of the money-changers and overturned their tables. And he told those who sold the pigeons, "Take these things away; do not make my Father's house a house of trade." His disciples remembered that it was written, "Zeal for your house will consume me." (John 2:13–17)

---

[3] "What Do Muslims Believe about Jesus?," https://www.islam-guide.com/ch3-10.htm.

In this passage, Jesus is declaring that God is his father, which is a bold statement for someone to make. The Jews challenge his actions because they recognize the significance of what he has just said:

> So the Jews said to him, "What sign do you show us for doing these things?" Jesus answered them, "Destroy this temple, and in three days I will raise it up." The Jews then said, "It has taken forty-six years to build this temple, and will you raise it up in three days?" But he was speaking about the temple of his body. When therefore he was raised from the dead, his disciples remembered that he had said this, and they believed the Scripture and the word that Jesus had spoken. (John 2:18–22)

In these texts, Jesus begins to show us something about God's process for transforming faith. First, he reveals something about himself; in this case he reveals his relationship to God by referring to the temple as "my father's house" without any further explanation (v. 16). None is needed because his disciples are able to draw upon their knowledge of the saying, "Zeal for your house will consume me" (v. 17), which is found in the Psalms (Ps. 69:9). Thus, the disciples begin to gain insight about Jesus's true nature from his brief statement about his father.

Then the Jews challenge his authority to refer to the temple in the way that he does. Jesus creates a different teaching moment by foretelling his resurrection from the dead. The demonstration of divine power that supports his claim made here will not come true until after his death. At that time, his disciples will remember this incident. Only then will they understand that he was referring to his own body as the temple in this current exchange.

Through these two texts, it becomes apparent that in undertaking the work of transformation, God does not merely sit an individual down to give a comprehensive course about himself and his son Jesus Christ and expect them to walk away and understand it all. Throughout the story of Peter, we will see that Jesus teaches crucial doctrines a little bit at a time through a series of increasingly explicit teaching moments, which are usually combined with increasing demonstrations of divine power. The purpose of this process is for Peter and the others to grasp the full significance of his teaching, of who he really is. As seen from the preceding texts, sometimes Jesus acts out of the divine authority that he has, and thus demonstrates something of who he really is. And sometimes manifestations of power will not actually occur until later (e.g., after Jesus's death and resurrection). However, Jesus continues to teach Peter and the others with great patience so that God's work of transformation will ultimately be successful—so that full understanding will eventually occur, which will enable them to go out and teach others the teachings of Jesus. Thus, we can see that the process of transforming our belief into genuine faith is accomplished in little events in the midst of daily life, and thus takes time.

New Birth Leads to Eternal Life

This pattern of a teaching moment followed by the manifestation of power through different signs and miracles continues in John's gospel, chapter 3. There we see a series of four teaching moments focusing on eternal salvation that leads to eternal life, followed by two manifestations of Jesus's power. The series of teaching moments begins when Jesus addresses Nicodemus, speaking about new birth:

> Jesus answered, "Truly, truly, I say to you, unless one is born of water and the Spirit, he cannot enter the kingdom of God. That which is born of the flesh is flesh, and that which is born of the Spirit is spirit. Do not marvel that I said to you, 'You must be born again.' The wind blows where it wishes, and you hear its sound, but you do not know where it comes from or where it goes. So it is with everyone who is born of the Spirit." (John 3:5–8)

PETER AND THE OTHER APOSTLES

He then continues with his teaching on eternal life:

No one has ascended into heaven except he who descended from heaven, the Son of Man. And as Moses lifted up the serpent in the wilderness, so must the Son of Man be lifted up, that whoever believes in him may have eternal life. (John 3:13–15)

Jesus then reveals the critical point of this teaching series:

"For God so loved the world, that he gave his only Son, that whoever believes in him should not perish but have eternal life. For God did not send his Son into the world to condemn the world, but in order that the world might be saved through him. Whoever believes in him is not condemned, but whoever does not believe is condemned already, because he has not believed in the name of the only Son of God." (John 3:16–18)

Finally, Jesus lays out the consequences of all that he has just said:

And this is the judgment: the light has come into the world, and people loved the darkness rather than the light because their works were evil. For everyone who does wicked things hates the light and does not come to the light, lest his works should be exposed. But whoever does what is true comes to the light, so that it may be clearly seen that his works have been carried out in God. (John 3:19–21)

Like any good teacher, in this series of teaching moments, Jesus addresses concepts that his disciples have not previously considered, thus laying the foundation for them to understand the doctrine

357

of eternal salvation. But his teaching is not yet detailed or specific enough for them to fully understand what he is saying.

It is crucial to notice the flow of the teaching moments as they lead to Jesus's ultimate lesson. He begins by contrasting physical life versus spiritual life when he talks with Nicodemus about being born again. He then moves on in the next text to temporal life versus eternal life by contrasting earthly things of a physical nature with heavenly things that are of a spiritual nature. Here we see Jesus helping the disciples see the reality of the kingdom of God—a spiritual worldview they do not yet have.

He then draws together these points with the universally known statement, "For God so loved the world, that he gave his only Son, that whoever believes in him should not perish but have eternal life" (v. 16). By this statement he continues to unpack the outcome of belief versus unbelief in the only Son of God, stating that whoever believes in him is not condemned, but whoever does not believe is condemned already (v. 18). Step by step through this series of teaching moments, Jesus leads up to making this one significant point, belief versus unbelief, which is critical for Peter to understand as God continues the work of transformation in his life.

After these four teaching moments, the story continues with Jesus manifesting different aspects of his divine power by performing two different sets of signs and miracles.

- In John 4:4–42, Jesus persuades a Samaritan woman about the truth of who he is by revealing to her the most significant things she has done in her life. Not only does she come to believe in Jesus, but she also brings to him many others from that town who believe in him because of her personal testimony.
- In John 4:46–54, Jesus instantaneously heals the nobleman's son from a great distance by merely saying, "Go; your son will live" (v. 50). When he returns home, his servants confirm that his son recovered his health at the same time that Jesus spoke to him. As a result, he and his entire household believe in Jesus.

At first glance, these two incidents appear to be significantly different, yet in each case, the outcome is the same: multiple individuals come to believe in Jesus because of his demonstration of divine power, which infers that they are saved unto eternal life by believing in him. In addition to resulting in the same outcome, we see in both situations that what Jesus says to one individual is passed along to others by that individual, resulting in *their* conversion. Thus, we see in the aftermath of personal testimony that others believe in Jesus.

These events connect directly with Jesus's teaching that those who believe in him are saved unto eternal life, and thus underscore and confirm for Peter and the other disciples what Jesus taught them in the previous series of four teaching moments about new birth, eternal life, and judgment.

Jesus Claims Who He Is

We can see this pattern in the gospel of Luke, chapter 4. Jesus teaches about himself in the synagogue of Nazareth, which is then followed by a manifestation of divine power:

> And he came to Nazareth, where he had been brought up. And as was his custom, he went to the synagogue on the Sabbath day, and he stood up to read. And the scroll of the prophet Isaiah was given to him. He unrolled the scroll and found the place where it was written,

> "The Spirit of the Lord is upon me,
>   because he has anointed me
>   to proclaim good news to the poor.
> He has sent me to proclaim liberty to the captives
>   and recovering of sight to the blind,
>   to set at liberty those who are oppressed,
> to proclaim the year of the Lord's favor."

And he rolled up the scroll and gave it back to the attendant and sat down. And the eyes of all in the synagogue were fixed on him. And he began to say to them, "Today this Scripture has been fulfilled in your hearing." And all spoke well of him and marveled at the gracious words that were coming from his mouth. And they said, "Is not this Joseph's son?" And he said to them, "Doubtless you will quote to me this proverb, 'Physician, heal yourself.' What we have heard you did at Capernaum, do here in your home-town as well." And he said, "Truly, I say to you, no prophet is acceptable in his hometown. But in truth, I tell you, there were many widows in Israel in the days of Elijah, when the heavens were shut up three years and six months, and a great fam-ine came over all the land, and Elijah was sent to none of them but only to Zarephath, in the land of Sidon, to a woman who was a widow. And there were many lepers in Israel in the time of the prophet Elisha, and none of them was cleansed, but only Naaman the Syrian." When they heard these things, all in the synagogue were filled with wrath. And they rose up and drove him out of the town and brought him to the brow of the hill on which their town was built, so that they could throw him down the cliff. But passing through their midst, he went away. (Luke 4:16–30)

In the third of the previous series of teaching moments in John, chapter 3, Jesus teaches that belief in the only Son of God, who is the long-awaited messiah, results in an individual receiving eternal life (John 3:16–18). Here in this teaching moment in Luke's gospel, Jesus infers that he is that long-awaited messiah, but he does not actually declare it. Those in the synagogue who hear him make this inference ask him to perform signs and wonders, just as he has done in Capernaum, in order to confirm what he has just said. His unwillingness to do so angers them. Why? His two-part response to their question requires some explanation.

First, he mentions that Elijah was not sent to Israel, but to a widow in Zarephath, a gentile town in the land of Sidon (v. 26) during a great famine. Second, he tells them that Elisha healed a leper, Naaman, the Syrian, also a gentile, rather than healing the many lepers in Israel. Remember, Jesus is speaking to Jews in a synagogue, and he refuses to give them the signs and wonders at this time that they ask for. Instead, he refers to these two stories about *gentiles* being saved or healed by God. The point he is making is this: eternal salvation is accomplished by God and is not dependent upon being a Jew. This would be an unacceptable teaching to the Jews who heard Jesus say these things.

This passage presents a new concept for Peter and the disciples, another building block in the foundation Jesus is laying for the transformation of their faith. It builds on what Jesus taught in the previous series of teaching moments. This time the main point is that one's natural heritage in being a Jew is no longer the critical factor in determining whether a person becomes saved unto eternal life.

In response to this, those who hear him say these things try to drive him out of town, and they attempt to kill him. Nevertheless, Jesus miraculously passes through their midst untouched and leaves. By doing so, he performs what they had asked him to do—a miracle. Most likely, this fact went unnoticed by those in the crowd. But the significance of what has just happened is not lost on his disciples, for this event has been included in Luke's gospel. Here again we see the pattern of Jesus's teaching being followed by a demonstration of his divine power, which God is no doubt using to further his work of transformation in Peter. And he is doing it one step at a time.

In chapter 4 of Luke's gospel, Jesus expands his claim of who he is by teaching again in a synagogue in Capernaum, and he then demonstrates his power by casting out a demon.

> And he went down to Capernaum, a city of
> Galilee. And he was teaching them on the

Sabbath, and they were astonished at his teaching, for his word possessed authority. And in the
synagogue there was a man who had the spirit of
an unclean demon, and he cried out with a loud
voice, "Ha! What have you to do with us, Jesus of
Nazareth? Have you come to destroy us? I know
who you are—the Holy One of God." But Jesus
rebuked him, saying, "Be silent and come out
of him!" And when the demon had thrown him
down in their midst, he came out of him, having
done him no harm. And they were all amazed and
said to one another, "What is this word? For with
authority and power he commands the unclean
spirits, and they come out!" And reports about
him went out into every place in the surrounding
region. (Luke 4:31–37; see also Mark 1:21–28)

In this text, there is no indication given as to what Jesus teaches.
All we know is that he has been teaching with authority, and that
those who hear his teaching are astonished. The focus of the text
immediately shifts to the demon that identifies Jesus as "the Holy
One of God" (v. 34). Jesus responds with a rebuke to the unclean
spirit and commands him to come out of the man. Those who see
this event recognize that he has unusual authority. It is interesting
to note that this interchange takes place in the synagogue, on the
Sabbath.

The less obvious issue is that the demon has spoken the truth,
so why does Jesus stop this true declaration of who he is? The most
logical answer is that it interrupts the work of transformation that
Jesus is accomplishing in Peter and the other disciples. Peter has not
yet come to this truth on his own; he cannot yet say the truth that
the demon has declared. So the work of transformation must continue, but Jesus intends for it to continue according to God's plan.
Therefore, Jesus commands the demon to be silent and to come out
of the man, thereby cutting off any discussion about what he has
declared. And it seems to work, because the people's comments are

then focused on the power that Jesus has just demonstrated by his authority over the unclean spirit. Neither Peter or anyone else presses Jesus about the declaration of who he is.

This is a crucial lesson concerning God's work of transformation. What Jesus is teaching Peter and the other disciples is not intended to be a mere abstract concept, a truth declared by another. Rather, he knows that they must come to their own conclusion about who he is *from their personal experience of him.* At this point they cannot yet make a declaration that they *know* he is the "Holy One of God" (v. 34). That is why Jesus silences the evil spirit. Once again, he manifests his power, with authority, after a teaching moment. His pattern for bringing about transformation in Peter continues.

Following this demonstration of Jesus's divine power, the three synoptic[4] gospel writers include the following events, which further demonstrate Jesus's divine power:

- Peter's mother-in-law   (Matt. 8:14-15, Luke 1:29-31, Luke 4:38-39)
- A leper   (Matt. 8:1-4, Mark 1:40-45, Luke 5:12-16)
- A paralytic   (Matt. 9:1–8, Mark 2:1–12, Luke 5:17–26)
- A lame man   (John 5:2-15)
- A withered hand   (Matt. 12:9–14, Mark 3:1–6, Luke 6:6–11)
- Multitudes by the sea   (Matt. 12:14–21, Mark 3:7–12, Luke 6:17-19)

---

4 *Synoptic,* "presenting or taking a similar view," https://www.merriam-webster.com/dictionary/synoptic. Matthew, Mark, and Luke are the three Synoptic gospels, which often tell the same stories about Jesus in similar terms, and in similar sequence. The Gospel of John stands in contrast to these three gospels, presenting a different perspective on the life and teachings of Jesus (https://biblehub.com/topical/s/synoptic.htm).

From the perspective of God's work of transformation, the focus of these events is not on the person healed, but rather on the manifestation of power by Jesus, which refocuses Peter and the other disciples' attention on who Jesus is. By these demonstrations of power, Jesus fulfills what the prophets and John the Baptist declared that the Messiah would do—heal the sick and free the oppressed (Luke 4:18, which references Isaiah 61:1). Demonstrating his power by fulfilling messianic prophecies is a logical next step in the flow of the process Jesus is using as he continues to broaden and deepen his teaching about who he is. Again, his teaching is moving forward, one step at a time, as he lays the foundation for the transformation of the disciples' faith.

Jesus's Main Purpose

The pattern repeats as Jesus teaches more about himself in Luke, chapter 4:

> And when it was day, he departed and went into a desolate place. And the people sought him and came to him, and would have kept him from leaving them, but he said to them, "I must preach the good news of the kingdom of God to the other towns as well; for I was sent for this purpose." And he was preaching in the synagogues of Judea. (Luke 4:42–44; see also Mark 1:35–39)

In this text, the people want to keep Jesus from leaving because they have seen a series of healings that he has performed among them. He responds that the main purpose of his life is not to heal their sicknesses, but rather to preach the good news of the kingdom of God. His purpose is not about himself, what he can and cannot do. It is about God and his kingdom. Through his teaching, he continues to refocus the people's attention on *this purpose*, the kingdom of God, thus keeping their eyes on what is ultimately most important, and not on demonstrations of power.

We see Jesus again teaching about himself in the sixth chapter of Luke:

On a Sabbath, while he was going through the grainfields, his disciples plucked and ate some heads of grain, rubbing them in their hands. But some of the Pharisees said, "Why are you doing what is not lawful to do on the Sabbath?" And Jesus answered them, "Have you not read what David did when he was hungry, he and those who were with him: how he entered the house of God and took and ate the bread of the Presence, which is not lawful for any but the priests to eat, and also gave it to those with him?" And he said to them, "The Son of Man is lord of the Sabbath." (Luke 6:1–5; see also Matt. 12:1–8, Mark 2:23–28)

In this text we find two teaching moments, during which Jesus continues to expand his teaching about himself as the Messiah. He refers to himself as "the Son of Man" (v. 5), which relates a twofold meaning. First, it is a reference to the prophecy in Daniel 7:13–14, where "Son of Man" is a messianic title referring to the one who receives dominion and glory and a kingdom. By using this phrase, Jesus is assigning the Son of Man prophecy to himself; he is proclaiming himself to be the Messiah. As Jews, his disciples would be intimately familiar with the phrase and to whom it referred. Second, he is identifying himself as a human being. God called the prophet Ezekiel "son of man" ninety-three times in order to emphasize that he was a human being. Jesus is applying this meaning to himself as well. These two points are new revelations about himself to his disciples.

Notice that with the last two passages, we see Jesus speak for the first time about the main purpose of his life, and then he infers that he is, indeed, the long-awaited messiah. These two new revelations about himself are the "next steps" in the gradual development of the foundation of truth that he is building for Peter and the others. He is intentional and systematic in his approach. He knows what he needs to reveal each step of the way in order to eventually lead them to the place of genuine faith.

Jesus Names the Apostles

Following these two teaching moments, Jesus then begins to focus upon the role that Peter will serve in the future, along with eleven other disciples:

> In these days he went out to the mountain to pray, and all night he continued in prayer to God. And when day came, he called his disciples and chose from them twelve, whom he named apostles: Simon, whom he named Peter, and Andrew his brother, and James and John, and Philip, and Bartholomew, and Matthew, and Thomas, and James the son of Alphaeus, and Simon who was called the Zealot, and Judas the son of James, and Judas Iscariot, who became a traitor. (Luke 6:12–16; see also Matt. 10:2–4, Mark 3:13–19)

By naming Peter and eleven other disciples as *apostles*, Jesus sets them apart from all of the other disciples (the larger crowds following Jesus) to serve specific roles. From the name alone,[5] they begin to understand that they will serve as messengers for him in the future. He is *the messenger* now, but they will become *the messengers* after his death. Thus we see a new topic emerge in Jesus's teaching for Peter and the others, that these twelve will become the messengers of his message. Setting them apart by naming them as apostles reveals the importance of what Jesus has been trying to teach them up to this point in time: they will be expected to go and teach others what Jesus is now teaching them. This calling has set them apart from the rest of the "disciples"—the larger group of followers.

---

[5] *Apostolos*, "a messenger, one sent on a mission, an apostle," *Strong's Concordance*, 652, https://biblehub.com/str/greek/652.htm.

This is an essential lesson concerning God's work of transformation. The importance of what God teaches an individual is revealed when it is seen in relation to God's call to that individual.

Apostles' Future Message

Jesus amplifies this point as he begins to teach Peter the critical elements of the message that he and the other apostles will carry to people once they begin to fulfill their roles as apostles. The heart of that message is set forth by Jesus in the Sermon on the Mount, as recorded in both Matthew's and Luke's gospels:

- Those who will be blessed—the Beatitudes (Matt. 5:3–12, Luke 6:20–26)
- Be righteous and keep commandments (Matt. 5:13–19)
- Be more righteous than scribes, Pharisees (Matt. 5:20–48; Luke 6:27–30, 32–36)
- Practice real righteousness (Matt. 6:1–18, Luke 11:2–4)
- Pursue only heavenly treasure (Matt. 6:19–24)
- Do not judge or condemn (Matt. 7:1–5, Luke 6:37–42)
- God answers your requests (Matt. 7:7–11)

These teachings are anchored in the reality of the kingdom of God and reveal how one is to live in this world if he or she is a disciple of Jesus. Each of these passages contains details about what Jesus will ask the apostles to teach others.

Jesus then focuses on the main point of these teaching moments by what he says next:

> "Why do you call me 'Lord, Lord,' and not do what I tell you? Everyone who comes to me and hears my words and does them, I will show you what he is like: he is like a man building a house, who dug deep and laid the foundation on the rock. And when a flood arose, the stream broke against that house and could not shake it, because

it had been well built. But the one who hears and does not do them is like a man who built a house on the ground without a foundation. When the stream broke against it, immediately it fell, and the ruin of that house was great." (Luke 6:46–49; see also Matt. 7:24-27)

Notice in this teaching that he links "hearing" and "doing" with being anchored on a rock that cannot be moved. This teaching is for the apostles, as well as for the larger crowds of followers. The primary focus of this teaching is that we should build our house upon the rock, referring to Jesus himself and his teachings. This anchoring is done when we hear his teaching, accept and embrace it as his teaching for us personally, and then obey his word by living by it.

This is another new line of teaching designed to further prepare Peter and the other apostles for what is coming. Jesus knows that they will replace him after his death and resurrection, that they will be responsible for delivering his message about who he is. Without saying it directly, he is revealing to the apostles that they will experience strong forces against them as they live out this call on their lives. In order to survive, they must be anchored by belief in *who he is.*

This is another critical lesson concerning the work of transformation. Jesus cannot teach Peter to build his house upon the rock until he understands *who the rock is.* God's work of transformation encompasses a process of layering one teaching moment upon another, until an individual begins to understand the total lesson. That is why Jesus began the first series of teaching moments with the topics of eternal life, salvation, and the kingdom of God, before moving on to referring to himself as both Messiah and Lord.

Then, as he has previously done, Jesus again manifests his power by performing the following signs and wonders to emphasize the truth of what he has just been saying about himself:

- Heals centurion's servant   (Matt. 8:5–13, Luke 7:1–10)
- Resurrects a woman's son   (Luke 7:11–17)

There are two important points to note about these two demonstrations of divine power. First, the magnitude of power is significantly greater than what has been seen in previous signs and miracles. Up to this point, Jesus has performed healings of different kinds. But when he heals the centurion's servant, he does so *long-distance*. Thus, he is demonstrating that the power of the kingdom of God is not restricted to just where Jesus is physically, but that his divine power can be manifested by him anywhere and everywhere. Then he performs the greatest example of who he is by resurrecting the woman's son from the dead.

In these two texts we see Jesus doing what no one has done or can do. His power far exceeds that of normal human power. Once again, Jesus is making an expanded point about who he is by these demonstrations of increased divine power. He continues to build the trust of the disciples *in him* as Messiah and Lord. As the importance and scope of his teaching moments continue to grow, so also does the magnitude of his manifestations of power.

Genuineness of Faith Tested

The teaching/power demonstration pattern begins again when John the Baptist sends two of his disciples to Jesus to ask him, "Are you the one who is to come?" (Luke 7:19), meaning the Messiah:

> And when the men had come to him, they said, "John the Baptist has sent us to you, saying, 'Are you the one who is to come, or shall we look for another?'" In that hour he healed many people of diseases and plagues and evil spirits, and on many who were blind he bestowed sight. And he answered them, "Go and tell John what you have seen and heard: the blind receive their sight, the lame walk, lepers are cleansed, and the deaf hear, the dead are raised up, the poor have good news preached to them. And blessed is the one who is not offended by me." (Luke 7:20–23; see also Matt. 11:2–6)

It is essential to notice that God uses John the Baptist to initiate this teaching moment by asking the question that we would expect Peter is asking within himself at this point: is Jesus truly the Messiah? Jesus has never answered this question directly. Moreover, he does not do so in this text either.

Notice that Jesus takes the opportunity to turn this unanswered question into a new teaching moment by reviewing what he has done. This review of his actions by divine power requires them to draw upon their knowledge of scriptural prophecies concerning the Messiah. So, instead of answering the question directly, he creates an opportunity for them to reach a conclusion themselves. He knows that genuine belief, rock-solid belief, must emerge from within the individual. This teaching moment is also a test of their transformation of faith process.

Jesus then challenges Peter and the others by saying, "Blessed is the one who is not offended by me" (v. 23). This is the ultimate point in this test of faith: many will be offended by what Jesus says and does, and as a result will turn away. So, we have to wonder, is Jesus making this point because Peter and the other apostles will become offended and turn away? Or will they continue to follow after Jesus?

This is an important point: in accomplishing the work of transformation, there are moments when God challenges us to test the genuineness of what we believe. If our faith is genuine, we will trust him regardless of our circumstances, accepting that what he allows to occur in our life is for our good. As we have pointed out in previous chapters, one can believe in abstract concepts, but until that belief becomes real to the individual, they cannot move beyond simple belief to genuine saving faith—trusting God and surrendering to God's will. As a part of the work of transformation, God sometimes places us in situations to test if what we say we believe is from genuine faith. If it is, that genuineness will manifest itself in actions that conform to our stated beliefs. We can say we trust Jesus, that we believe in him. However, we ultimately demonstrate our faith when we obey God's will.

Repentance and Forgiveness of Sin

Jesus then further expands on this teaching in Matthew's gospel, chapter 11, by showing that a failure of genuine belief results in negative consequences. He denounces the cities where he has performed mighty works, yet no one has repented:

> "Woe to you, Chorazin! Woe to you, Bethsaida! For if the mighty works done in you had been done in Tyre and Sidon, they would have repented long ago in sackcloth and ashes. But I tell you, it will be more bearable on the day of judgment for Tyre and Sidon than for you. And you, Capernaum, will you be exalted to heaven? You will be brought down to Hades. For if the mighty works done in you had been done in Sodom, it would have remained until this day. But I tell you that it will be more tolerable on the day of judgment for the land of Sodom than for you." (Matt. 11:21–24)

The important faith lesson here is that a lack of repentance is a sign of unbelief, which leads to eternal death. Thus, the opposite is also true: repentance reveals genuine faith, which leads to eternal life. It is essential to notice that Jesus is not speaking to residents of any of the cities that he is denouncing. Instead, once again Peter and the other disciples are the primary audience for this teaching moment. Here Jesus warns them of the consequences of unbelief, and thus continues to challenge them: do they genuinely believe in him as Messiah and Lord? Will they trust in him and thus surrender to his will? This is the ultimate challenge in God's work of transformation; trust that leads to obedience is evidence that faith is genuine.

The next teaching moment is found again in Luke's gospel, chapter 7. It occurs when Simon, a Pharisee, asks Jesus to eat with him. A woman of the city who is a sinner brings an alabaster flask of ointment, washes Jesus's feet with her tears, wipes them with her hair, kisses them, and then anoints them with the ointment. Her actions create an opportunity for Jesus to teach again:

> "A certain moneylender had two debtors. One owed five hundred denarii, and the other fifty. When they could not pay, he cancelled the debt of both. Now which of them will love him more?" Simon answered, "The one, I suppose, for whom he cancelled the larger debt." And he said to him, "You have judged rightly." Then turning toward the woman he said to Simon, "Do you see this woman? I entered your house; you gave me no water for my feet, but she has wet my feet with her tears and wiped them with her hair. You gave me no kiss, but from the time I came in she has not ceased to kiss my feet. You did not anoint my head with oil, but she has anointed my feet with ointment. Therefore I tell you, her sins, which are many, are forgiven—for she loved much. But he who is forgiven little, loves little." And he said to her, "Your sins are forgiven." Then those who were at table with him began to say among themselves, "Who is this, who even forgives sins?" And he said to the woman, "Your faith has saved you; go in peace." (Luke 7:41–50)

This text provides a clear illustration of what Jesus has been trying to teach Peter and the other disciples: the woman demonstrates the genuineness of her faith by her actions—cleaning, drying, and anointing Jesus's feet. Jesus points out that her actions stand in sharp contrast to the Pharisee's actions, thereby teaching that we have to look beyond someone's words and consider *what their actions communicate about their belief* in order to discern the real condition of the person's heart. In this case, the Pharisee's actions communicate a lack of respect for Jesus as a guest in his home, and thus reveal the true status of his heart. This is in contrast to the woman's actions that communicate genuine love and reverence for Jesus. Her actions reveal a deep heartfelt love for, and belief in, Jesus that we do not see in the Pharisee. His *lack of action* reveals a lack of genuine faith; her actions reveal genuine belief. She accepts who Jesus really is, and she honors him.

In his words in this text, Jesus again expands his previous teaching by going beyond talking about how our actions confirm our words, to declaring that the woman's sins are forgiven based on genuine faith. And it is her faith that saves her. Jesus is teaching that genuine faith leads to forgiveness of sin and eternal life.

Jesus then continues his teaching about genuine faith, through the following series of parables:

- The sower   (Matt. 13:3–9, Mark 4:3–9, Luke 8:5–8)
- How seed grows   (Mark 4:26–29)
- The weeds   (Matt. 13:24–30)
- The mustard seed   (Matt. 13:31–32, Mark 4:30–32)
- The leaven and other parables   (Matt. 13:33, Mark 4:33–34)

One way of viewing these parables is to see them as comparisons between good and evil: evil comes in to threaten the success of the good that has been sown. Another way of viewing these parables is to see them as descriptions of genuine saving faith, and false faith that does not save.

Disciples Seek Clarification

Right after this series of parables, when Jesus is alone with Peter and the others who are with him, a critical moment occurs concerning the work of transformation:

Then the disciples came and said to him, "Why do you speak to them in parables?" And he answered them, "To you it has been given to know the secrets of the kingdom of heaven, but to them it has not been given. For to the one who has, more will be given, and he will have an abundance, but from the one who has not, even what he has will be taken away. This is why I speak to them in parables, because seeing they do not see, and hearing they do not hear, nor do they understand. Indeed, in their case the prophecy of Isaiah is fulfilled that says:

""You will indeed hear but never understand,
    and you will indeed see but never perceive."
For this people's heart has grown dull,
    and with their ears they can barely hear,
    and their eyes they have closed,
lest they should see with their eyes
    and hear with their ears
and understand with their heart
    and turn, and I would heal them.'

But blessed are your eyes, for they see, and your ears, for they hear. For truly, I say to you, many prophets and righteous people longed to see what you see, and did not see it, and to hear what you hear, and did not hear it." (Matt. 13:10–17; see also Mark 4:10–12, Luke 8:10)

Peter and the others do not understand the purpose of Jesus teaching through parables. This creates another teaching moment. In this text, Jesus begins by teaching Peter the importance of the disciples being able to understand the parables: they contain the secrets of the kingdom of God. It seems Jesus is answering a question that they have not yet asked: why is he teaching them so many things? Here Jesus makes clear his purpose for all of his teaching moments: so that those whom he is teaching may come to know the secrets of the kingdom of God. By referring to them as secrets, he infers that not everyone is capable of understanding them. The important point is this: as the work of transformation continues in us, we will begin to have eyes that see and ears that hear. Thus our understanding of the parables will increase. Therefore, we can know that transformation of our faith is taking place when we begin to understand the meaning of the parables.

In this passage, Jesus expands his teaching about God. By referring to a prophecy by Isaiah, he is saying that it is God who gives individuals the ability to understand the parables. This is another crucial point in the work of transformation in Peter. Jesus is answering a logical question: "Why doesn't everyone to whom the gospel is preached respond to it?" He says, in effect, that it is because God has not given others ears to hear and eyes to see, but he has given this ability to the apostles.

Here is an essential point about how transformation works. God knows in advance the issues that will arise in someone's life as they follow and serve Jesus. He begins to prepare them for that service through many teaching moments, as we have seen so far in the story of Peter. Important points about life as a disciple of Jesus are taught and retaught over time until an individual understands and embraces all that has been taught. It is this understanding that leads to their transformed faith and actions.

Another Testing Moment

As the teachings of Jesus continue, we see Jesus creating a time of testing for Peter and the others:

> One day he got into a boat with his disciples, and he said to them, "Let us go across to the other side of the lake." So they set out, and as they sailed he fell asleep. And a windstorm came down on the lake, and they were filling with water and were in danger. And they went and woke him, saying, "Master, Master, we are perishing!" And he awoke

and rebuked the wind and the raging waves, and they ceased, and there was a calm. He said to them, "Where is your faith?" And they were afraid, and they marveled, saying to one another, "Who then is this, that he commands even winds and water, and they obey him?" (Luke 8:22–25; see also Matt. 8:18, 23–27; Mark 4:35–41)

At first glance, this incident could be seen as another in a series of manifestations of power by Jesus. But if that is the case, why does he ask them, "Where is your faith?" Peter and several of the others are fishermen by trade. Thus they should be able to handle themselves and the boat in a storm on the open water. Yet the severity of this storm is more than they can handle, which results in their expressions of fear and anxiety. Such reactions would be considered normal, except that they have already experienced various manifestations of power by Jesus, including that of resurrecting a woman's son from the dead. Therefore, how Peter and the others respond during the storm reflects that their trust in such situations still rests in themselves. They are still trying to resolve life problems in their individual strength and ability first, rather than immediately reaching out to Jesus for help. This further demonstrates the shallow nature of their faith in Jesus as Messiah and Lord at this time, in spite of all they have already seen and heard. Clearly, more of God's transforming work is needed in Peter's life and in the lives of the other apostles.

Notice, however, that Jesus turns a situation that begins as a test of faith into a manifestation of his power. Then, he proceeds to calm the storm. This demonstration of divine power is intended to continue to transform and strengthen their faith in who Jesus really is. It certainly causes them to question openly, "Who then is this?" (Luke 8:25). They are still grappling with who Jesus is, and he continues to demonstrate his divine power in a variety of ways to answer this question for them.

We see other examples of Jesus demonstrating more of his divine power by performing another series of signs and miracles by healing:

- a man with demon   (Matt. 8:28–34, Mark 5:1–20, Luke 8:26–39)
- a woman and Jairus's daughter   (Matt. 9:18–26, Mark 5:21–43, Luke 8:40–56)
- two blind men and a demoniac   (Matt. 9:27–34)

Through these actions, Jesus continues to reveal who he really is, his power and authority, to those close to him, in order to continue to build their faith and trust in him.

A Taste of What Lies Ahead

After these demonstrations of Jesus's divine power and authority, he takes the next step in continuing the disciples' preparation for the work they will eventually do in his name. He calls Peter and the others together and gives them power and authority over demons and diseases, to do as he has done. Then he sends them out to proclaim the kingdom of God and to heal, telling them to take nothing for the journey. He tells them that if they are not received in any town, they are to leave and "shake off the dust from their feet as a testimony against them" (Luke 9:5). So his disciples leave and go to various villages, preaching and healing as Jesus instructed (see Luke 9:1–6, Matt. 9:35–11:1, Mark 6:6–13).

Here we see Jesus using a different teaching method with Peter and the other apostles. He is creating opportunities to allow them to experience what they have learned from him up to this point, moving them from learning by hearing and observation to learning by personal experience. They are sent out to do what they will do as apostles following Jesus's death and resurrection. He is giving them a taste of what they have been called to do once he has finished preparing them for what lies ahead.

This is a crucial step in the work of transformation. Jesus is opening their eyes not just to good and exciting times that lie ahead, but to the rejection that will also occur. God's work of transformation is designed to prepare an individual for both the good and evil that they will encounter in daily life as his disciples. They will need to function in his power in order to be successful in what they will be asked to do.

Since this point is so important for Peter and the others to understand, Jesus continues to underscore it by performing more signs and wonders that further manifest his power in the following texts:

- Feeds five thousand (Matt. 14:13–21, Mark 6:30–44, Luke 9:10–17, John 6:1–13)
- Walking on water (Matt. 14:22–33, Mark 6:45–52, John 6:16–21)

It is important to notice that the power manifested in these texts is even greater than the power and authority that he has given to Peter and the others. In these two events, Jesus demonstrates that what he gave them was only a portion of the power and authority that they will one day possess; it is a foretaste of the power and authority that will be given to them by the Holy Spirit following his death and resurrection. However, Peter and the others are not yet ready to receive that level of power and authority, not until God completes the work of transformation in them.

Fallacy of Tradition

Then Pharisees and scribes come to Jesus asking him why his disciples break the tradition of the elders by not washing their hands when they eat. He challenges them in return by asking why they break the commandment of God for the sake of tradition. Then he seizes the opportunity to turn the situation into another teaching moment for Peter and the other apostles:

And he called the people to him and said to them, "Hear and understand: it is not what goes into the mouth that defiles a person, but what comes out of the mouth; this defiles a person." Then the disciples came and said to him, "Do you know that the Pharisees were offended when they heard this saying?" He answered, "Every plant that my heavenly Father has not planted will be rooted up. Let them alone; they are blind guides. And if the blind lead the blind, both will fall into a pit." But Peter said to him, "Explain the parable to us." And he said, "Are you also still without understanding? Do you not see that whatever goes into the mouth passes into the stomach and is expelled? But what comes out of the mouth proceeds from the heart, and this defiles a person. For out of the heart come evil thoughts, murder, adultery, sexual immorality, theft, false witness, slander. These are what defile a person. But to eat with unwashed hands does not defile anyone." (Matt. 15:10–20; see also Mark 7:1–23)

In this text, the Pharisees focus upon the importance of their ritual handwashing that the Jewish tradition teaches shall be done before every meal where bread is served (Mark 7:3). This tradition has nothing to do with personal hygiene, but rather is a purification rite that Scripture tells us was initially required for priests entering the temple (see Num. 8:5–7). The point Jesus is making is that the Pharisees' focus is on external purification, which represents "rules to live by," whereas Jesus focuses on the condition of an individual internally, the purity of the heart. He teaches Peter and the others that they should be more concerned about the condition of their hearts, rather than what they put into their stomachs and the manner in which they do it. In this, Jesus is challenging the teachings of the Pharisees that are rooted in tradition. He is teaching the disciples that there are fallacies in the teachings of the Pharisees, and therefore, *he is the one they need to listen to.*

Moving on in Matthew's gospel, we see that Jesus then emphasizes the importance of this new teaching by again manifesting his
power. He performs more signs and miracles:

- Heals daughter of Canaanite woman   (Matt. 15:21–28,
                                        Mark 7:24–30)
- Heals many   (Matt. 15:29–31)
- Feeds four thousand   (Matt. 15:32–38,
                                        Mark 8:1-9)

In these passages, Jesus continues to demonstrate divine power.
In doing so, he is proving he is more powerful than the Pharisees, and
therefore he is the one his disciples should listen to and trust.

In Matthew, chapter 16, Jesus expands on the teaching about
human traditions with the disciples:

> When the disciples reached the other side, they
> had forgotten to bring any bread. Jesus said to
> them, "Watch and beware of the leaven of the
> Pharisees and Sadducees." And they began dis-
> cussing it among themselves, saying, "We brought
> no bread." But Jesus, aware of this, said, "O you
> of little faith, why are you discussing among
> yourselves the fact that you have no bread? Do
> you not yet perceive? Do you not remember the
> five loaves for the five thousand, and how many
> baskets you gathered? Or the seven loaves for the
> four thousand, and how many baskets you gath-
> ered? How is it that you fail to understand that I
> did not speak about bread? Beware of the leaven
> of the Pharisees and Sadducees." Then they
> understood that he did not tell them to beware
> of the leaven of bread, but of the teaching of the
> Pharisees and Sadducees. (Matt. 16:5–12; see
> also Mark 8:14-21)

This passage presents another important lesson about the work of transformation. Jesus exhorts Peter and the others to listen critically to what the Jewish leaders are teaching. In essence, he warns that *their traditions* are the teaching of man, but may not be the same as the *commandments and teaching of God* contained in the Scriptures. This is the point of the previous teaching moment about purity of heart versus traditional actions.

Without a doubt, this is difficult for Peter and the others to hear. As good Jews, they would naturally accept as true and valid what they have been taught by their religious leaders, the Pharisees and Sadducees, since their youth. Just imagine the pressure that this teaching creates on Peter and the others! Yet this is an important part of God's work of transformation in them. He is equipping and empowering them to be able to test what they are taught against what the word of God actually teaches. Scripture is full of references to false prophets, false teachers, and false brothers. In this text Jesus is warning Peter and the others to not unthinkingly accept what they have been taught by the Jewish leaders. This teaching point is about the difference between worldly thinking versus "kingdom of God" thinking.

Consistency between Words and Actions

Following his exhortation about the leaven of the Pharisees, Jesus again tests the faith of Peter and the others:

> Now when Jesus came into the district of Caesarea Philippi, he asked his disciples, "Who do people say that the Son of Man is?" And they said, "Some say John the Baptist, others say Elijah, and others Jeremiah or one of the prophets." He said to them, "But who do you say that I am?" Simon Peter replied, "You are the Christ, the Son of the living God." And Jesus answered him, "Blessed are you, Simon Bar-Jonah! For flesh and blood has not revealed this to you for a reason, but my

Father who is in heaven. And I tell you, you are
Peter, and on this rock I will build my church,
and the gates of hell shall not prevail against it. I
will give you the keys of the kingdom of heaven,
and whatever you bind on earth shall be bound
in heaven, and whatever you loose on earth shall
be loosed in heaven." Then he strictly charged
the disciples to tell no one that he was the Christ.
(Matt. 16:13–20; see also Mark 8:27–30, Luke
9:18–21)

Peter answers Jesus's question correctly, that Jesus is "the Christ,
the son of the living God" (v. 16). Then Jesus commends him for
it, pointing out that he could only have answered in this manner
because God himself has revealed this truth to him. Then he takes
the opportunity to turn this time into a teaching moment, further
revealing the nature of the power and authority that Peter and the
others will receive following Jesus's death and resurrection.

At this point, we might question if Peter fully understands what
he has declared. Does he make his statement to indicate that he genuinely believes Jesus is the long-awaited messiah of the Jews? If so,
is the work of transformation in Peter complete at this point? As
the story of Peter continues through the gospels, we will see that his
actions and words are inconsistent, which indicates that the work
of transformation in him must continue. We will see that his future
actions clearly reveal that he has a great deal more to learn about Jesus
before he comes to a full understanding of who Jesus really is. Only
then will the work of transformation be completed; only then will we
see that Peter's actions become congruent with his words.

This is an essential point concerning the work of transformation, which we have seen in some of the lives of the other biblical
characters we have looked at in this work. It is important enough
to state it once again. An individual can know and be able to say all
the right words; yet like Peter, their actions may not be consistent,
or congruent, with their words. Satan himself can quote Scripture
correctly; likewise, the scribes and Pharisees knew the Scriptures and

could quote them correctly. Nevertheless, *their actions were not consistent with the words they spoke.* This eventually caused Jesus to call them hypocrites (Matt. 23:13). Thus, as the work of transformation progresses in an individual, their words and actions will begin to align and become consistent. Thus it is important to listen critically to what one says and compare their words with what their actions reveal.

This point about congruency between words and actions is demonstrated by what Peter does next:

> From that time Jesus began to show his disciples that he must go to Jerusalem and suffer many things from the elders and chief priests and scribes, and be killed, and on the third day be raised. And Peter took him aside and began to rebuke him, saying, "Far be it from you, Lord! This shall never happen to you." But he turned and said to Peter, "Get behind me, Satan! You are a hindrance to me. For you are not setting your mind on the things of God, but on the things of man." (Matt. 16:21–23; see also Mark 8:31–37, Luke 9:22–25)

After Jesus tests to see if the disciples are beginning to understand who he is, he then begins to teach them that he must go to Jerusalem, to suffer at the hands of the Jewish leaders, and die. Peter takes Jesus aside to rebuke him, revealing that he does not yet fully understand the significance of what it means to believe that Jesus is "the Christ, the Son of the living God" (Matt. 16:16). He cannot fathom that the Messiah, the one who is expected to free Israel from the geopolitical rule of Rome, would actually die before accomplishing this mission. Jesus immediately rebukes Peter severely for his failure to understand what Jesus has been teaching. Here we see that although Peter previously said the right words, his actions now do not support what he has declared he believes.

In Jesus's rebuke to Peter, he is saying that such inconsistency between words and actions is not acceptable for one of his followers. Once again, we can view Peter's actions as stemming from the world's way of thinking, rather than thinking that emerges from the kingdom of God. Peter is still seeing with human eyes, not "kingdom of God" eyes.

Cost of Discipleship

Jesus immediately moves on to another teaching moment that flows out of what has just taken place:

> Then Jesus told his disciples, "If anyone would come after me, let him deny himself and take up his cross and follow me. For whoever would save his life will lose it, but whoever loses his life for my sake will find it. For what will it profit a man if he gains the whole world and forfeits his soul? Or what shall a man give in return for his soul? For the Son of Man is going to come with his angels in the glory of his Father, and then he will repay each person according to what he has done. Truly, I say to you, there are some standing here who will not taste death until they see the Son of Man coming in his kingdom." (Matt. 16:24–28; see also Mark 8:34–9:1, Luke 9:23–27)

This text expands upon what Jesus has been trying to communicate to Peter and the others in the most recent series of teaching moments. He is beginning to teach them about the cost of discipleship. In the previous text, it was clear that Peter expected Jesus to fulfill his own expectations of what it means to be the Messiah. *This* is what Jesus's previous rebuke to Peter was about; he did not have true kingdom understanding of what the Messiah will do—what he must do. So, for Peter, dying to self means giving up his own expectations of the Messiah in order to follow Jesus. Peter has to give up

PETER AND THE OTHER APOSTLES

his expectations of a geopolitical leader in exchange for the idea of a dying savior. That would be difficult, and most likely painful, since it requires a significant change in his belief system. It would be much easier to deny that Jesus is the Christ and continue to search for a messiah who meets his own expectations of what the Messiah will do.

Knowing this, Jesus sets forth the cost of "exchanging expectations" by explaining that when the true messiah comes in his glory, he will repay each person according to what he has done. This demonstrates another critical lesson about the work of transformation: the person in whom the work of transformation is successful will give up everything of personal value in order to have eternal life in the kingdom of God. Jesus is trying to teach the disciples that this "exchange" is costly.

Having concluded a significant series of teaching moments, Jesus once again demonstrates *who he is* by manifesting his power, by performing more signs and miracles.

- The mount of transfiguration   (Matt. 17:1–9, Mark 9:2–10, Luke 9:28–36)
- Casts out demon when disciples can't (Matt. 17:14–21, Mark 9:14–29, Luke 9:37–43)

The important point made in the first event is that, even with the magnificent nature of what happens on the mountain when Moses and Elijah appear, it is evident that Peter has not yet learned the lesson. He still does not see or think from a kingdom of God perspective; rather, he continues to see and think from a human perspective. Thus, he wants to set up a tent for Jesus, Moses, and Elijah—one for each of them to live in. However, God the Father counters this error by saying, "This is my beloved Son…listen to him!" (v. 5). By speaking, God tells Peter to be quiet and listen, thus emphasizing that Peter still has much to learn, and thus, more transformation is needed.

In the second event, Jesus further emphasizes the need for ongoing transformation when he has to cast out a demon because Peter and the others are unable to do so. Jesus continues his teaching of the disciples by explaining that some demons can be cast out only by prayer. He is telling the disciples, in effect, that they still do not have the same power that he has or that they will eventually receive in the future. The role and power of prayer in the life of a disciple is something else that they still need to learn. Thus, more transformation is needed before they will be ready to do the work they will be asked to do in his name.

The Use of Repetition

Thus, Jesus teaches them another essential lesson: it takes time in order to learn all the lessons that one needs to learn through God's work of transformation. Jesus emphasizes the importance of this lesson when he repeats a previous teaching moment, as recorded in Matthew 17:22–23, "As they were gathering in Galilee, Jesus said to them, 'The Son of Man is about to be delivered into the hands of men, and they will kill him, and he will be raised on the third day.' And they were greatly distressed" (see also Mark 9:30–32, Luke 9:43–45). This is the second time Jesus has taught on his death and resurrection, thus demonstrating the necessity of repetition as the disciples' thinking is gradually being transformed from the world to the kingdom of God.

Jesus then returns a second time to teach about the cost of being his disciple:

> As they were going along the road, someone said to him, "I will follow you wherever you go." And Jesus said to him, "Foxes have holes, and birds of the air have nests, but the Son of Man has nowhere to lay his head." To another he said, "Follow me." But he said, "Lord, let me first go and bury my father." And Jesus said to him, "Leave the dead to bury their own dead. But as for you, go and proclaim the kingdom of God." Yet another said, "I will follow you, Lord, but let

me first say farewell to those at my home." Jesus said to him, "No one who puts his hand to the plow and looks back is fit for the kingdom of God." (Luke 9:57–62; see also Matt. 8:19–22)

This text along with the previous text from Matthew 17 clarify this point about repetition and the gradual nature of transformation. If an individual does not learn the lessons God is teaching in a specific moment, or in a series of teaching moments, God will repeat the lesson as many times as needed for *understanding, acceptance, and obedience* to occur. Repetition is necessary. Transformation is gradual; it takes time.

We now return again to chapter 8 in John's gospel, where Jesus begins a new series of teaching moments in which he expands on previous teachings about himself, and challenges the "knowing" of the Pharisees:

Again Jesus spoke to them, saying, "I am the light of the world. Whoever follows me will not walk in darkness, but will have the light of life." So the Pharisees said to him, "You are bearing witness about yourself; your testimony is not true." Jesus answered, "Even if I do bear witness about myself, my testimony is true, for I know where I came from and where I am going, but you do not know where I come from or where I am going. You judge according to the flesh; I judge no one. Yet even if I do judge, my judgment is true, for it is not I alone who judge, but I and the Father who sent me. In your Law it is written that the testimony of two people is true. I am the one who bears witness about myself, and the Father who sent me bears witness about me." They said to him therefore, "Where is your Father?" Jesus answered, "You know neither me nor my Father. If you knew me, you would know my Father also." These words he spoke in the treasury, as he taught in the temple; but no one arrested him, because his hour had not yet come. (John 8:12–20)

Jesus has already brought the disciples to the point of knowing that he is the Christ, the Son of the living God. He has continually referred to himself as the Son of Man. The disciples have seen that he has divine power, having performed many signs and wonders that are clearly beyond human ability. They have seen his authority in the way he teaches and casts out demons. Here Jesus further expands these teachings with a new description of himself: he is the light of the world, which refers to the source of spiritual enlightenment.

The Pharisees challenge the truth of his teaching, again from a human perspective: where is the second witness who can testify to the truth of his words? Jesus responds that his testimony about himself has met the requirements established by Jewish law in order to be considered true (see Deut. 17:6). There are, indeed, two witnesses of its truthfulness: he is the first witness, and God his father is the second. To accept his argument, the Pharisees must be able to "see" with spiritual eyes. Jesus declares that they do not see with spiritual eyes, for they do not know him or his father.

Jesus further expands this concept of the world versus the kingdom of God, as well as referring again to his death, and introduces new information about his relationship with his father in the next passage in John 8:

So he said to them again, "I am going away, and you will seek me, and you will die in your sin. Where I am going, you cannot come." So the Jews said, "Will he kill himself, since he says, 'Where I am going, you cannot come'?" He said to them, "You are from below; I am from above. You are of this world; I am not of this world. I told you that you would die in your sins, for unless you believe that I am he you will die in your sins." So they said to him, "Who are you?" Jesus said to them, "Just what I have been telling you from the beginning. I have much to say about you and much to judge, but he who sent me is true, and I declare to the world what I have heard from him." They did not understand that he had been speaking to them about the Father. So Jesus said to them, "When you have lifted up the Son of Man, then you will know that I am he, and that I do nothing on my own authority, but speak just as the Father taught me. And he who sent me is with me. He has not left me alone, for I always do the things that are pleasing to him." As he was saying these things, many believed in him. (John 8:21–30)

Remember that Jesus directs his statements in this text to the Pharisees, who have challenged the truth of his previous statement about being the light of the world. Yet it is reasonable to assume that Peter and the other apostles are likely present as well at this interchange. So when Jesus refers to what he has been telling them from the beginning, his disciples would naturally begin to go back over what Jesus has been teaching from the beginning about himself, which is far more than what he has said to this group of Pharisees. Jesus is telling Peter and the others that he knows they do not yet fully understand all that he has been teaching them, but they will understand after his crucifixion. He is also continuing to teach more about his father, thus seeking to gradually expand and deepen the understanding of the Pharisees and the others about his relationship with his father.

Notice from these last two passages in John 8 that Jesus is gradually bringing in more information, gradually expanding his teaching about himself and his father. This is an important point. Transformation leading to genuine belief, trust, surrender, and obedience is a process during which God guides an individual through one or more teaching moments, the content of which leads to an ever-increasing understanding of *who Jesus Christ really is*. The expanded information is intended to lead the individual to genuine belief and to completely trust his statutes and commandments, which enables one to completely surrender to God's will for their life. Each subsequent teaching moment contributes a different building block to the structure that becomes one's faith. Thus, each lesson must be grasped and understood in order for the work of transformation to be successful. That is why in this text, Jesus again repeats the teaching about his death. He has taught this to Peter and the others before, but for their understanding, it bears repeating, for he knows they still do not really understand what he is teaching them.

Then, following the pattern we have seen throughout this chapter, after this teaching, Jesus manifests his power as a demonstration of who he is by performing another outstanding sign and miracle: He heals a man who was born blind (John 9:1–7). We continue to see that as the scope and significance of Jesus's teaching moments increase, so too does the nature of the manifestation of his power, in order to emphasize and confirm what he is teaching them.

Extends Previous Teaching

We see in John's gospel that, having healed the blind man, Jesus gives the disciples another lesson about himself and the cost of discipleship:

> "Truly, truly, I say to you, he who does not enter the sheepfold by the door but climbs in by another way, that man is a thief and a robber. But he who enters by the door is the shepherd of the sheep. To him the gatekeeper opens. The sheep hear his voice, and he calls his own sheep by name and leads them out. When he has brought out all his own, he goes before them, and the sheep follow him, for they know his voice. A stranger they will not follow, but they will flee from him, for they do not know the voice of strangers." This figure

of speech Jesus used with them, but they did not understand what he was saying to them.

So Jesus again said to them, "Truly, truly, I say to you, I am the door of the sheep. All who came before me are thieves and robbers, but the sheep did not listen to them. I am the door. If anyone enters by me, he will be saved and will go in and out and find pasture. The thief comes only to steal and kill and destroy. I came that they may have life and have it abundantly. I am the good shepherd. The good shepherd lays down his life for the sheep. He who is a hired hand and not a shepherd, who does not own the sheep, sees the wolf coming and leaves the sheep and flees, and the wolf snatches them and scatters them. He flees because he is a hired hand and cares nothing for the sheep. I am the good shepherd. I know my own and my own know me, just as the Father knows me and I know the Father; and I lay down my life for the sheep. And I have other sheep that are not of this fold. I must bring them also, and they will listen to my voice. So there will be one flock, one shepherd. For this reason the Father loves me, because I lay down my life that I may take it up again. No one takes it from me, but I lay it down of my own accord. I have authority to lay it down, and I have authority to take it up again. This charge I have received from my Father." (John 10:1–18)

In this text, Jesus's teaching reveals more about himself, in particular about his role as a shepherd of the flock of God. He affirms that he loves his sheep, they know his voice, and they follow him.

Then, during the teaching, he shifts to describing how he cares for the sheep, in contrast to hired hands who leave the sheep when wolves attack. Who are the hired hands in this story? They are the ones who take over for the shepherd in his absence. Jesus is again revealing that Peter and the other apostles will take over following his death and resurrection. He is teaching them about how to conduct themselves as his replacements and about what to expect when they do: they and the sheep will be attacked. Thus, they must decide for themselves whether to defend the sheep like good shepherds or run like hired hands and abandon the sheep in the face of life-threatening situations. Jesus clarifies in this teaching that a shepherd takes responsibility for the safety of the sheep; it is his life's work. A hired hand may not, for shepherding is only a job.

As the work of transformation progresses, we are challenged to decide whether or not we will fulfill the role for which God is preparing us. That means considering the responsibility inherent in that role and counting the cost of fulfilling that role. In this teaching, Jesus has again returned to the topic of the cost of discipleship but has extended that teaching to reveal more clearly what that cost might be.

Importance of Prayer

Returning once again to Luke's gospel, chapter 11, we see that the disciples create an opportunity for the next teaching moment:

> Now Jesus was praying in a certain place, and when he finished, one of his disciples said to him, "Lord, teach us to pray, as John taught his disciples." And he said to them, "When you pray, say:

> "Father, hallowed be your name.
> Your kingdom come.
> Give us each day our daily bread,
> and forgive us our sins,
>   for we ourselves forgive everyone who is indebted to us.
> And lead us not into temptation."

And he said to them, "Which of you who has a friend will go to him at midnight and say to him, 'Friend, lend me three loaves, for a friend of mine has arrived on a journey, and I have nothing to set before him'; and he will answer from within, 'Do not bother me; the door is now shut, and my children are with me in bed. I cannot get up and give you anything'? I tell you, though he will not get up and give him anything because he is his friend, yet because of his impudence he will rise and give him whatever he needs. And I tell you, ask, and it will be given to you; seek, and you will find; knock, and it will be opened to you. For everyone who asks receives, and the one who seeks finds, and to the one who knocks it will be opened. What father among you, if his son asks for a fish, will instead of a fish give him a serpent; or if he asks for an egg, will give him a scorpion? If you then, who are evil, know how to give good gifts to your children, how much more will the heavenly Father give the Holy Spirit to those who ask him!" (Luke 11:1–13; see also Matt. 6:9–13)

Here is perhaps the first evidence that the work of transformation has begun to be successful in Peter and the others. Jesus challenged them in the previous teaching moment, asking if they will defend the sheep like a good shepherd, even at the cost of their own lives. And now, as they watch him pray, they realize that prayer will be important in fulfilling their call. They want to learn from Jesus how to pray. So he teaches them this surprisingly simple and direct prayer, yet he does not stop there. He goes further to assure them that if they ask, God will answer their prayer, thus teaching them that what he is calling them to do, they do not have to do based on their own strength and ability. Instead, just as for Jesus himself, guidance, direction, and empowerment will be provided by God in answer to their prayers.

Here is another important lesson learned through God's work of transformation: as our transformation continues over time, we learn that we cannot do what we have been called to do *in our own effort* and that God will provide his power and ability *to those who ask in prayer*. As we are being prepared to live out God's will for our lives, we learn the critical importance of prayer in our lives and in fulfilling our calling.

Fear versus Trust

Then, this series of teaching moments reaches its climax with Jesus's next teaching moment:

> "I tell you, my friends, do not fear those who kill the body, and after that have nothing more that they can do. But I will warn you whom to fear: fear him who, after he has killed, has authority to cast into hell. Yes, I tell you, fear him! Are not five sparrows sold for two pennies? And not one of them is forgotten before God. Why, even the hairs of your head are all numbered. Fear not; you are of more value than many sparrows.
> "And I tell you, everyone who acknowledges me before men, the Son of Man also will acknowledge before the angels of God, but the one who denies me before men will be denied before the angels of God. And everyone who speaks a word against the Son of Man will be forgiven, but the one who blasphemes against the Holy Spirit will not be forgiven. And when they bring you before the synagogues and the rulers and the authorities, do not be anxious about how you should defend yourself or what you should say, for the Holy Spirit will teach you in that very hour what you ought to say." (Luke 12:4–12)

This text reveals that Jesus has perceived the concern of Peter and the others since this series of teaching moments began. He extends his teaching to address how to handle the fear that they are beginning to experience. He seeks to put their fear of being put to death by the Jewish leaders in proper perspective: do not fear losing your earthy life; fear more the one who can kill the soul as well. He is telling them that they need to fear spiritual death more than physical death. Thus, God is to be feared more than any human being. Again, Jesus is comparing worldly thinking with "kingdom of God" thinking.

Then Jesus expands his teaching by telling them that he will speak on their behalf to God. But those who deny him—the same ones who will seek to kill them—will be denied by him before God. This is an additional reason not to fear human beings who can only kill their bodies, for even if they die a physical death, Jesus will intercede for them with God, thereby assuring acceptance by God unto eternal life.

Finally, he further amplifies his teaching about what they will experience by assuring them that even when the rulers and authorities question them, they need not fear, for God himself through the Holy Spirit will teach them in that moment what to say. In this we see a connection between the needs of those who will continue Jesus's work in the world and God's wisdom being made available to them to accomplish that work.

The ultimate focus of this teaching moment is trust. Jesus is encouraging Peter and the others to trust God as Father, Son, and Holy Spirit, both in their individual lives and in relation to what they are called to do as apostles. By this point in the story, they are beginning to accept that Jesus is who he says he is, and they are learning about God the Father. But their fear raises the question as to whether they *trust their lives to God*. So Jesus brings in an expanded teaching about the Holy Spirit.

This issue of trust is a crucial lesson concerning the work of transformation: it is designed to move a person beyond simple belief, mere mental ascent about God, to the point of trusting that he is alive and active in one's life, thus becoming real to that person. When this work of transformation has occurred, when a person does trust God, they will be willing to surrender to God's will for them during both the good and evil experiences in their lives, regardless of the potential threat they may face.

This question of trust becomes increasingly difficult due to the triune nature of the Godhead as Father, Son, and Holy Spirit. The Jewish authorities believe in God the Father but not in Jesus as the Son of God. And apparently some blaspheme the Holy Spirit by effectively denying his existence and work in their lives. This text places equal importance on each of the three members of the Godhead, even though their roles are different. Jesus is exhorting Peter and the others to fully and equally recognize each member of the Godhead and their respective roles, thereby creating a balanced understanding leading to greater trust and surrender to the Godhead as a whole. This too is a crucial component of the work of transformation: all three members of the Godhead are to be accepted, embraced, and trusted so that true surrender to the will of God can occur.

Jesus again follows this series of teaching moments where he has revealed more about who he is, who the Father is, his relationship with his father, the work of the Holy Spirit, their fear, death, etc., when he again manifests his power by healing a disabled woman on the Sabbath (Luke 13:10–17). The significance of this sign is not just that Jesus has the power, authority, and ability to cast out the disabling spirit from this woman, but that he does so on the Sabbath. In doing so he demonstrates that his authority is higher than the Jewish law. He continues to convey to Peter and his disciples the validity of his teachings about who he is.

Repetition and Extension of Previous Teachings

In Luke, chapter 13, we see that Jesus begins another series of teaching moments:

> He went on his way through towns and villages, teaching and journeying toward Jerusalem. And someone said to him, "Lord, will those who are

saved be few?" And he said to them, "Strive to enter through the narrow door. For many, I tell you, will seek to enter and will not be able. When once the master of the house has risen and shut the door, and you begin to stand outside and to knock at the door, saying, 'Lord, open to us,' then he will answer you, 'I do not know where you come from.' Then you will begin to say, 'We ate and drank in your presence, and you taught in our streets.' But he will say, 'I tell you, I do not know where you come from. Depart from me, all you workers of evil!' In that place there will be weeping and gnashing of teeth, when you see Abraham and Isaac and Jacob and all the prophets in the kingdom of God but you yourselves cast out. And people will come from east and west, and from north and south, and recline at table in the kingdom of God. And behold, some are last who will be first, and some are first who will be last." (Luke 13:22–30)

In this text, Jesus expands his teaching regarding the kingdom of God when asked about whether the number saved will be few. He responds that many will seek entry, but few will be able to achieve it. He then goes on to explain that God governs entry into the kingdom rather than what an individual has or has not done. He is again teaching that the status of one's heart, one's true relationship with God, is more important than one's actions.

Here then is a new and crucial point concerning the work of transformation: if God does not know a person, entry into the kingdom will not be possible. Being "known" by God gives evidence of the successful completion of God's work of transformation in someone. It is not our knowing about God that leads to entrance into the kingdom of God, but rather *God knowing us, by his choosing*. Casual experiences with God, hearing Jesus's teaching *without transformation of the heart* that comes from an intimate relationship with God is not sufficient for entering the kingdom of God. This teaching of Jesus is essential for Peter and the others to learn in order to be able to teach it to others in the future, in order to continue the work of Jesus in the world after his death.

In Luke, chapter 14, Jesus returns once again to further expand on his previous teaching about the cost of discipleship:

> Now great crowds accompanied him, and he turned and said to them, "If anyone comes to me and does not hate his own father and mother and wife and children and brothers and sisters, yes, and even his own life, he cannot be my disciple. Whoever does not bear his own cross and come after me cannot be my disciple. For which of you, desiring to build a tower, does not first sit down and count the cost, whether he has enough to complete it? Otherwise, when he has laid a foundation and is not able to finish, all who see it begin to mock him, saying, 'This man began to build and was not able to finish.' Or what king, going out to encounter another king in war, will not sit down first and deliberate whether he is able with ten thousand to meet him who comes against him with twenty thousand? And if not, while the other is yet a great way off, he sends a delegation and asks for terms of peace. So therefore, any one of you who does not renounce all that he has cannot be my disciple." (Luke 14:25–33)

Here is unambiguous and straightforward teaching about the cost of discipleship from a different perspective. This teaching naturally follows and expands upon his previous teaching about entry into the kingdom of God; entering by the narrow gate is the same as being Jesus's disciple. He makes it clear that only an individual who loves him more than all earthly possessions, more than members of one's own family, even more than their own life, can meet the requirements needed to enter the narrow gate into the kingdom of God. He concludes this teaching by stating that anyone who does not renounce all that he has cannot be his disciple and, therefore, is lost and cannot gain entry through the narrow gate into the kingdom of God. This is the cost of discipleship.

Jesus continues this teaching in chapters 15–17 of Luke's gospel. Through a series of parables, Jesus continues to reveal how things of this earth can be more important to us than the kingdom of God:

- Parable of the lost sheep   (Luke 15:3–7)
- Parable of the lost coin   (Luke 15:8–10)
- Parable of the lost son   (Luke 15:11–32)
- Parable of dishonest manager   (Luke 16:1–13)
- The law and the kingdom of God   (Luke 16:14–17)
- The rich man and Lazarus   (Luke 16:19–31)
- Temptations to sin   (Luke 17:1–4)

All of these parables are examples of how we seek that which we most value. Remember in the previous passage in Luke 14, Jesus said clearly, "Any one of you who does not renounce all that he has cannot be my disciple" (v. 33). He has also taught that true disciples will have ears to hear and eyes to see kingdom truths. Thus, the response of a genuine disciple, one who has eyes to see and ears to hear the invitation to costly discipleship, who recognizes the invaluable worth of Jesus, will respond with deep heartfelt repentance. When this occurs, they will receive forgiveness and thus enter into eternal life in the kingdom of God. They will count the cost and then willingly set aside all that this world has to offer to be a disciple of Jesus.

Recognition of Need for More Faith

In response to these parables, and with increasing understanding, the disciples realize they need more faith. Thus, another opportunity for a teaching moment occurs when Peter and the other apostles say to Jesus, "'Increase our faith!' And the Lord said, 'If you had faith like a grain of mustard seed, you could say to this mulberry tree, "Be uprooted and planted in the sea," and it would obey you'" (Luke 17:5–6).

The fact that Peter and the others recognize that they do not yet have enough faith, and thus ask Jesus for more, reveals that the work of transformation is progressing in them. It indicates some movement from simple belief toward genuine saving faith. Jesus's response to their question is to teach them just how powerful genuine faith is, that with only a very small amount, they can do what is humanly impossible.

Jesus continues to respond to their request for more faith in John's gospel, chapter 11. Here we see a unique opportunity for Jesus to expand his teaching about God and himself when Martha and Mary come to alert Jesus that their brother Lazarus is ill:

> Now a certain man was ill, Lazarus of Bethany, the village of Mary and her sister Martha. It was Mary who anointed the Lord with ointment and wiped his feet with her hair, whose brother Lazarus was ill. So the sisters sent to him, saying, "Lord, he whom you love is ill." But when Jesus heard it he said, "This illness does not lead to death. It is for the glory of God, so that the Son of God may be glorified through it."
>
> Now Jesus loved Martha and her sister and Lazarus. So, when he heard that Lazarus was ill, he stayed two days longer in the place where he was. Then after this he said to the disciples, "Let us go to Judea again." The disciples said to him, "Rabbi, the Jews were just now seeking to stone you, and are you going there again?" Jesus answered, "Are there not twelve hours in the day? If anyone walks in the day, he does not stumble, because he sees the light of this world. But if anyone walks in the night, he stumbles, because

the light is not in him." After saying these things, he said to them, "Our friend Lazarus has fallen asleep, but I go to awaken him." The disciples said to him, "Lord, if he has fallen asleep, he will recover." Now Jesus had spoken of his death, but they thought that he meant taking rest in sleep. Then Jesus told them plainly, "Lazarus has died, and for your sake I am glad that I was not there, so that you may believe. But let us go to him." So Thomas, called the Twin, said to his fellow disciples, "Let us also go, that we may die with him." (John 11:1–16)

Notice that as this text begins, Jesus wants to use the imminent death of Lazarus as a teaching moment for the disciples, to bring glory to God and to himself, and to further strengthen their faith. As he begins, it immediately becomes clear that Peter and the others understand neither what he is trying to teach them nor what he has previously taught them.

Still thinking from a human perspective, they lock in on his intent to return to Judea and are fearful he will be killed there. They completely miss his point about the purpose of Lazarus's illness: "to bring glory to God" (v. 4). When Jesus states two days later that it is now time to go to Judea, it is clear that the disciples still do not understand what he meant about glorifying God. Even as Jesus patiently attempts to clarify for them what he is saying, they continually fail to understand; they then state that if Lazarus has fallen asleep, he will wake up. When Jesus finally tells them bluntly that Lazarus has died, which is why he now wants to go to Judea, they remain focused on the issue of whether he will be killed. Their thinking is still rooted in worldly concerns; Jesus continues to work to show them kingdom truths.

In order to understand, and therefore learn, what Jesus is trying to teach them, Peter and the others need to focus on the point of his teaching rather than allowing themselves to be distracted by other fears and concerns. Understanding is a critical element in the process of transformation; it enables us to know more fully who God is, and thus to trust him, and then surrender to and obey his will for our lives. In order to understand, they need to be continually asking themselves, "What is Jesus trying to teach us?" In our own lives, when we experience the same faith challenges again and again, we also need to ask what kingdom principles and truths God might be trying to teach us.

But Peter and the others don't do this, and Jesus knows that their faith is not yet entirely genuine. So he continues to teach them as he prepares to raise Lazarus from the dead:

> Then Jesus, deeply moved again, came to the tomb. It was a cave, and a stone lay against it. Jesus said, "Take away the stone." Martha, the sister of the dead man, said to him, "Lord, by this time there will be an odor, for he has been dead four days." Jesus said to her, "Did I not tell you that if you believed you would see the glory of God?" So they took away the stone. And Jesus lifted up his eyes and said, "Father, I thank you that you have heard me. I knew that you always hear me, but I said this on account of the people standing around, that they may believe that you sent me." When he had said these things, he cried out with a loud voice, "Lazarus, come out." The man who had died came out, his hands and feet bound with linen strips, and his face wrapped with a cloth. Jesus said to them, "Unbind him, and let him go." (John 11:38–44)

Jesus performs another miracle of power and authority at the tomb of Lazarus, which is designed to bolster not only the faith and belief of his sisters but that of Peter and the others as well. We have seen at times that they say the right things, calling him Lord. But Jesus knows that they still lack genuine understanding and belief that will lead to trust, surrender, and obedience. Thus, before calling Lazarus out of the tomb, Jesus pauses to pray so that everyone watching will believe that God has given him the power to raise Lazarus from the dead. Then Jesus calls Lazarus from the tomb. In this demonstration of divine power and authority over death, Jesus reaffirms all that he has been teaching them about who he is. We see here, again, that when the disciples do not grasp the lesson about faith Jesus has been teaching them, he knows he must continue to teach the point again *so that* they will understand—and truly believe.

Teaching about the Kingdom of God

After this display of divine power, another teaching opportunity arises when Jesus is asked by the Pharisees about the coming of the kingdom of God. Jesus responds, "The kingdom of God is not coming in ways that can be observed, nor will they say, 'Look, here it is!' or 'There!' for behold, the kingdom of God is in the midst of you" (Luke 17:20–21). Even though the question comes from the Pharisees, Jesus seizes upon the opportunity for a critical teaching moment and responds that the kingdom of God is in their midst. Alternate translations of the Greek text indicate that Jesus could have meant the kingdom of God is within them.[6] Jesus is explaining that the kingdom of God is ultimately a matter of the heart, rather than an external, physical world event that will be obvious to everyone. The critical lesson Jesus is teaching is that the kingdom comes to an individual as a result of genuine belief, trust, and surrender to God and his Son Jesus Christ.

In various passages, Jesus continues to teach about the kingdom of God from other perspectives in the following series of parables:

- The coming of God's kingdom   (Luke 17:22–27)
- The persistent widow   (Luke 18:1–8)
- Pharisee and the tax collector (Luke 18:9–14)

---

[6] *Entos*, "within, inside; in the midst of," https://biblehub.com/str/greek/1787.htm.

- Let the children come   (Matt. 19:13–15, Mark
                                 10:13–16, Luke 18:15–17)
- Rich young ruler   (Matt. 19:16–30, Mark
                                 10:17–31, Luke 18:18–30)
- Laborers in vineyard   (Matt. 20:1–16)

Notice that often Jesus's parables provide different perspectives on the same biblical or theological point. Each of these parables represents Jesus "repeating" the teaching point we just saw in Luke 17. They describe in different ways the coming of the kingdom of God and the essence of God's kingdom.

Another Effort to Bring Understanding

Moving on to Luke, chapter 18, we find Jesus returning to a topic he has previously taught, his imminent death and resurrection:

> And taking the twelve, he said to them, "See, we are going up to Jerusalem, and everything that is written about the Son of Man by the prophets will be accomplished. For he will be delivered over to the Gentiles and will be mocked and shamefully treated and spit upon. And after flogging him, they will kill him, and on the third day he will rise." But they understood none of these things. This saying was hidden from them, and they did not grasp what was said. (Luke 18:31–34; see also Matt. 20:17–19, Mark 10:31–34)

Even at this point, Peter and the others still do not grasp what Jesus continues to teach them, that *he must die* in order to fulfill his earthly mission. By repeating his teaching, it is evident that this is a crucial truth that is important for them to understand.

The extent of their lack of understanding becomes evident when the mother of James and John comes up to Jesus with her sons and, kneeling before him, asks him to promise that her two sons will sit at his right and left hands in his kingdom. Her question reveals that she too is thinking from a human perspective about the status of being in close relationship with a king or ruler. Jesus answers her question from a "kingdom of God" perspective:

> Jesus answered, "You do not know what you are asking. Are you able to drink the cup that I am to drink?" They said to him, "We are able." He said to them, "You will drink my cup, but to sit at my right hand and at my left is not mine to grant, but it is for those for whom it has been prepared by my Father." And when the ten heard it, they were indignant at the two brothers. But Jesus called them to him and said, "You know that the rulers of the Gentiles lord it over them, and their great ones exercise authority over them. It shall not be so among you. But whoever would be great among you must be your servant, and whoever would be first among you must be your slave, even as the Son of Man came not to be served but to serve, and to give his life as a ransom for many." (Matt. 20:22–28; see also Mark 10:35–45)

By their response, it is evident that James and John do not yet fully understand what Jesus has been teaching them about the cost of discipleship, for they do not understand the "cup" that Jesus will drink. Neither do Peter and the other apostles, based on their anger at James and John. And none of them yet understand the cost to Jesus to fulfill his role as messiah—he must give up his earthly life.

Rather than continuing to debate the issue with them, Jesus begins a new teaching moment on the nature of leadership. In contrast to how Gentile leaders hold their power and authority over those subject to them, he teaches them that leaders in God's kingdom are to be servants of those over whom they have authority. He goes on to explain that, as the Son of Man, he is serving them all by his death. Thus, he is setting the example for Peter and the others to follow after his death.

Notice that even as Peter and the others continue to be distracted, focusing on issues that they think are important from a human perspective, Jesus continues to focus on teaching them the lessons that they need to learn from a kingdom perspective. The lessons he is teaching are necessary for them to be ready to fulfill their calling.

In chapter 19 of Luke's gospel, Jesus further extends this teaching moment during his encounter with Zacchaeus:

> He entered Jericho and was passing through. And behold, there was a man named Zacchaeus. He was a chief tax collector and was rich. And he was seeking to see who Jesus was, but on account of the crowd he could not, because he was small in stature. So he ran on ahead and climbed up into a sycamore tree to see him, for he was about to pass that way. And when Jesus came to the place, he looked up and said to him, "Zacchaeus, hurry and come down, for I must stay at your house today." So he hurried and came down and received him joyfully. And when they saw it, they all grumbled, "He has gone in to be the guest of a man who is a sinner." And Zacchaeus stood and said to the Lord, "Behold, Lord, the half of my goods I give to the poor. And if I have defrauded anyone of anything, I restore it fourfold." And Jesus said to him, "Today salvation has come to this house, since he also is a son of Abraham. For the Son of Man came to seek and to save the lost." (Luke 19:1–10)

This text reveals that Peter and the others do not yet understand the purpose of Jesus's earthly mission. Notice that Luke records "they all grumbled" (v. 7) when he invited himself to stay at Zacchaeus's house, who as a tax collector was considered to be a "sinner." The comment that all grumbled necessarily includes Peter and the others who are with Jesus.

As the episode continues, we see that Zacchaeus's attitude and actions demonstrate the true nature of his faith. He eagerly seeks out a place from which to see Jesus, even though his action, climbing a tree, could be embarrassing to one of his stature in the community. When Jesus calls him down out of the tree, he responds in joyful, unquestioning obedience. When in his home, in a relational setting, he addresses Jesus as "Lord" (v. 8) and then states the ways in which he lives as one who believes in Jesus is called to live: giving to the poor and making restitution when needed, which reflects honesty, integrity, and generosity. Here we see the true status of his heart. Thus, Jesus declares, "Salvation has come to this house" (v. 9).

It seems the reality of the kingdom of God is emerging in Zacchaeus, and thus serves as an example of what Jesus has previously taught the disciples. Jesus seizes upon this moment to begin to teach about the nature of his earthly mission, which is "to seek and save the lost" (v. 10). Interestingly, Jesus first provides the example of his mission through his encounter with Zacchaeus, who is considered to be a sinner *and* one in whom the kingdom of God is emerging, before he clearly states his mission.

Trusting Jesus, Trusting God

Following the encounter with Zacchaeus in Jericho, the climax of Jesus's earthly mission approaches. Jesus enters Jerusalem riding on a young donkey, thus fulfilling an Old Testament prophecy (see Zech. 9:9). As he approaches the city, a large crowd of his disciples take branches of palm trees and go out to meet him, celebrating his arrival as the one "who comes in the name of the Lord, even the King of Israel!" (John 12:13). In his gospel, John comments that Peter and the others do not understand these things at first, but later they will understand after Jesus's ascension and glorification (John 12:16).

Realizing that Peter and the others do not yet understand the significance of what is happening, Jesus again teaches about his death:

> "Now is my soul troubled. And what shall I say? 'Father, save me from this hour'? But for this purpose I have come to this hour. Father, glorify your name." Then a voice came from heaven: "I have glorified it, and I will glorify it again." (John 12:27–28)

Jesus takes this opportunity to reassure Peter and the others that what is happening is necessary in order for him to fulfill the purpose of his life. God the Father confirms his statement by speaking in response to Jesus's prayer. John states that some in the crowd hear thunder, and others believe an angel spoke to him (John 12:29). Jesus states that this experience is for the sake of those with him, designed to continue building their trust in who Jesus is and in what he has been teaching them. Building their trust moves them beyond simple belief to genuine faith, which will enable them to obey God. This is necessary in order for them to fulfill their calling in the coming days.

Then Jesus continues to build their trust by further expanding his teaching regarding his earthly mission:

> And Jesus cried out and said, "Whoever believes in me, believes not in me but in him who sent me. And whoever sees me sees him who sent me. I have come into the world as light, so that whoever believes in me may not remain in darkness. If anyone hears my words and does not keep them, I do not judge him; for I did not come to judge the world but to save the world. The one who rejects me and does not receive my words has a judge; the word that I have spoken will judge him on the last day. For I have not spoken on my own authority, but the Father who sent me has himself given me a commandment—what to

say and what to speak. And I know that his commandment is eternal life. What I say, therefore, I
say as the Father has told me." (John 12:44–50)

Jesus explains that believing in him is the same as believing
in God the Father; seeing Jesus is the same as seeing God. This is
the foundation for the disciples' ability to trust him, to trust God.
Further, he explains that he has spoken not on his authority but on
God's authority, for it is God, his father, who tells him what to say.
Moreover, he came not to judge but to save the lost, reiterating what
he had previously taught Peter and the others about the purpose of
his earthly mission. A crucial part of the work of transformation is
to build an individual's trust in Jesus as the only Son of God; Jesus
seeks to do this very thing for the disciples—so they will genuinely
believe in him.

Trusting Jesus, Not Hypocrites

After this, other things that Jesus told the disciples were going
to happen begin to happen, as he responds to a series of questions by
the Pharisees designed to discredit him:

-   About his authority   (Matt. 21:23–27)
-   About paying taxes   (Matt. 22:15–22)
-   About the resurrection   (Matt. 22:23–33)
-   About the great commandment   (Matt. 22:34–40)

The Pharisees' efforts to discredit Jesus are not successful. So
Jesus asks them a single question in return:

Now while the Pharisees were gathered together,
Jesus asked them a question, saying, "What do
you think about the Christ? Whose son is he?"
They said to him, "The son of David." He said to

them, "How is it then that David, in the Spirit, calls him Lord, saying,

"'The Lord said to my Lord,
"Sit at my right hand,
until I put your enemies under your feet"'?

If then David calls him Lord, how is he his son?" And no one was able to answer him a word, nor from that day did anyone dare to ask him any more questions. (Matt. 22:41–46; see also Mark 12:35–37, Luke 20:41–44)

From the perspective of Peter and the others, in this text, Jesus demonstrates that his theological understanding is superior to that of the Pharisees, thus providing a practical lesson that illustrates why they should place their trust *in him* as opposed to the Jewish leaders. The Pharisees can quote Scripture, but do they understand it? Jesus never attended the schools that they did, yet he has a greater understanding than they do.

Then Jesus continues to expand his teaching to Peter and the others about the scribes and Pharisees:

Then Jesus said to the crowds and to his disciples, "The scribes and the Pharisees sit on Moses's seat, so do and observe whatever they tell you, but not the works they do. For they preach, but do not practice. They tie up heavy burdens, hard to bear, and lay them on people's shoulders, but they themselves are not willing to move them with their finger. They do all their deeds to be seen by others. For they make their phylacteries broad and their fringes long, and they love the place of honor at feasts and the best seats in the synagogues and greetings in the marketplaces and being called rabbi by others. But you are not to be called rabbi, for you have one teacher, and you are all brothers. And call no man your father on earth, for you have one Father, who is in heaven. Neither be called instructors, for you have one instructor, the Christ. The greatest among you shall be your servant. Whoever exalts himself will be humbled, and whoever humbles himself will be exalted." (Matt. 23:1–12; see also Mark 12:38–40, Luke 20:45–47)

Notice that in this text Jesus uses the negative example of the scribes and Pharisees to once again teach Peter and the others about servant leadership, further expanding what he has previously taught them. Here he clearly warns them to not follow the actions, the practices of the scribes and Pharisees. They lord their position over people; they want to be seen in order to show off. Jesus's teaching is simple and direct: "Don't be like them."

Then he emphasizes this point by providing another practical example for them when he comments about a widow's offering:

Jesus looked up and saw the rich putting their gifts into the offering box, and he saw a poor widow put in two small copper coins. And he said, "Truly, I tell you, this poor widow has put in more than all of them. For they all contributed out of their abundance, but she out of her poverty put in all she had to live on." (Luke 21:1–4; see also Mark 12:41–44)

Here, Jesus draws a sharp contrast between the rich who give offerings out of the abundance of their possessions as required under the law and the poor widow who gives all that she has to live on out of the abundance of her heart. Jesus is pointing out that what is important is not *how much* one gives, but *the attitude* with which it is given. Once again, Jesus is emphasizing the importance of the true state of one's heart. The sacrificial giving of the widow has far more value in God's eyes than the obedient offerings given by the rich. The key lesson for Peter and the others is that she has almost nothing, but she gave all that she had to God. Jesus has just given the disciples an example to follow; this is how they should conduct their own lives.

Here is another important point about the process of transformation. Jesus provides these teachings *so that* we will learn the spiritual lesson *and implement changes in our behavior*, so that our lives gradually become congruent with his word to us. The degree to which we implement his teaching is evidence of God's continuing work of transformation in us.

Final Preparation of Disciples

Following this, Jesus turns to teach Peter and the others about the end times through the following series of stories and parables:

- Not one stone left standing (Matt. 24:1–2, Mark 13:1–2, Luke 21:5–6)
- The signs of the times (Matt. 24:3–9, Mark 13:3–10, Luke 21:7–13)
- Do not prepare a response (Mark 13:11, Luke 21:14–15)
- You will be hated and betrayed (Mark 13:12–13, Luke 21:16–19)
- Enduring to the end (Matt. 24:10–14)
- False christs (Matt. 24:23–28, Mark 13:21–23)
- What to do when false christs appear (Matt. 24:15–22, Mark 13:14–20, Luke 21:20–24)
- The fig tree (Matt. 24:32–35, Mark 13:28–31, Luke 21:29–33)

- As in the days of Noah   (Matt. 24:37–42, Mark
                                    13:33, Luke 21:34–36)
- The master of the house   (Matt. 24:43–44)
- The faithful and wise servant   (Matt. 24:45–51,
                                    Mark 13:34–37)
- Ten virgins   (Matt. 25:1–13)
- The talents   (Matt. 25:14–30)
- The sheep and the goats   (Matt. 25:31–46)

Admittedly, this is a very long list of teachings. We have listed them all here simply because the volume of these teachings indicates their importance. And their importance is this: Jesus is revealing what his disciples will experience and what will be required of them in the future. Additionally, it is important to remember that Jesus is moving toward the fulfillment of his mission and has little time left to revisit these important teachings. So it is important for him to say everything he needs to say to his disciples while he still has time.

We have seen throughout this chapter that Jesus has typically performed one or more signs and/or miracles to reinforce in various ways his teaching and to demonstrate that he is who he says he is. However, at this point he no longer performs signs and miracles. Instead, because his time to do what he came to do is near, he gives them these short teachings to reinforce what he has already taught them. Some of the lessons of the stories and parables listed above can be summarized as follows:

- the kingdom is within them;
- they should keep their eyes focused on God;
- they should not depend on their understanding or that of others, but on the guidance and direction of the Holy Spirit;
- when the end times occur, they will know because there will be a signal that they will understand, but the world will be blind to it;

- they should not sit back and wait, but instead be atten- tive, looking for the sign to occur;
- they need to use what they have been taught to teach others; and
- there will be a separation of good and evil when the end finally comes.

In essence, these stories and teachings are Jesus's last major attempt to teach his disciples all they need to know before he leaves them.

Reality Begins to Dawn

When he finishes all these sayings, Jesus says to Peter and the others, "You know that after two days the Passover is coming, and the Son of Man will be delivered up to be crucified" (Matt. 26:1–2; see also Mark 14:1–2, Luke 22:1–2). He continues to inform the disciples about what is coming and letting them know his time with them is very short.

A little later, Jesus is reclining at the table in the house of Simon the leper at Bethany, when a woman comes up to him with an ala- baster flask of costly ointment and pours it on his head. Peter and the others become indignant, saying that it could have been sold for a large sum and given to the poor. However, Jesus explains that she has done a beautiful thing to him; she is preparing him for burial. What she did was a loving act toward Jesus as Lord (see Matt. 26:6–13, Mark 14:3–9, John 12:2–8).

We have previously stated that understanding Jesus's teachings reveals that the work of transformation is progressing in a person; true, full understanding leads to a changed heart, which leads to changed actions. Here we see that Peter and the others still do not fully understand what Jesus has taught them about his impending death. The woman gets it; they do not. So, the work of transforma- tion is still not complete in the disciples.

As the story of Jesus's journey to fulfill his mission on earth con- tinues, we see the disciples coming to Jesus, saying, "Where will you have us prepare for you to eat the Passover?" He tells them what to do, and they follow his direction, preparing the Passover meal (Matt. 26:17–19; see also Mark 14:12–16, Luke 22:7–13). Then we read this in John's gospel:

> Jesus knew that his hour had come to depart out of this world… knowing that the Father had given all things into his hands, and that he had come from God and was going back to God, rose from supper. He laid aside his outer garments, and taking a towel, tied it around his waist. Then he poured water into a basin and began to wash the disciples' feet and to wipe them with the towel that was wrapped around him. He came to Simon Peter, who said to him, "Lord, do you wash my feet?" Jesus answered him, "What I am doing you do not understand now, but afterward you will understand." Peter said to him, "You shall never wash my feet." Jesus answered him, "If I do not wash you, you have no share with me." Simon Peter said to him, "Lord, not my feet only but also my hands and my head!" Jesus said to him, "The one who has bathed does not need to wash, except for his feet, but is completely clean. And you are clean, but not every one of you." (John 13:1, 3–10)

Peter still does not understand the purpose of what Jesus is doing. So after delivering this mild rebuke to him, Jesus seizes the opportunity to conduct another teaching moment to further expand his previous teaching about servant leadership:

> When he had washed their feet and put on his outer garments and resumed his place, he said to them, "Do you understand what I have done to you? You call me Teacher and Lord, and you are right, for so I am. If I then, your Lord and

Teacher, have washed your feet, you also ought to wash one another's feet. For I have given you an example, that you also should do just as I have done to you. Truly, truly, I say to you, a servant is not greater than his master, nor is a messenger greater than the one who sent him. If you know these things, blessed are you if you do them." (John 13:12–17)

Peter has *heard* all the words that Jesus has said to him and the others; he has *seen* all of the signs and miracles that Jesus has performed during his earthly ministry. Yet when he manifests servant leadership to them by washing their feet, *Peter still does not understand.* So, Jesus explains it to him and the others once again: the one they call Lord has served them; they are to follow his example and serve one another.

Here is an essential lesson concerning the work of transformation. It is not sufficient to hear the words that Jesus teaches or to observe him manifest his power throughout the gospels. Real understanding that results in genuine transformation of the heart occurs when an individual takes time to reflect and meditate upon what has been heard and seen, in order to grasp the lessons being taught, in order to *truly understand*, and then to apply them to one's life. The truth that leads to heart-level understanding is found in the lessons Jesus teaches.

Jesus emphasizes this point by what he says next:

"I am not speaking of all of you; I know whom I have chosen. But the Scripture will be fulfilled, 'He who ate my bread has lifted his heel against me.' I am telling you this now, before it takes place, that when it does take place you may believe that I am he. Truly, truly, I say to you, whoever receives the one I send receives me, and whoever receives me receives the one who sent me." (John 13:18–20)

Once again, Jesus manifests his infinite power by telling Peter and the others that one of them will betray him; he is demonstrating that he knows what will happen in the future. Thus, he is again emphasizing who it is that is teaching them these things. He does this in order to continue to build their trust that he is indeed the Christ, the Son of God. Jesus then continues his teaching:

> Now as they were eating, and Jesus took bread, and after blessing it, broke it and gave it to Peter and the disciples, and said, "Take, eat; this is my body." And he took a cup, and when he had given thanks he gave it to them, saying, "Drink of it, all of you, for this is my blood of the covenant, which is poured out for many for the forgiveness of sins. I tell you I will not drink again of this fruit of the vine until that day when I drink it new with you in my Father's kingdom." (Matt. 26:26–29; see also Mark 14:22–25, Luke 22:19–20)

This event, known as the Lord's Supper, has great significance within the Christian Church. But for Peter and the others, the most considerable significance lies in the final words that Jesus speaks. In order to continue to build their trust, Jesus tells them with confidence that there is an end-time coming when he will be with them again in his father's kingdom. By giving them the Lord's Supper to celebrate every time they come together, Jesus is telling them that his death is not the end. It is intended to be an encouragement and to serve as a reminder for them to trust him and all that he has taught them, regardless of what happens. He wants them to know that things are not as they seem.

Here is another critical lesson concerning the work of transformation. As we have seen throughout this chapter with Peter, true understanding may not occur during a teaching moment; it can be delayed for quite some time. Thus, *trust in God and surrender to his will* for one's life is more important than understanding what his will is at any point in time. Some measure of true understanding must come before trust can emerge, but it is trust that leads to full acceptance of and surrender to God's will.

Apostles' Failure, Jesus's Reassurance

After his last supper with his disciples, Jesus again manifests his infinite power by predicting that Peter will deny him three times:

> And when they had sung a hymn, they went out to the Mount of Olives. Then Jesus said to them, "You will all fall away because of me this night. For it is written, 'I will strike the shepherd, and the sheep of the flock will be scattered.' But after I am raised up, I will go before you to Galilee." Peter answered him, "Though they all fall away because of you, I will never fall away." Jesus said to him, "Truly, I tell you, this very night, before the rooster crows, you will deny me three times." Peter said to him, "Even if I must die with you, I will not deny you!" And all the disciples said the same. (Matt. 26:30–35; see also Mark 14:26–31, Luke 22:31–34, John 13:36–38)

Jesus is telling them that, because of what is about to happen, they will soon be filled with such fear and dread that every one of them will forsake him and run away, concerned for their own safety. He is warning them that they will stumble in their faith—that they risk "falling away" (see John 16:1), that they will begin to question and doubt whether he is the Messiah. Jesus knows that Peter and the others do not yet fully understand who he is and what he has taught them; he knows that their actions will not be consistent with their words until the work of transformation is complete in them.

Here we see that the apostles are about to experience a stumble in their faith journey. A "stumble" is a failure of a test of faith; our actions are not congruent with what we say we believe. When we stumble, it is wise to ask what we should focus our attention on: our failure of faith—and seek to correct it, deny it, cover it up as Peter and the others do here, or trust God—continue to depend on his grace and mercy to accomplish the work of transformation in us. Rather than focusing on ourselves and our failure, we need to keep our focus on Jesus and God the Father. We need to keep asking, what is God trying to teach me about Jesus, about himself, by allowing me to experience this failure of faith?

After this, Jesus begins his final teaching series with Peter and the others:

> "Let not your hearts be troubled. Believe in God; believe also in me. In my Father's house are many rooms. If it were not so, would I have told you that I go to prepare a place for you? And if I go and prepare a place for you, I will come again and will take you to myself, that where I am you may be also. And you know the way to where I am going." Thomas said to him, "Lord, we do not know where you are going. How can we know the way?" Jesus said to him, "I am the way, and the truth, and the life. No one comes to the Father except through me. If you had known me, you would have known my Father also. From now on you do know him and have seen him."
> (John 14:1–7)

After revealing to them in the previous passage his knowledge that they would all soon turn away, stumbling in their faith in him, in this passage, Jesus continues to focus on building their trust in him and in God. He knows that they expect him to drive out the Romans and restore the kingdom to Israel; in this belief, they still fail to understand that he must die in order to establish God's kingdom. Thus, he knows they will be devastated when his death occurs. Therefore, building their trust in him and what he has taught them becomes the sole focus of his final teaching series with them.

To this end, we see in the passage above that he begins by clearly stating the nature of his relationship with God the Father and what that means for them. Jesus then continues to expand on this teaching:

> Philip said to him, "Lord, show us the Father, and it is enough for us." Jesus said to him, "Have I been with you so long, and you still do not know me, Philip? Whoever has seen me has seen the Father. How can you say, 'Show us the Father'? Do you not believe that I am in the Father and the Father is in me? The words that I say to you I do not speak on my own authority, but the Father who dwells in me does his works. Believe me that I am in the Father and the Father is in me, or else believe on account of the works themselves." (John 14:8–11)

Philip's question in response to Jesus's previous statement indicates that Peter and the others still do not fully understand his divine nature, that he is one with the Father, although he has tried to teach them this truth from the beginning. Even after performing all of the signs and miracles in which he manifested his divine power to them, they still have not made the connection, that the manifestation of divine power reveals who he is. So here Jesus draws it all together and challenges them: do they still not know that he and the Father are the same? His question to them clearly indicates that the work of transformation is not yet complete in Peter and the other disciples.

It is evident from these passages that one source of the fear that Peter and the others are experiencing is that following Jesus's death, they will be left alone. This is another reason Philip asks him to show them the Father. Understanding this, Jesus continues to seek to build their trust at this point by again addressing their fear:

> "These things I have spoken to you while I am still with you. But the Helper, the Holy Spirit, whom the Father will send in my name, he will teach

you all things and bring to your remembrance all
that I have said to you. Peace I leave with you; my
peace I give to you. Not as the world gives do I
give to you. Let not your hearts be troubled, neither let them be afraid. You heard me say to you,
'I am going away, and I will come to you.' If you
loved me, you would have rejoiced, because I am
going to the Father, for the Father is greater than
I. And now I have told you before it takes place,
so that when it does take place you may believe."
(John 14:25–29)

The essence of this teaching moment is that even after his death,
after his resurrection to be with the Father, Peter and the others will
not be left alone. The Holy Spirit will be sent by God to continue to
teach them and to remind them of everything that Jesus has already
taught them. Jesus is reassuring them that they will not be alone as
they fear. He continues to seek to reinforce his teachings and further
build their trust. He continues with his reassurance:

"I am the true vine, and my Father is the vine-
dresser. Every branch in me that does not bear
fruit he takes away, and every branch that does
bear fruit he prunes, that it may bear more fruit.
Already you are clean because of the word that I
have spoken to you. Abide in me, and I in you.
As the branch cannot bear fruit by itself, unless
it abides in the vine, neither can you, unless you
abide in me. I am the vine; you are the branches.
Whoever abides in me and I in him, he it is that
bears much fruit, for apart from me you can
do nothing. If anyone does not abide in me he
is thrown away like a branch and withers; and
the branches are gathered, thrown into the fire,
and burned. If you abide in me, and my words
abide in you, ask whatever you wish, and it will

be done for you. By this my Father is glorified, that you bear much fruit and so prove to be my disciples. As the Father has loved me, so have I loved you. Abide in my love. If you keep my commandments, you will abide in my love, just as I have kept my Father's commandments and abide in his love. These things I have spoken to you, that my joy may be in you, and that your joy may be full." (John 15:1–11)

In this passage, Jesus uses a concept that they should be able to understand by talking about the relationship between a vine and its branches. Jesus continues to find different ways to get through to them *so that they will understand.*

These men have walked daily with Jesus for three and a half years; he has taught them these lessons before in different ways. He has repeatedly performed signs and wonders in order to manifest his power to them again and again, demonstrating that he is who he says he is. And yet, as his moment of death becomes imminent, he knows that they still do not fully understand; their trust is still not sufficient to sustain them in the days ahead. So, he diligently continues to build sufficient trust in them through teaching moments such as this. Here we see another important element in the work of transformation: God knows their condition; he knows that without sufficient trust, they will fall away after Jesus's death. So Jesus continues to teach them in order to build their trust. In doing so, the work of transformation continues in them.

Jesus then speaks to the question of Peter's and the others' fear from a different perspective:

"If the world hates you, know that it has hated me before it hated you. If you were of the world, the world would love you as its own; but because you are not of the world, but I chose you out of the world, therefore the world hates you. Remember the word that I said to you: 'A ser-

vant is not greater than his master.' If they per-
secuted me, they will also persecute you. If they
kept my word, they will also keep yours. But all
these things they will do to you on account of my
name, because they do not know him who sent
me. If I had not come and spoken to them, they
would not have been guilty of sin, but now they
have no excuse for their sin. Whoever hates me
hates my Father also. If I had not done among
them the works that no one else did, they would
not be guilty of sin, but now they have seen and
hated both me and my Father. But the word that
is written in their Law must be fulfilled: 'They
hated me without a cause.'

"But when the Helper comes, whom I will
send to you from the Father, the Spirit of truth,
who proceeds from the Father, he will bear witness about me. And you also will bear witness,
because you have been with me from the beginning." (John 15:18–27)

This time Jesus addresses the source of their fear: their growing
realization that if the Jewish leaders hate Jesus so much that they
want to kill him, they will undoubtedly do the same to Peter and
the others. In this teaching moment, Jesus challenges the depth of
their belief and trust that he and the Father are superior to the Jewish
leaders.

This is an important point: before the work of transformation
can be successful, we must reach the point of genuinely believing and
trusting that Jesus is more important, more powerful, than anyone
or anything in the world. Without this unshakable belief, obedience
will never become truly unconditional; there will always be "others"
(things or people) vying for our attention and allegiance, our trust.

The purpose of this series of teaching moments is that Jesus is
seeking to reassure Peter and the others that he understands their
fear—their desire to run and hide. He knows the sorrow that will

come upon them, how devastated they will feel when he is no longer with them. Thus, he must continue to build their trust in him so that they can overcome their fear. The only way to do so is through genuine belief and trust in God the Father so that the work of trans- formation can continue to take place in them. Jesus begins to explain all of this to them:

> "I have said all these things to you to keep you from falling away. They will put you out of the synagogues. Indeed, the hour is coming when whoever kills you will think he is offering service to God. And they will do these things because they have not known the Father, nor me. But I have said these things to you, that when their hour comes you may remember that I told them to you.
>
> "I did not say these things to you from the beginning, because I was with you. But now I am going to him who sent me, and none of you asks me, 'Where are you going?' But because I have said these things to you, sorrow has filled your heart. Nevertheless, I tell you the truth: it is to your advantage that I go away, for if I do not go away, the Helper will not come to you. But if I go, I will send him to you. And when he comes, he will convict the world concerning sin and righteousness and judgment: concerning sin, because they do not believe in me; concern- ing righteousness, because I go to the Father, and you will see me no longer; concerning judgment, because the ruler of this world is judged.
>
> "I still have many things to say to you, but you cannot bear them now. When the Spirit of truth comes, he will guide you into all the truth, for he will not speak on his own authority, but whatever he hears he will speak, and he will

declare to you the things that are to come. He will glorify me, for he will take what is mine and declare it to you. All that the Father has is mine; therefore I said that he will take what is mine and declare it to you." (John 16:1–15)

In this passage, Jesus is focusing on preparing Peter and the others for the moment when, following his ascension, the Holy Spirit will come to replace him in their lives. Yet he knows that the Spirit must first become real for them for the Spirit's work to be effective. Thus, in this text, Jesus seeks to prepare Peter and the others for what will happen at Pentecost when the Holy Spirit's power will be manifested in their midst—so that the work of transformation will continue in them, so that in that moment, they will truly believe.

Notice also that Jesus is aware that they will still need to learn more truth from him after his death. He knows the work of transformation in them is not yet complete; they still do not have genuine faith that leads to obedience to the will of God. This is why he tells them that they will continue to learn from the Holy Spirit who will guide them "into all truth" (v. 13).

Jesus continues to explain to them the purpose of his teaching moments:

"I have said these things to you in figures of speech. The hour is coming when I will no longer speak to you in figures of speech but will tell you plainly about the Father. In that day you will ask in my name, and I do not say to you that I will ask the Father on your behalf; for the Father himself loves you, because you have loved me and have believed that I came from God. I came from the Father and have come into the world, and now I am leaving the world and going to the Father."

His disciples said, "Ah, now you are speaking plainly and not using figurative speech! Now we know that you know all things and do not need anyone to question you; this is why we believe that you came from God." Jesus answered them, "Do you now believe? Behold, the hour is coming, indeed it has come, when you will be scattered, each to his own home, and will leave me alone. Yet I am not alone, for the Father is with me. I have said these things to you, that in me you may have peace. In the world you will have tribulation. But take heart; I have overcome the world." (John 16:25–33)

In this text, Jesus continues to seek to overcome the disciples' fear of being left alone, and to build their trust in him and his father, so that the work of transformation can continue in them. He knows that soon their trust in him will fail—they will fall away from him, and he will be alone. But he also knows that the Father will be with him. By using himself as an example, Jesus wants them to understand that what will happen to him will also happen to them: when everyone else deserts them, God will remain with them because he too loves them.

Fulfilling His Earthly Mission

Having said these things, Jesus then turns to pray, during which he states more clearly his mission in the world, the reason for his life:

When Jesus had spoken these words, he lifted up his eyes to heaven, and said, "Father, the hour has come; glorify your Son that the Son may glorify you, since you have given him authority over all flesh, to give eternal life to all whom you have given him. And this is eternal life, that they know you, the only true God, and Jesus Christ whom you have sent. I glorified you on earth, having accomplished the work that you gave me to do.

PETER AND THE OTHER APOSTLES

And now, Father, glorify me in your own presence with the glory that I had with you before the
world existed." (John 17:1–5)

In his prayer, Jesus sets forth the ultimate objective of the work
of transformation in Peter and the others: that they may receive eternal life, which is to know the only true God and his Son Jesus Christ.
In Greek, the term *know* does not mean merely taking in knowledge about God, nor having merely a casual familiarity with him.
Instead it refers to having a deep personal relationship with God, not
unlike experiencing the intimacy that occurs in a sexual relationship
between man and wife.[7] Such intimacy and the trust it engenders
can overcome all obstacles and remain steadfast and true. It is this
intimate "knowing" that enables trust to emerge, and thus results in
eternal life with God.

At this point, Peter and the others begin to experience the reality of everything that Jesus has told them would happen, as the following events occur:

- Jesus prays in Gethsemane for God's will to be done
  (Matt. 26:36–46, Mark 14:32–42, Luke 22:39–46,
  John 18:1)
- Jesus is betrayed and arrested
  (Matt. 26:47–56, Mark 14:43–52, Luke 22:47–53,
  John 18:2–11)
- Jesus is condemned by Caiaphas
  (Matt. 26:57–68; Mark 14:53–65; Luke 22:54,
  66–71; John 18:15)
- Peter denies Jesus
  (Matt. 26:58, 69–75; Mark 14:54, 66–72; Luke
  22:54–62; John 18:15–18, 25–27)

---

[7] *Ginōskō*, to "experientially know," which can mean by sexual intimacy. For
example in Luke 1:34, "And Mary (a virgin) said to the angel, 'How will this
be since I do not *know* a man?'" (italics added). (https://biblehub.com/str/
greek/1097.htm).

- Jesus is condemned by the Sanhedrin
  (Matt. 27:1–2; Mark 15:1; Luke 22:66–71, 23:1)
- Judas kills himself
  (Matt. 27:3–10, Acts 1:18–19)
- Jews force Pilate to condemn Jesus
  (Matt. 27:15–26, Mark 15:6–15, Luke 23:13–25,
  John 18:39–19:16)
- Jesus is mocked by Roman soldiers
  (Matt. 27:27–31, Mark 15:16–20)
- The crucifixion
  (Matt. 27:32–56, Mark 15:20–41, Luke 23:26–49,
  John 19:17–30)
- The burial
  (Matt. 27:57–60, Mark 15:42–47, Luke 23:50–56,
  John 19:38–42)
- The women come to anoint Jesus, but the tomb is
  open
  (Matt. 28:1–4, Mark 16:1)
- The women tell the disciples what they have seen
  (Luke 24:9–12, John 20:2–10)
- Jesus appears to Mary
  (Mark 16:9–11, John 20:11–18)
- Jesus appears to other women
  (Matt. 28:9–10)
- Jesus appears on the road to Emmaus
  (Mark 16:12–13, Luke 24:13–35)

Manifesting the Truth of His Teachings

After all of these events occur, Peter and the others gather together in a room behind locked doors because they fear the Jews—what has actually been done to Jesus might also be done to them. Then Jesus comes and stands among them and greets them, but they are startled and frightened, thinking they are seeing a spirit. Knowing that they are troubled because of doubts in their hearts, he shows them his hands and feet, encouraging them to touch him and thus realize that he is not a spirit. Because they still do not believe, Jesus asks them for something to eat. They give him a piece of broiled fish, which he then eats before them, proving that he is indeed with them in a resurrected body and that he is not a ghost (see John 20:19–25, Mark 16:14, Luke 24:36–43).

Then Jesus reminds them that he previously told them that everything written about him in the law of Moses, in the prophets, and in the Psalms must come true. Luke's gospel continues:

> Then he opened their minds to understand the Scriptures and said to them, "Thus it is written, that the Christ should suffer and on the third day rise from the dead, and that repentance for the forgiveness of sins should be proclaimed in his name to all nations, beginning from Jerusalem. You are witnesses of these things. And behold, I am sending the promise of my Father upon you. But stay in the city until you are clothed with power from on high." (Luke 24:45–49; see also Acts 1:3–5)

In John 20:26–29, we see that eight days later, Peter and the others are again inside behind locked doors, still afraid for their safety. This time Thomas is with them, who was not with them when Jesus first appeared to them, and thus doubts that what they have told him is true. Although the doors are locked, Jesus comes again and stands among them and greets them. He tells Thomas to examine his hands and his side, encouraging him to believe. Thomas answers him, "My Lord and my God!" (v. 28). Jesus immediately responds, "Have you believed because you have seen me? Blessed are those who have not seen and yet have believed" (v. 29).

In these successive occurrences of Jesus revealing himself to his disciples, we can see that he is still working to deepen their faith so that they will trust what he has said to them, trust that he is who he has always said he is, and to encourage them that all is not lost. Jesus is still preparing them to begin to live out the call on their lives, to do the work that he was preparing them for before his death.

Jesus reveals himself a third time to the disciples by the Sea of Tiberias. Peter, Thomas (called the Twin), Nathanael of Cana in Galilee, the sons of Zebedee, and two other disciples have been fishing all night, but have caught nothing. Just as morning dawns, Jesus is standing on the shore and says to them, "'Children, do you have any fish?' They answered him, 'No.' He said to them, 'Cast the net on the right side of the boat, and you will find some.' So they cast it, and now they were not able to haul it in, because of the quantity of fish" (John 21:5–6). Up to this point, neither Peter nor the others realize who is speaking to them. But at Jesus's words, John says to Peter, "It is the Lord!" (v. 7). When Peter hears that it is Jesus who is speaking to them, he puts on his outer garment and throws himself into the sea to swim to shore. The other disciples come to shore in the boat, dragging the net full of fish (see John 21:7–8).

When they get on land, they see a charcoal fire with fish cooking and bread. At Jesus's suggestion, Peter brings some of the fish they have just caught. Then Jesus invites them to come and have breakfast. When they do, Jesus takes the bread and gives it to them, along with the fish (see John 21:9–14).

It is important to notice in this third revelation of himself to the disciples that, even though Jesus is only one hundred yards away from Peter and the others (see John 21:8), they should recognize him, or at least recognize his voice. But they do not, not until John declares who he is. This lack of recognition reveals that the work of transformation is still not complete in them, even at this point. They do not yet have eyes to see who Jesus is. Their eyes of faith have not yet fully developed. Knowing this, Jesus continues to appear to them following his resurrection in order to continue the work of transformation in them.

After they finish breakfast, we find Jesus gently leading Peter on in the development of his faith:

> When they had finished breakfast, Jesus said to
> Simon Peter, "Simon, son of John, do you love
> me more than these?" He said to him, "Yes,

Lord; you know that I love you." He said to him,
"Feed my lambs." He said to him a second time,
"Simon, son of John, do you love me?" He said
to him, "Yes, Lord; you know that I love you."
He said to him, "Tend my sheep." He said to him
the third time, "Simon, son of John, do you love
me?" Peter was grieved because he said to him
the third time, "Do you love me?" and he said to
him, "Lord, you know everything; you know that
I love you." Jesus said to him, "Feed my sheep.
Truly, truly, I say to you, when you were young,
you used to dress yourself and walk wherever you
wanted, but when you are old, you will stretch
out your hands, and another will dress you and
carry you where you do not want to go." (This
he said to show by what kind of death he was
to glorify God.) And after saying this he said to
him, "Follow me." (John 21:15–19)

This interchange with Peter, which counters his earlier three
denials of Jesus, provides another crucial lesson concerning the work
of transformation. Even though Peter does not understand the purpose of Jesus's questions, and therefore becomes frustrated with him,
Jesus continues to lovingly work with Peter and the other disciples to
transform their faltering faith, until they are all able to willingly fulfill
their calling as apostles. As revealed by Jesus's final prayer for them,
that calling is to glorify God with their lives as Jesus did through his
earthly life (see John 17).

It is important to note that the work of transformation is not
complete in them until they *glorify God by being obedient to the call
on their lives*. As Scripture teaches, Jesus chose his disciples and called
them to follow him. As has been evident throughout the story of
Peter and the others, Jesus has conducted multiple series of teaching moments with them, followed by manifestations of his power
to demonstrate the truth of who he is, in order to prepare them to
undertake their roles as apostles. Thus, even when Peter and the oth-

ers stumble (as they all did), the work of transformation continues. It would not glorify God if, having stumbled, they are allowed to fail to fulfill their calling. The ultimate focus of God's work of transformation is not just for the sake of the individual, but even more so for the individual's ability to fulfill God's call on their life, and thus glorify God. That is why Jesus continues time after time to appear to Peter and others after his death and resurrection, to continue the work of transformation in them.

From Calling to Commission

Jesus reinforces the critical point about fulfilling God's call when he appears to Peter and the others in Galilee:

> Now the eleven disciples went to Galilee, to the mountain to which Jesus had directed them. And when they saw him they worshiped him, but some doubted. And Jesus came and said to them, "All authority in heaven and on earth has been given to me. Go therefore and make disciples of all nations, baptizing them in the name of the Father and of the Son and of the Holy Spirit, teaching them to observe all that I have commanded you. And behold, I am with you always, to the end of the age." (Matt. 28:16–20)

In this text, Jesus gives a straightforward commission to Peter and the other apostles to fulfill God's calling on their lives: *now* they are to go into all the world and proclaim the gospel to all nations.

In Mark's gospel, chapter 16, we see that in this commission and call, eternal life and death are at stake. Jesus states,

> "Whoever believes and is baptized will be saved, but whoever does not believe will be condemned. And these signs will accompany those who believe: in my name they will cast out demons;

they will speak in new tongues; they will pick up serpents with their hands; and if they drink any deadly poison, it will not hurt them; they will lay their hands on the sick, and they will recover." (Mark 16:16–18)

In this passage, Jesus is still teaching the apostles about the realities of God's kingdom. These are amazing statements from a human perspective, but they are normal events in the kingdom of God.

In the first chapter of Acts, we then find the apostles asking Jesus if he is now ready to restore the kingdom of Israel (v. 6). In response, Jesus does not get impatient with them. Instead he simply says to them:

"It is not for you to know times or seasons that the Father has fixed by his own authority. But you will receive power when the Holy Spirit has come upon you, and you will be my witnesses in Jerusalem and in all Judea and Samaria, and to the end of the earth." And when he had said these things, as they were looking on, he was lifted up, and a cloud took him out of their sight. (Acts 1:7–9; see also Mark 16:19, Luke 24:51)

Jesus lets them know that God the Father is the one responsible for the timing of events in the world. Indirectly, he is saying that even he does not know the answer to their question. He then redirects their attention to the power that will come to them, power to carry out this commission they have been given, power to live in kingdom reality. He then does what he has been doing all along: after a teaching, he demonstrates his power by ascending into heaven.

Notice that even though Jesus has appeared to Peter and the other apostles four times since his crucifixion, and he has now commissioned them for their work as apostles, they are still focusing on receiving an answer to the question of when Jesus will restore the kingdom to Israel. This indicates that even now they *still* do not comprehend who he really is and the true reason for his earthly life. They are still seeing and thinking from a worldly perspective rather than from a kingdom perspective. The work of transformation is still not complete in them *even though they have now been commissioned to fulfill the call on their lives.* So, we see that the work of transformation will continue even after Jesus is taken from their sight one last time.

Infused with God's Power

The final part of God's work of transformation from simple belief to genuine faith in Peter and the others happens when Pentecost occurs:

> When the day of Pentecost arrived, they were all together in one place. And suddenly there came from heaven a sound like a mighty rushing wind, and it filled the entire house where they were sitting. And divided tongues as of fire appeared to them and rested on each one of them. And they were all filled with the Holy Spirit and began to speak in other tongues as the Spirit gave them utterance.
> Now there were dwelling in Jerusalem Jews, devout men from every nation under heaven. And at this sound the multitude came together, and they were bewildered, because each one was hearing them speak in his own language. And they were amazed and astonished, saying, "Are not all these who are speaking Galileans? And how is it that we hear, each of us in his own native language? Parthians and Medes and Elamites and residents of Mesopotamia, Judea and Cappadocia, Pontus and Asia, Phrygia and Pamphylia, Egypt and the parts of Libya belonging to Cyrene, and visitors from Rome, both

Jews and proselytes, Cretans and Arabians—we
hear them telling in our own tongues the mighty
works of God." And all were amazed and per-
plexed, saying to one another, "What does this
mean?" But others mocking said, "They are filled
with new wine." (Acts 2:1–13)

Just as Jesus promised, the Holy Spirit comes upon Peter and
the others, releasing divine power upon them. Their ability to speak
in tongues, so that individuals from every nation are able to understand in their own language what is being said, is the immediate
proof of this infusion of divine power. However, there are some in
attendance who do not understand the meaning of what is happening; some even assume that the apostles are drunk.

However, as Peter explains to the rest of them what has just
happened, it is evident that God's work of transformation is finally
complete in him:

But Peter, standing with the eleven, lifted up his
voice and addressed them: "Men of Judea and all
who dwell in Jerusalem, let this be known to you,
and give ear to my words. For these people are
not drunk, as you suppose, since it is only the
third hour of the day. But this is what was uttered
through the prophet Joel:

"'And in the last days it shall be, God declares,
that I will pour out my Spirit on all flesh,
and your sons and your daughters shall prophesy,
and your young men shall see visions,
and your old men shall dream dreams;
even on my male servants and female servants
in those days I will pour out my Spirit, and they
shall prophesy.
And I will show wonders in the heavens above
and signs on the earth below,

blood, and fire, and vapor of smoke;
the sun shall be turned to darkness
    and the moon to blood,
    before the day of the Lord comes, the great and
    magnificent day.
And it shall come to pass that everyone who calls upon the
    name of the Lord shall be saved.'" (Acts 2:14–21)

Here we see Peter suddenly "connecting the dots." He finally *understands* beyond intellectual assent—by way of personal experience—what the prophet Joel had prophesied. Not only does he "get it," he is also able to articulate it clearly to the others with him who do not yet understand. Here we see Peter beginning to emerge into the fullness of God's call on his life. Transformation from simple belief (mental assent) to genuine saving faith that leads to obedience to the will of God is now visible in him.

The fact that God's work of transformation is now complete in Peter becomes further evident as he preaches to those who have observed this stunning event:

> "Men of Israel, hear these words: Jesus of Nazareth, a man attested to you by God with mighty works and wonders and signs that God did through him in your midst, as you yourselves know—this Jesus, delivered up according to the definite plan and foreknowledge of God, you crucified and killed by the hands of lawless men. God raised him up, loosing the pangs of death, because it was not possible for him to be held by it. For David says concerning him,

> "'I saw the Lord always before me,
>   for he is at my right hand that I may not be shaken;
> therefore my heart was glad, and my tongue rejoiced;
>   my flesh also will dwell in hope.
> For you will not abandon my soul to Hades,

or let your Holy One see corruption.
You have made known to me the paths of life;
    you will make me full of gladness with your presence.'

"Brothers, I may say to you with confidence
about the patriarch David that he both died and
was buried, and his tomb is with us to this day.
Being therefore a prophet, and knowing that
God had sworn with an oath to him that he
would set one of his descendants on his throne,
he foresaw and spoke about the resurrection of
the Christ, that he was not abandoned to Hades,
nor did his flesh see corruption. This Jesus God
raised up, and of that we all are witnesses. Being
therefore exalted at the right hand of God, and
having received from the Father the promise of
the Holy Spirit, he has poured out this that you
yourselves are seeing and hearing. For David did
not ascend into the heavens, but he himself says,

"'The Lord said to my Lord,
"Sit at my right hand,
    until I make your enemies your footstool.'"

Let all the house of Israel therefore know for certain that God has made him both Lord and Christ,
this Jesus whom you crucified." (Acts 2:22–36)

We see here evidence of a deep and profound transformation in
Peter; he is no longer the person he was before this infusion of divine
power. And the effect of that power, through his preaching, is seen by
what happens next. Those who hear his words are convicted in their
spirits and say to Peter and the others:

"Brothers, what shall we do?" And Peter said to
them, "Repent and be baptized every one of you

in the name of Jesus Christ for the forgiveness of your sins, and you will receive the gift of the Holy Spirit. For the promise is for you and for your children and for all who are far off, everyone whom the Lord our God calls to himself." (Acts 2:37–39)

Peter is immediately able to compress and summarize much of what Jesus has taught the disciples over the past three and a half years. His message is quite succinct and to the point. No fear is apparent in him as he declares what must be done to be saved.

Peter continues to exhort them, saying, "Save yourselves from this crooked generation" (v. 40). As a result of his words, about three thousand souls are baptized. From these passages from Acts 2, it is evident that the work of transformation is indeed complete in Peter, and that he is now beginning to undertake in obedience the work to which God has called him.

Lessons Learned from the Story of Peter

Peter's story is our story; God has called us to be his disciples. He is at work in various ways in our lives to prepare and equip each of us to accomplish his higher purposes, not just for us individually, but for countless others through us. We encourage you to take some time to reflect further on the parallels between Peter's story and your faith transformation process. Here are some things to consider as you reflect on your journey with God in light of what we learn from Peter's story:

1. The process of transformation that leads to genuine belief, trust, surrender, and obedience is a process by which God leads an individual through one or more series of teaching moments. The content of these teaching moments leads to an ever-increasing understanding of who Jesus Christ really is over time, *so that* we are able to have genuine belief in him, to completely trust his commandments and stat-

utes, and to wholeheartedly surrender to his will for our life. Crucial doctrines are taught through separate series of increasingly explicit teaching moments, until we fully understand what the gospel teaches, what it is that God wants us to understand. Those teachings are not intended to be mere abstract concepts. True understanding does not come from just hearing the words that Jesus teaches or observing manifestations of his power throughout the gospels. True understanding comes only when we take time to reflect and meditate upon what has been heard and seen in order to grasp the lessons being taught. And when the truth is understood, we can then choose to act in accordance with that truth. This is the process by which Jesus becomes real to us. Such understanding may not occur during a teaching moment, but can be delayed for quite some time. Thus, as the work of transformation progresses, our words and actions will gradually become congruent and become consistent with what the gospel teaches. Moreover, we will be challenged to decide whether we will fulfill God's call on our lives for which he is preparing us.

Consider: As you reflect on your personal faith journey, consider how reading about the transformation of Peter's faith has challenged or changed your perspective about how God is leading you to an ever-increasing understanding of who Jesus Christ really is? How has God challenged you to decide whether or not to fulfill the role for which he is preparing you?

2. Part of God's work of transformation is intended to prepare us for both the good and evil that will occur in our lives. Therefore, throughout the process of transformation, God gives us a taste of what we have been called to do. An important part of that preparation is to open our eyes not just to the joy of living out God's call, but also to the rejection that will also occur. That is why God will repeat

specific lessons that we did not learn the first time. He will do so until understanding, trust, surrender, and obedience occur. As the work of transformation progresses in our lives, we move beyond mere mental ascent about God to trusting that he is alive and active in *our* life. Only then will we be willing to surrender to his will for us, trusting God completely—even through times of pain and suffering.

Consider: In what ways has God given you, or is now giving you, a taste of what you have been called to do once he finishes preparing you for what lies ahead? In what ways is he opening your eyes to the good and exciting times, as well as the challenges and possible rejection that will also occur?

3. Scripture is full of references to false prophets and false teachers. Therefore, Jesus exhorts us to *listen critically* to what we are being taught, rather than blithely accepting what is being taught by our pastors and teachers. When we evaluate what they are preaching and teaching in light of the commandments and teaching of God contained in Scripture, we guard ourselves against what is really only the teaching of man. We naturally accept as true and valid what we are taught by our leaders. Yet it is an important part of our transformation process to test what we are being taught against what the Word of God teaches.

Consider: In what ways has God been teaching you to listen critically to what you are being taught by others? In what way is God working to transform your mind so that by testing you can discern whether what is taught is good and acceptable and perfect (Rom. 12:2)?

Our prayer is that Peter's story will inspire and challenge you to search for God's active involvement in your life's circumstances. We encourage you to see what is happening at every moment of your life as part of God's bigger plan to transform and strengthen your faith, *so that* you will partner with him as he works through you to accomplish his plans and purposes for his world—*so that* your obedience to his will for your life will bring glory to God.

CHAPTER 10
What Do I Do Now?

God's Transforming Process

Throughout this book, we have focused on the question "How does transformation of basic belief into genuine saving faith take place?" In chapter 1, we saw that Jesus attributes the transformation that occurs in a person who is "born again" to the work of the Holy Spirit (John 3:4–8). Jesus then explains in John 6:63–65 that God does not just *provide the means* of salvation and transformation, but that God is also the *provider*, the agent, of this transforming work. Thus, transformation that leads to genuine saving faith is not the work of human effort and will; it is only the work of God through his Holy Spirit. This fact is repeated continuously in Scripture: to become a genuine believer, a person's simple belief must undergo the process of transformation. And many texts make it explicit that it is God who does the work of transformation.

As we bring this book to a conclusion, you might be wondering how to recognize God at work in your life. Although Scripture is clear that God does this work of transformation through the Holy Spirit, there is no straightforward answer about *how* that work is accomplished. However, we believe that the stories of the biblical characters we have examined in this book provide excellent examples of how God works in and through everyday life events to reveal himself to us to transform our faith. God desires that this transformation bring us to the point where we are willing to unconditionally obey God's guidance and direction to us. That transformation results in increasing intimacy with God over time and deepening dependence on God and not on ourselves.

This deepening intimacy and dependency happens as God becomes real to us amid life's challenges. Moreover, Scripture is full of promises to his people, which he uses to reveal himself to us. In the process of fulfilling those promises over time, he proves his faithfulness, thus revealing more of his character to us and thus transforming and strengthening our faith. As we experience God's presence with us and learn more about his character, he works within us to enable us to trust him more. As our trust grows, we find we are willing and able to surrender our plans for our life, and instead accept and embrace God's plans for us. We can do this only to the degree that we trust his goodness toward us, his love, grace, mercy, and forgiveness. It is *his* plan for our lives that enables us to live fully as the person he has created us to be and to live out his call on our lives, as he works to accomplish his purposes in his world through us.

As we have seen in several of the biblical stories that we have examined, the process of transformation requires us to experience difficult and painful life circumstances designed to turn the eyes of our hearts toward God alone, *so that* we experience more of *who God is*. In various life challenges, we struggle (and often fail) to be consistent in our lived-out faith by not trusting God. However, growth *is* taking place even in what appears to be inconsistent progress. We can trust that God is, indeed, working in our lives to continually reveal his presence and his character to us, to make himself known to us for the sake of transforming our faith, so that we can and will trust in him alone throughout our lives.

As we examined some of the familiar biblical stories of well-known and important individuals, we focused on how God brought about his transforming work through daily life events to move them from simple, objective belief to genuine faith anchored in deep trust, which enabled them to unconditionally obey God. Through it all, we kept asking again and again, "Where is God in this?" to see how he was actively involved in daily life events, working to transform each one into the individual he created them to be. As we worked through these biblical stories, we saw that the transformation process is unique to each individual; there is no "one way" for everyone. Even though we saw similarities in the transformation process of the different characters, there were also noticeable and important differences.

We hope that as you read each story, you asked how God might be working in your own life in similar ways to transform your simple belief into genuine faith. That is why we provided a summary of some of the lessons learned at the end of each chapter, with questions to consider for each lesson. Our purpose in doing so is to provide you with tools to help you discover how God is at work to transform your faith and, therefore, your life.

What Do I Do Next?

In that regard, we offer the following recommendations. First, we recommend that you use the lessons provided at the end of each chapter to begin to examine your own life story from the perspective of your personal faith. If you consider yourself to already be a genuine believer, we still encourage you to continue to use the Lessons Learned to further confirm the genuineness of your faith. Or, use these questions for reflection to help reveal the ways in which God may be testing that faith. If you have questions about the genuineness of your faith, the Lessons Learned sections can be used to help you identify areas in your faith in which you need the transforming work of God to occur.

Second, we recommend that you engage the specific prayer process[1] provided below, as God reveals to you each area of faith that he wants to address. By praying in this manner, you will open up to the guidance of the Holy Spirit, thus enabling you to be sensitive to the areas of your faith that God desires to transform.

Acknowledge: As you identify specific areas in your faith that need transformation, we recommend that you acknowledge that you

---

[1] The basic structure of this prayer process comes from John Piper, which we have modified to specifically apply to God's work of transformation of faith. See Piper's audio sermon on 1 Thess. 2:13-16, "The Word of God is at Work in You" (January 7, 2012), https://www.desiringgod.org/messages/the-word-of-god-is-at-work-in-you#full-video.

may not be a genuine believer. You may say all the right things and do what you think is right but recognize that your words and actions are not congruent, that your actions do not match what you say you believe. If this is the case, then start by acknowledging that you have a faith issue. But acknowledging does not stop there.

You also need to ask yourself, "Is God real for me?" When you examine yourself against the biblical stories studied in this book, you may recognize that you cannot see God at work in your life, or you may realize that you do not know God *experientially*—that you do not yet trust him with your life to the point of obedience. It is important to acknowledge that God is not a "genie in the bottle" that you can keep on the shelf until you have a problem that you cannot solve in your own strength. God does not work that way. God wants us to acknowledge that only he, through the work of the Holy Spirit, can transform us into a genuine believer.

Petition: Petition is the simplest part of the whole process. This is where we ask God in prayer specifically for what we want him to do for us—that which we cannot do for ourselves. It first declares, "Lord, I do not want to remain as I am, a professing Christian in name only. So, I ask you through the power of the Holy Spirit to transform me so that I become a genuine believer. Please transform these specific areas of my faith (and others that I cannot yet identify) so that I can have genuine faith." Can there be a more simple, direct prayer than that?

Trust: Trusting is the hardest yet most essential part of the whole process. It is one thing to acknowledge that God is God, the Lord of the universe—to have simple belief in him. But simple belief is purely mental assent, whereas trust comes from the heart. If you do not trust that God is who he says he is, that he will do what he says he will do (e.g., keep his promises), then how different is it to believe in God than that George Washington was the first president of the United States? Trust involves risk. That is why Scripture says that we must die to self in order to genuinely trust God. When we do, Satan's deception is no longer effective. He can get us to acknowledge a lot of doctrinal teaching week after week, yet most of the sermons we hear have been forgotten by the time we get to our car. So, if they have been forgotten, or were never really heard because we were thinking of other things, or we slept through the message, how then can it transform us? If the only part of the Bible we read each week is the text from our pastor's message, how can we expect God to transform us through his Word? We need to read all of God's Word in order to know who God really is, as he reveals himself to us in Scripture. Only then can we say, "Yes, I trust you, Lord. Therefore, I am willing for you to transform my life."

Remember that transformation is an ongoing process and that it does not happen automatically. It is very difficult to genuinely trust somebody to the point that you are willing and able to surrender your life to them. But if transformation is to occur in our lives, then we must trust what Jesus says—that it is God, through the power of the Holy Spirit, who is the only one who can do that work in us. And that work must be done so that our faith will be transformed.

Act: It is then important to begin acting according to what you have asked God to do for you. If you are not willing to change your behavior, then why ask at all? You can look at a chair and think, yes, it looks like a chair, it stands on legs like a chair, and then *say* that you can trust that it will support you. But how do you really know if that trust is genuine until you *take action* and sit down in the chair, and experience the reality of it?

We have a supernatural faith because the Holy Spirit is real, and the work of the Holy Spirit is real. Thus, we can trust that God *will act* in us to transform our faith. But being transformed is not magical, as Satan would have us believe. Even though God could transform us with a word, the stories from Scripture that we have examined reveal that he does not, in most cases, immediately do so simply because we have asked. Remember that in Greek, the word for *transform* is *metamorphoó*, which is the root for the English word *metamorphosis*. This word brings to mind an image of a caterpillar that climbs onto a branch and begins to spin a cocoon around itself. After a certain number of days, if you open the cocoon, there will be a butterfly inside, but it cannot survive. The process and struggle to break out of the confines of the cocoon are essential to make the butterfly capable of flight. The same is true for a little chick breaking out of its egg. So too God puts us in cocoon-like situations from which we must struggle in order to be able to walk in the ways of God. We must choose to take action in the process of transformation. When we are able to trust God, we are then able to accept God's will and thus act accordingly.

Thank: It is important to thank God daily for *his desire* to transform our faith, for his faithfulness, and for his process of transformation, which he initiates. Transformation requires that we die to self, which is hard to do. But, as the work of transformation progresses, we will come to realize that the benefits of being transformed by God far outweigh the costs. Thus, we can thank God daily that he will enable us to do what he invites us to do, and thus with a willing heart participate with God in the transformation process.

Does that prayer process seem too simple? Perhaps, but it works. And you must work it. It is not magic. As we have repeatedly seen in the stories examined in this book, the process of transforming us into the person God created us to be takes time. We live in an instant gratification society. We have been told that we can have things our way and have them now. But God is not in that business. The time that transformation requires is inconsequential to God; thus, we must be patient with the process. That is why we must repeat this prayer daily until God completes his work in us, until the transformation that we desire, and that God desires for us, becomes evident in our daily lives.

A Final Word

The purpose of putting the thoughts and words to paper in this book has been to share what we have personally experienced and observed so that others may benefit from those insights. Through our respective ministries, we have found this information especially helpful for anyone who has or is currently struggling to understand the pain, suffering, and wilderness experiences of daily life—for those who are asking, "Where is God in this?" It is our genuine desire and prayer that as you read and ponder the contents of these chapters, the insights shared about the transformation process will bless your life as it has our own.

ACKNOWLEDGMENTS

Together we give praise, honor, and glory to God the Father, Son, and Holy Spirit for bringing this work into being. May his purposes be fulfilled, and may he be glorified in and through this work to the praise and glory of his name.

Jeff, I wish to acknowledge and thank my wife, Krisi, without whose loving support and encouragement I could not have undertaken this work.

Julie, although this has been a team effort, I want to thank Jeff for bringing me into this project, which is mainly his work. He spent about eighteen months studying and teaching this material in an adult Sunday school class, which was recorded for transcription. He then asked me to take the transcribed draft of the manuscript and prepare it for submission for publication. Along the way, he gave me the freedom to add my own perspective to his work. Very quickly I lost the distinction between his words and mine. However, I worked to maintain his *voice* and to honor his *thought* throughout the manuscript. I am deeply thankful for this opportunity to participate in bringing his work to print.

Additionally, I am thankful for many friends in various parts of my life for the prayer support and encouragement they have provided throughout this process. Members of my Wednesday group ("The Five") entered this project with me more than two years ago. During the past year, my Thursday night group and the women in my Friday morning group have also been encouraging and supportive through prayer. And I am thankful to the following people who have supported this endeavor in various ways: Judy Lind, Lynn Johnson, Gwen Ingram, Claudia Rowe, Corinne Kershaw, Terri Hewitt, Shelley Abel, Dorothy Crockett, Karen Woo, and Cathy

Thornton. I am deeply indebted to all of you—prayer warriors and faithful friends. This work exists largely because of your faithfulness in prayer. Bless you all!

A special thank-you to the few who read a portion of the manuscript and gave their feedback and encouragement: Dorothy Crockett, Karen Woo, Jerri Meier, and Lynn Johnson. I am grateful to Hank and Tina Rhoads who generously made their mountain cabin available to me for writing retreats when I needed to get away to focus for extended periods of time, and to Jeff and Kristi Etchberger who made possible several weeklong writing retreats at their home in Florida. And with humble gratitude, I thank Alice Kincheloe and Maire Paserba, whom God sent to me as personal intercessors during this time. You both are true angels!

ABOUT THE AUTHOR

After forty years of being a professing Christian, Jeff went through an intense wilderness experience that resulted in his becoming a genuine, born-again believer. He then felt called to attend seminary and received a Master of Divinity degree from Fuller Theological Seminary in 1994. He pastored churches in California and Mexico, all in need of renewal and revitalization. However, there were more wilderness experiences, including a visual handicap that increasingly limited his ability to preach and teach. Jeff began to see God's direction in his life and to focus on *God's transforming process to genuine faith* through the ministry of pastoral counseling and mentoring. He studied Scripture to understand God's work in the lives of biblical characters. As a result, God's process of transformation has been the focus of his study and thinking for the past twenty-five years.

In 2017, in collaboration with Julie Lopes, a colleague and friend since seminary, he began writing his groundbreaking book, *Beyond Simple Belief: God's Transforming Process to Genuine Faith*. Recently, Jeff began a second writing project to adapt one of Jonathan Edward's major works from 1747 for the modern church. It too focuses on the differences between simple belief and genuine saving faith.

CPSIA information can be obtained
at www.ICGtesting.com
Printed in the USA
LVHW050529180221
679369LV00002B/52

9 781098 059644